THOMAS AQUINAS AND HIS PREDECESSORS

The Philosophers and the Church Fathers in His Works

THOMAS AQUINAS AND HIS PREDECESSORS

The Philosophers and the Church Fathers in His Works

Leo J. Elders

THE CATHOLIC UNIVERSITY OF AMERICA PRESS
Washington, D.C.

Originally published as *Thomas d'Aquin et ses prédécesseurs: la présence des grands philosophes et Pères de l'Église dans les oeuvres de Thomas d'Aquin*
Copyright © 2015 by Les Presses Universitaires de l'IPC, Paris

English translation Copyright © 2018
The Catholic University of America Press
All rights reserved

Library of Congress Cataloging-in-Publication Data
Names: Elders, Leo, author.
Title: Thomas Aquinas and his predecessors : the philosophers and the church fathers in his works / Leo J. Elders.
Other titles: Original title: Thomas d'Aquin et ses predecesseurs
Description: Washington, D.C. : The Catholic University of America Press, 2018. | Includes bibliographical references and index.
Identifiers: LCCN 2017058267 | ISBN 978-0-8132-3316-1 (pbk)
Subjects: LCSH: Thomas, Aquinas, Saint, 1225?–1274. | Fathers of the church—Influence. | Philosophy, Ancient—Influence.
Classification: LCC B765.T54 E3513 2018 | DDC 189/.4—dc23
LC record available at https://lccn.loc.gov/2017058267

CONTENTS

Preface   vii
Introduction   ix
Abbreviations   xiii

1. Plato's Philosophy   1

2. Aristotle   20

3. The Commentaries on the Works of Aristotle   39

4. The *Stoa*, Seneca, and Cicero   67

5. Gnosticism and Neoplatonism: Philosophy   84
   in the First Centuries and Gnosis

6. The Fathers of the Church; Saint Augustine   101

7. Saint Jerome   127

8. Saint John Chrysostom   157

9. The Commentaries on Two Treatises of Boethius   178

10. Saint Gregory the Great   193

11. The Platonism of Pseudo-Dionysius   220

12. The Metaphysics of the *Liber de causis*   241

13. Saint John Damascene and Saint Anselm   262
    of Canterbury

14. Avicenna   283

15. Averroes   306

16. Jewish Philosophy: Avicebron and Maimonides   332

    Works Cited   351
    Index of Names   373
    General Index   377

PREFACE

The great interest in the thought of Thomas Aquinas shown by scholars in the Western world, both at the individual level as well as in the centers of the study of medieval philosophy, has led to the publication of a great number of books and articles in specialized journals on this great medieval philosopher and theologian. Nevertheless a book has still been lacking which would bring together in one volume detailed studies on the relation between Thomas and his sources: the leading philosophers from ancient Greece until the twelfth century of the Middle Ages, as well as the Fathers of the Church most present in his work. Such a study would be a certain supplement to the introductions to the life and work of Aquinas, which cannot give detailed descriptions of his position with regard to the most important authors with which he is dealing in his writing.

This lacuna has led me to examine the relation between the great philosophers and theologians of the past on the one hand and Thomas Aquinas on the other. This book is an attempt to bring together what Thomas appreciated and has eventually taken over from the conclusions of his great predecessors, and also to show what he rejected. Amidst numerous other publications on the relationship between Thomas and such philosophers/theologians as Plato, the Stoics, Neoplatonists, Boethius, and so on, our study discusses the latter is so far as they are present in his works. For this reason it is based mainly on the references to and the thousands of citations to works of these authors as found in the different treatises of Thomas and on the analysis which Thomas himself gives of their doctrinal positions.

Prof. Jörgen Vijgen (Tiltenberg) has made an important contribution to the research needed for completing this study, indicating several relevant articles and books and suggesting a number of useful additions. I hope that this book, the fruit of many years of research and in which a number of previously published articles have been inserted, may help the readers to understand better the unequaled greatness of Aquinas as a philosopher and a theologian.

INTRODUCTION

Some years ago the director of studies of the University of Santo Tomás, Santiago (Chile), invited me to give a series of conferences on St. Thomas Aquinas and other philosophers. This invitation led me to pursue the subject and to write a series of studies on the presence of the great philosophers in the works of Thomas Aquinas. It is true that there exist a considerable number of publications on the relation of Thomas with these authors taken individually, as for instance, with Aristotle, Pseudo-Dionysius, Avicenna, and others, but to the best of my knowledge the *presence of the thought* of the more important of those authors *in the works of Aquinas* nowhere is examined in detail, on the basis of the quotations Thomas himself gives of them. Here are meant Plato, Aristotle, the Stoics, Cicero and Seneca, Neoplatonism, St. Augustine, Boethius, Pseudo-Dionysius, St. Anselm, and such Jewish and Arab philosophers as Avicenna, Averroes, Avicebron, and Maimonides. To these have been added chapters on the theology of such Church Fathers as Augustine Hieronymus, John Chrysostom, Gregory the Great, and John Damascene, as they are referred to by Aquinas.

It seemed useful to bring together in one book the appraisal Thomas has made of their thought, to indicate agreements on points of doctrine, to show those elements of their thought Thomas appreciated, and those which he criticized and rejected. It was not our purpose to give a complete account of the philosophy and theology of the authors with whom Thomas entered into a dialogue, but to show his agreement with certain points of doctrine and his critique of other theories, as this becomes apparent in his works. In other words, our intention is to show the extent to which the thought of these authors is present in the works of Aquinas, and is appreciated or discarded by him. To this effect we have studied the thousands of references to them in the texts of Aquinas. It was not our intention to present a historical study of these predecessors in their own cultural milieu. To give an example, the so-called Latin Averroism of the thirteenth century is mentioned, as referred to by Thomas, but the reader will not find a specific study of the question whether this supposed Averroism is the true doctrine of the Arab philosopher himself. Thomas has given his critical view of what in his time the masters of the Faculty of Arts in Paris presented as the doctrine of Averroes.

A second restriction we have applied in this study is to limit our examination to those philosophers and theologians who occupy a considerable place in the works of Aquinas and to leave out the authors whose influence on Western thought has not been very considerable. One may think here of the Mutakallimun, Al-Kindi, Al-Farabi, and Algazel. Correspondingly only those Church Fathers have been mentioned whose presence in the works of Aquinas is substantial and who have made a considerable contribution to his doctrinal synthesis. Thus the reader will not find chapters on St. Hilary of Poitiers, St. Ambrose, Origen, and so on.

For the same reason I have not examined the presence in the works of Aquinas of some Latin theologians of the twelfth and the first decades of the thirteenth century, such as the authors of the abbey of Saint-Victor in Paris, William of Auvergne, William of Auxerre, Alexander of Hales, Bonaventure, or St. Albert the Great.

The presentation of the thought of these predecessors of St. Thomas is each time preceded by a short introduction of the author in question, of whom we are going to examine the passages where Thomas mentions their doctrine. These short exposés are followed by the study of the references in the works of Aquinas and the latter's observations, and eventual critical notes.

The commentaries of St. Thomas on some twelve works of Aristotle, the *De Trinitate* and the *De Hebdomadibus* of Boethius, the *Divinis nominibus* and *De Caelesti Hierarchis* of Dionysius are analyzed with regard to agreements and eventual disagreements. To facilitate the reading of these doctrinal texts, each chapter is divided according to certain themes. To give an example, the observation of Thomas on the doctrines of Avicenna consists of the following sections: "Being and the One," "Truth," "God," "Creation," "The intelligences," "The souls of the celestial spheres and their causality," "The human soul," "Moral life," "The cosmos according to Avicenna," "Matter, form and the body," and "The animals."

As to the discussion of the presence of Aristotle, Boethius, and Pseudo-Dionysius, the most important observations of Aquinas on these texts are reproduced insofar as he himself formulated them in his commentaries of their works. Because of the extraordinary importance of Aristotle's philosophy, a special chapter has been devoted to these Aristotelian commentaries.

For the evaluation of the doctrine of these different authors, many of the available publications on the various subjects treated have been examined. In several chapters I have used previous articles published in different philosophical reviews, as will be indicated in the respective chapters. Publications on the various doctrines of Aquinas are so extraordinarily numerous that I can only hope that at least the more important ones have been taken into consideration. The final conclusion which imposes itself after the following detailed survey is that St. Thomas studied and evaluated the doctrine of these authors with perfect objectivity, grasped the essential elements, and examined the extent of their being well-founded and true.

ABBREVIATIONS

All works are by Thomas Aquinas unless otherwise noted. For Thomas's commentaries on Aristotle and some other works, the number of the book (e.g., the first book of Aristotle's *De anima*) appears before the rest of the title (*In I De anima*); the abbreviation for Thomas's commentary on the second book of the *De anima* would be *In II De anima*, and so on.

ST	Summa theologiae
SCG	Summa contra Gentiles
PG	Migne, Patrologia Graeca (collection of texts)
PL	Migne, Patrologia Latina (collection of texts)
Anal. Post.	Analytica Posteriora (Aristotle)
Catena in Ioan.	Catena aurea in Ioannem
Catena in Lucam	Catena aurea in Lucam
Catena in Marcum	Catena aurea in Marcum
Catena in Matth.	Catena aurea in Matthaeum
De civ. Dei	De civitate Dei (Augustine)
De div. nom.	De divinis nominibus (Pseudo-Dionysius)
De doct. christ.	De doctrina christiana (Augustine)
De Gen. ad litt.	De Genesi ad Litteram (Augustine)
De lib. arb.	De libero arbitrio (Augustine)
Epist. ad Lucilium	Epistulae morales ad Lucilium (Seneca)
Enarr. in Ps.	Enarrationes in Psalmos (Augustine)
Hom. in Evang. Matth.	Homilae in evangelia (Gregory the Great)
Hom. in Ezech.	Homilae in Ezechielem Prophetam Libri Duo (Gregory the Great)
In Boetii De Hebdomadibus	Expositio in librum Boethii *De hebdomadibus*
In Boetii De Trinitate	Super Boetium De Trinitate

In De causis	Expositio super librum *De causis*
In De divinis nominibus	Expositio super Dionysium *De divinis nominibus*
In De generatione et corruption	Exposition super *De generatione et corruptione*
In De sensu et sensato	Sententia Libri *De Sensu et sensato*
In De anima	Sententia Libri *De anima*
In De caelo	Sententia super librum *De caelo et mundo*
In Metaph.	Sententia super Metaphysicam
In Peri Hermeneias	Expositio libri Peri hermeneias
In Polit.	Sententia libri Politicorum
In Sent.	Scriptum super libros Sententiarum
In Post. Anal.	Expositio in libros Posteriorum Analyticorum
In Ethic.	Sententia libri Ethicorum
In Psalm.	Postilla super Psalmos
In Phys.	Expositio in libros *Physicorum*
QD de anima	Quaestio disputata de anima
QD de malo	Quaestiones disputatae de malo
QD de potentia	Quaestiones disputatae de potentia
QD de spir. creat.	Quaestio disputata de spiritualibus creaturis
QD de unione Verbi	Quaestio disputata de unione verbi incarnati
QD de veritate	Quaestiones disputatae de veritate
QD de virtutibus	Quaestiones disputatae de virtutibus
Quodl.	Quaestiones de quodlibet I–XII
Reg. past.	Liber Regulae pastoralis (Gregory the Great)
Sermo sup.	Sermo super orationem dominic (Augustine)
Super 1 Cor.	Super I Epistolam B. Pauli ad Corinthios lectura
Super 1 Thess.	Super I Epistolam B. Pauli ad Thessalonicenses lectura
Super 1 Tim.	Super I Epistolam B. Pauli ad Timotheum lectura
Super Col.	Super Epistolam B. Pauli ad Colossenses lectura

Super Eph.	Super Epistolam B. Pauli ad Ephesios lectura
Super evang. Ioan.	Super Evangelium S. Ioannis lectura
Super evang. Matth.	Super Evangelium S. Matthaei lectura
Super Galatas	Super Epistolam B. Pauli ad Galatas lectura
Super Hebr.	Super Epistolam B. Pauli ad Hebraeos lectura
Super Isaiam	Expositio super Isaiam ad litteram
Super Philemon	Super Epistolam B. Pauli ad Philemonem lectura
Super Romanos	Super Epistolam B. Pauli ad Romanos lectura
Super Titum	Super Epistolam B. Pauli ad Titum lectura

THOMAS AQUINAS AND HIS PREDECESSORS

The Philosophers and the Church Fathers in His Works

1 ❧ PLATO'S PHILOSOPHY

Until fairly recently Thomists were accustomed to underline the continuity of the philosophical thought of Thomas Aquinas with Aristotelianism. They recognized, however, that Thomas's philosophy was not just a re-formulation of doctrines of the Stagirite, and that he had further developed or modified certain of his positions. It was even said that he was more of an Aristotelian than Aristotle himself (*Aristotele aristotelior*). Although Thomists were convinced of a substantial agreement of Aquinas's doctrines with the basic positions of Aristotle, some authors, however, were of a different opinion and called attention to the presence of Platonic theories in the works of Aquinas. Cornelio Fabro was one of the protagonists of this line of interpretation and insisted on the borrowing by Thomas of the doctrine of participation. Other authors studied the influence of the Platonism of the *De divinis nominibus* of Dionysius and the *Liber de causis*, which represent the Platonism of the end of the classical age, which were examined in detail by Thomas.

The Christians and the Greek Fathers were no Aristotelians.[1] Thomas himself writes that with regard to philosophical theories not related to the faith, Sts. Basil and Augustine follow the opinions of Plato.[2] Nevertheless, in a somewhat later text, he writes that when Augustine, in philosophical questions, quotes the views of Plato, he does not subscribe to these, but only mentions them.[3] In doctrinal questions Augustine follows the opinions of Plato to the extent that the faith allows him to do so.[4]

On the other hand Thomas was well aware of the difficulties which

---

1. Cf. Leo Elders, "The Greek Christian Authors and Aristotle," in *Aristotle in Late Antiquity*, ed. Lawrence P. Schrenk (Washington D.C.: The Catholic University of America Press, 1994), 111–42.
2. *In II Sent.*, d. 14, q. 1, a. 2: "Basilius et Augustinus et plures sanctorunm sequuntur in philosophicis, quae ad fidem non spectant, opiniones Platonis."
3. *Summa theologiae* (*ST*) I, q. 77, a. 5, ad 3: "In multis autem quae ad philosophiam pertinent, Augustinus utitur opinionibus Platonis, non asserendo sed recitando."
4. *QD de veritate*, q. 21, a. 4, ad 3: "... quantum fieri potest secundum fidei veritatem."

certain positions of Aristotle may cause with regard to the Christian faith, but accepted nevertheless the substance of his philosophy instead of subscribing to the Augustinian Platonism which dominated among the theologians of his time.[5] The reason for this choice is his certitude that the greater part of Aristotle's positions are true, and that the latter had used the right method in the study of nature. Despite his appreciation of Plato's greatness and of the value of certain of his theories, Thomas was convinced that Aristotle offers a greater clarity, stays within the limits of available evidence and demonstrates with greater certitude the existence of immaterial beings.[6] On the other hand, the way in which Aristotle elaborated his philosophy is not without defects.[7] Notwithstanding the contrast between the two Greek philosophers in their respective doctrines of nature and of man, Thomas wants to see a substantial agreement insofar as both acknowledge the existence of a superior principle from which spiritual and material things depend, and both accept a certain form of divine providence.[8] As points of difference between the two philosophers with regard to the principles of reality, he mentions that Plato taught the existence of intelligible forms separate from the material world, in which we participate while we are thinking, a theory not admitted by Aristotle, who also did not place a considerable number of separate substances between the First Principle and our world. It should be noticed that Thomas sees a substantial agreement between the two philosophers with regard to separate substances and the causes of the world.

What Thomas knew of Plato is summarized in his commentary on the *Metaphysics*, I, chapter 6, lesson 10: Plato was the immediate predecessor of Aristotle who was his disciple; in many questions Plato followed the earlier Greek philosophers of nature, such as Empedocles, Anaxagoras, and so on, but he developed certain doctrines as peculiar to him, in particular in his use of theories of the Pythagoreans. In his insatiable thirst for knowledge, he visited various countries in search of the truth. So he wanted to be instructed in the Pythagorean doctrines by Archytas of Taranto.

---

5. See Étienne Gilson, "Pourquoi saint Thomas a-t-il critiqué Augustin?" *Archives d'Histoire doctrinale et littéraire du Moyen-Age* 1 (1926–27): 126.
6. *De substantiis separatis*, chap. 2, 2: "ideo Aristoteles manifestiori et certiori via processit ad investiganum substantias a materia separatas, scilicet per viam motus."
7. Ibid., nn. 53–57.
8. Ibid., chap. 3, nn. 58–60.

The desire to discover a considerable correspondence between the positions of the two great ancient philosophers in the field of metaphysics is noticeable in the commentaries of the Neoplatonist authors on the writings of Aristotle. Thomas himself followed this line of interpretation, but for him Aristotle's method of investigation and his interpretation of nature were irreplaceable for establishing a real philosophy of man and for the understanding of nature,[9] the organization of ethics, and political science. In addition Aristotle also provided the concepts and principles to be used in the study of the doctrine of the faith and the elaboration of the science of the faith. Thomas also wanted to develop this Aristotelianism in order to provide the intellectual framework for the building of a new society, the first lines of which began to appear in his time.

Some authors have argued that toward the end of his life Thomas showed a growing interest in Platonism, a trend which, according to them, shows in the fact that in the last years of his life he wrote a commentary on the Neoplatonic treatise *Liber de causis*. The redaction of this text, however, can be explained very well by the importance attached to it at the University of Paris. It was at first thought to be part of the *Corpus aristotelicum*, and for this reason it was perhaps appreciated more than for it intrinsic value.[10] According to Otto Bardenhewer, the treatise would have exercised a decisive influence on Thomas, but as we shall see, this opinion is not correct.[11] Karl Prantl argued that Thomas corrupted his Aristotelianism by the mysticism of the *De causis*.[12] The treatise belonged to a group of Greek writings and had been translated into Arabic in the eleventh century. Thomas showed that it depends on the *Elementatio* of Proclus, and on numerous occasions he draws attention to the Platonic character of the text. He may have wanted to write his commentary so as to help students to understand what is valuable in the *De causis*, and to bring Neoplatonic theories in harmony with the fundamentals of Aristotelianism, correcting some erroneous statements and clarifying certain theo-

---

9. Cf. *De substantiis separatis*, chap. 2: "Aristotle's position is more certain since he does not considerably deviate from what is evident to the senses."

10. Shortly before 1240 this text was put on the list of those works of Aristotle which were obligatory reading at the University of Paris. Its frequent use is shown by the fact that some 237 manuscripts are still extant.

11. Otto Bardenhewer, *Die pseudo-aristotelische Schrift über das reine Gute, bekannt unter den Namen* Liber de causis (Fribourg i. Br.: Herdersche Verlagshandlung, 1882 (lLater edition, Frankfurt: Minerva, 1961).

12. Karl Prantl, *Geschichte der Logik im Abendlande*, vol. 3 (Leipzig: Verlag von S. Hirzel, 1870), 114.

ries. In his commentary Thomas refers frequently to Pseudo-Dionysius, since he wanted to bring together different theories inspired by Neoplatonic metaphysics which were accepted by many theologians of his time in order to transpose them in the framework of the philosophy of being.[13]

When we inquire about the influence of Plato's philosophy on St. Thomas Aquinas, our examination is rendered difficult by the particular nature of the writings of Plato. While the *Corpus aristotelicum* presents the various doctrines in precise formulae, Plato is looking for approximations which are often different and often does not give a definite solution. With regard to certain questions, his position is far from evident. An interesting example of this lack of clarity became visible in a recent publication of the papers presented in a symposium on the Idea of the Good as placed above Being. Several speakers rejected the esoteric interpretation of the School of Tuebingen, which however was defended by others. Nevertheless the reader gains the impression that the qualification of the Good as beyond (ἐπέκεινα) our knowledge is more than just a metaphor and must be considered a thesis of Plato and his School.[14]

Undoubtedly it was more difficult for Thomas than for us to know Plato's doctrine in detail, since he had only a few dialogues at his disposition and had to look for the substance of his information in the works of Aristotle, Augustine, and other sources. We must nevertheless admire the way in which he succeeded in drawing a fairly complete picture from these sources and in formulating a solid and truthful judgment about essential points of Plato's doctrine. One must, however, notice that Thomas repeatedly mentions under the name of Plato theories proper to Middle- and Neoplatonism. To give an example, he writes that according to Plato there are two substances separated from matter: God, the Father of the world, and his Intellect or Spirit, in whom all the Ideas or essences of things are present. This is a view of later Platonism. Characteristic of the thought of Plato himself is that the higher one mounts in the hierarchy of beings, the more impersonal things become.

But Thomas familiarized himself with the intellectual universe of Platonism in an admirable way. In the following pages the reader will find a survey of the doctrines and opinions of Plato accepted or rejected by Thomas. In Chapter 5 his attitude in respect of Middle- and Neo-

---

13. See chapter 12 of this book on the metaphysics of the *Liber de causis*.
14. *New Images of Plato: Dialogues on the Idea of the Good*, ed. Giovanni Reale and Samuel Scolnicov (Sankt Augustin, Germany: Academia Verlag, 2002).

platonism will be examined. Generalizing we could say that a main reproach of Thomas to Platonists is that they did not show much interest in the study of the material world and did not have a precise knowledge of it. In his *Commentary* on Aristotle's *De generatione et corruptione*, he writes that the Platonists spoke too easily about material things, while using logical categories.[15] The same criticism is found in other texts: in their study of the material world, the Platonists chose as their point of departure certain categories of our intellect, whereas other philosophers started from an analysis of sensible things.[16]

The following survey of Plato's doctrines as Thomas saw them is based on the study of about one thousand texts in which Plato is mentioned.[17] Yet the separation between the doctrine of Plato himself and the theories of later Platonists is difficult. Sometimes when Thomas speaks of Platonists in general, he has in mind Plato himself.

Plato's Theory of Knowledge

In the first part of the *Summa theologiae*, where Thomas examines the question whether we can know sensible things, he calls to mind the hopeless situation of the Greek philosophers because of the theory of Heraclitus: if all bodies are constantly subject to changes, it would seem that we cannot acquire a certain knowledge of them. In this situation Plato entered the scene (*superveniens Plato*), says Thomas. Plato introduces the theory of forms or Ideas as realities separated from the material world. When we partake in the Ideas we can acquire a certain knowledge of the essence of material things. But Thomas explains immediately the insufficiency of this theory: how can we know material things which are in motion by means of immaterial and immutable forms? Why should we, while we try to know the things surrounding us, resort to these forms which cannot be the substance of perceptible things? Plato's error is that he thought that "what is abstract in our intellect, is also so in reality."[18] According to Plato the formal content of the known things is present in

---

15. *In I De generatione et corruptione*, a. 1, lesson 3.
16. *QD de spir. creat.*, a. 3.
17. For an almost complete collection of texts on Plato and the Platonists in the works of Aquinas, see R. J. Henle, *Saint Thomas and Platonism: A Study of Plato's and Platonic Texts in the Writings of Saint Thomas* (The Hague: M. Nijhoff, 1956).
18. *QD de spir. creat.*, a. 3: "estimaverunt enim quod quidquid est abstractum in intellectu sit abstractum in re." (Translations throughout are by the author himself, unless otherwise noted.)

the same way in the person who knows it and in the things itself.[19] But in reality, Thomas says, the forms of material things are in a different way in our intellect, for in our mind they are immaterial and immobile, conforming to the principle that whoever receives a form receives it in conformity with his own way of being.[20]

The Origin of Our Knowledge: The Ideas

Plato had understood that our intellect has universal concepts which express the essences of individual things. This means that he had grasped the existence of the immaterial, but he thought that these concepts, being universal, must exist independently and separated from the material things of which they are said. The reason is that things exist as individuals. Taking up the "hunting of the essences," initiated by Socrates,[21] and the introduction of the spirit (νοῦς) by Anaxagoras,[22] we can arrive at the conclusion that the pure immutable essence of things, as we think it, must exist outside this material world which is always in motion. The collection of all essences or universal forms constitutes the so-called world of Ideas which is immaterial and immutable and exists outside and above sensible things.

Thomas observes that Plato did not see how our intellect can abstract forms which as they exist in nature are not abstract. On the other hand, he said that what is abstract according to our intellect, is also so in reality, that is to say, in the world of Ideas.[23] He says explicitly that they exist independently; for him they are not the ideas of God.[24] Resorting to this theory of universal and immaterial forms or Ideas allowed Plato to explain the presence of universal concepts in our mind. What is universal and immutable, as are the essences, cannot come from our world of material and individual beings. This made Plato conclude that our human soul, which existed forever outside and above the material world, must have known these forms before entering in a body. Apparently it has forgotten them and must recover them from oblivion.[25]

---

19. *QD de veritate*, q. 21, a. 4: "quae possunt separari secundum intellectum, ponebant enim etiam secundum rem esse separata."
20. *ST* I, q. 84, a. 1. The principle is frequently mentioned by Aquinas.
21. The expression is Aristotle's, *Metaphysics*, 1078b27, and following.
22. Fragments 12 and 13.
23. *In II Phys.*, lesson 3.
24. *Super evang. Ioan.*, chap. 1, lesson 1.
25. *QD de potentia*, q. 3, a. 5. This is the well-known theory that knowledge is reminiscence:

Assuming the existence of a collection of universal Ideas, which exist outside the material things, is a theory, says Thomas, in conflict with the Christian faith. He points to a contradiction: the forms of material things exist outside these beings without having matter. If so, how could they be their essential forms? Another difficulty: the Ideas do not have any matter, but the essences of material things do have matter. Thomas even ascribes to Plato the theory according to which these forms exist in the mind of God. In this way they can be the causes of our knowledge and of the being of all things. But as we shall show it later, this opinion results from a later development and originates from the beginning of the Christian era.[26] Thomas stresses that Plato did not accept ideas of accidents,[27] but notwithstanding this general view he spoke of ideas of moral virtues, such as piety, justice, and so on, and also of the idea of equality, although the latter is an accidental determination of two substances which resemble each other.

The theory of Ideas insists on the fact that we know the immutable essence of things, and that these essences must exist, since according to Plato the mode of our knowledge corresponds to the mode of the existence of these objects,[28] whereas what our senses allow us to perceive are uninterrupted changes. Heraclitus had in fact argued that everything is in a continuous flux.[29] In consequence of this pessimistic view concerning physical reality, Plato turned away from what our senses tell us, to consider only the universal Ideas in our intellect which represent immutable essences. In this way he developed his philosophy of separate forms and built a barrier between the physical world and the world of thought. Thomas explains that it is not necessary that the way in which we think the thing be the same as the way in which it exists.[30]

Plato conceived the theory of immaterial and subsistent forms to ex-

---

learning is to remember, being ignorant results from oblivion. Plato explains the theory in his dialogue *Meno*.

26. *ST* I, q. 15, a. 1. In *In II Sent.*, d. 1, q. 2, a. 5 Thomas says that the error of Plato was that he placed these forms outside God. On the origin of the theory, see Willy Theiler, *Die Vorbereitung des Neuplatonismus* (Berlin: Weidmann, 1934), 34; Audrey N. M. Rich, "The Platonic Ideas as Thoughts of God," *Mnemosyne* 7 (4th series), no. 4 (1954): 123–33. Seneca writes that God possesses in himself the models of all things (*Epist.* 7, 28).

27. *QD de veritate*, q. 3, a. 1.

28. *ST* I, q. 85, a. 1 ad 1. See R. J. Henle, *Saint Thomas and Platonism*, 328. In questions 84 and 85 just referred to, Thomas totally opposes what he considered the essential doctrines of the *via platonica*.

29. *QD de spir. creat.*, a. 10, ad 8.

30. *ST* I, q. 85, a. 1 ad 1: "Est enim absque falsitate ut alius sit modus intelligentis in intelligendo, quam modus rei in essendo."

plain the presence in our mind of universal concepts which express the essences of the existing things. The concepts in our intellect originate from these forms or Ideas which exist separately from our material world. Consequently, our intellect does not receive its knowledge from what the senses present to it, but through a contact with or a participation in these ideal forms. They are present in our intellect, before our soul enters into our body, as also are the virtues.[31] When our senses perceive material things, the intellect remembers the corresponding Ideas in which these material things participate. In this way, to know is to remember.[32] Thomas criticizes this opinion severely. It is *dupliciter falsum*: the immaterial and immobile Ideas exclude all knowledge of motion and of matter; it seems preposterous to resort to other entities in order to know what is manifest, that is, sensible things.[33]

Following a text of Aristotle in his *Metaphysics*, Thomas points out that the Ideas do not contribute anything to what happens in the world of material things. They are not causes of motion and do not explain the knowledge we have of it.[34]

With regard to sense knowledge, Plato is of the opinion that this knowledge is not completely (*totaliter*) the result of the contact of the senses with material things. They wake up the senses; these are actualized by the causal influence of our soul and in this way the intellect can begin to think. The material things do not communicate their properties to the senses. Aristotle agreed with Plato in respect of the essential difference between sense knowledge and intellectual knowledge, but he was opposed to Plato in so far as he taught that the senses cannot perceive their objects if the material things do not communicate themselves to them.[35]

In his commentary on the Aristotelian treatise *De sensu et sensato*, Thomas criticizes the Platonic theory of sense perception: according to Plato our eyes would see things by emitting rays which would be reverberated by the object, a theory conceived by Democritus, but utterly im-

---

31. *ST* I, q. 84, a. 4; *SCG* II, 98. This way of presenting the origin of our concepts differs somewhat from the theory according to which our soul, before entering into the body had already seen the Ideas. It may have been influenced by Neoplatonism.

32. *In I Post. Anal.*, lesson 3. Cf. *In III Sent.*, d. 33, q. 1, a. 2: "Addiscere non est aliud quam recordare."

33. *ST* I, q. 84, a. 1.

34. *In I Metaph.*, lesson 15, no. 226: "quod non prosunt ad motum; secundo quod prosunt ad scientiam."

35. *ST* I, q. 84, a. 6.

possible. If it were true, we should see things even in the dark.[36] Thomas also criticizes Plato's theory of the way in which the sense of touch functions. According to Plato we would feel bodies by stretching out toward them. If this were the case, Thomas says, we would not know the size of these bodies. It is also a fact that we can represent bodies in their different sizes, which presupposes that we have known them by touch.[37]

Plato thought that in this life we can know the immaterial substances, but Thomas denies this.[38] From the presence of the universal forms of material things in our intellect, Plato concluded that the names we give are not arbitrary symbols, but represent the nature of these things,[39] a conclusion rejected by Thomas.[40]

The Causality of the Ideas

The manner in which the forms or Ideas exercise their causality is a debated question. In Plato's dialogues we encounter divergent descriptions. In his earlier dialogues Plato speaks of a certain immanence of the Ideas in physical things, while he later mentions the imitation of the Ideas, which means that the forms remain outside the things.[41]

Thomas shows a very great interest in Plato's theory of participation in the Ideas. We notice that he modifies Aristotle's very strong negation of participation in the second book of the *Metaphysics*, and even criticizes some sayings of the Stagirite. For instance, when Aristotle writes that the Platonists encountered serious difficulties in their attempts to explain what participation is, Thomas says that they attempted to find what participation is and to define its causes.[42] In his commentary on a treatise of Boethius, the *De Hebdomadibus*, Thomas deals *in extenso* with the Platonic participation. The standard example of participation is that of Socrates participating in human nature, but Thomas observes that in the strict sense of the term we cannot say that Socrates participates in human nature, since he possesses it essentially.[43] But in a secondary meaning one

---

36. *In I Metaph.*, lesson 3; *In I De anima*, lesson 4.
37. *In I De anima*, lesson 7.
38. *In I Post. Anal.*, lesson 30.
39. See Plato, *Cratylus*, 425d: names signify things by means of a certain imitation.
40. *In I Peri Hermeneias*, lesson 4.
41. See David Ross, *Plato's Theory of Ideas* (Oxford: Clarendon Press, 1951), 208.
42. *In II Metaphys.*, lesson 10.
43. *In Boetii De Hebdomadibus*, I. 2. Cf. *In VII Metaph.*, lesson 3.

may speak of participation insofar as Socrates does not actually possess all that is virtually contained in human nature. For instance, he is not a woman, nor an African. Thomas explains that certain central doctrines of Aristotle can be expressed with the help of the term "participation": in the way a substance participates in its accidents, as matter does in the substantial form and potency in the act which determines it. The value of the doctrine of participation consists in the fact that it is useful to express the causality of God with regard to the world. If a creature does not receive the influence of God's causality to its full extent, we may speak of participation.

Nevertheless there a considerable difference between this use of the term and Plato's theory of participation. Participation as put forward by Plato is at the level of formal causality—beautiful things, for instance, have a part of the form of beauty—while according to Thomas created beings receive their being from God insofar as he is their *efficient cause*. In their case we speak of participation since the perfections received from God are realized in different degrees. If beautiful things did not have a common cause and source of their beauty, one could not explain why beauty is present in different degrees.[44] Aristotle had noted as against participation in a common source that a predicate as good or beautiful has a different meaning according to the different categories of being in which it is found. Thomas solves the difficulty noticing that there exists a transcendent source of goodness, beauty, etc., which communicates it to the different beings.[45] Everything which participates in another being is in a situation of potency to act.[46] This means that even in the evaluation of the doctrine of participation, Aristotle has the last word insofar as one of the central elements of Plato's philosophy is subsumed under the doctrine of act and potency.

The Origin of the World

Concerning the formation of the world as Plato described it in the *Timaeus*, Thomas notes that the demiurge is not the cause of matter and that consequently one cannot speak of Plato's account as creation in the strict

---

44. *In De causis*, lesson 9. The principle involved is used in the fourth way of demonstrating the existence of God in the *ST* I, q. 2, a. 3.
45. *In I Ethic.*, lesson 6; *ST* I, q. 44, a. 1.
46. *SCG* II, 53.

sense of the word.⁴⁷ Thomas adds that Plato never intended to say that the world has been created, he just wanted to describe its composition.⁴⁸ With regard to the disorderly movement which Plato ascribed to the receptacle and the elements, we must see it as a description of the world in the supposition that God did not impose order. One should not understand Plato's text in its literal sense, as if according to him the world would have been made. On the contrary, according to Plato the world is imperishable.⁴⁹ According to the *Timaeus*, 29a, the demiurge made a most beautiful thing. Thomas reads a principle of being in the sentence: It is proper to the best cause to produce the best.⁵⁰

In this connection Thomas also mentions the second ontological principle of Plato, namely, the Great and (the) Small, sometimes called the Indeterminate Dyad or the Infinite. He considers it a disposition of matter, as quantity is for Aristotle.⁵¹ But at this point Thomas takes up a criticism of Aristotle which is mentioned several times by him: Plato did not distinguish between matter and privation, and considered matter as a not-being.⁵² In the treatise on creation of the *Summa theologiae* I, question 44, article 2, we read that subsequently to a first group of philosophers important progress was made in philosophy, that is to say that the philosophers began to understand that changes of the *essences of things* do occur. According to some these are due to the movement of the sun in the ecliptic plane, whereas others attributed these changes to the causality of the Ideas. Aristotle and his School belong to the first group, Plato and his disciples to the second.⁵³

Thomas writes that certain thinkers continued in this direction and accepted a cause of the being of things. This passage of the *Summa theologiae* says in covert terms, without giving the names of the philosophers which came after Plato and Aristotle, that neither Plato nor Aristotle acknowledged God as the cause of the being of things. Plato could not acknowledge the creation of the world, since cosmic space, the receptacle which he considered a first principle, is uncreated.⁵⁴ Thomas thinks

---

47. *De articulis fidei.*
48. *In I De caelo*, lesson 23.
49. Ibid., lesson 22.
50. *QD de potentia*, q. 5, a. 1: "optimi est optima adducere." This means that one should resort to it with some reservations: a perfect mode of being does not flow spontaneously from God.
51. *ST* III, q. 77, a. 2.
52. *In De divinis nominibus*, chap. 3, lesson 1.
53. See the *De generatione et corruptione* of Aristotle; and the *Phaedo*, 96a, of Plato.
54. *ST* I, q. 15, a. 5, ad 3.

that Plato restricted divine causality to all *immaterial* substances.[55] Notwithstanding the above quoted texts, he writes elsewhere that Plato and Aristotle did acknowledge the cause of all beings.[56] We may understand this text as meaning that some authors who took the principles of these two great authors as their starting point arrived at the conclusion that the world has been created.[57] This seems to be the explanation of why in some other texts Thomas writes that according to Plato the world received its being from God.[58] Thomas attributes to Plato the idea that God could not have made a better world than ours, an idea taken over by Dionysius.[59] In the *Summa theologiae* I, question 44, number 1, this same conclusion is proposed—before any multitude there has to be oneness—in conjunction with Aristotle: what is being in the highest degree and what is true in the highest degree is the cause of whatever exists and of whatever is true.[60] Thomas wants to indicate a line of thought in the philosophy of the two great masters that may lead to the formulation of the doctrine of creation.

At this point the question comes up again of whether according to Thomas Plato recognized the existence of God. In the *Quaestiones disputatae de potentia* he suggests that Plato did arrive at the acceptance of a universal cause of being, for before all plurality there must be a unity, both in thought and in natural things.[61]

The Hierarchy of Beings

As we have seen above, Plato taught the existence of the forms of the different material substances, which partake in those universal forms. This theory is also formulated in somewhat different terms by Thomas: it is necessary that the abstract forms in which things participate, exist previously to matter.[62] But in addition to the forms or Ideas, there are also oth-

---

55. *De substantiis separatis*, chap. 3: "summus Deus causa est omnibus immaterialibus substantiis."

56. *In VIII Phys.*, lesson 2.

57. This is probably the meaning of *QD de potentia*, q. 3, a. 5—a reference to Augustine, who does not say that Plato himself taught the creation of the world by God, but that "certain authors followed Plato and other philosophers who deserve praise."

58. *In I De caelo*, lesson 29.

59. *In I Sent.*, d. 44, q. 1, a. 1.

60. Aristotle, *Metaphysics*, II, chap. 1, 993b25–28.

61. *QD de potentia*, q. 3, a. 5.

62. *QD de spir. creat.*, a. 5: "Plato vero est alia via usus ad ponendum substantias incorporeas."

er substances separated from our sensible world, namely, the mathematical entities. In this way he distinguished a hierarchy of beings: between the Ideas and the material things, subject to continuous change, there are the mathematical entities and the ideal numbers. Even in the world of Ideas, the supreme reality, there reigns a certain order. The Good and/or the One occupy the highest place and are the first principle of things. If a person does not have the idea of the One, he knows nothing. But Plato was mistaken, Thomas observes, in that he considered the One as a transcendental principle to be the same as the number one.[63]

This places us before the question whether Plato did place God at the summit of this hierarchy of beings. In certain texts Thomas confirms it, but it is difficult to distinguish between doctrines of Plato himself and theories taught by later Platonists. A beautiful text in Thomas's commentary on the *De divinis nominibus* might also apply to Plato himself: what Dionysius says about the participation in a First Principle, the Good, is very true and in agreement with the Christian faith.[64]

The Platonists elaborated the theory of as hierarchy of all beings.[65] According to Plato himself the first principles are impersonal and universal; the more we descend in this hierarchy the more the ontological content decreases.[66]

Plato assigned to the human souls a rank superior to that of the celestial bodies. He also mentions intermediary beings or demons, but references to these in his works are few and vague and the subject has been elaborated by later Platonists.[67] According to Thomas Plato would have assigned souls to the celestial bodies, which would be the cause of their revolutions,[68] but this attribution to Plato seems to have been influenced by the writings of Neoplatonists. Likewise what he writes on the Platonic theory of divine providence seems to have been influenced by the writings of Neoplatonists. Thomas observes on one point that this doctrine is in contradiction with the Christian faith, insofar as it says that not all beings would be directly subordinated to divine providence.[69] Finally Thomas notes that regarding the number of the celestial sphere, Aristotle

63. *ST* I, q. 11, a. 1.
64. *In De divinis nominibus*, prologue.
65. See chapter 5 of this book.
66. *SCG* I, 13.
67. In his commentary on *Metaphysics* III, lesson 11; and V, lesson 10, Thomas speaks of the demons as being a doctrine of the Platonists.
68. *ST* I, q. 70, a. 3.
69. *SCG* III, 76.

had limited the number of movers, while Plato had not set any limit.[70] Certain cosmological theories which Thomas assigns to Plato himself seem to belong to later currents of Platonism, as for instance that of the *animalia aerea*. Thomas was aware of this, for he wrote in his *De substantiis separatis* that he has drawn the themes he is discussing from different sources (*ex diversis scriptis collegimus*).

The Doctrine of the Soul

Plato's theory of the human soul is one of the most discussed themes of the history of ancient philosophy. Thomas stresses that according to Plato the soul is a principle of the movement of bodies and also the source of the soul's self-motion. In addition to the motions and changes caused by souls, there is also a disorderly movement in the world, which is inherent to the receptacle or cosmic space, which already existed when the souls were made.[71] The moving power ascribed to the soul comprehends different activities, among which are thinking and appetite, so that the soul is thought to be a mover which also moves itself. In this line of thought God is also thought to move himself.[72] For Plato the soul is a complete substance and the source of the activities and movements of the body on the one hand, and of thought and sensation on the other. By itself the soul is the human being.[73] Its relation with the human body resembles that of a captain to his ship.[74] Repeatedly Thomas observes that according to Plato the souls are not the forms of their respective bodies, but causes of the motions of the latter and that they direct their bodies as the first mate steers his ship.[75] For this reason, as Nemesius notes, the definition of man is that of a soul which uses a body.[76] Thomas also quotes the formula *anima utens corpore*[77] and concludes that for Plato the soul is united

---

70. *De substantiis separatis*, chap. 2.
71. *In XII Metaph.*, lesson 6.
72. ST I, q. 18, a. 3 ad 1; *In I Sent.*, d. 8, q. 3, a. 1 ad 2; d. 45, a. 1, a. 1. In his *QD de potentia*, q. 10, a. 1, Thomas almost excuses this view, which is wholly impossible according to Aristotle's principles: "According to our way of speaking, we say that a thing which acts by itself and in itself, is alive. In this way Plato said that the First Mover moves itself."
73. *QD de anima*, a. 1.
74. *In II Sent.*, d. 1, q. 2, a. 4, ad 3 (according to Nemesius, *De natura hominis*).
75. SCG II, 57.
76. *In II Sent.* d. 17, q. 2, a. 2.
77. SCG II, 57; ST I, q. 75, a. 4.

with the body against its nature.[78] The soul is not the substantial form of the body, and its connection with the body is so tenuous that it is assured of an eternal existence because it is not drawn down into corruptibility by the body.

Since it is the moving principle in man, Plato even speaks of a tripartition of the human soul, since the different types of motion demand different movers,[79] namely, the thinking soul, a second soul which is the seat of energy and courage, and, finally, the concupiscent soul. For Plato it was not so strange to speak of a multiplicity of souls, since according to him the soul is an extrinsic principle and cause of motions and not an intrinsic form united with matter.[80] Thomas notes that according to Plato sensitive souls, and even those of irrational animals, are immortal, since they are sources of movement,[81] a conclusion which Thomas considers outright as impossible.[82]

As has been explained, for Plato the soul is an extrinsic principle.[83] Our souls have existed forever at the edge of the world of Ideas and have arrived on earth in consequence of a fall and entered a body. In agreement with the general line of his philosophy, Plato thinks that we must ascend from the soul as the cause of motion to the source of motion, a soul or a first being which is moving itself in all its purity. This has led to the elaboration of the theory of the world soul. In line with this view Plotinus considered the universal soul as the principle of the individual souls.[84] The world soul has no vegetative nor sensitive activities; its thought is marked by a circular movement,[85] a conception criticized by Thomas, who argues that thought has a beginning and a term, in which it rests. Plato was to such a point absorbed by his study of our thought, Thomas says, that he did not pay sufficient attention to the question of the way in which the soul is united to the body. With regard to this point, his doctrine is deficient.[86]

Pythagorianism has influenced the doctrine of the soul of Plato to

---

78. *In I De anima*, lesson 8: "Anima unitur corpori contra naturam suam."
79. This tripartition is mentioned in the *Phaedrus* and in the *Timaeus*. Thomas deals with it in *SCG* II, 58.
80. *ST* I, q. 67, a. 3.
81. *SCG* II, 57. Thomas comments "quod quidem improbabile videtur."
82. *SCG* II, 57 and 82; *QD de anima*, a. 19.
83. *ST* I, q. 67, a. 3.
84. *In II Sent.*, d. 18, q. 2, a. 3.
85. *In I De anima*, lesson 8.
86. *ST* I, q. 85, a. 1; *In I De anima*, lesson 8.

such a point that the latter even assigned a number to the soul and to its operation. The human soul is composed of the Same and the Other, so that it can, on the one hand, know the immutable Ideas, and, on the other, material, corruptible things. The same being known by the same, the Ideas must be present in the soul. Numbers are the causes of things. Plato did hold this since he did not make a distinction between unity as a transcendental property of beings and the one as the principle of numbers. In accordance with this view, he considered the Ideas as being composed of numbers because of the causality of the One. He assigned to the intellect the number one, to science two, to opinion three, and to the body, which has a pyramidical form with four sides, the number four.[87] It is surprising that Thomas tried to discover a meaning in these unusual theories. Plato's notion of the soul is directly related to the theory of numbers.[88]

Another form of composition attributed by Plato to the soul is that of the Same and Otherness. By these two principles the soul can know what is above her—the world of immutable forms—and the sensible things, subject to incessant movements.[89]

Cosmology

Philoponus writes that according to Plato the world is the outcome of a process of generation and is corruptible by its very nature, but Thomas observes that the text quoted by the commentator can be explained differently, for instance, as signifying dependence on a higher cause.[90] The first heaven participates in the motion of the world soul.[91] With regard to the position of the fixed stars and the planets, Plato seems to have adopted the theory of Eudoxus. Nevertheless he thought that the sphere of the fixed stars contained fire because of the light of the stars.[92] As for the question whether Plato accepted the immobility of the earth in the center of the world, Thomas voices some doubts.[93] The souls of a lower grade, movers of the planets, imitate the world soul.[94] With regard to Pla-

87. *In I De anima*, lesson 4.
88. Ibid., lesson 9.
89. *In De anima*, lesson 4.
90. *In I De caelo*, lesson 6.
91. *In I De caelo*, lesson 6.
92. Cf. *In I De caelo*, lesson 4.
93. *In II De caelo*, lesson 21.
94. *In I De anima*, lesson 7.

to's cosmology Thomas mentions the principle that whatever exists in the world has been modeled after the world of Ideas.[95] The world is one as is its model. There are four elements in the sublunar region, whereas the heaven consists of fire.[96]

Aristotle draws attention to the difficulties that Plato met in his attempts to explain the processes of the generation and corruption of things. Thomas quotes the criticism that the Platonists were *indocti* about the things of nature.[97] It is hard to see how mathematical entities could be the substance of natural things.

Thomas criticizes certain statements of Plato, such as a text of the *Phaedo* where we read that all the rivers and the water of the seas come together in a place underneath the earth.[98] According to a theory generally accepted in Greece, natural things would have been formed in the way an artisan makes his products, a view which Thomas rejects as wrong.[99] Thomas also mentions the theory according to which time would have had a beginning, and notes that this must be the case if one understands the formation of the world by the demiurge in a literal sense.[100] But Thomas knows that Plato did not teach the creation of the world by God, since in his view matter of the receptacle precedes the activity of the demiurge.[101] For Plato the world is eternal.[102]

What Plato says about the first heaven is hardly different from Aristotle's doctrine, except that he does not speak of a *quinta essentia*.[103] The body of the first heaven contains fire, since it radiates light, but he does not say that it consists of fire.[104] Plato thinks that place is a material thing, insofar as it is identical with the receptacle. When he writes that there is in the world an above and a below, he is just following the way of speaking of people in general.[105] He denies that outside our world there would be an infinite mass of matter; he attributes infinity only to the forms which have attained the highest degree of perfection.

---

95. *SCG* I, 54.
96. *Quodl.* IV, q. 2, a. 3.
97. *In De generatione et corruptione*, lesson 3.
98. *In I Meteor.*, lesson 3.
99. *In I Metaph.*, lesson 15.
100. *In II Sent.*, d. 12, q. 1, a. 5 ad 2.
101. *De articulis fidei*.
102. Cf. the *De aeternitate mundi*.
103. *ST* I, q. 66, a. 2.
104. *In I De caelo*, lesson 4. In *Quodl.* IV, q. 2, a. 2, however, we read that according to Plato the nature of the first heaven consists of fire.
105. *In IV Phys.*, lesson 5.

The Moral Doctrine

The reader of the works of Aquinas is surprised by the almost total absence of references to the moral doctrine of Plato. It would seem that he did not possess translations of the dialogues which deal with these themes, such as the *Republic*, the *Laws*, and so on. In the second part of the *Summa theologiae*, Plato is mentioned about twenty times, but several of these references do not concern the question of the moral life. Just like the Ideas of the essences of things, those of the virtues are also always present in our souls.[106] Occasionally Thomas mentions Plato's view of pleasure which would be a process, that is to say, an activity.[107] On this point Plato was mistaken: he considered certain forms of sensitive pleasure, for instance, the pleasure of eating and drinking, activities, whereas in reality pleasure is the completion of an activity.[108] According to Plato, Thomas observes, not all forms of pleasure are bad—as the Stoics would say—nor are all good, as the Epicureans would hold.[109]

Thomas mentions the theory of the *Republic*, which says that all wives and children must be possessed in common. On the other hand, Plato also holds that women should be free to organize reunions and festivities. Another suggestion made is that the state should forbid drunkenness.[110] Whoever wants to grow in the virtues should begin by practicing them in his youth.[111] The purpose of all laws is to render citizens more virtuous.[112] The authorities of the state must forbid products and activities connected with immoral purposes.[113]

At the beginning of the *Nicomachean Ethics*, Aristotle writes that Plato was used to distinguishing between arguments from principles and those of which the starting points are the effects. Thomas comments that the two methods are used in moral philosophy. We must always begin from that which is most evident for us. Sometimes this is a principle, but on other occasions it is the effect of an action.[114]

Aristotle criticized Plato for arguing that human happiness consists

---

106. *QD de virtutibus*, q. 1, a. 8.
107. *In I Sent.*, d. 1, q. 4, a. 1; *In IV Sent.*, d. 49, q. 3, a. 3 qc. 3, ad 2.
108. *ST* I-II, q. 34, a. 3.
109. Ibid.
110. *In II Politic.*, lesson 17.
111. *In II Ethic.*, lesson 3.
112. *In II Politic.*, lesson 14.
113. Ibid., lesson 8.
114. *In I Ethic.*, lesson 4.

in the common idea of the good, since this idea does not exist: there is an order of good things according to more and less, and good things are place in the different categories.¹¹⁵

Conclusion

This chapter in which we examined the evaluation of Plato's main doctrines by Thomas might create the impression that for Thomas Plato's philosophy had only a negative value. Critical statements and corrections dominate, something almost inevitable because of the fact that Thomas had to rely mainly on the exposés Aristotle gives of Plato's physics, of his theory of knowledge, and of his doctrine of the soul, exposés which are frequently quite negative. Nevertheless in certain texts the admiration Thomas felt for the figure of Plato appears, namely, when he speaks of the good and of God, of the quest for a universal cause of being,¹¹⁶ the principle that before any multitude there must be unity,¹¹⁷ of certain other principles, and of the theory of participation. Thomas recognized the merits of Plato in his rejection of the materialism of the Presocratics, in the development of a philosophy of the mind, the doctrine of the immortality of the human soul, and of a destiny of man beyond life on earth. He has taken over Plato's theory of the four principal moral virtues. Thomas also knew that Plato and his school had exercised an enormous influence, in general for the good, and had contributed to the development of Christian theology, as we shall see in chapters 5, 11, and 12.

115. Ibid., lesson 6.
116. *QD de potentia*, q. 3, a. 5.
117. *ST* I, q. 44, a. 1.

2 ❧ ARISTOTLE

Aristotle's Philosophy in the Thirteenth Century

In the thirteenth century two contrary doctrinal positions collided at the University of Paris, Platonism and Aristotle's realism. According to the followers of the Augustinian tradition, Aristotelianism exalted to such a degree the value of creatures that the glory of God and the doctrine of the faith came out diminished, and were even threatened. The Aristotelians on their side were of the opinion that their adversaries did not have a correct scientific method, were not able to explain the physical world, and got lost in unreal speculations. This divide largely coincided with the structure of the university faculties of liberal arts and theology: in the teaching of theology, after Holy Scripture, the works of Augustine and Dionysius were most prominent, but the studies at the Faculty of Arts were organized around the works of Aristotle.[1]

The Christian authors of the first centuries and the Church Fathers were not Aristotelians.[2] They did not know the so-called school writings of Aristotle and drew their information from the collections of the sentences of the great authors. They knew that Aristotle had taught the eternity of the world, that his idea of God was confused, and that he denied divine providence with regard to the sublunar world. An additional reason for this lack of enthusiasm for the study of the works of Aristotle was the very technical character of his academic writings. During the time of the Fathers the dominant thought was a sort of mixture of Platonism and

---

1. One should notice that at the beginning of the thirteenth century Latin translations of the more important works of Aristotle were at the disposition of the medieval doctors. These translations did not offer a critical text. It is remarkable that Thomas so well grasped what Aristotle had written.

2. Cf. Leo Elders, "The Greek Christian Authors and Aristotle," in *Aristotle in Late Antiquity*, ed. Lawrence P. Schrenk (Washington D.C.: The Catholic University of America Press, 1994), 111–42.

Stoicism, with some influence of Gnosticism. Clement of Alexandria and Origen were close to Plato's philosophy; and the Cappadocian Fathers, Gregory of Nazianzus and Basil, who had received their philosophical education in Athens, still worked in a Platonic climate but began to use the categories of thought elaborated by Aristotle. The fact that heretics, and especially the Arians, used the Aristotelian logic—although in a totally unjustified way—in order to attack the orthodox expression of the mysteries of the Trinity and Christ as a Divine Person, increased the reserve of Christians with regard to Aristotle. But gradually the value of the Aristotelian philosophy was discovered. Moreover during the first centuries the masters in the different schools, even the Platonists, taught Aristotle's logic and physics, but preferred Plato in metaphysics and theology.

Thomas writes that in respect of philosophical theories not related to the faith Basil and Augustine followed the views of Plato.[3] But in a later text he notes that when in philosophical questions Augustine mentions the theories of Plato, he does not subscribe to them, but limits himself to mentioning them.[4] In the fields of theology Augustine accepts the views of Plato in so far as the faith allows it.[5] In order to examine the substantial incorporation of Aristotle's philosophy, we must study the relation between St. Thomas and Aristotle.

As was Aristotle himself, Thomas was convinced of the fact that the subject matter of all the sciences is the universal and the necessary. The universal essences are abstracted from the individual things perceived by the senses. The latter are the source of whatever we know. Thomas accepted the theory of the sciences as formulated by Aristotle in the *Posterior Analytics*. Thomas made his own the doctrine of the categories of being—of substance and accidents—formulated in the *Categories* as well as the rules for scientific reasoning and proofs of the *Prior Analytics*. We may quote John Henry Newman's words on the value of Aristotle's contribution to scientific reasoning:

While the world lasts, will Aristotle's doctrine on these matters last, ... for the great Master does but analyze the thoughts, feelings, views, and opinions of human kind. He has told us the meaning of our own words and ideas, before we

---

3. *In II Sent.*, d. 14, q. 1, a. 2: "Basilius et Augustinus et plures sanctorum sequuntur in philosophicis quae ad fidem non spectant, opiniones Platonis."

4. *ST* I, q. 77, a. 5, ad 3: "In multis autem quae ad philosophiam pertinent, Augustinus utitur opinionibus Platonis, non asserendo sed recitando."

5. *QD de veritate*, q. 21, a. 4, ad 3: "... quantum fieri potest secundum fidei veritatem."

were born. In many subject-matters, to think correctly, is to think like Aristotle; and we are his disciples whether we will or no, though we may not know it.[6]

Aristotle's philosophy is intellectualistic and assigns the first place to knowledge. In the first sentence of his *Metaphysics*, he declares that "all men by nature desire to know." The last end of man is the contemplation of truth. Aristotle is optimistic as regards the possibility of knowing the beings in the world and the presence of finality. He draws attention to the first principles of the speculative intellect—such as the principles of contradiction and causality—which are at the basis of all demonstrations.

The first task of philosophy is the study of the processes of becoming in the world which must be analyzed according to the four genera of causality. In connection with his doctrine of the four causes, Aristotle developed the theory of act and potency, a theory which became the key for a profound understanding of physical reality.

The doctrine of the first principles of the speculative intellect lays the foundation of all scientific knowledge. Thomas shows that, in addition to these principles, there are also first principles of the practical intellect, which are the basis of natural law and moral science.[7] In contrast with the view of Plato and the First Academy, Aristotle underlines the priority of being with regard to the good. First philosophy is the science of being as being.

Aristotle developed the theory of the analogy of being: the word "being" is used in different meanings and is divided according to the ten categories. Substance is the basic reality, the other categories are a determination of the substance and are beings in the substance.

In his philosophy of nature, Aristotle fought atomism, monism, and materialism. Following closely what nature teaches us, he elaborated hylomorphism, a doctrine accepted by Thomas. Aristotle analyzed the meaning of motion, of place and time, of generation and corruption. He was the first to attempt to construct a scientific cosmology and to develop the study of life in its different forms. Important also is his theory of the soul and its powers, in particular of the cognitive faculties. One may add to this listing of important accomplishments Aristotle's work as a pioneer in biology and his doctrine of the First Unmoved Mover.

---

6. This text is found in one of the conferences pronounced in connection with the project to establish a Catholic university in Dublin, *The Idea of a University* (1852; Notre Dame, Ind.: University of Notre Dame Press, 1982), 82–83.

7. *In V Ethic.*, lesson 12.

He worked out the art and science of logic in an unsurpassed way, and composed the first scientific treatises on ethics and political science. According to his moral doctrine man's last end is happiness, which consists primarily in contemplation. The Stagirite also explained which factors may restrict or impede our free choices, and he developed a theory of the virtues as being the substance of the moral life. His theory of the state is based on the thesis that man is a social animal who must live in a political society. Aristotle also submits a detailed study of the different political regimes, of their respective good properties, and of their defects. Finally one must also remember his investigations in the field of poetry, literary criticism, and rhetoric.

Needless to recall that one encounters in the works of Aristotle certain doctrinal positions which cause problems to a Christian reader. Theories such as that of the eternity of the world, and the apparent negation of creation and of divine providence, as well as his description of certain moral theories, seem to contradict the Christian virtue of humility.. His definition of the magnanimous man is unacceptable to Christians. In his *Hexaemeron* Robert Grosseteste warned against the danger of trying to baptize Aristotle. In his *Collationes*, conferences given at the University of Paris between 1267 and 1273, St. Bonaventure censured certain theories of Aristotle which he considered contrary to the faith. As we said above, the Christian authors in antiquity and the Church Fathers, such as Basil and Augustine,[8] were not Aristotelians.[9]

Thomas did not ignore the difficulties that certain doctrinal positions of Aristotle could pose for the Christian faith, but he nevertheless accepted the substance of Aristotle's philosophy instead of subscribing to the Platonic Augustinianism which was dominant among the theologians of his time.[10] The reason for his choice was his certitude that the greater part of Aristotle's doctrinal positions are true and that he had used the right method in the study of nature.

Notwithstanding his appreciation of the greatness of Plato and of the value of certain of his doctrines, Thomas thinks that Aristotle offers a greater clarity and stays within the limits of the available evidence, and

8. See above note 3.
9. See above note 1.
10. Cf. Étienne Gilson, "Pourquoi saint Thomas a-t-il critiqué Augustin?" *Archives d'Histoire doctrinale et littéraire du Moyen-Age* 1 (1926–27): 126.

also demonstrates the existence of immaterial beings with greater certitude than Plato.[11] Nevertheless the way in which Aristotle had elaborated metaphysics was not without shortcomings and defects.[12] Despite the contrast between the two Greek philosophers in their doctrines about physical nature and man, Thomas sees a substantial agreement in so far as both acknowledge the existence of a supreme principle, on which spiritual and material beings depend and also accepted a certain form of divine providence.[13]

In the commentaries of Neoplatonist authors on the writings of Aristotle, we also notice a trend to seek and to see a substantial agreement between the two philosophers in the field of metaphysics, a discipline which they had not developed very much. Thomas followed this line of interpretation. But for him Aristotle's method of investigation and interpretation of nature were of irreplaceable value for the development of a true thilosophy of man, the understanding of nature, and the organization of ethics and political science. They also provide the concepts and principles useful or necessary in the study of the doctrine of the faith and the elaboration of the science of theology.

In this perspective one appreciates the enormous task of the composition of very detailed commentaries on the main works of Aristotle, a task Thomas undertook despite the already heavy workload imposed on him as master of theology: the redaction of biblical commentaries to be used in his classes of theology, finishing the *Summa theologiae*, the composition of occasional treatises, and the organization, conducting, and eventual publication of the various disputed questions. At the beginning of his commentary on the *Physics*, Albert the Great explains his intention in undertaking this enormous task: to put the text of Aristotle's works with his comments and explanations at the disposition of his students.[14] We may assume that it was also Thomas's intention to explain the often difficult texts of Aristotle for students. But he commented on these writings in a novel way: each sentence was explained. We may assume that at the same time he wanted to point the way which one should follow to elaborate the philosophy of nature, anthropology, and metaphysics, and a

---

11. *De substantiis separatis*, chap. 2: "Et ideo Aristoteles manifestiori et certiori via processit ad investigandum substantias a materia separatas, scilicet per viam motus."

12. Ibid., nos. 53–57.

13. Ibid., nos. 58–63.

14. See Albert the Great, *Physica, Pars 1,. Libri 1–4*, ed. Paul Hossfeld, Alberti Magni Opera Omnia 4/1 (Münster: Aschendorff Verlag, 1987), bk. I, tract. 1, chap. 1.

moral philosophy of universal value. While writing his commentaries, he could also remove misunderstandings and erroneous interpretations of Aristotle's doctrines by masters of the Faculty of Arts.[15]

Aristotle and the Christian Faith

Thomas was well aware of the opposition of numerous theologians and ecclesiastic authorities against certain doctrines of Aristotle and of a fairly general mistrust against his *rationalistic* method. This attitude was an obstacle against the elaboration of philosophy and of theological science. Thomas did acknowledge of course that there are certain conflicts between the doctrine of the faith and what Aristotle taught, but he tried to find explanations. By way of an example one may refer to the *De caelo et mundo*, a treatise in which Aristotle tries to show with several arguments the eternity of the world. Thomas explains the arguments of Aristotle, but then he writes that these arguments do not prove that the world did not have a beginning but only show that the world did not begin to exist in the way the other philosophers had imagined, namely the world did not begin by a process of generation and is not destined to perish. This explanation by Thomas is generous since certain arguments of Aristotle aim at excluding any possibility of a beginning of the world.

Thomas also distances himself from the theory of the eternity of the celestial bodies. He notes that on this point Aristotle expresses himself similarly to Plato, who called divine not only God, the First Cause, but also other beings. The reader gets the impression that Thomas is saying that we may as well follow Aristotle, because Plato was also mistaken. Also in some other texts Thomas associates Aristotle with Plato, to protect him against one-sided criticisms. We find an example of it in the *Quaestiones disputatae de potentia* (q. 3, a. 5) where we read that Plato and Aristotle, and those who followed them, concluded the existence of a universal being, the cause of all things, as Augustine affirms.[16] Here Thomas quotes Augustine to guarantee that the principles of Aristotle's philosophy lead to the admission of the creation of the world.[17] One

---

15. Cf. Jean Isaac, "Saint Thomas, interprète des œuvres d'Aristote" in *Scholastica ratione historico-critica instauranda* (Rome: Pontificium Athenaeum Antonianum, 1951), 360–61. See Albert the Great, *Physica, Pars 1, Libri 1–4*, bk. I, tract. 1, chap. 1.

16. Augustine, *De civitate Dei*, VIII, chap. 4.

17. Another example is found in the *Commentary on the Letter to the Hebrews*, 1:10–11:

should notice that in a parallel text, *Summa theologiae* I, question 44, article 2, Thomas writes that Plato and Aristotle had not arrived at the consideration of the universal Being.[18] The difference between the two texts disappears if one reads in them that it was the disciples (*sequaces*) of the two philosophers who had drawn these conclusions from the principles established by their masters.

When Aristotle writes that God and nature do nothing in vain, Thomas comments that Aristotle admits implicitly that God is the cause which made the celestial bodies. A sentence in which Aristotle says that "nature provides" seems to imply that Aristotle is thinking here of divine providence as watching over the world (*hic sentit*).[19] At the beginning of the *Physics*, Aristotle writes that we must always look for the supreme cause. Thomas uses these words to add that we must pursue our investigations until we arrive at the supreme Cause. These additions are an example of the way in which Thomas invites us to read in texts of Aristotle an opening toward the acknowledgment of the existence of God. In an analogous way, the statement that "nature always acts in view of an end" is understood by Thomas as meaning that nature is the project of divine art, which God placed within the things he made.

In the *De caelo* III, chapter 4, Aristotle demonstrates that there is no perfect infinite. Thomas adds a remark to emphasize that this conclusion does not apply to God,[20] since here Aristotle is considering only the order of material things. In his commentary on the *Physics*, he also adds a correction of a passage, in which Aristotle seems to admit a direct influence of the celestial bodies on the immaterial faculties of man: such an influence on the soul is not possible, and if there is an influence on the human body, it cannot impose any necessity on the spiritual faculties of man.[21]

We find similar corrections in the other great commentaries on the treatises of Aristotle. According to the *Nicomachean Ethics*, man is himself the cause of his beatitude, a theory which was condemned at Paris in 1277. Thomas writes that in the first place Aristotle is speaking of the

---

"Dicendum est quod secundum Augustinum et Philosophum in qualiber mutatione est generatio et corruptio."

18. It is tempting to explain the difference between the two texts by the fact that for the *Summa theologiae*, being destined originally for the students of the Dominican *Studium* in Rome, Thomas did not need to present Aristotle in the most favorable light, as he had to do later in Paris.

19. *In II De caelo*, lesson 15.

20. *In III De caelo*, lesson 7, no. 348.

21. *In VIII Physic.*, lesson 4, no. 1003.

imperfect happiness of our life on earth and that in another text he concedes that beatitude is a gift of the gods.[22] At 1099b12 of his treatise Aristotle does indeed make an observation which goes in this direction, but the sentence might just be a concession to the way people speak about happiness. As he does on other occasions, Thomas looks for similar sentences in Aristotle's writings to corroborate his interpretation. Assuming that there is a perfect coherence between the various writings, he avails of such sentences to submit an interpretation which goes beyond what Aristotle is saying in a particular passage.

One comes across a certain number of this type of correction in the other great commentaries, in particular in that on the *Nicomachean Ethics*. In Thomas's time masters of the Faculty of Arts criticized the Christian view of virginity and appealed to Aristotle: they argued that virginity could not be a virtue because of its rejection of all sexual pleasure. Thomas answers that those who observe virginity are not deprived of all pleasure.[23] Thomas also corrects a text which says that a person who commits suicide to escape from great evils should not be condemned; he reads it as meaning that a man must sometimes bear great evils. We also encounter this type of rectification in what Aristotle says about certain virtues such as liberality, magnificence, and, above all, magnanimity. According to Aristotle a magnanimous person is looking for honors. Can a Christian do that? Thomas says "yes" in so far as he accepts and acknowledges his condition as a creature.[24]

In the commentary on the *Metaphysics*, we find several examples of this kind of interpretation of texts of Aristotle, which aim at removing in as far as possible any appearance of opposition to the Christian faith. We have already mentioned the problem of the theory of the eternity of the world. To this we may add that in *Metaphysics* XII, chapter 9, Aristotle excludes knowledge of the world from the First Mover. Thomas answers that what Aristotle excludes is that God would receive his knowledge about the creatures he made from the creatures themselves. We may add a remark on the theory of plurality of unmoved movers in chapter 8 of Book XII. It is somewhat surprising to see that in the prologue to

---

22. *In I Ethic.*, lesson 14, nos. 165–76.
23. *In II Ethic.*, lesson 2, no. 263 Cf. Proposition 169 of the list of propositions condemned in 1277: "Perfecta abstinentia ab actu carnis corrumpit virtutem et speciem." See Roland Hissette, *Enquête sur les 219 articles condamnés à Paris, le 7 mars 1277* (Louvain: Publications universitaires, 1977).
24. *In IV Ethic.*, lesson 8, nos. 735–49.

his commentary as well as in some other texts, Thomas preserves the plural—*"primas rerum causas"*—leaving open for the time being the question of the uniqueness of the First Principle. He affirms this uniqueness only in the commentary on Book XII, chapter 8, where he notes that the plurality of first movers is not necessary to explain the motions of the celestial bodies and that it is only an astronomical theory, which has no more than some probability. In a following section Thomas distinguishes between the Unmoved First Mover and other immaterial substances, but he avoids a hasty correction of texts and respects the need for a patient examination. This method has been called *reverenter exponere*.

Thomas's Choice in Favor of Aristotelianism

Thomas was well aware of the difficulties which the introducing of Aristotelian doctrines in philosophy and theology would bring along, but he decidedly opted in favor of the principles of Aristotle's philosophy. The Platonists were mistaken in various questions, but in the field of metaphysics there was a certain convergence: Plato and Aristotle, Thomas says, agreed on the existence of a unique principle, on which things depend. Spiritual beings have no matter, but are nevertheless composed of their essence and the act of being. Thomas goes to the point of saying that both philosophers accepted divine providence.[25]

When trying to qualify Thomas's relation with Aristotelianism, one could speak of a "going beyond." Thomas penetrates the various doctrines to their core and uses the fundamental principles of the Stagirite, but in some places he goes beyond Aristotle in his conclusions. Thomas also established a greater coherence between the different doctrines, especially in anthropology, ethics, and metaphysics. The thousands of quotations, in Thomas's writings, from the *Organon*, *Physics*, *Metaphysics*, *On the Soul* (*De anima*), and *Nicomachean Ethics* show the importance Thomas attached to these writings of Aristotle. As a master in sacred theology, Thomas had extensive obligations and had also to carry out other tasks besides teaching. He nevertheless undertook the enormous task of composing commentaries on twelve of Aristotle's major works, explaining their doctrinal contents, analyzing the texts in their smallest details, not

---

25. See *De substantiis separatis*, chap. 3. Thomas bases his affirmation on certain texts of Aristotle.

avoiding difficulties, and rejecting interpretations which disagreed with the letter of the text and the intention of Aristotle. He also drew attention to texts of which the arguments seemed to disagree with the doctrine of the faith. The quality and accuracy of these commentaries show that Thomas also wanted to compose the elements of an anthropology, metaphysics, and ethics that could serve in higher institutes of learning.

In his explanations he places the text to be commented upon in the light of the principles of Aristotelian philosophy as a whole. In these commentaries one frequently encounters the expression *secundum intentionem Aristotelis*.[26] These words may signify the meaning of a sentence as an intelligent reader sees it, but can also refer to a more profound meaning which one discovers when meditating on the particular text or when one compares it with what Aristotle writes in other places. The expression does indeed sometimes refer to what Aristotle says in another place. On a few occasions Thomas shows that the apparent opposition between texts disappears when one reads them very carefully, but there are cases where a particular affirmation is irreconcilable with the Christian faith. Thomas frequently completes what Aristotle says in a particular passage by adding a paragraph which begins with the words *sciendum est autem, notanndum est autem* or *advertendum est autem*.[27]

In order to illustrate how, on certain occasions, Thomas goes beyond the text of Aristotle, one should recall the treatment of analogy in *Metaphysics* IV, lesson 2, where Thomas explains the analogous meanings of "healthy" by pointing to its relation to the efficient and the final cause, and also to that of an accident with a substance. When Aristotle criticizes the Platonic doctrine of participation, Thomas weakens Aristotle's words in order to open the way to a new form of participation, namely, that of creatures in God's being. Also in the field of metaphysics Thomas developed the theory of the transcendental concepts and demonstrated as the central thesis of metaphysics the real distinction, in all created beings, between their act of being (their existence) and their essence.

In this connection we should also mention the important text of the *Peri Hermeneias*, in which Thomas goes beyond what Aristotle wrote with regard to the act of being. He uses a sentence of Aristotle (the verb

---

26. Cf. for instance *De substantiis separatis*, chap. 14, where Thomas writes that when one attentively considers the words of Aristotle, his intention appears to be different.

27. Cf. *In VI Metaph.*, lesson 1, where Thomas contradicts Aristotle's theory that material things are not comprehended in the subject of first philosophy.

"is" also signifies a composition)²⁸ to stress that the main meaning of the verb "to be" is that of being real in an absolute way.

The amplification of Aristotle's doctrine is very noticeable in the commentary on the *De anima*. Thomas accepts Aristotle's doctrine of the soul and its faculties, as well as of the process of knowledge and of the appetitive powers, but he goes beyond Aristotle, and shows why the essence of material things constitutes the object of the intellect. He gives a fine explanation of the role of the agent intellect, which goes much beyond the scarce indications provided by Aristotle: the agent intellect is located in the soul itself, since the Creator gives to the natural things the faculties they need to accomplish the tasks proper to their nature.

In the third book of the *De anima*, Aristotle's exposition is very concise, but owing to the commentary of Thomas the text becomes more complete, yet remains faithful to what Aristotle sets forth. Thomas goes much beyond Aristotle in the way he elaborates the theme of the spiritual soul of man, which is the substantial form of the body, but is not totally submerged in the body; it is and remains a subsistent reality (*aliquid subsistens*). Thomas explains also why it is united to the body, and related to this he demonstrates that the soul survives after the death of a man, a conclusion doubted by Aristotle.²⁹

In his works on moral theology, Thomas stresses, more than Aristotle had done, the scientific nature of this discipline. In his commentary on the first book of the *Nicomachean Ethics*, Thomas declares that in ethics it is absolutely necessary to determine what is man's last end.³⁰ Aristotle thinks that in our conclusions in moral science we cannot attain more than a moral certitude concerning the goodness or badness of our actions, but Thomas points out that moral science is not only called to shed light on our actions, but it is also a form of scientific knowledge which lies at the level of the theoretical disciplines. In fact, Thomas transposes the prudential type of knowledge, described by Aristotle, to the level of the theoretical sciences. Aristotle mentions criteria which help us to determine whether an action is good or bad, such as the just mean, the

---

28. *In I Peri Hermeneias*, lesson 5 no. 73: "Hoc verbum est consignificat compositionem quia eam non principaliter significat, sed ex consequenti."

29. See Endre von Ivanka, "Aristotelische und thomistische Seelenlehre," in *Aristote et saint Thomas d'Aquin; journées d'études internationales*, ed. Paul Moraux (Louvain: Publications universitaires de Louvain, 1957), 221–28.

30. Cf. Leo Elders, "St. Thomas Aquinas's Commentary on the Nicomachean Ethics," in Elders, *Autour de saint Thomas*, vol. 1, *Les commentaires sur les oeuvres d'Aristote; La métaphysique de l'être* (Paris: Fac-Editions, 1987), 77–122.

wise man, right reason, the eye of the soul; but Thomas delves deeper and insists on the first principles of practical reason, which are parallel to the first principles of theoretical reason. They are the basis of the law of nature, whereas Aristotle does not mention them.

Thomas read the texts of Aristotle in the light of his own philosophy of being. Thus the question arises to what extent this philosophy of being is identical to Aristotle's thought. As is known, Aristotle composed his writings to reproduce reality. He avoided as much as possible providing explanations from a subjective point of view. This explains why his writings lent themselves to be assimilated, and at times remodeled, by Thomas in a more systematic way. Thomas could often show all that is contained in the reality of natural beings, and point out structures which Aristotle had not seen.

Aristotle's texts lend themselves to this more profound understanding because they are close to reality. Thomas made considerable efforts to analyze the texts of Aristotle, sentence by sentence, to discover their profound meaning, to draw from them whatever is true, and to insert it into the framework of a more coherent philosophy, which he considered to be the authentic Aristotelianism. Thomas's intention might well have been to lay the foundation of a true philosophy which would help students to understand the world, build the city of men, and defend the doctrine of the faith.[31]

When one emphasizes the great value of Aristotle's philosophy, one clashes with the fact that his cosmological theories are in large part erroneous. As to this point one must distinguish between the philosophy of nature and natural sciences. In Aristotle's text this distinction is hardly made, but Thomas was aware of the different approaches. In certain texts he notes that Aristotle's cosmological system is only a hypothesis and that, through later discoveries and more precise observations, new hypotheses might eventually be formulated.[32] The natural philosophy of Thomas, which aims at certitude in its analyses and arguments, is independent of these scientific theories.

---

31. These pages reproduce our study "Saint Thomas d'Aquin et Aristote" in *Revue thomiste* 88, no. 3 (1988): 357–76.

32. *In II De caelo*, lesson 17, no. 451: "licet talibus suppositionibus factis apparentia salvarentur, non tamen oportet dicere has suppositiones esse veras; quia forte secundum aliquem alium modum, nondum ab hominibus apprehensum, apparentia circa stellas salvantur." Cf. *ST* I, q. 32, a. 1, ad 2; *In II De caelo*, lesson 3, no. 28.

Aristotle's Philosophy as an Aid in the Study of Theology: Aristotle's Presence in the *Summa theologiae*

In the first question of the *Summa theologiae*, Thomas examines whether philosophy has a role in theological science. In his answer he stresses that theology also uses human reason, not in order to demonstrate the faith—reason does not have any direct authority in theology—but to clarify certain things which accompany what has been revealed and are connected with it.

Reason must be at the service of the faith, but is not a source of theological knowledge. Aristotle—called in most places the Philosopher[33]—is mentioned more than two thousand times. In order to explain this huge number of references to Aristotle, we should remember that he had given a fairly precise description of the world. In our investigations, Thomas writes, we must follow the nature of things, except with regard to what God has revealed, since as for these things we have to do with what is above nature.[34] A theologian must also turn to the study and analysis of natural things, to discover analogies with supernatural realities.

Texts of Aristotle are frequently quoted in the objections put forward at the beginning of an article or in the answers Thomas gives at the end. The objections and answers help to understand better the theme which is studied. The references to Aristotle quoted in the arguments *sed contra* deserve to be mentioned separately.[35] Differently from the arguments *sed contra* brought forward in the *Disputed Questions*, those in the *Summa theologiae* have usually a different function, namely, they formulate the doctrine of the faith on a particular point (texts of the Bible, the magisterium of the Church, tradition, and the *consuetudo Ecclesiae*). On the other hand, when a doctrine accessible to reason is examined, the argument *sed contra* may formulate a definition or a thesis which contains a truth defined by reason. In such cases Aristotle may provide the argument. For example, in *Summa theologiae* I, question 12, article 1, he helps to establish that God's existence as such is not known to man per se, since no

---

33. The fact that Aristotle is called "the Philosopher" shows that for Thomas he is not just any thinker, but one of objective philosophical thought who gives a correct and true analysis of reality.

34. *ST* I, q. 99, a. 1.

35. Cf. Leo Elders, "Structure et fonction de l'argument *Sed contra* dans la *Somme théologique*," *Divus Thomas* 80 (1977): 245–60.

one can affirm the contrary of what is known per se, as some people do in respect of God.[36] It is superfluous to say that certain themes lie entirely outside the field of philosophy, such as the dogmas of the Divine Trinity, the Incarnation and Redemption, and the sacraments. With regard to these themes, we do not find any references to Aristotle. There also are none in the treatise of the theological virtues (*ST* II-II, qq. 1–46) except for the question whether with the virtue of faith one can believe something which is not true. Here Aristotle reminds us that a virtue as such is always ordered to the good.[37]

In order to explain that unbelief may take different forms, a text of Aristotle tells us that honesty has just one form, but that the contrary vices are many.[38] In *Summa theologiae* II-II, question 24, article 5, the question is raised whether a simple form like charity can increase. Aristotle reminds us that a simple form does not grow by addition. In II-II, questions 27–31, where friendship is studied Aristotle intervenes in two arguments *sed contra*, since he has given an excellent explanation of its nature.

In the long treatise of the moral virtues, Thomas quotes texts from Gregory the Great and Augustine to affirm that he is now speaking of supernatural virtues. But in a more detailed treatment of these cardinal virtues and their subdivisions, Aristotle is repeatedly invited to provide explanations.[39] He had in fact elaborated these themes in an unsurpassed way, as also Cicero, Macrobius, and Seneca had done. Thomas quotes these authors to develop and clarify his treatise, since the naturally acquired virtues are taken up and incorporated in the corresponding supernatural virtues. To understand the latter, one must examine the former. The supernatural virtues are not just a duplication, but place moral life on the level of divine grace and allow us to conduct a life in conformity with our Christian vocation.[40] The acquired virtues reach their fulfilment in the supernatural ones and lead us to the beatitudes promised by Christ.

In theological questions Aristotle can provide some technical assistance, as, for instance, to determine the meaning(s) of the term "word" or

---

36. Aristotle says as much in *Metaphysics* IV, 1005b1; cf. Aristostle, *Anal. Post.*, 76b23.

37. *ST* II-II, q. 1, a. 3, sed contra.

38. Aristotle, *Nicomachean Ethics*, 1106b35.

39. The supernatural moral virtues, which develop in those having received supernatural grace, follow the substructure of their natural counterparts. Cf. *QD de veritate*, q. 6, a. 5, ad 3: "Actus autem virtutum gratuitarum habent maximam similitudinem cum actibus virtutum acquisitarum."

40. *ST* I-II, q. 63, aa. 3–4; q. 65, a. 3. They help us to live as fellow citizens of the saints (Eph. 2:19).

that of the human body in the treatise of the Second Person of Holy Trinity.[41] To show how subtle the way is in which Thomas resorts to Aristotle, we must notice that in *Summa theologiae* I, question 26, where Thomas studies divine beatitude, Aristotle is not quoted, although he has a telling text in *Metaphysics* XII, chapter 7, 1072b24, where he writes that God is always in the state of the best and most pleasant contemplation. Thomas may have avoided a reference in order not to come in contradiction with what Aristotle says in the first objection-difficulty of the article, namely, that beatitude is the reward of a virtuous life—which does not apply to God. It is also possible that he did not want Aristotle to say something about the center and summit of divine life, in a question which prepares the transition to the study of Holy Trinity.

In *ST* I, question 44, article 1, Thomas formulates the thesis that all things have been created by God. God is subsistent being itself, and this cannot but be unique. He quotes Plato and Aristotle in confirmation, but the text of *Metaphysics*, α, 993b27 which he puts forward is not very clear. Aristotle only writes that of all beings the eternal beings must always be most true. In the second article of this question on creation, Thomas examines if prime matter has been created by God. In his central exposition he presents a summary of the development of philosophical thought with regard to the question of the first principles of things. As we have indicated before, Thomas suggests that Plato and Aristotle did not mention the cause of the being of all things, something which later philosophers have done.

About the middle of the thirteenth century, the masters of the University of Paris showed a tendency to give a benign interpretation of Aristotle's position and his apparent denial of a beginning of the world. Even Bonaventure wrote that although Aristotle had not reached the conclusion that the world was created by God, he had nevertheless come close to it.[42] This explains why in academic texts such as the *Quaestiones disputatae de potentia* and in his commentaries on certain treatises of Aristotle, Thomas is inclined to give a positive interpretation of Aristotle's position as to this point, while in the *Summa theologiae*, which was originally conceived as a manual for the students of the Dominican School in Rome, he felt free to draw attention to the insufficiencies of certain theories of Aristotle.

41. *ST* I, q. 34.
42. *In II Sent.*, d. 1, p. 1, a. 1, q. 1.

Has the world existed forever?⁴³ Aristotle affirms that it is eternal. Thomas looks for an opening in Aristotle's texts which would allow him to reconcile what Aristotle writes with the doctrine of the faith, which says that the world began to exist. Thomas himself accepted, of course, the dogma that the world had a beginning, but defended the theoretical possibility of a world dependent on God, but coexisting from all eternity with him. He even got involved in an academic debate on this theme with John Peckham.⁴⁴

The arguments advanced by Aristotle in defense of his view do not have the value of a demonstration, but show that the proofs advanced by others in favor of the world's eternal existence are defective.⁴⁵ To our surprise we discover in the text of the article and in the answers to the various difficulties brought forward, fifteen references to different works of Aristotle, something which suggest that Thomas wants to associate Aristotle with his own position. These quotations help to correct too simple affirmations and attribute some value to what Aristotle writes about the existence of the world. Aristotle himself moreover suggests that the question of the eventual eternal existence is treated by the dialecticians.⁴⁶ Certain authors argued that according to Aristotle prime matter has no cause, since it does not have a contrary from which it would have been derived,⁴⁷ but Thomas replies that Aristotle only wants to say that it has not come to existence by natural generation.

One of the treatises of the *Summa theologiae* where the presence of Aristotle is very dense is I, question 76, concerning the union of the human soul with the body. Can the soul, which is immaterial, be the substantial form of the body? Several Parisian professors seem to have denied it, and affirmed instead that the relationship of the soul with the body is that of a captain with his ship.⁴⁸ But more important is the argument of Aristotle, quoted in the *sed contra*: the spiritual soul *must* be the substantial form of man, because that which constitutes the formal difference of man is precisely the fact that his is a rational being. This is the effect of his soul.⁴⁹ Thomas explains it in greater detail in the central

---

43. *ST* I, q. 46, q. 1. On Aristotle's doctrine see *De caelo et mundo*, I, chap. 12.
44. See his short treatise *De aeternitate mundi contra murmurantes*.
45. Aristotle, *Physics* VIII, 1; Aristotle, *De caelo et mundo*, I, chap. 12.
46. Aristotle, *Topics* I, 194b16.
47. Aristotle, *Physics* I, 102a28.
48. See Hissette, *Enquête sur les 219 articles condamnés à Paris, le 7 mars 1277*, 200.
49. Aristotle, *Metaphysics* VIII, 1043a2–10.

part of the article, which presents Aristotle's doctrine of what in fact is the soul and what it does, namely, the first principle by which we nourish ourselves, have sense knowledge and local motion, and by which we think. This unique principle is the center from which flow forth our operations.[50] In the answer to the first difficulty—the intellect and the soul are immaterial[51] and for this reason cannot unite themselves to a body as its form—Thomas shows his extraordinary familiarity with the writings of Aristotle in a quote from *Physics* II, 194b12, where Aristotle writes that the human soul is separate from matter because thought is not a function of bodily organs, but that in the generation of a human being, the body is involved, for man is begotten by man in and out of matter.

In *Summa theologaie* I, question 76, article 2, the question examined is if a plurality of human souls is possible. The multiplication of individuals in a species is the effect of matter. Again in the argument *sed contra* Aristotle gives the solution: the soul is a particular cause and the same soul cannot be the form of several human beings, individually different.[52] Could there be several substantial forms in man as Plato had suggested and Avicebron confirmed? Aristotle rejects this view, but he does not express himself very clearly in respect of the question whether the function of thought is separated from other functions of the soul, not only with regard to what it is, but also locally.[53] The polyvalence of the human soul is illustrated by a text of Aristotle, which explains that the greater numbers contain also the smaller ones.[54] There is a presence of Aristotle in all the articles of our question.

Turning now to the second part of the *Summa theologiae*, the reader will notice that in his study of happiness in the first questions Thomas introduces numerous references to Aristotle, although the treatise is about understanding the characteristics of the supernatural virtues. This shows Thomas's conviction that the supernatural order is in harmony with nature, which it perfects. This provides also an answer to the question why Thomas has not treated the virtues starting from what Holy Scripture tells us about them, but follows the divisions given by Cicero and Macrobius: the supernatural realities adapt themselves to the articulations of the natural order. To understand the nature and the characteristics of the

50. Aristotle, *De anima* II, 414a12.
51. Ibid., III, 429a27.
52. Aristotle, *Physics* II, 195b26.
53. Aristotle, *De anima* II, 413b22.
54. Ibid., 414b28.

supernatural virtues, we must turn to the analysis of the corresponding natural virtues.[55] In this way Thomas could consider the *Nicomachean Ethics* as a fundamental treatise for the study of our moral life. The number of references to the writings of Aristotle is so considerable in this part of the *Summa theologiae* that the reader wonders how Thomas succeeded in finding so many texts in the works of Aristotle which bear on the different subjects discussed.

The presence of Aristotle is also remarkable in the *Summa theologiae* II-II. To determine that the traditional, four cardinal virtues mentioned by philosophers are also Christian virtues, Thomas quotes texts from the Church Fathers. In question 47, article 4, Gregory the Great is invited to tell us that prudence is a virtue, while Aristotle explains that it has its seat in practical reason and that it is concerned with individual actions. To situate justice and to determine its nature, Aristotle provides the basic information, but it is Gregory who tells us that it is a virtue, that is, that for us its practice unfolds at the level of supernatural life. Aristotle, however, provides the basis for the more precise description of its nature in article 9 of question 58: justice does not concern the passions, but our actions. Augustine asserts that fortitude is a virtue (q. 123, a. 1), while Aristotle provides the basis for a more precise description of its object (a. 4). Augustine, again, tells us that temperance is a virtue (q. 141, a. 1), but Aristotle determines more precisely its object in the *sed contra* argument of the second article.

These examples show the full extent of the role which Thomas assigns to Aristotle as well as its limits. The very numerous references show an unbelievable familiarity with the works of the Stagirite. Another aspect of turning to Aristotle is that in this way Thomas could show that on certain points Aristotle was close to the truth and to the teachings of Christianity[56] and that in any case he accompanies us in our analyses and investigations of nature and the supernatural order. On a few occasions Thomas sees a relation of a text of Aristotle to what Holy Scripture or Augustine tell us.[57]

With regard to the presence of references to Aristotle's works in the *tertia pars* of the *Summa theologiae*, the Philosopher is mentioned in more than sixty places. In III, question 63, article 2, Thomas tries to relate the

---

55. Cf. *QD de veritate*, q. 6, a. 5, ad 3 (see above note 34).
56. Cf. the reference to Aristotle, *Politics* II, in *ST* I-II, q. 105, a. 1.
57. For instance *ST* I-II, q. 37, a. 1, arg. 2.

entitative nature of the sacramental character which some sacraments impress on the receivers to one of Aristotle's categories of being. We find another example in question 66, article 4, where the question is raised if seawater can serve as matter in baptism. The greater part of these references is in questions 73–83 on the Eucharist.[58] To give an example of the use of Aristotle, Thomas recalls that according to Aristotle blood is part of the human body,[59] so that the question comes up why there is a separate consecration of the wine. There is a confrontation of what happens miraculously in this sacrament and Aristotle's physics. If having the accident of quantity also gives a body a location, how can the whole Christ be present in each particle of the consecrated bread (a. 76, a. 3, arg. 3)? Thomas points out that Christ is present *secundum modum substantiae*. In question 77 on the state of the accidents after the conversion of bread and wine, there are several references to Aristotle. Thomas stresses that it is impossible that the accidents exist without a subject in which they inhere and which they determine. He quotes the Aristotelian thesis *accidentis est inesse*[60] to explain that by God's omnipotence the Eucharistic accidents are maintained in existence as individual beings and as objects of sense perception, owing to quantity, the first accident, by which they are sustained. In question 77, article 5, Thomas has recourse to the Aristotelian doctrine, that the corruption of one thing is the generation of another, to conclude that something new must be formed when the species of bread and wine are corrupted. In his treatise on the sacrament of penance, Thomas uses what Aristotle wrote on the virtues of justice and temperance to illustrate the distinction between the different parts of penance.[61]

---

58. See Jorgen Vijgen, "Aquinas' Use of Aristotle in the Sacramental Theology of the *Summa theologiae* III, qq. 60–90," *Divinitas* 57, no. 2 (2014): 187–241.
59. Aristotle, *History of the Animals* I, lesson 4, 489a30; Aristotle, *On the Parts of Animals* II, 2, 647b12.
60. *QD de potentia*, q. 8, a. 2.
61. *ST* III, q. 90, a. 2.

3 ⁕ THE COMMENTARIES ON THE WORKS OF ARISTOTLE

During the seven last years of his life, Thomas wrote commentaries on twelve treatises of Aristotle. The first commentary is that on the *De anima*, which Thomas wrote at Rome when he was redacting the first part of the *Summa theologiae*, and the last commentaries were written in Naples. Of these commentaries those on the *Peri Hermeneias*, the *De generatione et corruptione*, the *De caelo*, the *Politeia*, and the *Meteora* remained unfinished. Before Thomas Albert the Great had written a paraphrase of all the works of Aristotle, in order to render "the Master of all those who think" more accessible to students.[1]

The commentaries of Thomas distinguish themselves by the fact that he explains the text, sentence after sentence, does not sidestep difficulties, and, thanks to his knowledge of the entire *Corpus aristotelicum*, succeeds in placing the contents of the individual treatises in the context of the whole of Aristotle's thought. The fundamental principles on which Thomas bases his work as a commentator are respect for the literal meaning of the text, concern to have at his disposal the best translations and the classical commentaries, a general sympathy with the thought and the method of Aristotle, the desire to bring out the profound meaning of the particular texts and the intention of showing that in general the philosophy of Aristotle is reconcilable with the Christian faith. To this effect he sometimes suggests conclusions which Aristotle himself had not imagined. I would nevertheless like to point out with Gilson that, in his commentaries on the works of the Stagirite, Thomas wanted above all to give a faithful exposition of the latter's philosophy.[2]

That Thomas undertook to comment on the most important works of Aristotle is the more surprising since as a master of sacred theology

---
1. See chapter 15 of this book on the commentaries of Averroes.
2. Étienne Gilson, *The Philosopher and Theology* (New York: Random House, 1962), 210.

he was burdened with several tasks, as we have explained in the previous chapter and as Thomas himself notes in his exposition of the *Peri Hermeneias*.[3] Obviously, commenting on the often difficult texts of Aristotle was a challenge, and Thomas wanted also to show that Aristotle's philosophy was not fundamentally opposed to the Christian faith, but rather represented an aid in the study of numerous theological questions. At the background of Aquinas's project lies the conflict which raged at that time between theologians who adhered to the Platonizing thought of St. Augustine and the masters of the Faculty of Arts who considered Aristotle their most important authority. In the framework of this study we cannot enter into details about the debate of the last decades on the question whether the commentaries faithfully represent Aristotle's thought, and whether Thomas wants to make out that his thought expresses the truth. Some scholars seem to think that these commentaries are, in the first place, pedagogical texts (except in cases when Aristotle's texts are in conflict with the doctrine of the faith). Others, however, suggest that they contain the philosophy of Thomas himself.[4] Our position is that in its substance the philosophical content of Aristotle's writings is accepted by Thomas, who, however, has prolonged Aristotle's reflections, clarified what he says, and marked theories in conflict with the Christian faith.

Obviously an exhaustive treatment of the contents of the different commentaries is not possible in this study. We must limit ourselves to mentioning the most important points and the way in which Thomas proceeds to comment on difficult texts.

The Commentary on the *Peri Hermeneias*

The *Peri Hermeneias* is a relatively short treatise, in which Aristotle examines the form of our affirmative and negative statements and the nouns and verbs of which they consist. Contrary to what Plato affirms in the *Cratylus*, Aristotle notes that nouns are not based on the nature of things, but are given to indicate things by convention. In classical antiquity the *Peri Hermeneias* attracted the attention of numerous scholars. In the Latin West Boethius commented on it in the translation of Marius Vic-

---

3. In the dedication of this work he wrote: "... inter multiplices occupationum mearum sollicitudines."

4. On this debate see John Jenkins, CSC, "Expositions of the Text: Aquinas's Aristotelian Commentaries," *Medieval Philosophy and Theology* 5, no. 1 (1996): 39–62.

torinus, but later himself made a new translation. Several masters wrote a commentary on the treatise.[5] In his exposition Thomas quotes almost exclusively the ancient commentators. His sources are Ammonius, translated by William of Moerbeke, and the two commentaries by Boethius. Boethius seems to draw on a Greek manuscript which contained the observations of various authors, such as Aspasius, Syrianus, and Alexander, and which presented the common doctrine of the schools of Athens and Alexandria. For studing the commentary of Thomas, we have now at our disposal the new edition of the Leonine by R.-A. Gauthier and the commentaries of Boethius as published by L. Minio-Paluello.[6]

Thomas wrote his commentary at the request of a student who had been nominated provost of the Church of St. Peter in Louvain at the end of 1269 or in 1270. This makes it possible to determine the time of composition. In his dedication Thomas declares that he wants to explain the more difficult passages (*altiora*) of the text in order to facilitate its study. The method he uses is that of explaining the *littera, sensus, et sententia* of the text.[7]

About the title of the treatise, he says that *interpretatio* is used to indicate that certain words have a sense. In this way one may call nouns and verbs interpretations, but says Thomas, they are the principle of an interpretation rather than the interpretation itself. One who declares that a thing is true or false "interprets." Our intellect has two operations, the simple apprehension of concepts and the composition or division of concepts in the judgement. Nouns and verbs are parts of such a judgement. A verb by itself is just a noun and does not yet tell us whether the thing it indicates exists. In connection with this passage Thomas explains that the verb "to be" does not signify in the first place a composition, but being real, that is that being enters the mind as that which exists in absolute way.[8]

The reality (*actualitas*) which the verb "to be" signifies is the actuality of all forms; the verb is in fact used to indicate the reality of each form. In the following lessons affirmative and negative sentences are examined. The sentences on contingent future events pose a problem. Those which concern necessary events are true, but as for statements about

---

5. See Jean Isaac, *Le Peri Hermeneias en Occident de Boèce à saint Thomas* (Paris: J. Vrin, 1953).

6. R.-A. Gauthier, *Expositio Libri Peryermeneias*, rev. ed. (Rome-Paris: Vrin, 1989).

7. See Hugh of Saint-Victor, *Didascalicon*, PL 176: 771D.

8. *In I Peri Hermeneias*, lesson 5: "Significat enim quod primo cadit in intellectu per modum actualitatis absolutae."

future contingent events there is a difficulty: they are necessarily either true or false. Thomas gives a remarkable explanation: "true" signifies that one declares that which is, or that something is true in the way it exists. A future contingent event does not yet have existence in itself, but exists in its cause, which is sometimes as yet undetermined. In a long parenthesis Thomas defends the presence of contingent events and contingent beings in the world, while for God, who exists entirely outside the order of time, the whole future is present in the eternal instant of his being. This is illustrated by the well-known phrases: "There will be a sea battle tomorrow" or "The battle will not take place." One of the two propositions is absolutely true, only we do not yet know which. The commentary of Thomas on the *Peri Hermeneias* remained unfinished and ends abruptly at the tenth chapter.

The *Expositio in Libros Posteriorum Analyticorum*

At the beginning of his commentary on *Posteriorum Analyticorum*, Thomas used the translation of the text by James of Venice, but somewhat later that that of Moerbeke, which could mean that he began his commentary in 1271 at Paris and finished it at Naples in 1272 or 1273. In his proem he explains the relationship between the *Categories*, the *Peri Hermeneias*, and the two *Analytics*, by referring to the operations of the intellect: the *Categories* explains what we do in the first operation, the *Peri Hermeneias* considers the operations of composition and division, and the other treatises of logic the third operation of the mind, namely, reasoning. The *Analytics* studies our reasoning in so far as it leads to certain conclusions and the other books of the *Organon* in so far as it ends at probable conclusions and provides material for discussion.

In so far as certitude is reached by the form of our reasoning—the syllogism—this is examined in the *Prior Analytics*, and with regard to its matter, that is "propositions per se and necessary," the theme is studied in the *Posterior Analytics*. The central theme of this last treatise is explaining where *scientific* knowledge begins, namely, in what was known before. Non-scientific knowledge is rendered possible by what our senses make known. But in order to reason one must know that something is and secondly what it is.

In a certain sense the conclusion of a syllogism is known in the premises, so that a demonstration does not go on without end by looking all the time for something which is previously evident, the point of departure must be evident by itself and immediately known. For scientific knowledge, however, this point of departure cannot be a contingent intuition.

This takes us to the consideration of the first principles of the speculative intellect, in particular the principle of contradiction. The first principles are immediately known. With regard to the development of the different sciences, Aristotle explains how we come to the knowledge of the universal and the necessary: from sense knowledge we go to reminiscence, when we remember having already perceived something before. Then, when this perception is reiterated and we notice the same thing repeatedly, we acquire experience (about it), called *experimentum*, for instance that a particular sort of herb helps to heal a particular disease. When this is confirmed, we deduce a general rule from it (for example, the use of certain things as medicine); and if this has to do with what is always the case and happens all the time in the same way, science is born. Therefore, the universal principles of the sciences are known by induction.[9]

The Commentary on the *Physics*

Aristotle's treatise called the *Physics* exercised a profound influence on the study of nature until the time of Galileo, but for many moderns it is no more than a historical document. Several authors have affirmed that it does not give a true knowledge of nature.[10] This places us before the question of what Thomas thought of this treatise of Aristotle and up to which point he subscribes to the arguments and explanations of Aristotle. Does he accept superseded theories?[11] Thomas seems to have written his commentary in Paris in 1268–69; he used the new translation by William of Moerbeke, while still comparing it with the older translation (called the *Vetus*) by James of Venice. M. Grabmann suggested 1268 as

---

9. *In II Post. Anal.*, lesson 20, no. 595.

10. See Jonathan Barnes, "An Aristotelian Way with Scepticism" in *Aristotle Today: Essays on Aristotle's Ideal of Science*, ed. Mohan Matthen (Edmonton: Academic Printing & Publishing, 1987), 75. Francis Cheneval and Ruedi Imbach consider the *Physics* as without value for scientific studies (*Thomas von Aquin: Prologe zu den Aristoteles-Kommentaren* [Frankfurt am Main: Klostermann, 1993], xiii).

11. For more details see Leo Elders, "St. Thomas Aquinas's Commentary on Aristotle's *Physics*," *The Review of Metaphysics* 66, no. 4 (2013): 713–48.

the *terminus a quo* of the redaction of this commentary, since Thomas took into account certain positions of Siger of Brabant, whose commentary on the *Physics* dates to 1268. Thomas describes the order of the eight books of which the *Physics* is composed as follows: Book I presents a general introduction and explains the place of the philosophy of nature and studies next the principles of the things subject to change. Aristotle examines the principles of this science in Books II and III. In Book IV motion and what is consequent on it is studied. Books V and VI deal with the parts of motion, while Book VII deals with motions in their relation to the movers and the bodies set in motion. Surprisingly Thomas does not mention Book VIII. Did he consider it the continuation of Book VII? This interpretation is difficult since he does set the book apart.[12] The reason why is given at the beginning of the commentary on Book VII, where Thomas writes that Aristotle first demonstrates the existence of a First Mover and a first motion in order to pass, in Book VIII, to the investigation of the nature of the First Mover and the first movement.[13] It would seem that Thomas is implying that in Book VIII we are passing to the field of metaphysics.

In order to determine up to which point Thomas accepts the contents of the *Physics*, one has to examine from close quarters what he says about many of the arguments. We notice that he often criticizes the demonstrative value of several of them. Some examples: in Book I, lesson 12, number 98, we read that up to chapter six of the first book Aristotle proceeds as if he were involved in a dispute, but that now he begins to determine the truth.[14] Thomas is receptive to the fact that certain arguments have little value and that further on in this text sometimes Aristotle formulates with greater precision a topic he had discussed previously without reaching certitude.[15] Repeatedly Thomas draws attention to Aristotle's habit of proceeding from the suppositions of other authors, before formulating his own theory.[16]

Thomas even explains this way of proceeding and of resorting to

---

12. *In VIII Phys.*, lesson 2, no. 972.

13. *In VII Phys.*, lesson 1.

14. See also ibid., Book I, lesson 13, no. 114: "Sic igitur patet quod priores sermones disputati ad utramque partem fuerunt, secundum aliquid veri, sed non totaliter." A similar remark is found in Book IV, lesson 3, no. 422.

15. With respect to the argument in *Physics* VII, chap. 1, lesson 2, Thomas observes that there is a better one in Book VIII, chap. 5, lesson 9.

16. Ibid., Book III, chap. 5, lesson 8, no. 353: "Semper antequam probet id quod est suae opinionis procedit ex suppositione opinionis aliorum communis."

what people in general think: the human mind, guided by a natural inclination, sometimes is tending to the truth, although the particular person in question does not understand well why he does think so.[17] He is also very attentive to occasional real or supposed contradictions in the text,[18] and draws attention to a *sophisma consequentis*.[19] The reader discovers the same critical analysis of certain arguments on the First Mover and the motion of the first heaven. In several places Thomas uses the expression *secundum intentionem Aristotelis*. This is often a reference to Aristotle's philosophical thought in general or to his principles. This allows Thomas to advance interpretations which go beyond the text he is commenting upon.[20] Quite frequently Thomas corrects or completes Aristotle's arguments. Sometimes he quotes the comments of Averroes on a particular text to criticize them, such as the statement that it is impossible for a thing to receive its perpetual being from another.[21] Thomas wants to show that Averroes's explanations are not always conformable to Aristotle's thought.

With regard to the question whether Thomas accepts the essential part of Aristotle's theories, the answer is affirmative: the doctrine of primary matter and substantial form, of which physical bodies are composed; the distinction between substances and their accidents; the definition of motion as the actualization of a being in potency in so far as it remains in potency, a definition which Thomas calls excellent;[22] the division of motion into its species; the analysis of place and time; and Thomas makes his own the argument which leads to the existence of the Prime Mover. He says that the demonstration of the First Principle on the basis of an analysis of motion is most effective. One must admit its existence when the world and movement are eternal, and even more when they are not.[23]

---

17. Ibid., Book I, chap. 5, lesson 10, no. 79: "Ita interdum intellectus humanus quadam naturali inclinatione tendit in veritatem licet rationem veritatis non percipiat."
18. Ibid., Book I, chap. 4, lesson 9, no. 66.
19. Ibid., Book IV, chap. 2, lesson 3, no. 424.
20. Ibid., Book VIII, chap. 1, lesson 21, no. 1153, where he says that there is no potency to not-being in the simple substances.
21. Ibid., Book VIII, chap. 5, lesson 21, nos. 1152–53.
22. Ibid., Book III, chap. 1, lesson 2, no. 285.
23. Ibid., Book VIII, chap. 1, lesson 1, no. 978.

The Commentary on the *De caelo et mundo*

Thomas's exposition on the *De caelo* is one of his last commentaries. Its date of composition is approximately known since William of Moerbeke finished his translation of the commentary of Simplicius on the book of Aristotle on June 15, 1271.[24] Thomas used this commentary from the beginning to the end of his exposition (which goes until the third chapter of the third book). This means that he wrote his commentary between July 1271 and the fall of 1273, when he put an end to all his writing. Thomas had access to the translation of Aristotle's text made by Gerard of Cremona, from an Arab version (before 1187) and also to that of Robert Grosseteste (which went as far as the beginning of Book III).[25]

The *De caelo* is a treatise on cosmology: in the first two books Aristotle deals with the nature and the movement of the celestial bodies and their eternal being, while in Books III and IV he treats of the four elements of the sublunar world and their movements and of the theories of the generation and the behavior of the heavy and the light bodies. A first question is whether Thomas accepted as an established fact the ingenious cosmological system of Eudoxus, as corrected by Callippus and taken over by Aristotle, whose contribution to the system was that of assigning physical reality to the homocentric spheres of Eudoxus:[26] from the point of view of physical science the theory of isolated and dispersed bodies, moving through the void, does not make sense.[27] In Aristotle's system the center and the circumference of the universe are its most important parts.

Did Thomas make his own the ingenious, but mistaken reconstruction, its geocentrism, and immutable fixed stars circulating around the earth? With regard to this point we must notice that for Thomas the theory had only the value of a hypothesis, which explained a number of phenomena, but which could be replaced by another theory resulting from new observations. He writes in effect that "although what we observe can be saved by the elaboration of this kind of hypotheses, one should not say that these hypotheses are true, since the appearances regarding the stars

---

24. Cf. Martin Grabmann, *Die Werke des hl. Thomas von Aquin*, 3rd ed. (Münster: Aschendorff, 1949), 276.

25. Fernand Van Steenberghen, *Aristotle in the West* (Louvain: Nauwelaerts, 1970), 94.

26. See Leo Elders, *Aristotle's Cosmology. A Commentary on the De Caelo* (Assen: Van Gorcum, 1966), 8.

27. *De caelo et mundo*, Book II, chap. 8.

may perhaps be satisfactorily explained in a different way, which man has not yet conceived."[28]

The hypotheses which have been made in the past are possible, and one may retain them as long as they are not contradicted by the facts.[29] Thomas, however, studies and writes to discover the truth rather than to describe the different opinions about a certain question. He says so in as many words in his comments on Book I, lesson 2: "Whatever one thinks of these interpretations [of Simplicius and Alexander] does not have much importance for us, because the purpose of the study of philosophy is not to come to know what people have thought, but how things are in reality."

If the exposition by Thomas of a theory of Aristotle is not immediately followed by a refutation, it does not mean that Thomas agrees with all that Aristotle wrote. One should read with attention the rest of the commentary on a passage. In Book II, chapter 3, lesson 3, Thomas comments on the theory of the animation of the heavens, to note that Aristotle deals with this theme according to his own opinion (*secundum opinionem suam*). Somewhat further on he writes that Aristotle supposes (*supponit*) that the world is animated, basing himself on his doctrine of the First Mover, who moves in so far as desired.

The presence of arguments characterized by considerations of a geometrical nature, places the reader before a new difficulty. Aristotle is convinced that local motions must describe a circle, a straight line, or a figure composed of these two. But is that not an extrapolation to a different genus of reality (geometry instead of physics)? Thomas thinks that this is not the case: geometrical figures do not constitute a genus different from that of physical bodies, since the latter add sensible matter to figures which in a certain way they contain.[30] This answer opens the way to the application of mathematical principles in physics. He admits the finiteness of the world and its unicity.

Owing to the commentary of Simplicius, Thomas knew the theory of Heraclides Ponticus, who taught that the earth revolves about the sun, but he did not consider it a probable alternative since most "modern" astronomers did not admit it.[31] All through his treatise Aristotle affirms on the one hand the finitude of the heavens and on the other its eternity, a thesis which contradicts the Christian faith. The question of the eternity

---

28. *In II De caelo*, chap. 12, lesson 17, no. 451.
29. *In I Meteor.*, chap. 7, lesson 11, no. 68.
30. *In I De caelo*, chap. 2, lesson 3, no. 24.
31. *In II De caelo*, chap. 8, lesson 1, no. 396.

of the world is connected with the thesis of its incorruptibility. Aristotle thought that he could demonstrate the latter on the basis of observation: during the entire expanse of time no change has been observed to take place in the heavens, but Thomas says that this argument gives only a certain probability.[32] Simplicius mentions the theory of the Christian commentator Philoponus, who thinks that the celestial bodies have the same matter as other bodies. Thomas does not follow him but notes that Aristotle's arguments only show that the world did not begin to exist in the way certain authors had said.[33]

About those texts in which the world is considered to be divine, Thomas writes that Aristotle just states the common convictions of people or expresses himself in the way of Plato and those pagans who called the world divine because of its incorruptibility.[34] In order to explain the motion of the celestial bodies, attributed to special movers or souls, Thomas writes that it is better to admit as mover a substance outside the world, whose power is not limited to the latter.[35] He suggests that one understand the passages on the eternity and the divinity of the heavens in such a way that there is no conflict with the Christian faith. Thomas delves deeper to rejoin the principles of his philosophy of being.

When Aristotle tries to give an explanation of the rotation of the first heaven—a fundamental fact for him—Thomas suggests that the First Principle of all things might very well be its cause.[36] On another occasion he quotes the phrase "God and nature do nothing in vain" to say that here Aristotle himself admits that God is the cause who made the celestial bodies.[37] Here as well in other places, Thomas takes Aristotle's texts in their literal sense in order to remind the reader that Aristotle's main theories agree with the doctrine of the Christian faith. All through his commentary Thomas uses the commentary of Simplicius as an indispensable source of information, but he rejects resolutely Simplicius's penchant to assign souls to the heavenly bodies. On several occasions he also mentions the opinion of Alexander, as Simplicius presents it. Thomas's commentary witnesses to an extraordinary understanding of the theories proposed by Aristotle in the *De caelo et mundo*.[38]

---

32. *In I De caelo*, chap. 3, lesson 7, no. 76.
33. *In II De caelo*, chap. 1, lesson 1, no. 289.
34. *In I De caelo*, chap. 3, lesson 7, no. 75; *In II De caelo*, chap. 3, lesson 4, no. 334.
35. *In II De caelo*, chap. 2, lesson 3, no. 315.
36. *In II De caelo*, chap. 5, lesson 7, no. 363.
37. *In I De caelo*, chap. 4, lesson 8, no. 91.
38. See also Leo Elders, "Le commentaire de saint Thomas d'Aquin sur le De caelo d'Aristote,"

The Exposition on the *De generatione et corruptione*

The commentary of Thomas on the very popular treatise of Aristotle *De generatione et corruptione* remained unfinished.[39] Thomas only commented on the first five chapters of Book I. His commentary is later than his expositions on the two preceding works of Aristotle, since in the *De generatione et corruptione* he refers to them. For this reason we must place it in the last period of his life, when he was in Naples. Thomas used a text which was close to the *translatio nova* of the writings of Aristotle. This new translation of the *De generatione et corruptione* is a revision of the *translatio vetus* and is attributed by J.K. Otte to Burgundio of Pisa, but to Moerbeke by others.[40]

The purpose of Aristotle's treatise was the scientific explanation of the becoming of substances.[41] In his proem Thomas determines the place of the text amidst the treatises on nature. In his *Physics* Aristotle examines mainly motion in general as common to all bodies; in the *De caelo* he studies local motion; then there are other movements which are not proper to all bodies, but to those of lower rank. Among these movements, generation and corruption are the most important. Alteration and augmentation are subordinated to generation and corruption. When studying the latter we must consider these changes first in their most fundamental form, that is to say, as transformations of the four elements which are at the basis of all changes of material substances.

After a survey of what the ancient philosophers said about this question, Thomas examines Aristotle's theory of generation and corruption

---

in *Proceedings of the World Congress on Aristotle (Thessaloniki August 7–14, 1978)* (Athens: Ministry of Culture and Science, 1981), 173–87; James A. Weisheipl, "The Commentary of Saint Thomas Aquinas on the *De caelo* of Aristotle," *Sapientia* 29 (1974): 11–34.

39. See Johannes M M H Thijssen, "The Commentary Tradition on Aristotle's *De generatione et corruptione*: An Introductory Survey," in *The Commentary Tradition on Aristotle's* De Generatione et corruptione, ed. Johannes M.M.H. Thijssen and Henricus A.G. Braakhuis (Turnhout: Brepolis, 1999), 99–20.

40. See Joanna Judycka, "L'attribution de la *Translatio nova du De Generatione et corruptione* à Guillaume de Moerbeke," in *Guillaume de Moerbeke: Recueil d'études à l'occasion du 700e anniversaire de sa mort*, ed. Josef Brams and Willy Vanhamel (Leuven: Leuven University Press, 1989), 247–252.

41. See Bertrand Carroy, "Héritage et différences: Thomas d'Aquin et Albert le Grand, commentateurs du *De generatione et corruptione*," in *Lire Aristote au Moyen Âge et à la Renaissance. Réception du traité sur la Génération et la corruption*, ed. Joëlle Dacos and Violaine Giacomotto-Chorra (Paris: H. Champion, 2011), 102–117.

and next of alteration and augmentation. In addition to the generation of the four elements, there is also that of complex beings and the countless intermediary generations, such as those which occur between the seed and the full-grown animal. Such accidental qualities as warm and cold, humid and dry have an essential role in the formation of new substances and in their decomposition.

It appears that Thomas hardly used other commentaries while writing his exposition.[42] Bertrand Souchard draws attention to some examples with a theological connotation: Thomas would have wanted to make an allusion to the transformation of bread and wine in the Eucharist and the production of natural residues during the corruption of the accidents of bread and wine. Furthermore characteristic of Thomas is his seeing a parallelism between light and the act of being.[43]

The Commentary on the *Libros Meteorologicorum*

The commentary on the *Meteora* by Thomas also remained unfinished. Thomas commented on the text up to chapter 8 of the second book.[44] In this treatise Aristotle deals with cosmological processes which take place in the atmosphere and on the earth, but first he gives a survey of what he had established in his previous works on the cosmos and the elements. Thomas used the translation by William of Moerbeke and wrote his commentary either during his second period at the University of Paris or at Naples.

At the beginning of his exposition Thomas explains that in order to have a perfect scientific knowledge of a subject one must not only know it in general, but also in its division into species. For this reason Aristotle examined in this work the elements in the higher regions of the world, such as falling stars, comets, and the rain, but also phenomena which

---

42. See Bertrand Souchard, "Le commentaire de Thomas d'Aquin du *De generatione et corruptione* d'Aristote: de la critique aristotélicienne des matérialistes à la critique thomasienne des spiritualists," in Giacomotto-Chorra, *Lire Aristote au Moyen Âge et à la Renaissance*, 55–83.

43. Souchard, "Le commentaire de Thomas d'Aquin du *De generatione et corruptione* d'Aristote," 73.

44. Cf. Antoine Dondaine and Louis-Jacque Bataillon, "Le commentaire de saint Thomas sur les *Météores*," *Archivum fratrum praedicatorum* 36 (1966): 81–152. See also the study of Kevin White, "Three Previously Unpublished Chapters from St. Thomas Aquinas's Commentary on Aristotle's *Meteora*," *Medieval Studies* 54 (1992): 49–93.

happen in the lower part of the world on the earth as earthquakes, lightning, thunder, etc. In his exposition Thomas does not refer to other authors except once to a theory of Plato mentioned in the *Phaedo* on the formation of rivers and the sea.

The Commentary on the *De anima* of Aristotle

Thomas wrote his exposition on the three books of the *De anima* in Italy, probably in 1268, before his departure for Paris. The detailed study of Aristotle's doctrine of the soul and its faculties was useful during the composition of the questions on man in the first part of the *Summa theologiae*. The text of the *De anima* consists of three parts or books. The first is a general introduction and provides a survey of the opinions of Aristotle's predecessors about the soul and its operations. Book II gives a definition of the soul and its faculties (potencies) in general, to deal next with sense knowledge. In Book III Aristotle examines the *sensus communis* and the imagination to pass from there to the study of the intellect and the way in which thought in us originates so that we think. In the last chapter of this book Aristotle deals with movement as we observe it in sensitive beings.

The *De anima* was frequently discussed already from the end of the second century B.C. Posidonius studied it, as did later Alexander of Aphrodisias. Plotinus, Porphyry, and Themistius refer to it. About 1030 Avicenna wrote a Platonizing synthesis of the question of the human soul, and Averroes left us three commentaries on Aristotle's treatise.

Thomas was the first commentator in the West to use the new translation by Moerbeke. He takes over some views of Averroes but blames him for a number of serious errors. Thomas does not add a proem to his commentary, since the first chapter of the text serves in this capacity. Thomas begins by praising the intellectual culture and the value of the sciences which are the perfection of man. Subsequently he points out that thought is not a product of a bodily organ: the role of the latter is limited to providing objects to the intellect.[45] Thought is the act of the soul which has, in a certain way, the character of a substance, which exists by itself, although it forms a unity with the body.

---

45. *In I De anima*, chap. 1, lesson 2, no. 19: "... indiget obiecto corporali."

In the second book Aristotle determines what in his view and in reality the human soul is (*"secundum propriam opinionem et veritatem"*). The way in which Thomas expresses himself suggests that Aristotle's exposition lets us know what the soul is. Then he explains the first definition of the soul, namely, the first act of a physical and organic body. On the following pages the faculties of sense cognition and the way in which this knowledge is generated are studied. At this point Thomas reminds us that the one who actually knows something, *is* the object he knows.[46]

Thomas begins his commentary on Book III at the third chapter of the text: How does thought come about? The intellect does not mix with matter: it cannot have the nature of the things which it is coming to know, and therefore it is not some particular thing; it is nevertheless in potency with regard to all things.[47] The intellect is not a particular specific thing, and it is totally different from the material order: it is *separate*. In the fourth lesson Thomas develops the theory of the agent intellect, which fertilizes the (possible) intellect with the cognitive object it abstracts from the images of the imagination. He shows that the agent intellect is not a substance separated from man but a faculty of the soul. He refutes the theory of Averroes according to whom we think in so far as the representations of our imagination enter into contact which the concepts present in a common separate intellect outside us. Further on in his commentary, Thomas tries to show that the possible as well as the agent intellect continue to exist after the death of the body.[48] He also writes that whatever transcends sensible things is not known by us, except in a negative way.[49]

He explains the two operations of the intellect—forming concepts and judgements. As to the difference between the intellect and the senses, Thomas notes that the intellect is moved as soon as it seizes a good or bad object, while in the senses pleasure or aversion make their appearance and the objects are subsequently desired or rejected. In the intellect this also happens, but the senses do not form a real judgments but make a quasi-comparison.[50] In the following part of this lesson, Thomas speaks of abstraction and observes that Aristotle did not do what he promised, namely, to explain how we know the things which are separated from matter in their being.

46. *In II De anima*, chap. 5, lesson 12, no. 377.
47. *In III De anima*, chap. 4, lesson 7, no. 681.
48. Ibid., chap. 5 lesson 10, nos. 742–43.
49. Ibid., chap. 6, lesson, 11, no. 758.
50. Ibid., chap. 7, lesson 12, no. 771.

In lesson seven the principle, often quoted by Thomas, is mentioned: the soul is, in a way, all things (*"anima est quodammodo omnia"*). This principle is explained in the following way: all things are either objects of thought or are perceived by the senses. In the process of knowledge, the soul becomes these objects in a certain way. Thomas adds a few lines on the finality of knowledge. We are given a soul instead of all the forms of nature so that in a certain way we can become the totality of all things.[51]

This section of the chapter presents what one might call the empiricism of Aristotle. Thomas formulates it as follows: "Nothing is in the intellect which was not before in the senses;" it is indeed a fact that whatever we know comes to us from the senses and that our thought is always accompanied by sense knowledge, but in the material which it receives from the senses, the intellect can discover things which the senses do not perceive; it can formulate laws of being and with the help of the first principles conclude that immaterial being exists.

The Commentaries on *De sensu et sensato* and *De memoria et reminiscentia*

The composition of the two commentaries *De sensu et sensato* and *De memoria et reminiscentia* is to be placed in Italy during the years 1267–68, a short time before Thomas returned to Paris. The text deals first with the senses in general and their organs to study next light and colors, and, in the nineteenth lesson, the taste and smell of things. The question is raised whether sensible qualities are infinitely divisible. In the sixteenth lesson Thomas examines if the sensible qualities affect the medium before the senses themselves. The answer is that where there is a medium this is often affected gradually. The last three lessons consider whether two senses can perceive something at the same time. In his other works Thomas refers some twenty times to the *De sensu et sensato*.

The commentary on the *De memoria et reminiscentia* contains eight lessons. In a fine introduction Thomas writes that we observe in nature a gradual progress to more perfect beings. When one compares plants to animals, they seem almost without life, but in comparison with minerals it is evident that they are living beings. Likewise when we pass from the

---

51. Ibid., chap. 8, lesson 13, no. 790: "Anima data est homini loco omnium formarum, ut sit homo quodammodo totum ens."

animals to man, we see certain properties by which they approach human beings. In certain animals one observes a behavior with resembles prudence and which shows that they have memory. There is however a difference, for human beings possess in addition reminiscence.

In the fourth lesson of his commentary, Thomas explains what according to Aristotle reminiscence is: it is not a simple receiving of some knowledge, nor a simple evocation of what one has perceived before.[52] It is an act which makes us remember what we have perceived before. It presupposes a vague memory and is an effort to find and to recall what we had known earlier. In order to recall something more easily, we must introduce a certain order in this subject, impress it profoundly on the mind, recall it several times, and start this process of recalling from the beginning.[53] In the works of Thomas there are some fifteen references to this treatise.[54]

The Commentary on the *Metaphysics*

The exposition on the twelve books of the *Metaphysics* is a voluminous and very important work, which occupies a central position among the Aristotelian commentaries of Aquinas. With regard to its date of composition and the translations used by Thomas, investigators have met with great difficulties. Father Jean-Pierre Torrell writes that Thomas used some five translations.[55] With respect to the date of composition, we notice that as from the exposition on Book VII he designates Book Λ as Book XII. But it is only after 1271 that the new translation by Moerbeke appears which introduced Book K as Book XI, so that Λ becomes Book XII. If this is correct, Thomas would have written his commentary at Paris or at Naples.[56] Thomas may have reworked certain sections, such as Books II and III. He ends his exposition at the end of Book XII (Λ), in

---

52. Ibid., chap. 2, lesson 4, no. 335: "... quod reminiscentia non est memoriae resumptio nec nova acceptio."

53. Ibid., chap. 2, lesson 5, no. 371.

54. See Kevin White and Edward M. Macierowski, introduction to Aquinas, *Commentaries on Aristotle's* On Sense and What Is Sensed *and* On Memory and Recollection, trans. Kevin White and Edward M. Macierowski (Washington, D.C., 2005).

55. See Leo Elders, "Le commentaire sur le quatrième livre de la *Métaphysique*," in *San Tommaso d'Aquino nel suo settimo centenario. Atti del Congresso Internazionale Roma-Napoli, 17–24 aprile 1974*, vol. 1 (Naples: Edizioni domenicane italiane, 1975–76), 207–14, where it is shown by numerous examples that Thomas used several translations.

56. See Jean-Pierre Torrell, OP, *St. Thomas Aquinas*, vol. 1, *The Person and His Work*, 2nd ed., trans. Robert Royal (Washington, D.C.: The Catholic University of America Press, 2005), 231 ff.

which Aristotle demonstrates the existence of God. Thomas summarizes the arguments of Aristotle with the sentence that therefore there exists a supreme governor of the world, who is the first mover, the first intelligible, and the first good, who is God blessed for ever and ever.[57] Thomas does not comment on Books XIII and XIV, which are a study of the doctrines of Plato and his successors at the Academy, Speusippus and Xenocrates.

In his proem Thomas unites the different conceptions of first philosophy as Aristotle mentions them in Books A, Γ, and E: it is the science that gives the greatest certitude; it is the knowledge of the first causes and the science whose subject is furthest removed from the domain of the senses. In Book Γ Aristotle writes that it is the science of being qua being, and in Book E, where he presents a tripartition of the theoretical sciences, metaphysics becomes theology, the science of the immaterial and unmoved, namely, the divine. Thomas says that the science of being qua being and theology are the same since, when studying the causes of being, we arrive at the First Cause of all things.

Contrary to what some texts of Aristotle say, Thomas points out that in metaphysics we also study material things, abstract from matter.[58] That we are able and allowed to abstract the concept of common being (*ens commune*) from material things and to leave behind the material world is shown by the existence of such immaterial entities, as the human mind and soul. The proem is in perfect agreement with the *Expositio super librum Boethii De trinitate*, question 5, articles 2 and 3. Thomas does not use a historical approach to explain Aristotle's partly divergent conceptions of the nature of first philosophy in the different books of the metaphysics.[59]

With regard to the method applied by Thomas, it appears that the commentary is a gigantic effort to understand the doctrine exposed by Aristotle in the successive books. Thomas tries to make us understand and see the contents of the different texts. He points out the activity of the intellect which can study things in different ways. In his explanations

---

57. *In duodecim libros Metaphysicorum Aristotelis exposition*, Book XII, chap. 10, lesson 12, no. 2663. In this text Thomas does not say that according to Aristotle the First Unmoved Mover is also the Creator of the world.

58. *In VI Metaph.*, chap. 1, lesson 1, no. 286.

59. Cf. John F. Wippel, "Thomas Aquinas' Commentary on Aristotle's *Metaphysics*," in *Uses and Abuses of the Classics: Western Interpretations of Greek Philosophy*, ed. Jorge J. E. Gracia and Jiyuan Yu (Burlington, Vt.: Ashgate, 2004), 138–64.

Thomas stays within the limits of what a text demands from us and avoids digressions. His commentary is a patient and very precise analysis, line by line, of this very difficult philosophical treatise. Thomas wants to explain the text because of its valuable contents and the truth contained in it. He tries to discover an order in the arrangement of the different books, and on particular points he gives numerous references to other parts of the book found in the Stagirite's other works. Thomas freely uses Aristotle's doctrinal expositions and statements in other books of the latter's works. He shows that some particular texts do not necessarily exclude a truth such as the creation of the world by God. In such cases, however, one cannot say that he surreptitiously corrupts the text, because it is always clear to the reader from the context that in a particular text he goes beyond what Aristotle said, although he does not always explicitly say so, contrary to what a modern commentator would do.[60]

Some critics, such as J. Owens, say that Thomas reads his own philosophy of being into Aristotle's treatise.[61] It is true that in this commentary as well as in some of his other works Thomas says that in his text Aristotle acknowledges that things depend on God, who is the source of their being. We have already mentioned this question in the previous chapter where we quoted texts from the *Summa theologiae* and the *Quaestiones disputatae de potentia* on creation. In these texts there was no question of a direct commentary on a text of Aristotle. I wish to draw attention to the reserve of Thomas in his exposition of *Metaphysics* XII, chapter 10. In the last sentence of the commentary, quoted above, Thomas summarizes what Aristotle says of God in Book Λ: God is the First Mover and the Primary Good. He does not add that he is the source of the being of things.

Another example of the way Thomas comments on the *Metaphysics* is his treatment of the doctrine of participation. He subscribes to Aristotle's criticism of the theory of Ideas, but avoids the latter's total rejection of the notion of participation, which in Thomas's view expresses the relationship of created beings with God in the field of efficient causality. The way in which Thomas deals with the question of separate substances also illustrates the character of his commentary. In his proem he mentions God and the *intelligentiae* as beings (*res*) studied in metaphysics. On several occasions he speaks of these separate substances. In chapter 8 of

---

60. See Leo Elders, "St. Thomas Aquinas's Commentary on the Metaphysics of Aristotle," *Divus Thomas* 86 (1983): 307–26.

61. Cf. James Doig, *Aquinas on Metaphysics: A Historico-doctrinal Study of the Commentary on the Metaphysics* (The Hague: Nijhoff, 1972).

Book Λ, Aristotle even appears to admit a plurality of immaterial substances which move the different celestial spheres. In the first chapter these movers are called universal and first causes, and further on we read that man, in uniting himself to them, finds his ultimate happiness. In the second ook the knowledge of these substances is called the end of our intellectual life.⁶² In his commentary Thomas keeps the plural (the immaterial substances), until he arrives at chapter 9 of Book XII, where Aristotle himself raises the question whether the separate and immobile substances are one or several. Thomas does not object to Aristotle's theory that each sphere needs a mover, even if he thinks that a superior and unique substance is able to produce several different motions. Thomas concludes that Aristotle did arrive at the view that a unique, unmoved Mover is the cause of the movements and activities in the world. Out of respect for Aristotle, he refrains from adding at this place that this mover is also the cause of the being of things.

At the end of Book XII, chapter 6, and at the beginning of chapter 7, the conclusion is reached that there is a first being, whose substance is to be in fully in act. From this it follows that the First Mover must be unique, as Aristotle himself says for reason of the good government of the world which requires a unique supreme cause.⁶³ Thomas adds a reflection on the nature of God, the first intelligible object, who as Aristotle says is at the same time thought in act and an intelligible object. In this connection Thomas quotes the principle that the cause of an attribute is itself more what the attribute is than what its effects are.⁶⁴ Divine qualities, such as thought and joy, are present in a much higher degree in God.⁶⁵ In his commentary on Book XII, chapter 9, where Aristotle excludes from God that he knows the world, instead of correcting right away what Aristotle says, Thomas writes that what is excluded from the First Mover is that he would receive his knowledge from the things in the world outside him. In his commentary on Book XII Thomas does not say that (for Aristotle) God is being itself, existing by itself.⁶⁶

In Book XII, 1070a13, Aristotle rejects the Platonic theory of Ideas,

---

62. *In II Metaph.*, chap. 1, lesson 1, no. 286.
63. *In XII Metaph.*, chap. 10, lesson 12, no. 2663.
64. Aristotle, *Anal. Post.* I, chap. 2, 72a29: "Semper id magis tale est propter quod unumquodque est tale."
65. *In XII Metaph.*, chap. 7, lesson 7, no. 2543.
66. "*Ipsum esse per se subsistens.*" See *ST* I, q. 4, a. 2. Also *ST* I, q. 3, a. 4, and other places in the *Summa*.

noting that in certain cases the form does not exist separately from the composite substance (e.g., the form of a house), except in the art of the one who constructs it. Thomas observes that when we consider the form as existing in the mind of the builder, it exists outside matter.[67] By this observation he keeps the door open for the doctrine of God's creative activity: according to Thomas the Ideas of all things are present in God's intellect. But he does not say so explicitly and only mentions the plan of the house present in the mind of the builder, while he indicates the importance of his remark by the words *sed ego dico*.

In chapter 6 of Book XII Aristotle brings the argument that if there is an eternal motion, an eternal substance must exist. Thomas accepts the argument in the case where the movement of the first heaven would indeed be eternal.[68] But at the end of the chapter he adds a *sed tamen est sciendum*: the reason given for the eternity of motion and the accompanying argument to show that time is eternal, which are taken over from *Physics* VIII, do not have the value of a demonstration. But what Aristotle writes about the eternal and necessary being of the First Mover is valid. If the world is not eternal, it must have been made by a being which existed before it.

In the last chapter of Book XII that in the world it is as with a family, in which free persons do not act by whim, but conduct a very regular life. Thomas adds the following sentence: "In the nature of all things there is a certain inclination, placed there by the First Mover, which directs them to the end proper to each of them. This shows that natural things act in view of an end, even if they do not know it, for they receive their inclination to this end from the First Intellect."[69]

Thomas's commentary on the *Metaphysics* is a philosophical text. It is a patient and careful analysis, line after line, of a difficult treatise. He explains what Aristotle wrote because of the value of the text. That the exposition is a philosophical commentary is confirmed by the way in which Thomas deals with the question of the separate substances and the First Mover in Book XII. Thomas himself would undoubtedly have written a different treatise, but he restricts himself to a commentary. It is right that in certain passages he attempts to find an opening toward the doctrine of the Christian faith, but in such cases the intention is to show that a particular text does not exclude a truth of the faith. Contrary to what Joseph

---

67. *In XII Metaph.*, chap. 7, lesson 3, no. 2448.
68. Ibid., no. 2492.
69. Ibid., chap. 10, lesson 12, no. 2634.

Owens and James Doig suggest, one does not find an intrusion of Thomas's own doctrine of being.[70] This moreover was not necessary because Aristotle does not place his book on the level of a study of being qua being. He makes no statements on being as the perfection of all perfections nor a definition of God as the being subsistent in itself.

Thomas employs subtle means to indicate his own position or to make certain clarifications or corrections, namely, short phrases such as *sciendum est autem* or *considerandum est*, but he also creates a certain distance between the text and his own thought by such words as *hic dicit, hoc excludit*, and *hic supponit*. For the attentive reader the commentary is a mine of information on Aristotle's metaphysics. Owing to his knowledge of the entire *Corpus aristotelicum* and his penetrating grasp of the meaning of the text, Thomas's commentary has no equal.

The Exposition on the Ten Books of the *Nicomachean Ethics*

The *Commentary on the Books of the Ethics* was composed by Thomas at Paris in the years 1271–72. To determine these dates the completion of the translation by Moerbeke and a certain parallelism with the writing of the *secunda secundae* are decisive. Thomas's commentary explains what Aristotle is saying.[71] A difficulty arises from the fact that Aquinas's own moral theology is inspired by the Gospel and the doctrine of the faith, while Aristotle moves on a level and in a climate where not God but man is at the center. This fact has given rise to divergent evaluations of this commentary of Thomas. Is it true that from the very beginning Thomas places himself in a Christian perspective, as certain critics say?[72] May we use the commentary as a source of the ethics of Thomas himself? H. V. Jaffa thought that the exposition was of little value for the study of the text of Aristotle, since it was contaminated by what is proper to Thomas's Christian ethics.[73] Other scholars, however, say that the com-

---

70. This is confirmed by John F. Wippel, who declares, contrary to Doig's view, that he has not found any passage in which Thomas comments on the text through the spectacles of his own philosophy of being. See Wippel, "Thomas Aquinas' Commentary on Aristotle's *Metaphysics*," 146.

71. We now have access to the text in the splendid Leonine edition by R.-A. Gauthier, Sententia libri Ethicorum, 2 vols. (Rome: Ad Sanctae Sabinae, 1969).

72. Torrell, *The Person and His Work*, 228.

73. Harry V. Jaffa, *Thomism and Aristotelianism: A Study of the Commentary by St. Thomas Aquinas on the Nicomachean Ethics* (Chicago: University of Chicago Press, 1952).

mentary is very useful to help us in the study of the *Nicomachean Ethics*,[74] and even to learn about it.[75] Recently some students of the commentary such as M.-D. Jordan insisted on the difference between the contents of the *Nicomachean Ethics* and Aquinas's own moral thought.[76] Several of the differences pointed out by Jordan disappear, however, when one keeps in mind the nature of medieval commentaries, which could be an exposition of the thought of the author of the text commented upon, but also an interpretation or adaptation of other views. The texts commented on were in the first place considered as a road to moral knowledge.

Thomas's commentary on the *Ethics* is not preceded by a proem: the two first chapters of the text function as such. Aristotle stresses the distinction between the theoretical and non-theoretical sciences. In this second group human action is the end to which the sciences are ordered. Ethics is ordered to show the way to a morally good life. Thomas, for his part, stresses, more than Aristotle had done, the cognitive nature of this discipline: man should have a true knowledge of the end he must attain.[77] In his commentary Thomas shows, against what Jacques Maritain and others said, that an independent moral science is possible: our reason can discover that we are ordered to the contemplation of God as our last end, and it can also discern the more important obligations of natural law, as flowing forth from our human nature. But since we do not really know the nature of our last end and of our happiness, ethics remains an imperfect science. On several occasions Thomas draws attention to the imperfect nature of the happiness of which Aristotle speaks.

Thomas points out the difference between ethics as a practical science and the virtue of prudence: in so far as it is a science, ethics belongs to the speculative intellect, whereas prudence has its seat in the practical intellect.[78] Regarding the role of the reason and of desire in determining the last end, Aristotle is not very clear, but Thomas notes that desires should be orientated according to the inclinations of human nature.

---

74. Ralph McInerny, *Aquinas on Human Action: A Theory of Practice* (The Catholic University of America Press: Washington D.C., 1992). See also James Doig, *Aquinas's Philosophical Commentary on the Ethics* (Dordrecht: Kluwer Academic Publishers, 2001).

75. Cf. Christopher Kaczor, "Thomas Aquinas's Commentary on the *Ethics*: Merely an Interpretation of Aristotle?" *American Catholic Philosophical Quarterly* 78, no. 3 (2004): 353–76.

76. Mark D. Jordan, "Thomas Aquinas's Disclaimers in the Aristotelian Commentaries," in *Philosophy and the God of Abraham: Essays in Memory of James A. Weisheipl, OP*, ed. R. James Long (Toronto: Pontifical Institute of Mediaeval Studies, 1991), 99–112.

77. *Sententia libri Ethicorum*, Book I, lessons 2 and 3.

78. Ibid., Book VI, lesson 7 (p. 357 of the Leonine text). Cf. also Book I, lesson 1; and Book II, lesson 2 (Leonine, 81, 71–78).

This takes us to the question of how to determine the morality of our actions. Aristotle proposes several criteria, such as those of the wise man and the right mean,[79] but Thomas weakens this position, by writing that the wise man is *as* a criterion of what one should do.[80] On first view Thomas seems to accept the theory of a mean between excess and deficiency, but he notes that Aristotle's theory applies only to the moral virtues, where excess and deficiency occur and we can therefore speak of a mean. Rather than being a mediate position, a virtue is a correct attitude which establishes the right mean.[81] Aristotle also mentions right reason as a criterion of the morality of our actions. Thomas agrees with Aristotle and stresses the role of reason in establishing the norms of conduct. For Thomas this is an objective process, and he uses the term *ratio recta* in order to underline the objective character of our reason insofar as it is a norm of our conduct.

At this point he introduces the concept of *synderesis*, the habitus of the first principles of the practical intellect, the first of which is that what is good must be done, and what is evil avoided. In several texts of the exposition he mentions these first principles of the practical intellect.[82] These principles, he says, constitute what is naturally right; we cannot ignore them, since they have been naturally impressed on our minds. Aristotle, however, did not develop the role of these principles.

Aristotle writes that once a person has become unjust, he no longer has the possibility of changing. Thomas attenuates this declaration: it is not possible to change only by a decision of the will without making efforts.[83] Aristotle mentions the opinion according to which it is not possible to change the way the good and the bad present themselves to the intellect, but he rejects it, since one can control one's own moral development: we are responsible for the judgments we make of the morality of our actions.[84] Thomas distinguishes between a general theoretical knowledge, which is independent from the particular dispositions of the agent and is acquired by reasoning, and, on the other hand, a moral prac-

---

79. Aristotle, *Nicomachean Ethics*, 1134b7. Other criteria mentioned are the eye of the soul and the mean between excess and deficiency.
80. *Sententia libri Ethicorum*, Book III, lesson 10, (Leonine, 148).
81. Ibid., Book II, lesson 6 (Leonine, 96).
82. Ibid., Book II, lesson 4 (Leonine, 88); Book V, lesson 12 (Leonine, 304); lesson 15 (Leonine, 319).
83. Ibid., Book III, lesson 12 (Leonine, 154).
84. Aristotle, *Nicomachean Ethics*, 1114a31–1115a6.

tical knowledge concerning the actions one wants to perform.[85] In this case one forms the judgment that a particular thing is good for oneself. Such a judgment can be based on a passion or on a habitual state of mind as, for example, some vice. This note by Thomas is a development of the theory of Aristotle.

In Book V Aristotle makes a distinction between what is right by its nature and what is so by positive law. What is naturally right has everywhere the same value (τὸ φυσικὸν δίκαιον), since it does not depend on what people think, but is derived from man's nature. Thomas explains that natural law is valid because it refers to human nature which is everywhere the same, while positive law is only valid for those who live under the jurisdiction of the particular state which issues it.[86] Thomas adds that natural justice consists in the first principles of the practical intellect and the principles closely connected with them. He mentions some negative principles such as that one should not unjustly cause damage to others and that one must not steal the goods of others. To prevent a reader of Aristotle's text from thinking that legal justice is arbitrary, Thomas adds that it is derived from natural law and corroborates this remark by a reference to Cicero.[87]

Thomas's commentary contains important developments of Aristotle's theory of natural justice and of legal justice and of the criteria of our actions. The following books of the *Nicomachean Ethics* study the virtues of fortitude, temperance, liberality, magnanimity, etc. According to Aristotle virtues are perfections and so a virtuous man will not commit bad actions, whereas in a Christian vision life remains a struggle, even for a virtuous person.[88] More important is the fact that the description of certain forms of conduct according to a few of the virtues mentioned by Aristotle is difficult, or even unacceptable to Christians. How does Thomas comment on these passages? Here are some examples: when Aristotle writes that death seems to be the greatest evil and that the dead lose everything, Thomas adds: "that is of the things belonging to our present life and which we know, but we have no knowledge of those things which belong with the state of souls after death."[89] Likewise when Aristotle writes

---

85. *Sententia libri Ethicorum*, Book III, lesson 13 (Leonine, 156f).
86. Ibid., Book V, lesson 12 (Leonine, 304).
87. Ibid. (Leonine, 306).
88. Aristotle, *Nicomachean Ethics*, 1100b34; 1105a26–1105b12. Cf. Jean-Yves Jolif, "Le sujet pratique selon saint Thomas d'Aquin," In *Saint Thomas d'Aquin aujourd'hui*, ed. Association des Professeurs de Philosophie des Facultés catholique de France (Paris: Desclée de Brouwer, 1963), 29.
89. *Sententia libri Ethicorum*, Book III, lesson 14 (Leonine, 161).

that the courageous man defends his position in combat even if there is no hope that he will win (because it is so beautiful to act in this way), Thomas adds that when a courageous person defends his position in such a case, he does so in order that some good may come from it.[90]

According to Aristotle it is painful for a courageous person to be deprived of his life, an opinion contradicted by the Stoics. Thomas adds this commentary: "We must nevertheless consider that because of their hope in a future life, death can become desirable for some virtuous persons, but that is not what the Stoics said and the Philosopher also had nothing to say about what belongs to man's state in another life."[91]

In lessons 19 and 20 of Book III, Thomas comments on what Aristotle says about the virtue of temperance. The text of the *Nicomachean Ethics* shows some signs of a dualistic conception of man, since the pleasures of our lower faculties are entirely separated from those of the intellectual soul. On this point Thomas stresses the unity of man, such as it is conceived in the hylomorphistic doctrine: what the senses perceive prepares the way for intellectual knowledge, and for this reason we experience some pleasure in the conformity of sensible things with our senses, even if in certain cases this conformity is not ordered to sustain our natural life.[92] With regard to the virtue of liberality, Thomas shows that it has a more extensive use than the one indicated by Aristotle, who restricts it to that of money. It is more important to regulate the desire to possess material things. The virtue of magnificence leads to spending large sums of money for important purposes and undertakings. It would seem that a poor person with no money cannot possess this virtue. Thomas's answer is that our inner attitude is more important.

Next Aristotle treats the virtue of magnanimity which, he says, makes us seek honors and to know our own value, an attitude which seems to enter into conflict with humility. For Aristotle humility is the attitude of mediocre people who admit that they do not deserve great honors. For Thomas, on the other hand, humility is the virtue which makes us acknowledge our condition as a creature, yet, he says, it is not necessarily contrary to magnanimity. The magnanimous person finds little pleasure in the honor which is given him and does not attach much value to it.[93] Thomas tries to make the text acceptable.

90. Ibid., lesson 15 (Leonine, 166).
91. Ibid., lesson 18 (Leonine, 178).
92. Ibid., lesson 19 (Leonine, 182).
93. Ibid., Book IV, lesson 9 (Leonine, 230–31).

In Book VI Aristotle examines the intellectual virtues. This section of the text shows the influence of Plato's thought. In the seventh lesson Thomas explains the order in which one should learn the different subject matters which complete our formation. The study of mathematics and physics must come before that of moral philosophy. In Book VII continence and moral weakness are examined. Thomas sheds light on what Aristotle says about moral weakness. We must distinguish between a perversity of the appetite which does not affect practical reason and the case when everything is corrupted by it.[94] With regard to pleasure Thomas takes over Aristotle's definition: pleasure is the unobstructed act of a habitus in conformity with our nature.[95] Thomas defends Aristotle's evaluation of pleasure by noting that something which all men are seeking cannot be bad. Nature itself does not move us to what is bad or erroneous.[96]

The subject discussed in Books VIII and IX is friendship. Thomas explains with great clarity Aristotle's beautiful doctrine on this theme. But the friendship between God and man lies beyond Aristotle's horizon, which is that of "the friendship of which we are speaking now." This sentence qualifies the level on which Aristotle in moving in his ethics.[97] In Book IX Aristotle discusses the properties and the effects of friendship. The virtuous man, he writes, lives in peace with himself and has no reason ever to have regrets. Thomas comments: he will not easily feel regret.[98]

In Book X Aristotle comes back to the discussion of pleasure to explain that happiness is found above all in contemplation. Thomas comments on the arguments of Aristotle observing that happiness accompanies the activity of the intellect, which is the highest in us. This conclusion is above all directed against the Averroists who placed the intellect outside us.

Thomas shows that he has grasped the profound intention of Aristotle's text, the grandeur of which he admits. But on certain themes he goes beyond what Aristotle writes and offers a more systematic view of ethics, without however, substituting his own philosophy of moral life for that of Aristotle. The fact that Aristotle's text lends itself to a certain deeper

---

94. Ibid., Book VII, lesson 1 (Leonine, 380).
95. Ibid., lesson 12 (Leonine, 429).
96. Ibid., lesson 13 (Leonine, 423).
97. Ibid., Book VIII, lesson 7 (Leonine, 465).
98. Aristotle, *Nicomachean Ethics*, 1166a29; *Sententia libri Ethicorum*, Book IX, lesson 5 (Leonine, 514).

comprehension of the subject treated and to a systematic ordering is to be explained by the high degree of truth of his thought on the subject. It is true that on several occasion Thomas opens up the text toward the direction of Christian doctrine, but Thomas does not use considerations based on revelation to modify what Aristotle wrote. He shows a profound respect for Aristotle's treatise and does not insist on omissions to make the text more complete. The order of the ten books and of the themes treated is not that of Thomas himself. But he shows the profound truth in a great deal of what Aristotle tells us.[99]

The *Sententia libri Politicorum*

The commentary on the *Sententia libri Politicorum* by Thomas remains unfinished and ends at lesson 6 of Book III. The rest of the text was completed by Peter of Auvergne. But the original text in its recent editions goes back to Louis of Valence (Rome, 1492) and is not very reliable. Thomas uses the translation by William of Moerbeke and seems to have known the commentary by Albert the Great. Thomas's commentary probably dates to his second Parisian sojourn.[100]

In Book I Aristotle discusses the communities of people, in particular in domestic life and basic economy which makes us need others and collaborate; he speaks of property and its acquisition. The city, a unit formed of several villages, is a community which has reached full autarchy. Aristotle concludes from this that the city is the natural fulfilment of the social life of man, who is therefore destined to live in a political community. Aristotle speaks next of the domestic economy and of serfdom. In Book II the different constitutions of the Greek city states are examined. In Book III Aristotle studies what being a citizen implies and what the duties of citizens are.

The commentary of Thomas follows the text closely. In general Thomas accepts the doctrine manifested, but may express some restrictions. He introduces the concept of the law of nations[101] and makes important observations. As to certain questions such as the legitimacy of making profit in

---

99. See Leo Elders, "St. Thomas Aquinas's Commentary on the Nicomachean Ethics," in *The Ethics of St. Thomas Aquinas*, ed. Leo Elders and Klaus Hedwig (Vatican City: Libreria Editrice Vaticana, 1984), 9–49.
100. See Torrell, *The Person and His Work*, 233 ff.
101. *Sententia libri Politicorum* I, lesson 4.

business deals, Thomas proposes a broader view in the *Summa theologiae*. With regard to serfdom which in classical antiquity provided the needed manpower in families as well as in cities, Thomas speaks of it in the third and fourth lessons of the commentary on Book I.[102]

---

102. See Fabrizio Casazza, "Il Commento di San Tommaso d'Aquino alla Politica di Aristotele," *Archivio teologico torinese* 10, no. 2 (2004): 325–42. Cf. also *Tomás de Aquino, Comentador de Aristóteles*, ed. Héctor Velázquez (Mexico: Universidad Panamericana, 2010).

4 ~ THE STOA, SENECA, AND CICERO

Stoicism is one of the three philosophical schools of Greece which exercised a great and lasting influence on Western thought and culture. Zeno, the founder of this school, was not a Greek, although he developed his doctrine in Athens, where he established his school. He followed the lessons and attended the conferences of Theophrastus, the successor of Aristotle in the Lyceum, and those of Polemon, the head of the academy after the death of Xenocrates. But he was also profoundly influenced by the cynic Crates and developed his thought in opposition to Epicureanism, the philosophy developed by Epicurus some fifteen years earlier. Zeno taught in a public hall, the so-called *Stoa poikile*, after which his school was named.

Zeno was of Phoenician origin, which marked his thought in that in his view the practice of philosophy must serve our moral life and have a practical and social purpose. In order to organize our lives according to his teachings, Zeno says that we are helped by *physics*, which lets us know the world in which we live, our own human nature, and the ultimate cause of all things, the fundamental law, the cosmic law, and divine providence. All reality is corporeal; it is one material reality characterized by a vital force, the *pneuma*, consisting of air and fire. This pneuma is active in all things, giving them a vital tension and making living beings grow; it conserves minerals and is the cause that all things work together (συμπαθεία). It is the moving principle of all beings, and so it is called god. This means that religion and the science of divine beings (theology) are part of physics. Stoic philosophy is nevertheless thoroughly religious. Stoics are pantheists who speak of the divine *logos* as a unifying force which shows different faces. But above all they are materialists.

The things of the material world send impressions to our senses and in this way knowledge begins to develop in us and we assent to what we perceive. Then we grasp what we have perceived, and this is called comprehension. We elaborate logic, the art of thinking well, which helps us to make proper discourses and to distinguish between what is true and what is false. For Aristotle logic is the art we use in the sciences, but for the Stoics it is more than that: it is the way of life of the wise man, it helps him to discover how the world is organized—which to them means that it allows him to describe the influence of the *pneuma* in all the articulations of the world. This *pneuma* must transmit what we observe to our central faculty, the faculty of judgment, the so-called *hegemonikon*. For the Stoics our entire inner life unfolds itself at the level of matter and of the senses.

Our attitude, however, with respect to the world is more than a simple receiving of impressions. The *logos*—reason in us as a participation in and expression of the universal cosmic reason and law—considers and compares these impressions before giving its assent. This process is called συγκατάθεσις,[1] which makes us form general representations (ἔννοιαι). This process is at first incomplete, since the logos unfolds itself in us in an imperfect way and we have no more than a certain anticipation—πρόληψις—of the order we must follow. Later the faculty of representation in us becomes active. Connected to perception we grasp the way in which what we have perceived affects us in our innermost being, a process the Stoics call συναίσθησις. At this point we begin to seek what can lift up our life to a higher level and put what we perceive in relation with ourselves. This process is called οἰκείωσις, our inclination to approve and to appropriate what is useful. The *logos*, which is active in us, is also the basis of the universal order which creates sympathy between all beings. It is the law of the world and also its destiny (fate); it is the principle which assigns a place to each thing.

Opposing Epicurus, Zeno argues that if a man follows his passions and instincts, he places himself at the level of the animals, while in reality he is different and must conduct his life under the direction of the *logos*. The *logos* also determines what is the purpose of his life. This is a life conformed to the order of the world and in harmony with ourselves—ὁμολογουμένως ζῆν. Physics instructs us about the order of things. Zeno also said that in following our nature we must discern and accept the most profound and strongest inclination in us which presses us to keep

---

1. Cicero speaks of *assensio* (*Academica priora*, 37–39). For a survey of ancient Stoicism, see Max Pohlenz, *Die Stoa. Geschichte einer geistigen Bewegung* (Göttingen: Vandenhoeck & Ruprecht, 1948).

ourselves alive and to develop ourselves in accordance with our natural inclinations. But this fundamental inclination is not limited to the promotion of our own well-being, it extends also to other human beings and all human kind.

Acting in agreement with nature places us in the order of the morally good. Man's life should be highly consistent under the guidance of the *logos*. Chrysippus expressed Zeno's maxim of acting consistently by pointing out that we should be consistent not only with ourselves, but also with nature (τῇ φύσει). Now human nature shows a dual aspect, namely, what belongs to the physical and animal nature of man, and secondly what is proper to the domain of reason. Good is what renders man morally good; when a person does what is good the *logos* manifests itself in his conduct, namely, when he is acting according to the order and the law of the universe. For the Stoic the good is a life in accordance with the logos, a life in which we practice the virtues, which include friendship with one's fellow men. External goods, such as wealth, power, comfort, and pleasure, are in reality indifferent things (ἀδιάφορα).[2] Yet among these indifferent things some are more important than others. The wise man, for instance, prefers to be in good health rather than to be sick and suffering. So certain of the morally indifferent things are preferable (προηγμένα), while others are not.

We must allow reason to do its work in us and to direct our actions. Passions are movements in us which turn us away from a life according to reason and must be extirpated. The Stoics mention four basic passions among many other feelings: pleasure, pain, desire, and fear. On the other hand, the virtues render our lives morally good. The virtues are dispositions produced in us by the *pneuma* and give the right tension to the soul. The first of them is wisdom, meaning good common sense and prudence, which puts our life in order. It becomes the virtue of fortitude when it helps us to bear the difficulties which we encounter and to face dangers, while it becomes temperance when it lets us choose what is really desirable. Lastly it is justice when it regulates our relations with other human beings. The relations between these virtues are so close that one may wonder whether the four virtues are really different dispositions of the soul.[3]

---

2. *Stoicorum veterum Fragmenta*, III, 117.
3. Cf. Pohlenz, *Die Stoa*, 123–28.

Three periods are distinguished in the history of Stoicism. Instead of periods, some speak of three forms which Stoic thought has taken. There is the ancient Stoicism of the founder, Zeno, his successor Cleanthes, and of the great organizer Chrysippus. The next period is that of the so-called Middle Stoa, from about 200 BC until the beginning of the Roman Empire, during which Posidonius and Panaetius are the most important representatives of the school. Finally there is the Stoa during the Roman Empire, represented by Seneca, Epictetus, and the emperor Marcus Aurelius. The School of the Stoics preserved its system and coherence beyond these first five hundred years and continued to exercise its influence even after the collapse of the Roman Empire.

Because of its insistence on the value of the virtuous life, the discharging of one's duties, and the presence of the *logos* in human life, Stoicism has found many sympathizers and even influenced Christian authors. In his discourse before the Areopagus in Athens, the apostle Paul follows a line of thinking familiar to the Stoics. He evokes man's natural knowledge of God and the historic evolution of religion such as Posidonius had described it. There are also a good number of reminiscences of Stoic positions in Clement of Alexandria's works.[4] Of the Christian authors who knew and used certain Stoic views, one may mention Tertullian, Lactantius, Ambrose, Jerome,[5] and Augustine.[6] Stoicism played an important role in the West by its moral teachings, especially before the imposing entry of Aristotle's philosophy at the end of the twelfth century. The message of Stoicism, addressed to all men, promised an inner liberation: according to its view most people live in a sort of slavery by pursuing insignificant, if not bad ends. What is important is to establish in us the realm of reason and to insert ourselves in the order of the universe.

After this general introduction we must return to our central theme, Thomas Aquinas and Stoicism.

---

4. Cf. Pohlenz, *Die Stoa*, 415–24.

5. Jerome calls Seneca "noster Seneca" (*Adv. Jovanianum* I, 49: PL 23: 28). In his commentary on the prophet Isaiah, he says of the Stoics "qui nostro dogmati in plerisque concordant" ("Commentariorum in Esaiam," *Corpus christianorum, series latina*, 73: 151).

6. As for Augustine, he rejects Zeno's definition of knowledge (*Contra Academicos*, chap. 4, 18). Charles Baguette even speaks of a Stoic period in the evolution of Augustine's thought in "Une période stoïcienne dans l'évolution de la pensée de saint Augustin," *Revue des Études Augustiniennes et Patristiques* 16, nos. 1–2 (1970): 44–77. For a detailed treatment of the presence of Stoicism in the Latin authors, one may consult Marcia L. Colish, *The Stoic Tradition from Antiquity to the Early Middle Ages, 2: Stoicism in Christian Latin Thought through the Sixth Century* (Leiden: Brill, 1990). See also Michel Spanneut's great book *Permanence du Stoïcisme. De Zénon à Malraux* (Gembloux, Belgium: Duculot, 1973).

The Sources from which Thomas Has Drawn His Knowledge of Stoicism[7]

In the Middle Ages the writings of the great personalities of ancient Stoicism had already been lost for a long time. The only Latin Stoic philosopher of whom Thomas had read several works is Seneca. He does not seem to have known Epictetus and Marcus Aurelius. For a considerable part of his information, he depends on authors such as Cicero, Augustine, Hieronymus, and Boethius (in the *De consolatione philosophiae*). Cicero is without doubt his most important source, but Thomas also knows Pseudo-Andronicus's *De passionibus*, the *De natura hominis* of Nemesius, and texts of Isidorus and others.

Cicero and Thomas Aquinas

On the question of Cicero as a source of information, C. Vansteenkiste points out that Thomas integrated a considerable part of the moral doctrine of Cicero in his system, by combining it with Aristotelianism and Neoplatonism.[8] But with M. Spanneut we must stress that Thomas did not consult the *De finibus* nor the *De legibus* of the great Roman orator and philosopher. Vansteenkiste found three hundred quotations from or references to Cicero in the works of Aquinas. But in these, Stoic doctrines as such are not greatly emphasized. There are references to the Stoic theory of fate, to which all things are subordinated.[9] Thomas repeatedly recalls that Cicero followed the Stoic theory according to which all passions are diseases of the soul.[10] He also refers to Cicero for the theory of the cohesion of the virtues[11] and recalls that for the Stoics all virtues are equal.[12]

According to another theory mentioned by Cicero, all sins are also equal.[13] Cicero thinks that the Stoics would have reached this conclusion since they considered sins under the aspect of being privations. Thomas

---

7. See Michel Spanneut, "Influences stoïciennes sur la pensée morale de saint Thomas d'Aquin," in *Ethics of St.Thomas Aquinas*, ed. Leo Elders and Klaus Hedwig (Vatican City: Libreria Editrice Vaticana, 1984), 50–79.

8. Clemens Vansteenkiste, "Cicerone nell'opera di S. Tommaso," *Angelicum* 36 (1959): 343–82. Cf. also Edward K. Rand, *Cicero in the Courtroom of St. Thomas Aquinas* (Milwaukee: Marquette University Press, 1946): and Michel Spanneut, *Permanence du Stoïcisme*.

9. *SCG* III, 94. The reference is to the *De divinatione*.

10. *ST* I-II, q. 24, a. 2; q. 59, a. 2, ad 2; q. 71, a. 3; *QD de malo*, q. 12, a. 1, ad 12.

11. *ST* I-II, q. 65, a. 1 (reference to the second book of the *De Tusculanis disputationibus*).

12. Ibid., q. 73, a. 2.

13. Ibid., q. 73, a. 2.

mentions that Cicero is mistaken in rejecting the Aristotelian doctrine of the possibility that the wise man may have moderate passions.[14] He is more severe is his criticism of a passage in the *De divinatione* where Cicero writes that, if God foresees all things, the outcome of whatever happens in the order of causes is certain and there is no room left for our free will.[15] This remark is superficial and not well thought out, says Thomas. It subtracts human life from divine providence.[16] But in general Thomas is quite positive with regard to Cicero's thought and associates his doctrine with that of the Peripatetics. He often uses what Cicero writes on the cardinal virtues and on the circumstances of the moral acts. By its very nature, moral virtue seeks the mean; it is a habitus in accordance with reason.[17] Thomas valued and quoted the divisions of the main virtues into subordinate virtues proposed by Cicero, as, for instance, those of prudence, justice, fortitude, and temperance. He made his own the division of prudence into integral parts as mentioned by Cicero, namely, *memoria, intelligentia, providentia*.[18] Likewise we find correspondences with what Cicero writes about justice, fortitude, and temperance in chapters LIII and LIV of his *De inventione*.[19]

Thomas and Seneca

The only direct source of Stoic philosophy which Thomas has consulted was Seneca who enjoyed a good reputation under the Christian authors of the first centuries. Seneca was also thought to have been in contact with the apostle Paul, and it was even suggested that he converted to the Christian faith; but Thomas does not take these rumors into account. In some eighty-five places he mentions Seneca and his doctrines, especially in the *Summa theologiae*, II-II, where the moral virtues are studied. Thomas quotes certain definitions and descriptions. He follows Seneca in his beautiful exposition of clemency[20] and of friendliness toward all.[21] The four cardinal virtues are each a genus, the other virtues are species

---

14. Ibid., q. 24, a. 2.
15. *SCG* III, 94 (*De divinatione*, a text which Thomas read in Augustine's *De civitate Dei*, V, chap. 9).
16. *ST* I, q. 22, a. 2, ad 4.
17. *ST* II-II, q. 47, a. 7.
18. *ST* II-II, q. 48, a. 1. Cf. Cicero, *De inventione* II, 53, 159.
19. Cicero himself borrowed much from the philosophical tradition and also from Aristotle. See Olof Gigon, "Cicero und Aristoteles," *Hermes* 87, no. 2 (1959): 143–62. Cf. also M. Spanneut, "Influences stoïciennes sur la pensée morale de saint Thomas d'Aquin," 70–72. In his treatment of these virtues Thomas goes beyond his sources.
20. *ST* II-II, qq. 157–59.
21. *ST* II-II, q. 168, a. 4.

of them.²² According to Seneca, reason alone is sufficient to make us act with the virtue of fortitude, so one does not need the help of a passion such as anger. Such a total rejection of the passions is criticized by Thomas who writes that this position of Seneca shows that he is a member of the "sect" of the Stoics and puts him in direct conflict with teachings of Aristotle.²³ This critical position in respect of the passions is recurrent in Seneca's works. Such passions as fear which paralyzes and anger which enrages us are worse, he says, than the desires of concupiscence.²⁴

The *Stoici* in the Works of Thomas

In his treatises and commentaries, Thomas mentions the *Stoici* some ninety-five times. He sometimes borrows his information from the writings of Augustine, but frequently also from other sources. Once he mentions Aulus Gellius, quoted from Augustine. What Thomas says to be Stoic doctrine has probably for the greater part been taken from Cicero, Seneca, Macrobius, Augustine, Boethius, and Nemesius, as well as from anthologies and collections current in his day. It is noteworthy that Thomas does not distinguish between the different Stoics, probably in order to simplify the study of their doctrines. He prefers to speak of Stoicism as being one typical philosophy. We see this also, notes Spanneut, in that he kept silent about the name of Epictetus as defending the theory that the images of our imagination penetrate in the interior of our soul without this process being subject to our control.²⁵ Rational knowledge in us is actually caused by the impressions things make on our senses (*cognitio intellectus causari ex sensu*).

One of the main doctrines mentioned by Thomas as being characteristic of Stoic philosophy is that of fate: all things in our world happen necessarily, and the concatenation of the different causes is necessary. Thomas also mentions the opinion that things are governed by certain spirits, which the Stoics called gods. We are repeatedly reminded that the wise man is free from passions, and, on the other hand, that the virtues are to such an extent connected to one another that they seem to be just one habitus. In this connection we must also mention that Thomas recalls that for the Stoics all sins are equal.

22. *In II Ethic.*, lesson 8.
23. *ST* II-II, q. 123, a. 10, ad 2.
24. *ST* II-II, q. 155, a. 2, obj. 2.
25. Augustine, *De civitate Dei*, IX, 4, mentions Epictetus. See Spanneut, "Influences stoïciennes sur la pensée morale de saint Thomas d'Aquin," 50–79.

There are no other true goods than those of the soul. The things which people at large consider to be good, are called "convenient" (*commoda*) by the Stoics, while for the Peripatetics they are real goods, although of lesser worth than those of the mind.[26] External goods are of less worth than those of the soul which occupy the first place. The goods connected with the body lie in the middle.[27] The wise man seeks happiness in an active life.

An Examination and Evaluation of Stoic Theories

Fate and Fatalism

The term "fate" is used by the Stoics in the sense of the activity of the main cosmic cause, which is necessary when considered from the point of view of the effects it is producing. In some texts, however, it denotes a series of causes. As John Rist writes, under the Stoics and the authors close to their school, there is much confusion in the way they conceived the precise meaning of the causality of fate.[28]

A basic text for studying Thomas's position with regard to Stoic philosophy is his commentary on the *Peri Hermeneias* of Aristotle, where the latter examines the question of the truth of statements concerning contingent future events. According to the Stoics there is an unbreakable connection between a cause and its effect. If the cause exists, the effect follows necessarily. All future events happen necessarily, and there is a necessary concatenation of causes.[29] Thomas objects that not all causes are of such a nature that their effects cannot be impeded.[30] The Stoics define the necessary and the impossible according to external criteria; according to them, that which cannot be impeded is necessary, and that which is always impeded is impossible. Thomas observes that the necessary is that which is determined in its nature; the impossible is that which is determined not to be.[31] According to the Stoics the celestial bodies exercise a determining causal influence on the life of man, but Thomas says

---

26. QD de veritate, q. 26, a. 8, ad 9.
27. In I Ethic., lesson 12.
28. John Rist, *Stoic Philosophy* (London: Cambridge University Press: 1969), 112–32.
29. QD de malo, q. 16, a. 7, ad 14.
30. In I Peri Hermeneias, lesson 14, no. 185.
31. Ibid., lesson 14.

they can only have a limited influence on corporeal things, including the human body, but none on our spiritual faculties.[32]

According to the Stoics our life is conducted by an inevitable necessity.[33] But Thomas objects that our life would no longer be human if our choices were determined by cosmic and material factors, as the Stoics say, who speak of fate—εἱμάρμενη. Some of them say that everything is subjected to divine providence and determined beforehand.[34] While Thomas affirms that for God all is determined in the immovable instant of his eternity, he explains that God wills that certain events and causal processes happen in a contingent way, and others in a necessary way. It would be contrary to God's way of proceeding if there were no fortuitous events in the world, since there must be all different degrees of being in nature, both the contingent and the necessary. Moreover, if everything were necessary, there would not be any corruptible things.[35] Not only effects but also their causes are subject to divine providence, which does not exclude fortune and chance (*fortuna et casus*). There often is a concourse of several causes, and there is also causality per accidens.[36] Prayer is not useless, as the Stoics say, as if our will and our desires were not included in the order of divine providence.[37] The final outcome of the causal processes in our world is certain for God; but God transcends necessary and contingent events and beings, and he wills that certain processes in the world be necessary and others contingent. God is the cause which encloses all that is real and all differentiations.[38]

Connected with these theories about fate is the Stoic denial of free will in man. Thomas, however, affirms that divine providence does not exclude free choice in man. The human will acts according to the objects presented to it by the intellect, which receives a great number of such objects. This means that man must choose between them. So he is free. Furthermore, if there were no free will, one could not praise a person for the virtuous acts he accomplished. Thomas adds that if freedom of the will would be denied the virtue of prudence would no longer make sense[39]

---

32. Ibid., no. 189.
33. SCG III, 84. See Gérard Verbeke, *The Presence of Stoicism in Medieval Thought* (Washington, D.C.: The Catholic University of America Press, 1983), 71–95.
34. *In I Peri Hermeneias*, lesson 14, no. 191; and SCG III, 94.
35. SCG III, 72.
36. SCG III, 74.
37. SCG III, 96.
38. *In I Peri Hermeneias*, lesson 14: "... causa quaedam profundens totum ens et omnes eius differentias."
39. SCG III, 73.

and our life would not be a human life any more, since it would be driven by a fatal necessity.[40]

Cognition

In line with their materialism, the Stoics say that our cognition is a sense activity. Apprehending the objects which we know is the work of the senses with the assistance of the celestial beings,[41] whose direct influence on human beings is denied by Thomas.[42] The images of the bodies are printed on our senses as drawings are put on a sheet of paper.[43] These impressions are interiorized and make us give our assent to them (συγκατάθεσις).[44] In this process the logos in us is awakened, and the impressions become an active factor in our lives. Then we form general representations owing to repeated similar impressions. These the Stoics call κοιναὶ ἔννοιαι. As children we have at first only a general anticipation of them, called πρόληψις. Gradually we make these "concepts" as well as our natural inclinations our own. A propensity to them appears as does an approval (οἰκείωσις) of certain fundamental inclinations of our being. We become familiar with what we are and with the demands of our nature such as the preservation of our life, the union of male and female, the development of knowledge. Against the background of this psychology, the Stoics developed their famous doctrine of the natural law. Our human activity and moral life develop from our human nature and its structure. Reason in us—which is the universal divine reason—grasps the fundamental laws we must observe in our life. There is in us a fundamental inclination which makes us accept our condition and the obligations flowing from it.

Natural Law

Thomas Aquinas did not accept this Stoic reduction of human knowledge to sensualism. The activity of the agent intellect transforms the content of the representations into universal concepts. What is naturally good becomes a good of our reason, and we formulate the principles and laws of human action. According to Thomas,

---

40. *SCG* III, 85.
41. *SCG* III, 84.
42. *In I Peri Hermeneias*, lesson 14, no. 191. Cf. *QD de veritate*, q. 6, a. 6: "opinio stoicorum qui ponebant res omnes regi quibusdam spiritibus quos deos vocabant."
43. *SCG* III, 84.
44. Cicero calls it *assensio* (*Academica* II, 37–39).

as being is the first thing that falls under the apprehension simply, so good is the first thing that falls under the apprehension of the practical reason, which is directed to action; since every agent acts for an end under the aspect of good. Consequently the first principle of the practical reason is one founded on the notion of good, viz. that good is that which all things seek after. Hence this is the first precept of the law, that good is to be done and pursued and evil is to be avoided. All other precepts of the natural law are based upon this: so that whatever the practical reason naturally apprehends as man's good (or evil) belongs to the precepts of the natural law as something to be done or to be avoided.

Since, however, good has the nature of an end, and evil the nature of a contrary, hence it is that all those things to which man has a natural inclination are naturally apprehended by reason as being good, and consequently as objects of pursuit, and their contraries as evil and objects of avoidance. Therefore according to the order of natural inclinations, is the order of the precepts of natural law. Because in man there is first of all an inclination to the good in accordance with the nature which he has in common with all substances: inasmuch as every substance seeks the preservation of its own being, according to its nature: and by reason of this inclination, whatever is a means of preserving human life and of warding off the obstacles (to its preservation, belongs to the natural law. Secondly, there is in man an inclination to things that pertain to him more specifically, according to that nature which he has in common with other animals, such as sexual intercourse, education of offspring and so forth. Thirdly there is in man an inclination to good, according to the nature of his reason, which nature is proper to him: thus man has a natural inclination to know the truth about God and to live in society: and in this respect, whatever pertains to this inclination belongs to the natural law; for instance, to shun ignorance, to avoid offending those among whom has to live, and other such things, regarding the above inclination.[45]

It has been pointed out that this famous text in which Thomas mentions the fundamental precepts of the natural law, is influenced by Stoic moral thought and, in particular by Cicero. According to the doctrine of the Stoics, the fundamental universal law which must govern the conduct of all men has not been made by man, but given to him with his nature. What this law prescribes is nothing else but what is conformed to our nature.[46] This fundamental law is the same for all men. There are no hu-

---

45. *ST* I-II, q. 94, a. 2 (translation by the Fathers of the English Dominican Province, from *Summa theological* [Westminster, Md.: Christian Classics, 1981]).
46. *Stoicorum veterum Fragmenta*, III, 519–20; III, 314–15.

man beings who are by their nature barbarians or slaves. Thus the point of departure of the moral life is a life in conformity with nature, which is the same for all, and which is conducted observing the same laws. Zeno pointed out that our first inclination is not the quest for pleasure, but the conservation and development of our being. The inclinations mentioned by Thomas are inclinations to the first goods of our nature, τὰ πρῶτα κατὰ φύσιν.⁴⁷ The Stoics put much stress on the community of all men. Man is a κοινωνικὸν ζῷον. Although in regard to other doctrines Cicero was not a Stoic, he made the doctrine of the natural law his own and, with his theory of natural right, exercised a great and wholesome influence.⁴⁸ Thomas writes that we consider good what corresponds to the fundamental inclinations of our nature, a conclusion which we find in Stoic philosophy.⁴⁹ As Spanneut writes, this is inserting natural law into a context of physical nature.⁵⁰ To live in conformity with nature is the same as a life according to reason. Nature is entirely penetrated by *logos*. The order of law is not what men have established but is given with nature: φύσει τε τὸ δίκαιον εἶναι καὶ μὴ θέσει.⁵¹

In nature at large the *logos* manifests itself and determines what should be done and from what we should abstain. The object—that which we choose to do—determines the goodness or badness of our actions, since reason determines whether or not these actions are in agreement with nature and its fundamental inclinations. This is in fact an Aristotelian doctrine,⁵² but taken over and propagated by the Stoics.⁵³

The Moral Life and the Virtues

According to the doctrine of the Stoics, the moral life consists in conduct established by reason and connected with the law of the cosmos and nature. Also according to Aquinas following reason is the first principle of the moral life. The words "nature" and "reason" appear often also in the

---

47. Ibid., III, 140–46.
48. Cicero, *De re publica*, III: "Est quidem vera lex ratio naturae congruens, diffusa in omnes, constans, sempiterna sed et omnes gentes et omni tempore una lex et sempiterna et immutabilis continebit;" cf. Cicero, *Pro Milone*, 4, 11: "Est igitur haec non scripta sed nata lex quam non didicimus, accepimus, legimus, verum ex nature ipsa arripuimus."
49. Cf. Cicero, *De finibus*, III, 33: "Cum enim ab iis rebus quae sunt secundum naturam ascendit animus, collatione rationis, tunc ad notionem boni pervenit."
50. Spanneut, "Influences stoïciennes sur la pensée morale de saint Thomas d'Aquin," 61.
51. *Stoicorum veterum Fragmenta*, III, 308.
52. Aristotle, *Nicomachean Ethics*, VI, chap. 2.
53. Cf. Seneca, *Epist. ad Lucilium* 66: "The senses cannot tell what is good and what bad ... Ratio ergo arbitra est bonorum et malorum."

writings of the first Christian authors. "The criteria of natural morality occupy a very important place in the writings of the Christian authors about the year 200."[54]

The Stoics distinguish four main moral virtues, which Plato had already mentioned: prudence, justice, fortitude, and temperance, Chrysippus subdivided these virtues into several auxiliary virtues, but all virtues form a unity: one who is courageous is also just, and the moderate person is prudent, because the virtues are the expression of the *logos* in us.[55] This mutual involvement is called the ἀντακολουθία of the virtues. They are corporeal in as much they are an expression of the *logos* in us,[56] but they are impassible inasmuch as they are effects of the *pneuma*.[57] If one has one virtue, one possesses also the other ones.[58] This last conclusion was accepted by such Christian authors as Lactantius, Ambrose, Jerome, and Augustine. Thomas makes a distinction: in their perfect form virtues are connected with one another, but one can possess a virtue also in an imperfect way, as an inclination to a category of good actions, without having the other virtues.[59] According to the Stoics virtues are the same in men and women and do not admit a more and less: if you possess the virtues, you have them in the highest degree.[60] Another particularity of the Stoic doctrine of the virtues is that we acquire them gradually, whereas according to Aristotle a strong decision makes us take the road of the virtues in that it makes us act against an inclination. Cicero says, however, that the Stoic theory makes it easier for us because it teaches the gradual acquisition of the virtues.[61]

It is also a thesis of the Stoics that contrary to what happens in the liberal arts, the virtues cannot be intensified. They are present in fullness, because the essence of the virtues is a maximum.[62] Thomas observes that when one considers a virtue from the side of the person in which it is

54. Spanneut, *Permanence du Stoïcisme*, 165.
55. *Stoicorum veterum Fragmenta*, III, 295 ff.
56. Seneca, *Epist. ad Lucilium*, 113, 1.
57. *In II Ethic.*, lesson 3: "Virtutes sunt quaedam impassibilitates." Cf. *In VII Phys.*, lesson 6.
58. Cf. Cicero, *De Tusculanis disputationibus* II, chap. 14: "Ecquid nescis virtutem si unam amiseris.nullam esse te habiturum?"
59. *ST* I-II, q. 65, a. 1.
60. *QD de virtutibus*, q. 5, a. 3.
61. *In II Ethic.*, lesson 11, no. 376: "Via stoicorum magis competit iis qui habent debilem et tepidam voluntatem."
62. *ST* I-II, q. 66, a. 1, according to Simplicius in his commentary on the *Categories* of Aristotle (*Stoicorum veterum Fragmenta*, III, 217). Cf. *ST* I-II, q. 52, a. 1: differently from the arts and sciences, virtues do not have a more or less.

present, it can be greater or less according the dispositions of the subject in question. With regard to this point, he says, the doctrine of the Stoics is defective.

In his commentary on Psalm 32, Thomas writes that according to Epicurus happiness is found in what is inferior to man, and according to the Stoa in the active life, while for the Peripatetics it consists in the contemplation of truth.

Conscience

Another zone of contact between Thomas and the doctrine of the Stoics is the recourse they make to the synderesis. According to the Stoics, human beings when still children have an inclination to affirm their nature and what comes with it; they approve their fundamental inclinations. The Stoics speak here of συνείδεσις, the awareness of one's fundamental inclinations.[63] Later some used also the term συντήρεσις, for instance Jerome in his commentary on *Ezechiel*.[64] The first obligations of man, as Thomas formulated them, become the habitus of the first principles of the practical intellect, which he calls *synderesis*. In his earlier works Thomas frequently speaks of the synderesis, but he seems to avoid the term in the *Summa theologiae*. The synderesis becomes the basis of conscience. In medieval theology the doctrine of conscience was well developed, and found its definitive formulation in Aquinas, who defines it as an act of the speculative intellect.[65] But in classical Stoicism the theory of man's individual conscience had hardly been developed. Saint Paul did not borrow his view of conscience from the popular language of his time.[66]

All Sins Are Equal; The Passions

The virtues constitute an indivisible whole for the Stoics who also taught that all sins are equal. They thought so because they considered sins as a privation of the rectitude of reason.[67] No privation has a more or less. The

---

63. *Stoicorum veterum Fragmenta*, III, 178 (a text of Diogenes Laertius).
64. I, 10 (PL 25: 22 B-C). Cf. Michael Waldmann, "Synteresis oder Syneidesis? Ein Beitrag zur Lehre vom Gewissen," *Theologische Quartalschrift* 119 (1938): 33–37.
65. *ST* I-II, q. 19, aa. 3–5. For Aquinas's doctrine on conscience, see Leo Elders, "La doctrine de la conscience de saint Thomas d'Aquin," *Revue thomiste* 83 (1983): 533–57.
66. See C. A. Pierce, *Conscience in the New Testament* (London: SCM Press, 1955). Seneca speaks of it (*De ira*, III, 36), but in his daily examination of conscience, he followed his master Sextius, who followed the practice of the Pythagoreans.
67. *QD de malo*, q. 2, a. 9.

Stoics know only one form of privation, total corruption.[68] In this connection Thomas reminds us that they made no distinction between the senses and the intellect, nor between the irascible and the concupiscible appetite.

Following Augustine[69] he writes that for the Stoics there are three good sentiments in the wise man (εὐπαθεῖαι): instead of inordinate desire there is good will; instead of pleasure there is joy; instead of fear there is the feeling of security. On the other hand, all passions are bad. Sadness, for instance finds no place in the soul of the wise man, since no evil can hit him: temporal goods are not true goods. Consequently, the contrary evils are not real evils. This is an error, Thomas writes, for things are goods or evils, even if they are small.[70] The theory of the Stoics is not reasonable, since man is composed of body and soul, and it is wrong to say that he is happy when he is tortured.[71] Whatever contributes to preserving the life of the body is also a human good, and what harms the body also affects man himself.[72]

According to the Stoics pity should be banished.[73] Anger is also condemned, in particular by Seneca in his *De ira*. Thomas notes that on this point Seneca is directly opposed to Aristotle, who says that a virtuous person may resort to anger.[74] The absence of anger may even be blameworthy.[75] Thomas refutes Seneca by observing that our reason uses the sensitive appetite as an instrument, and an instrument may well be inferior to the main agent.[76] Moreover such moral virtues as fortitude and temperance concern the passions directly, for instance fortitude must moderate presumption, ambition, and vainglory on the one hand, and faint-heartedness on the other. Patience must make us avoid and master softheartedness and stubbornness. Thomas also explains how temperance introduces order and measure in the contrary virtues.[77] Thomas finally reminds us again that according to the Stoics all our actions and choices are determined by fate.

68. *ST* I-II, q. 73, a. 2.
69. Augustine, *De civitate Dei* XIV.
70. *ST* II-II, q. 125, a. 4, ad 3. In his *Lectura super Ioannem*, XI, 33–35 Thomas writes: "Valde inhumanum videtur quod aliquis de morte alicuius non tristatur."
71. *In VII Ethic.*, lesson 13. According to the Stoics even unfortunate people are really happy.
72. *ST* I-II, q. 59, a. 3; *In III Ethic.*, lesson 18.
73. *QD de veritate*, q. 26, a. 7, s.c. 2.
74. *QD de malo*, q. 12, a. 1.
75. *In IV Ethic.*, lesson 13.
76. *ST* II-II, q. 123, a. 10 ad 2.
77. *ST* II-II, qq. 46–150 and following.

In the wise man there are no passions at all, according to the Stoics, since all passions are bad.[78] They promote, the ideal of ἀπάθεια, the total extinction of the passions, an ideal that was not accepted in the Western Church. On this point the Stoics are in direct contradiction with the Peripatetics, but in reality the difference between the two theories with regard to the passions and feelings is not so total.[79] Thomas restricts the affirmation of a total rejection of passions and feelings to *certain Stoics*, suggesting that their condemnation by later Stoics is no longer so absolute.[80]

Concerning their general moral philosophy, the Stoics committed three errors, Thomas says: a) they did not distinguish between that which is better and that which is good for a certain person; b) they did not realize that a passion may be consequent upon the judgment of reason and have some use; c) they did not distinguish the passions from other movements of the soul. Thomas stresses that the passions have their seat in the sensitive appetite.[81]

Stoic Cosmology[82]

In their reduction of all of reality to bodies, the Stoics affirm the existence of space, in which bodies exist, but this space in which the different parts of the world are located is surrounded by the absolute void.[83] The world consists of the four elements, which are in contact with each other by an adhesive force. Fire and air—the *pneuma*—penetrate everywhere, The *pneuma* keeps certain bodies in being and lets others grow. Between things there is a natural sympathy, and the Stoics profess a general optimism. However the world is not eternal. After a long period a general conflagration will occur. The souls which until then will have survived

---

78. *ST* I-II, q. 24, aa. 2 and 3.

79. Ibid. Cf. *QD de veritate*, q. 26, a. 8, ad 2: "As for the essential the Stoics do not say anything different from the Peripatetics. Macrobius and Cicero also know that these movements may occur in virtuous persons, their reason being dragged along."

80. *ST*, q. 34, a. 2; cf. *QD de veritate*, q. 26, a. 8, ad 2, where Thomas writes that certain Stoics considered the passions natural movements of our sensitive faculties, without approving or condemning them. Posidonius seems to have taught this moderate view. See Marie Lafranque, *Posidonius d'Apamée* (Paris: Presses universitaires de France, 1964), 412–14, and 432 ff.

81. *QD de malo*, q. 12, a. 7.

82. As an aside, on the subject of grammar, in his commentary on the *Peri Hermeneias*, Thomas mentions a difference with Aristotle's theory of grammar. According to Aristotle only a noun in the nominative case is a real noun, but for the Stoics and modern grammarians those in the other cases are also nouns.

83. *In I De caelo*, lesson 2.

will be dissolved in the whole. Some Christians, recalling a phrase of the apostle Peter,[84] accepted this theory of a final conflagration.[85]

In cosmology there is a certain correspondence of Thomas's doctrine with the Stoic theory of seminal forces (*rationes seminales*) in material things, by which these produce their natural effects. According to Thomas these are dispositions to receive specific forms in the processes of becoming and transformation, in particular in the generation of living beings. But these forces reside in the first place and primarily in God.[86]

According to the Stoics bodies are active by themselves, while Aristotle holds that they are so through their qualities,[87] owing to the impulse of the First Mover. According to the Stoics the sense faculties in man are not really different from one another; we know the different qualities, the objects of the senses, directly by ourselves.[88]

The above survey has drawn attention to the main points of contact between Aquinas's philosophy and Stoic thought. One may conclude that at the doctrinal level there is no dependence on the doctrine of the Stoics, except with respect to the theory of natural law and the classification of the moral virtues and some definitions. Thomas draws attention to the opposition in certain doctrinal points between Aristotle and Stoicism, and in particular Seneca. Thomas rejects Stoic materialism, along with their doctrine of the soul and its faculties, and he stresses that the Stoics ignore the immaterial nature of thought and deny man's free will. In what Thomas writes on divine providence he also shows his rejection of the Stoic doctrine of fate.

---

84. See 2 Pet 3:7–10.
85. Cf. *In IV Sent.*, d. 47, q. 2, a. 1.
86. *ST* I, q. 91, a. 2, ad 4; q. 115, a. 2; *In II Sent.*, d. 18, q. 1, a. 2.
87. Alexander of Aphrodisias, *Expositio in De sensu et sensato*, 10, 10.
88. *In De sensu et sensato*, 19, 13.

5 ∽ GNOSTICISM AND NEOPLATONISM

Philosophy in the First Centuries and Gnosis

The second century of our era was characterized by a general feeling of satisfaction by many citizens because of the grandeur of Roman civilization, its power, and the security it offered. It was an age of relative prosperity. In several of the larger cities in the provinces, schools were established. In Athens the emperor, Marcus Aurelius, founded an international university with chairs for each of the four main schools of philosophy. There was a renaissance of medical studies, astronomy, and optics. Yet studies were not marked by originality, and few new ideas were proposed.

In the field of religious life one observes a growing interest in religion, which showed in particular in the desire to have some personal experience of what was thought to be the divine. Since the imperial religion only demanded a certain loyalty and proposed a mixture of gods and goddesses whose identity was not very well known, and since the philosophers also did not give a satisfactory explanation of the nature for divinity, people went looking for answers elsewhere. One could see everywhere a thirst of revelations. Pythagorianism and the supposedly miraculous activities of Apollonius of Tyana were widely acclaimed. Educated people also looked for information in the books of the prophets of Israel and the Indian sages. Typical of this trend is the philosopher Numenius who studied the writings of the sages of Persia, Babylon, Israel, and Egypt, and became the father of what is called negative theology.[1] In that century Egypt was considered the cradle of religious thought. The Greek philosophers, in particular Pythagoras and Plato, were believed to have traveled to Egypt already ages ago to seek the source of wisdom.

---

1. See E. R. Dodds, "Numenius and Ammonius," in *Les sources de Plotin* (Geneva: Fondation Hardt, 1960), 3–32.

With regard to the idea of God in the second century, several accepted a supreme, transcendent God—ὁ πρῶτος Θεός—distinct from the Noûs. God is above what we can know of him. Theology, therefore, will be negative and cannot analyze and describe the divine attributes. In the first century the philosophers of the Academy and the Aristotelians transposed the world of Ideas (conceived by Plato) to the intellect of the supreme God. But parallel to these philosophical views a pseudo-philosophy appeared, the dualism of the Gnostics, who taught that there exists a second power, opposed to the first God and which is the source of evil. Contrary to this dualism Christian authors insisted that evil is a privation: before the creation of the world by God, there was no evil and God who is good does not create evil beings; evil cannot be but a privation of some good.

Contrary to this dualism Middle- and Neoplatonism moved in the direction of a monism, which stressed the kinship of man with divinity.[2] Among the philosophers of Plato's school, hostility against Christian doctrine became more virulent. In the third century Porphyry and Longinus openly attacked Christianity.

The Gnostics believed that with the help of magic we can enter into contact with the hidden forces of the universe, as is suggested by the term "gnosis." Gnosis is not a rational knowledge, but rather a form of piety with its formulae of prayer and ascetical practices. While in his study of nature Aristotle looked for facts, ordered them, and tried to discover their causes, the Gnostics, in their pseudo-science, tried to find secret forces, in particular in plants, in order to make use of them. The word "gnostic" was also used by some pagans who were interested in the Christian faith and who said that they were discovering a new science.

Some said that the world is permeated by the divine, while others believed that it is basically bad and that we must turn away from matter to approach God.[3] Oneirology was fashionable. As A.-J. Festugière writes, many did not distinguish between science and religion.[4] Regarding the doctrine of the soul, there was a general conviction that the soul comes from God or that it has detached itself from the Ideas or the stars. It enters into a body as the consequence of a sin. Life on earth serves as a probation

---

2. Édouard des Places, *Syngeneia. La parenté de l'homme avec Dieu d'Homère à la patristique* (Paris: C. Klincksieck, 1964).

3. E. R. Dodds, *The Greeks and the Irrational* (Berkeley: University of California Press, 1951), 246 ff.

4. A.-J. Festugière, *La révélation d'Hermès Trismégiste*, vol. 1, *L'Astrologie et les sciences occultes* (Paris: J. Gabalda, 1950), 84.

period. According to other Gnostics man has two souls, one good, the other evil. In the different Gnostic systems, things receive their existence from a first principle, called the demiurge. Some speak of a feminine principle, which would be the cause of multiplicity and difference.[5]

Thomas Aquinas and Dualism

Ever since the time of Pythagoras, there existed a rather strong current of dualistic thought in Greek philosophy. Pythagoras taught the table of the ten contraries, such as light and darkness, good and evil. Empedocles introduced two contrary cosmic forces, love and hatred. In his *Timaeus* Plato introduced the theory of matter as antagonistic to the good; it is cosmic space (χώρα), which is characterized by disorderly movements.

In Thomas's time Gnosticism was no longer a very active movement, except as present in the heresies of the Albigenses and the Cathars. The latter taught that matter is evil. They retained from the Christian faith the names of the Father, the Son, and the Spirit, but the Son and the Spirit were considered inferior to the Father. Christ, moreover, has only an apparent body. Concerning the Gnostics of the first centuries, Thomas knew about them through the writings of Irenaeus, Jerome, John Chrysostom, and other authors of the early Church. Especially in the *Catena aurea*, the names of a few Gnostics are mentioned, in particular Basilides who dared to write a gospel and rejected the Old Testament as did also Valentinus and Marcion.

Marcion is mentioned several times by Thomas. He taught that Christ did not take a human body from Mary, denied the passion of Christ, and rejected marriage. Valentinus taught at Rome between 130 and 160. At the center of his teaching is the theory that our world has been made by a malicious being, an antagonist to the good god.[6] The name Valentinus recurs forty-nine times in the works of Thomas. An important source for him was the *De haeresibus* of Augustine, who mentions Valentinus as one of the heretics who deny the human nature of Christ and say that he had a spiritual or, rather, an imaginary body.[7] In this line of thought Valentinus denies also the resurrection of Christ. As for the procession of the Word,

---

5. Cf. John M. Dillon, *The Middle Platonists* (London: Duckworth, 1977), 396.
6. *SCG* III, 140.
7. Cf. *ST* III, q. 5, a. 2; and *SCG* IV, 30.

Valentinus speaks of a *prolatio*, that is, an extension of the Father.[8] In his view we must be saved by an illumination.

Another heresy mentioned by Thomas is that of the Manicheans, a sect founded by a certain Mani, born in 216 of Persian origin, but living in Babylon. His doctrine, marked by an extreme dualism, spread in the northern part of Africa, but Mani also had disciples in Italy. In his youth Augustine was an adept of Manicheism, but later he combated it. In his writings Thomas mentions more than 260 times the theories of the Manicheans which partly coincide with those of Valentinus. In their extreme dualism the Manicheans considered the two first principles as entirely independent from each other, one was the good god, the other the evil one. The best of the spiritual beings were made by the good god,[9] while material things, on the contrary, were made by the evil god to whom they were subject.[10] The evil god is the God of the Old Testament and the prince of darkness,[11] while the good god is an infinite corporeal light spreading through space.[12] Creatures consist of a mixture of good and of a certain amount of evil.[13] In man only the soul proceeds from the good god, whereas his body is made by the second principle. Human souls have been made since all eternity and migrate from one body to another.[14] They are particles of the divine substance. In other texts Thomas writes that the Manichaeans deny free will in man: according to them people sin necessarily.[15] They have not understood, Thomas says, that what is evil may incrust the human being which is good by nature[16] and that the evil of sin does not exclude that man's nature is good.[17]

These theories affected the interpretation that the Manicheans gave of some fundamental truths of the Christian faith. Thomas mentions several times that for the Manicheans and Marcion Christ did not have a real human body and that, consequently, he was not born from the Virgin Mary. His body being a phantasm, he did not suffer on the cross.[18] The

8. *ST* I, q. 34, a. 2.
9. *De substantiis separatis*, chap. 16.
10. *QD de potentia*, q. 3, a. 16; *In I Sent.*, d. 39, q. 2, a. 2.
11. *QD de malo*, q. 16, a. 1.
12. *SCG* I, 20.
13. *In IV Sent.*, d. 47, q. 2, a. 1, ad 1.
14. Cf. *SCG* II, 38.
15. *In II Sent.*, d. 28, q. 1, a. 1; *QD de veritate*, q. 24, a. 12.
16. *SCG* III, 71.
17. Cf. *QD de malo*, q. 16, a. 4.
18. *In III Sent.*, d. 2, q. 1, a. 3, qc 2. In the *Catena in Matth.*, chap. 2, lesson 5, John Chrysostom is quoted as saying that Marcion denied that Christ had a real human body.

Manicheans also denied that all things have been created by the Son of God, and they condemned marriage.[19]

Thomas and the Platonists

The difficulties that Thomas experienced in discussing Plato's original philosophical thought and in evaluating it, as mentioned in the first chapter, are even greater in his discussion of later Platonism. By "later Platonism" a group of doctrines and an important philosophical movement and school are meant which extended from the death of Plato to the sixth century of our era and several hundred years later, if one also considers the *Liber de causis*, Avicenna, and other philosophers influenced by it. To a considerable extent Platonism determined the intellectual and religious climate of the Hellenistic period and the Roman Empire. Platonism went through evolutions and modifications but was accepted, at least partly, by Christian authors, Church Fathers, and the theologian Dionysius the Areopagite. Thomas speaks of the philosophers of this school by using, in general, the term *platonici*, which he uses very frequently in his works, but judging according to the doctrines which are ascribed to them, the term signifies not only the Academy of Plato, but also doctrinal movements of the first centuries.

In the rest of this chapter, the question is studied to what extent Thomas knew later Platonism, accepted it, or criticized its doctrine, on the basis of about five hundred texts of Thomas in which the name *platonici* is mentioned. This name, *platonici*, indicates several authors of a more or less Platonic doctrinal orientation.

The sources where Thomas found what he knew about Platonism, the Ancient and the New Academies, Middle Platonism, and Neoplatonism, in so far as we are able to reconstruct them on the basis of what he himself tells us, are Augustine (in the first place *The City of God*), Apuleius (*De somnio Scipionis*), Proclus (*Elementatio theologica*), Dionysius (in particular his *De divinis nominibus*), and the commentary by Simplicius on the *Categories* of Aristotle. For the Ancient Academy Aristotle is the most important witness.

The difficulty for Thomas was that he only had access to few direct sources and that, on the other hand, Middle and Neoplatonism show a

---

19. In the *Catena aurea* the reader finds many references to doctrines of the Manichaeans.

considerable variety of opinions. We see this in the texts where Thomas speaks of Plotinus, Porphyry and Proclus. Proclus is mentioned in the *De substantiis separatis*, the Commentaries on the *De caelo et mundo* as well as on the *Liber de causis*. More than half of the sixty-five texts in which Porphyry is mentioned, refer to the latter's *Isagoge*, the rest are taken from Augustine,[20] Simplicius, Jerome, and Boethius. Plotinus is mentioned twenty-four times. Thomas stresses in particular what the latter wrote about the virtues, which information he found in Macrobius. There are only two references to Iamblichus, taken from Syrianus's commentary on the *De caelo*.

Thomas distinguishes between several currents and speaks of *primi platonici et posteriores*.[21] We also read that certain Platonists taught that demons are beings gifted with sense cognition and with ethereal bodies.[22] Their dwelling place is the world space underneath the celestial bodies. Elsewhere he writes that some Platonists thought that the beginning of all passions is in our body, but that other Platonists did not share this view.[23] We find once the expression *gentiles platonici* by which Augustine designates some authors who practiced a cult of the demons and of all immaterial beings.[24] He also writes that several Platonists (*plures platonicorum*) hold that God made things from all eternity.[25] It would seem that Thomas attributes certain ambiguous theories of Plato to later Platonists, so that he could treat Plato himself with great respect, for example, the view that our human essence does not contain matter. If this were true, the Son of God would have adopted human nature in its universality, without matter and without individuality.[26]

Before considering in Aquinas's writings the various passages where he mentions the different doctrines of the Platonists, let us first examine whether Thomas himself has been influenced by Platonism. Attention has been drawn by some to the fact that he begins his theological exposi-

---

20. Augustine mentions twice the letter of Porphyry to Anebon (*De civitate Dei*, X).

21. *In De divinis nominibus*, chap. 11, lesson 4.

22. *SCG* II, 90. Cf. the well-known definition by Apuleius: "Animalia corpore aerea, mente rationabilia, animo passiva, tempore aeterna." Thomas borrowed it from Augustine. Cf. also *ST* I, q. 115, a. 5.

23. *QD de veritate*, q. 26, a. 3, ad 2. In q. 8, a. 9, he writes that according to *quidam platonici* the angels draw their concepts from material things, an opinion which contradicts a correct evaluation and the authority of the saints.

24. *QD de potentia*, q. 6, a. 6.

25. *In VIII Physic.*, lesson 2.

26. *ST* III, q. 2, a. 5, ad 2: "Sed tunc Filius Dei non assumpsisset carnem." Cf. *ST* III, q. 4, a. 4.

tions in the fourth book of the *Summa contra Gentiles* with a statement on the unity of God: the more a being is one, the greater is its power, whereas beings further removed from the One exhibit a greater diversity. For this reason whatever proceeds from God by emanation, must be one in him, a text which some critics have said is thoroughly Neoplatonic.[27] But when one studies the text and the rest of the chapter from close quarters, it becomes obvious that we are in the climate of Christian doctrine. That at this point Thomas stressed the unity of the First Principle may be explained by the fact that the *Summa contra Gentiles* was also to serve as an aid in the debate with non-Christian philosophers, many of whom were Muslims or Jews who considered the unity of the First Principle as the main philosophical truth.

Another example of the attribution of an ontological Neoplatonist scheme of thought to Thomas is that in the composition of the *Summa theologiae* he would have followed the Neoplatonist model of an emanation from the First Principle (*exitus*; in part I) and of return to it (*reditus*; in parts II and III).[28] But other authors have objected to this presentation arguing that in the *Summa theologiae* this scheme is biblical rather than Neoplatonist.[29] It is quite hazardous to draw conclusions about Thomas's doctrinal positions with regard to Platonism from his use of certain terms or of one or another point of their doctrine. Thomas has his own philosophy of being. The fact that on some occasions he approves a theory of the Platonists does not mean that he subscribes to Platonism, but it rather means that he found some sparks of the truth in other philosophical currents.

The Main Authors and Doctrines Mentioned by Thomas

Porphyry (234–304 or 305) was a native of Tyre and is known as the editor of the works of Plotinus, and for his commentary on the *Categories* of Ar-

---

27. Wayne J. Hankey, "Aquinas, Plato and Neoplatonism," in *The Oxford Handbook to Aquinas*, ed. Brian Davies and Eleonore Stump (Oxford: Oxford University Press, 2011), 55–64.

28. Marie-Dominique Chenu, *Introduction à l'étude de saint Thomas d'Aquin*, 2nd ed. (Paris: Vrin 1954), 255–276.

29. Cf. André Hayen, *Saint Thomas d'Aquin et la vie de l' Église* (Louvain: Publications universitaires, 1952); Albert Patfoort, "L'unité de la 'Ia Pars' et le mouvement interne de la Somme théologique de S. Thomas d'Aquin," *Revue des sciences philosophiques et théologiques* 47, no. 4 (1963): 513–44.

istotle, his *Life of Plotinus*, and a treatise in fifteen books, *Against the Christians*. In this last book he casts doubt on the historic reliability of several passages of the Old and the New Testaments. His name turns up about a hundred times in the works of Thomas, and in general in questions about logic, such as the doctrine of the five universals and the definition of the individual as the being which is distinguished by a set of accidents. Thomas also mentions Porphyry's affirmation that all men are one because of the human nature which they have in common. Some references to the works of Porphyry concern religious beliefs. In his youth Augustine thought that he had found, in the works of Plato and of Porphyry, some intimations of the Christian doctrine of the Divine Word, born from the Father,[30] but in general Porphyry was a pugnacious adversary of the Christians.

As to the religious doctrines of Porphyry, Thomas writes that he tried to assign the cause of certain effects produced by magicians to the celestial bodies.[31] There are spirits who deceive and help the magicians.[32] This is confirmed by Augustine, who says that by their nature the demons are beings full of deceit, but according to Thomas Porphyry thinks the demons to be this way because they are living beings of an animal nature, inclined to desire particular goods which in reality are bad.[33]

Another theory of Porphyry is that of the existence of deceitful spirits who imitate the gods.[34] The demons undergo the influence of the celestial bodies, as do also certain herbs.[35] Thomas, however, affirms that every nature is good and that it is impossible that one or another nature has an inclination to what is evil, except when it is considered under the aspect of a particular good. Concerning the question whether one can summon the demons, Thomas answers that demons are not forced, but that they intervene when they are called.[36] With regard to the use of certain melodies, stones, or herbs to solicit the help of demons, Thomas writes that certain effects which demons are thought to produce cannot be explained by material causes.[37] Repeatedly he mentions the thesis of Porphyry that in order to be happy man must avoid all contact with bodies.[38]

30. *QD de veritate*, q. 10, a. 13.
31. *De substantiis separatis*, chap. 2, where Thomas mentions a letter of Porphyry to Anebon.
32. *SCG* III, 107.
33. *ST* I, q. 63, a. 4.
34. *De substantiis separatis*, chap. 20.
35. *ST* I, q. 115, a. 1, ad 3.
36. *QD de potentia*, q. 6, a. 10, s.c. 2.
37. *QD de malo*, q. 16, a. 1.
38. *ST* I-II, q. 4, a. 6.

Another point where Neoplatonist theories show a certain correspondence with Gnosticism holds that the stars influence man's life, a theory quite wide-spread in antiquity. People were aware of an affinity between man's destiny and the universe. Thomas recalls that the Egyptians and the wise men among the Babylonians observed very attentively the planets and the stars, and proposed many credulities (*credulitates*) with respect to them. Thomas seems to make an allusion to the theory that the planets exercise some influence on man's life.[39] Thomas himself admits that a certain influence of the planets and the stars on the human body is possible and eventually also on man's senses,[40] but these faculties remain subject to our reason. On several occasions he quotes a phrase of Ptolemy: *Sapiens dominatur astris*.[41] One must therefore be much reserved with regard to the attribution of certain effects to the celestial bodies.[42]

With regard to this influence Thomas, as he writes in several places, thinks that during his sleep man is more susceptible to influences from above.[43] He could be basing himself on his own experience: when unexpectedly he had to prepare his inaugural lecture as master in sacred theology and could not decide which theme to choose, a Dominican appeared to him in a dream suggesting which one to choose.

Returning to the theme of the presence of Platonic doctrines in the writings of Thomas, we see that certain theories which are said to be taught by the Platonists, coincide with the doctrine of Plato himself, the Ancient Academy, Speusippus, and Xenocrates.[44] Other theories, however, deviate from Plato or are a later development of his views. Because of this the following summary may seem a certain repetition of what was imparted in the first chapter on Plato himself. The relation between the Platonic theories of Dionysius and the philosophical and theological doctrine of Thomas himself will be discussed in chapter 11 on *The Platonism of Pseudo-Dionysius in the Works of Thomas Aquinas*.

---

39. *In II De caelo*, lesson 1.
40. Cf. *In II Sent.*, d. 7, q. 2, a. 2, ad 6.
41. *ST* I-II, q. 9, a. 5, ad 3.
42. *In II Sent.*, d. 15, q. 1, a. 3. ad 4: "... cum non sit dubium dispositiones corporis humani impressiones corporum caelestium sequi, quamvis talibus praedictionibus non sit tutum nimis intendere."
43. Cf. *Super evang. Matth.*, chap. 2, lesson 13, no. 207: "In somniis dicitur apparere quia tunc homines ab actibus exterioribus cessant et talibus fit revelatio per angelos."
44. This applies in particular to the *platonici* mentioned in those books of Aristotle which Thomas commented upon.

As to the hierarchy of beings, the Platonists taught that numbers and geometrical magnitudes are located between the sensible world and the Ideas.[45] In Neoplatonism one went beyond this and considered numbers to be the causes, or even the substance of things.[46] Now all numbers, except the prime numbers, are produced from the number two.[47] The One, as also Being, is the principle of the prime numbers.[48] In a way analogous to the causality of the One, the point is the cause of all geometrical figures,[49] but numbers in their turn are the formal factors of magnitudes.[50] In this way the Platonists came to assert that numbers are the causes of things and even of the Ideas themselves, in particular the odd numbers which cannot be divided. Mathematical entities are even said to be the substance of things, since they delimit matter.[51]

This takes us to the theory of the dyad. This second principle, introduced by Plato himself in the *Timaeus*, belongs to the domain of matter. It is called "the Great and the Small" by reason of its divisibility. Disorderly movements are connected with it. In several texts Thomas notes that the Platonists did not distinguish between matter and privation and were therefore inclined to consider matter the source of evil, whereas in Aristotle's philosophy primary matter has an aptitude to the good.[52]

The One as the first Reality is called by certain authors the Father, and below him there is a substance called the intellect, a view which made Augustine think that these Platonists had an inkling of the doctrine of the Word of God.[53] We also see that in Plotinus's Platonism the world soul, from which the human souls come forth, makes its return.[54] After the One comes the order of the intelligibles or the Ideas, next the "intelligencies," then the souls and the demons, and last of all the corpo-

---

45. *In VI Metaph.*, lesson 1. But we read in *In VII Metaph.*, lesson 11, that some Platonists did not place the numbers between the sensible things and the Ideas. One wonders, indeed, how mathematical entities and universal concepts, which are separated from sensible things, can be the substance of the latter (cf. *In Boetii De Trin.*, q. 5, a. 3).
46. *In I Metaph.*, lesson 10; *In III Metaph.*, lesson 13.
47. Ibid.
48. *In III Metaph.*, lesson 12.
49. *In VII Metaph.*, lesson 7.
50. *In I Post. Anal.*, lesson 41.
51. *In I De generatione et corruptione*, I, lesson 13. The discussion of the Platonic doctrine of the principles is found above all in the commentaries of Thomas on Aristotle's treatises.
52. *ST* I, q. 5, a. 2, ad 1; a. 3, ad 3; *QD de malo*, q. 1, a. 2; *In VII Metaph.*, lesson 11.
53. *ST* I, q. 32, a. 1.
54. *In Boetii De Trin.*, q. 3, a. 4. In his texts on the First Mover, Aristotle mentions the theory of the Platonists, according to which every mover itself is moved ("omne movens movetur"), *In VIII Phys.*, lesson 9. This makes the World Soul, which itself is always in motion, a source of motion.

real things. The Ideas are the causes of the generation of the bodies and at the same time their exemplary causes. The demons are thought to be living beings gifted with reason (*animalia rationabilia*).[55]

A theory frequently mentioned by Thomas is that of the demons or intermediary beings who play an important role in later Platonism. They are defined as living beings, gifted with bodies composed of air. They are eternal and influence things at lower levels.[56] They live in the sphere of the air, but not in that of the celestial bodies. Their place is between the superior substances and human beings, and they are able to exercise some influence on the human soul.[57] According to the Platonists some of them are good, others evil. The Christians call those who are good, angels.[58]

In numerous texts of the Platonists, the view is expressed that the world is filled with hierarchically ordered beings. The first principle is the One, which by its very essence is identical with the Good.[59] The Good is prior to being, a thesis rejected by Thomas.[60] The highest God is the cause of all existing things. The doctrine of a unique first principle agrees with the doctrine of the faith and with the truth, but is not conformable to the theory of the Ideas.[61] In this connection Thomas also mentions a thesis which one finds in the Neoplatonism of certain Arab authors: from the One only proceeds what is one. In other words, the unique first principle cannot be the cause of the differences between things, but only of what they have in common.[62] This theory explains why those authors accepted the collaboration of secondary causes in the production of things. Thomas also corrects the view that God is above goodness and being. One may nevertheless call Him a *super ens*, inasmuch as he is infinite being.[63]

According to the Platonists there are, at a lower level, spiritual beings produced by God, who participate in the divine being. The next group in this hierarchy are the souls of the celestial bodies, the demons, and the human souls.[64] Thomas writes that the Platonists worshipped all these

---

55. *In V Metaph.*, lesson 10.
56. See *In IV Metaph.*, lesson 10, where Thomas quotes Apuleius: "Animalia corporea aerea, mente rationalia, animo passiva, tempore aeterna."
57. *QD de malo*, q. 16, a. 12, s.c. 1. Cf *ST* I, q. 115, a. 5: because of certain occult phenomena attributed to them, the demons were believed to have an aerial body.
58. *De substantiis separatis*, chap. 19.
59. *In I Ethic.*, lesson 7.
60. Ibid., lesson 1.
61. *In De divinis nominibus*, proœmium.
62. Ibid., chap. 5, lesson 3.
63. *In De causis*, lesson 6.
64. *ST*, II-II, q. 94, a. 1.

beings (*omnibus his cultum divinitatis exhibeant*).[65] In one of his other works, Thomas describes this hierarchy in the following way: the first order is that of the gods, that is of the immaterial forms; next there is the order of the intelligences separated from matter; finally there are the souls and the bodies.[66] Whatever is separated from matter is, or is considered, a god or a divine being.[67]

A theme which comes back often in the works of Thomas is that according to the Platonists the One is the cause and the essence of the Good. Moreover, the One is not only the cause of numbers, but also of quantity. The Platonists thought that the One, as the principle of numbers, is the same as the oneness of beings. Thomas notes that it is hard to see how from the One. quantity could proceed since quantity is characteristic of bodies and is by its very nature divisible.[68]

In yet another text Thomas draws attention to the doctrine of Middle Platonism or Neoplatonism according to which from God, the Father and Creator of all things, proceeds an intellect (*quaedam mens*), in which the forms of all things are present. From this intellect proceeds the world soul.[69] Thomas refers also to a text of Augustine in *Confessions* VII: the Platonists taught that "the principle [i.e., in the beginning] was the Word," although they did not use the same words as the evangelist.[70] The heretic Arius did in fact follow the Platonists with his false doctrine of the Divine Word.

As to the creation and the eternity of the world, the Platonists thought that things made by God can be eternal (*adeo quod semper fuit*), but according to Augustine, says Thomas, the world with all it contains has a beginning in time.[71] Especially the intellectual substances would receive from all eternity their being from the supreme God, a theory

---

65. On the different meanings of the word θεῖός in Plato's works see Jean Van Camp and Paul Canart, *Le sens du mot theios chez Platon* (Louvain: Bibliothèque de l'université, 1956).

66. *In De causis*, lesson 19.

67. *In I Politic.*, lesson 1: "Hic more platonicorum substantias separatas a materia deos nominat."

68. *In III Metaph.*, lesson 12. How can division proceed from the One? How can we come to know the One from what proceeds from it, if it is above all things? The One of Plotinus should be without any connection with what comes after it. See Richard T. Wallis, *Neoplatonism* (London: Scribner's, 1972), 91.

69. *SCG* IV, 6. Cf. *Super evang. Ioan.*, chap. 1, lesson 2: "Alii etiam platonici, ut Chrysostomus refert, ponebant Deum patrem eminentissimum et primum, sub quo ponebant mentem quamdam."

70. *ST* I, q. 32, a. 1, obj. 1.

71. *QD de potentia*, q. 3, a. 14, arg. 7.

which is in contradiction with the Christian faith.[72] According to the Platonists divine providence governs the world with the assistance of the demons as intermediaries.[73]

Repeatedly Thomas mentions the reason which brought the Platonists to affirm the existence of the Ideas. They noticed that in every species of things there is something common, and so they arrived at making what is common into a separate essence, separated from matter.[74] Another reason why they conceived the theory of the forms or Ideas was that considering the mutability of material things and the stability of the essences they accepted immutable Ideas of the latter.[75] The Ideas have more reality than the individual things which participate in them.[76] They are both the efficient and exemplary causes of the becoming of things.[77] The basis of this theory is the fact that whatever is divisible must be reduced to unity, and that what is *per accidens* to what is per se. From this it follows that what moves itself exists prior to that which is moved by another.[78]

Thomas also criticized the fact that the Platonists attributed the different perfections of a thing, for instance, its goodness and its beauty, to distinct principles (i.e., different Ideas), a theory defended in the West by Gilbert of Portiers.[79] With regard to the question whether the Platonists accepted Ideas of artefacts, Thomas's answer is generally negative.[80]

The human soul exists before the body, to which it is united. According to certain authors, the soul is eternal and returns, after the death of the body, to the stars which are kindred to it (*ad compares stellas*).[81] Certain Platonists defended the view that the soul, after the death of the body, unites itself to different other bodies.[82] Surprisingly some Platonists taught that the separated soul, after it has attained beatitude, desires nev-

---

72. *De substantiis separatis*, chap. 18.
73. *In IX Ethic.*, lesson 10.
74. *In I Ethic.*, lesson 14.
75. *In IV Ethic.*, lesson 10.
76. *In III Ethic.*, lesson 3.
77. *In VIII Ethic.*, lesson 7. Thomas wondered why the Platonists did not accept Ideas of the genera (*In VIII Metaph.*, lesson 14).
78. *In VIII Physic.*, lesson 9. Cf. *In I Ethic*, lesson 4: "Praeter haec diversa bona platonici aestimaverunt esse unum bonum quod est secundum se ipsum, id est quod est ipsa essentia bonitatis separata."
79. *Super Col.*, chap. 1, lesson 2.
80. *In XI Metaph.*, lesson 2.
81. *QD de veritate*, q. 18, a. 7; *SCG* II, 83: some Christian authors, Thomas writes, thought that the human soul, although not eternal, had been created simultaneously with (or before) the visible world.
82. *SCG* III, 80: "... diversis corporibus uniri."

ertheless to be with a body.[83] In general, however, they were of the opinion that the soul is complete by itself and that the union with the body is only an accidental one.[84] The soul unites itself with the body through a causal contact, and not as its substantial form.[85] Their theory opens the door to a multitude of substantial forms in man, an opinion defended by Avicebron.[86] In the latter's theory a form is more universal in so far as it is more material. Primary matter is the first effect of the First Principle, the Good.

Another opinion defended by Neoplatonists asserts that the human soul is united to a body through an intermediary: by its very nature the soul would first be united to an incorruptible body, which would be the link connecting it with a corruptible body.[87] Certain Platonists were of the opinion that the soul is deteriorated by its union with the body.[88] Because of this union it loses the knowledge it possessed before.[89]

With regard to the moral teachings of the Platonists, Thomas writes that for them the soul is already virtuous by its very nature. By practicing the virtues one overcomes the obstacles to a morally good life,[90] but, Thomas adds, the virtues do not only incline us to a life in conformity with reason (as the Platonists say), but they also accompany our reason in its activity.[91] Macrobius writes that according to Plotinus, who in his view holds together with Plato the first place among the philosophers, there are four levels in the practice of the main virtues: the virtues which are typical of God and a model for us; virtues in the social field; virtues which purify us; virtues which the already purified soul practices.[92] Aristotle mentions that the Platonists opposed the theory of Eudoxus, according to whom pleasure is our real good. For the Platonists pleasure has no determined value.[93] We must shun material things and find our happiness in the universal Good.[94]

---

83. Ibid., III, chap. 62. In *ST* I-II, q. 5, a. 4, Thomas notes that according to Origen, who followed the teachings of the Platonists, the soul, having attained beatitude, could become again unhappy.
84. *QD de potentia*, q. 3, a. 10, ad 5.
85. *ST* I, q. 70, a. 3.
86. *QD de spir. creat.*, a. 3.
87. *ST* I, q. 76, a. 7.
88. *In I De anima*, lesson 8.
89. *SCG* II, 83.
90. *ST* I-II, q. 63, a. 1.
91. Ibid., I, q. 58, a. 4, ad 3.
92. Ibid., I-II, q. 61, a. 5.
93. *In X Ethic.*, lesson 2. Cf. *In IV Sent.*, d. 49, q. 3, a. 4, ql. 3: "... omnem delectationem esse malam."
94. *In I Ethic.*, lesson 1.

Ontological Principles of Platonism

Among the numerous references to the doctrines of Platonism in Aquinas's works, we also encounter a number of principles such as the following:

- One might consider one of the first of these the principle that knowledge begins with what is best known to us, namely, sensible things, and then goes from them to what is most knowable in itself. Aristotle mentions this principle in his *Physics*, chapter 1, and in other texts. But it must be considered a heritage from Plato who tries to lead us from the uncertain knowledge of the material world to the contemplation of the Ideas.
- God governs beings on a lower level by those of a higher rank.[95]
- The higher a cause, the more beings it extends to.[96]
- Beings of higher rank are found in lower beings through participation.[97]
- The Good extends to more things than Being.[98]
- The universal exists before the particular. Since in our world forms and perfections appear always particularized, therefore immaterial and universal forms must necessarily exist.[99] This principle is also formulated as follows: before all multiplicity, oneness exists necessarily,[100] or in other words, the more universal something is, the more anterior it is.[101]
- Whatever is present in several things must be reduced to that which is first and by which other thing are such through participation.[102] One formulation says that they are more or less according to their distance from a maximum.[103] Another formulation of the principle is that the maximum in a genus is the cause of all beings in this genus.[104]

---

95. *Contra impugnantes*, 3, chap. 4.
96. *In De divinis nominibus*, chap. 4, lesson 3.
97. Ibid., chap. 4, lesson 5.
98. Ibid., chap. 5, lesson 1. Thomas determines the sense of this principle.
99. *QD de potentia*, q. 6, a. 6. Thomas uses the principle to demonstrate the existence of God.
100. *ST* I, q. 44, a. 1: "Ante omnem multitudinem necesse est ponere unitatem."
101. *In De causis*, lesson 2.
102. Ibid., lesson 16.
103. *ST* I, q. 2, a. 3.
104. Ibid. Cf. Vincent de Couesnongle, OP, "La causalité du maximum," *Revue des sciences philosophiques et théologiques* 38 (1954): 433–44; Leo Elders, "The First Principles of Being in the Philosophy of St. Thomas Aquinas," *Doctor Angelicus* 3 (2003): 59–95.

- The higher the level on which a cause exists, the further extends its causality.[105]
- Every effect returns to its cause.[106] The meaning of this principle is that each effect seeks its good, but this good proceeds from its cause and for this reason it aspires after its cause, when it seeks this good.[107] The Neoplatonist axiom that all things are in all is explained by Thomas as follows: Beings of a higher level are present in those of a lower level in so far as the latter participate in the higher ones; the lower being is in the higher one by the eminence of the latter.[108]
- The closer substances are to the First Good, the less numerous they are.[109]
- The higher a cause, the further its causality extends.[110]

Conclusion

Thomas sees a considerable distance between the doctrine of Plato and that of Aristotle, in the fact that the Platonists proceed from what the intellect presents (*ex rationibus intelligibilibus*), while the School of Aristotle takes its starting point in that which is perceived by the senses (*ex rebus sensibilibus*). Connected with this is Plato's thesis that what is known by the intellect as abstract and universal, exists in reality also as abstract (from matter). If this were not be the case, our intellect would be in error. This is the reason why Plato elaborated the doctrine of the Ideas.[111] Thomas observes that the way in which the Platonists treated these themes, was no longer in use in his time, since this way of proceeding was less scientific and logical.[112]

As to Thomas's definitive appreciation of Platonism, one must take into account that the works of the great Augustine are saturated with Platonic doctrines (*doctrinis platonicorum imbutus fuit*), but that this Church

---

105. *In De divinis nominibus*, chap. 4, lesson 2.
106. Ibid., chap. 1, lesson 3; *ST* I, q. 63, a. 4. See also chapter 12 of this book (*Liber de causis*).
107. This explanation is perhaps different from what Plotinus meant by the *reditus* to the First Principle.
108. *In De divinis nominibus*, chap. 4, lesson 5.
109. *QD de spir. creat.*, a. 1, ad 10. Thomas notes that Dionysius was of a different opinion.
110. *Quodl.* III, q. 3, a. 1.
111. *QD de spir. creat.*, a. 3.
112. *In De divinis nominibus*, proaemium: "... apud modernos est inconsuetus."

Father corrected what was not in conformity with the faith.[113] Other Church Fathers also followed Plato on many points. As did the Platonists, certain Christian authors taught that a number of spiritual beings govern the material substances.[114] Thomas notes that Gregory the Great follows the Platonists in his doctrine of the angels and for this reason thinks that the angels closest to the First Principle are less numerous, a view rejected by Thomas.[115] On several occasions Thomas writes that Platonism may lead to errors. Some medieval theologians arrived at the theory that the virtue of charity in the soul of Christians is uncreated.[116]

Our exposition shows that for Thomas Platonism was important. In certain erroneous theories he discovered a core of truth. Thomas valued the affirmation of the priority of the spiritual, of the immateriality of the human soul, and of the existence of a primary principle. But most important is the fact that Thomas used certain metaphysical principles in the field of formal causality and incorporated them into his own metaphysics.

---

113. *ST* I, q. 84, a. 5: "... imbutus doctrinis platonicorum;.in melius commutavit."
114. *ST* I, q. 110, a. 1, ad 3.
115. *ST* I, q. 112, a. 4, ad 2.
116. *ST* II-II, q. 23, a. 2, ad 1.

6 ~ THE FATHERS OF THE CHURCH; SAINT AUGUSTINE

The Fathers of the Church

"Fathers of the Church" is the name given to those Christian authors of the first period of the Church who distinguished themselves by their doctrine, their holy life, and their defense of the orthodox faith. In the West the period of the Fathers of the Church is closed by Isidore of Seville, and in the Eastern Church, by John Damascene. Such theologians as Origen and Tertullian are called Christian authors but not Fathers of the Church.[1] Thomas does not use the expression "Fathers of the Church" in the sense it has today, but speaks of *sancti doctores*, the meaning of which comes close to our Fathers of the Church, although he does not restrict this expression to theologians of the first six centuries. What is the relationship between the writings of the Fathers and the theology of St. Thomas? How does Thomas construct a bridge between the teachings of the Fathers which had a pastoral character and the scholastic theology of his time?[2] In the West theologians were familiar with most of the works of the Latin Fathers, but those of the Fathers of the Eastern Church were scarcely known and seldom quoted.[3]

In the study of sacred theology, Holy Scripture provides the principles. In the second place comes the authority of the Fathers of the Church, as a source proper to theology, but their doctrine as such is only probable. The writings of the Fathers are directly related to Scripture, since they were composed under the inspiring influence of the same Holy

---

1. Thomas and the other medieval theologians did not use this chronological delimitation of the period of the Church Fathers.

2. On this question see Martin Grabmann, *Die Geschichte der scholastischen methode*, 2 vols. (Graz: Akademische Druck und Verlagsanstalt, 1957).

3. For more details see Leo Elders, "Saint Thomas d'Aquin et les Pères de l'Église," in Elders, *Sur les traces de saint Thomas d'Aquin théologien* (Paris: Presses universitaires de l'IPC, 2009), 317–50.

Spirit.⁴ The Fathers are a source of Christian doctrine in so far as they propose what is contained in the Bible and their teachings have been received by the Church.⁵ There is a continuity of thought between them as representatives of the authority of the apostles and the Bible.⁶ To understand the profound contents of the *Sacra Scriptura* we need the explications proposed by the saints, although the totality of what they write may not have the same value. Moreover, in those things which do not belong to the faith, we may differ from them. A theologian must apply his mind with attention, assiduity, and respect to the texts of the great doctors of the past without denying or decrying what they say.⁷

In his proem to the treatise *Contra errores Graecorum*, Thomas writes that insofar as certain affirmations in the works of the Fathers seem doubtful, they can become an occasion for error, dispute, or disparagement. We must, however, first attempt to explain what is doubtful in those texts and show how we can take it into account as a starting point for teaching and defending the Catholic faith. Thomas explains why certain texts seem doubtful to us: the views of these Fathers and authors have sometimes been influenced by erroneous philosophical theories as well as by certain Platonic principles.⁸ More important is the fact that only after the appearance of the first heresies did the Fathers feel obliged to formulate what they wanted to write, with the greatest possible caution. Thomas himself is very respectful when he comments on certain unfortunate sentences, for instance that of St. John Chrysostom on the Virgin Mary when he writes that she was ambitious, or that of St. John Damascene when he says that the Holy Spirit does not proceed from the Son. Not even the consensus of several Fathers concerning a certain point gives absolute certitude.

Where did Thomas draw his knowledge of the Fathers from, especially that of the Greek Fathers? J. De Ghellink suggested that the theologians of the thirteenth century often obtained the texts they quoted from collections such as the *Tabula aurea in Augustinum*, the *Tabula in Damascenum*, etc. We must also draw attention to the *glosses of the Bible*, such as the

---

4. *Quodl.* XII, a. 26 (q. 17, a. unic.): "Dicendum est quod ab eodem Spiritu sunt expositae et editae."
5. Cf. *ST* II-II, q. 5, a. 3.
6. See J. G. Geenen, "Le fonti patristiche come 'autorità' nella teologia di S. Tommaso," *Sacra doctrina* 20 (1975): 18.
7. *ST* II-II, q. 49, a. 3, ad 2.
8. Cf. *In II Sent.*, d. 49, q. 3, a 2.

Glossa ordinaria, the *Glossa interlinearis*, and the *Glossa Petri Lombardi*. But Thomas was also able to use the writings of several Greek Fathers, of which he had found translations at the papal court at Orvieto or at the abbey of Monte Cassino during the immense preparatory work for the *Catena aurea*. He says that he had translations made of several Greek texts. Certain biblical commentaries or homilies of some Fathers, as well as the *De principiis* of Origen, had already been translated by Rufinus and Jerome. Toward the middle of the thirteenth century, Burgundio of Pisa wrote good translations of the homilies of Chrysostom on the Gospel according to John and Genesis, as well as of his commentary on the Gospel according to Matthew. We may add the Latin version of part of the *De natura hominis* of Nemesius (attributed to Gregory of Nyssa) and the third part of the *Fons scientiae* of John Damascene, which under the title of *De fide orthodoxa* exercised a considerable influence on theology in the Latin West.

The numerous quotations from the Fathers in the works of Aquinas were meant to establish the doctrinal elaboration of a theme on the solid foundation of the authentic tradition of the Church and to show the subjacent unity of all truly Christian thought. Thomas was not interested in a historical study of the Fathers, but in discovering, with their help, a more profound understanding of the mysteries of the faith. As Ignaz Backes writes: "The Fathers must make the road safer for this voyage to the most profound mysteries, they must clear up the darkness. St. Thomas wants to obtain knowledge from them and he wants to know what they say in order better to know the incarnate Word of God."[9]

Augustine and Thomas Aquinas

We can speak of a massive presence of Augustine in the different works of Thomas. He is quoted more than fifteen hundred times in the *Scriptum super libros Sententiarum*, more than two thousand times in the *Summa theologiae*, and very often in the *Disputed Questions*, the commentaries on the Gospels according to Matthew and John, as well as in those on the letters of St. Paul and the shorter theological treatises. In the *Summa contra Gentiles*, however, we find only thirty-seven references, a small num-

---

9. Ignaz Backes, *Die Christologie des hl. Thomas von Aquin und die griechischen Kirchenväter* (Paderborn, Germany: Schöningh, 1931), 123. For further information see Leo Elders, "Thomas Aquinas and the Fathers of the Church," in *The Reception of the Church Fathers in the West: From the Carolingians to the Maurists*, ed. Irena Backus (Leiden: E. J. Brill, 1997), 338–66.

ber which can be explained by the philosophical character of most of its arguments and the fact that in discussions with non-Christians on the mysteries of the faith the authority of the Fathers plays a minor role. As will become clear there is a real communion of mind between Augustine and Thomas, who fully accepts the former's extraordinary authority in theology, but repeatedly draws attention to mistaken *philosophical* doctrines and points out his affinity with some theories of Plato.

Divergent Philosophical Positions

Augustine did not know the doctrine of the pure potentiality of primary matter (*materia prima*) as Aristotle taught it. His conception of time is also different, seeing it as a series of successive instants, a crumbling of being. With the aid of our memory we are able to assemble these disparate moments of time into a unity.[10] We must lift ourselves up above this succession of moments and seek unity in God. More important is the question of the distinction between the soul and its faculties, in particular the intellect and the will. The soul is made after the image of the Triune God. In some texts Augustine is moving toward the view of a strict unity of the soul and its faculties, but elsewhere his position shows nuances on this question.[11] The later Franciscan tradition, which on this point follows Augustine, is also hesitant, but Thomas explicitly teaches the real distinction between the soul and its faculties, as between a substance and its accidents; and he explains the words of Augustine (implying an identification) as referring to known and loved objects, which in a certain sense are the knowing and loving person himself.[12] In his analysis of knowledge Augustine affirms clearly—and Thomas approves—that, according to our way of speaking, seeing and knowing is to have and to possess the known object.[13]

---

10. Cf. Jules Chaix-Ruy, *Saint Augustin. Temps et Histoire* (Paris: Études augustiniennes, 1956); Chaix-Ruy,"La Cité de Dieu et la structure du Temps chez saint Augustin," in *Augustinus Magister Congrès international augustinien, Paris, 21–24 septembre, 1954*, vol 2 (Paris: Etudes augustiniennes, 1954), 923–31.

11. Cf. Augustine, *De Trintate* IX, 4: "Mens, notitia et amor sunt substantialiter in anima vel ut idem dicam, essentialiter;" Augustine, *In Ioannis Evangelium*, tract. XV, 4, 19: "Non enim aliquid aliud est quam anima, sed aliquid animae est intellectus. Sic in anima nostra quiddam est quod intellectus vocatur."

12. *ST* I, q. 77, a. 1, ad 1.

13. Augustine, *Soliloquia* I, 1, 3: "Deum habet quisquis beatus est."

With regard to sense knowledge Augustine seems to deny the influence of the senses on the intellect. The reason which withheld him from accepting the full function of the senses is that sense knowledge is located at a different level and that material things cannot influence the spiritual soul.[14] Augustine emphasizes indeed the difference between the body and the soul.[15] But if so, the question arises why the soul unites itself to a body, if it can live all by itself. For Augustine this union remains a mystery.[16] Nevertheless with regard to this mystery of man, Augustine has already abandoned Platonism, because he sees the soul as a substance which uses the body as another substance. Origen taught the preexistence of the soul, but this theory was rejected by the common doctrine of Christians, who profess that the human soul is created by God. Augustine emphasizes that the soul is not part of God, as certain Gnostics said it is, nor does it come from the seed of the parents. Although Augustine is not very sure about the way in which the individual souls are formed,[17] he affirms their immortality in his *De immortalitate animae* and numerous other texts.

Augustine makes a distinction between what we know of the material world and our knowledge of immaterial beings: the first is acquired by the senses, the latter through an illumination.[18] God is the father of this spiritual light which enlightens our minds.[19] With regard to the Augustinian theory according to which all things are known by us in God, the First Truth, Thomas notes that we should not understand this in the sense that God would be the immediate principle by which we know and form propositions. The meaning of the text is rather that we know owing to a spiritual light that God has given us and which shows a certain similarity with the divine nature.[20] The soul does not think with the help of the body, but rather by distancing itself somewhat from it.[21] The soul is present in all the members of the body, but more so in some of them than in others.[22]

One of the basic presuppositions of the Christian faith is that man has

---

14. Augustine, *De Gen. ad litt.*, XII, 16.
15. Cf. Augustine, *Epistulae* 166, 2, 4.
16. Augustine, *De civitate Dei*, XXI, 10, 11: "Modus mirus est nec comprehendi ab homine potest, et hoc homo est."
17. Augustine, *Epistulae* 190, 1.
18. Augustine, *De Trinitate* IX, 3, 3.
19. Augustine, *Soliloquia*, 1, 2.
20. *In Boetii De Trinitate*, I, q. 3, ad 1.
21. Augustine, *De immortalitate animae*, 1.
22. Augustine, *Epistulae* 156, 2, 4.

a free will. Augustine has vigorously taught this doctrine.[23] All processes at the level of knowledge are co-determined by the will. The will has a fundamental inclination to the good, which shows in all our desires and decisions.[24]

In his meditations on metaphysical problems Augustine insists on transcendence, that is, the movement of things to the principles on which they depend. In this way unity, the concept of the One, characterizes all beings, since existing is nothing else but being one. Simple things exist because they are one, and composite things since they imitate unity. Augustine also makes an important contribution to the doctrine of truth, another transcendental concept. The truth of things comes from God and consists in a resemblance with Him. With the entire Catholic tradition Augustine affirms the goodness of things and with the other Christian authors he calls evil a privation. He meditates frequently on the beauty of things: a thing must be one and have a resemblance with its ideal model in God, and its parts must be united harmoniously.[25]

In his doctrine of being, Augustine comes close to Thomas. In this respect his view is not inspired by Plato, but by the Bible, which sees being as a reality and a perfection. God is not located above being, as the Neoplatonists hold, rather he is being itself.[26] Did Augustine know the real distinction between the essence of creatures and their act of being? The answer appears to be that in certain of his writings he is groping toward this distinction. God is for him the person to whom being belongs in the most total way. Divine being is at the same time full of power, justice, and goodness. God is simple but creatures—including angels—are composed of matter and their form.[27] Thomas agrees but indicates other components than those indicated by Augustine. In agreement with Platonism Augustine considers immutability the central characteristic of the divine being, or even another name for it.[28]

Another doctrine where there is agreement is that of participation: the

---

23. Augustine, *De duabus animabus*, X, 14.
24. Augustine, *Confessiones* XIII, 9, 10: "Pondus meum amor meus; eo feror quocumque feror."
25. Augustine, *De Gen. ad litt.*, I, 1, 1; I, 16, 59; Augustine, *De vera religione*, 32.
26. Cf. James F. Anderson, *St. Augustine and Being: A Metaphysical Essay* (The Hague: M. Nijhoff, 1965), 5 ff. John M. Rist reaffirmed this point in "Augustine, Aristotelianism and Aquinas," in *Aquinas the Augustinian*, ed. M. Dauphinais, Barry David, and M. Levering (Washington, D.C.: The Catholic University of America Press, 2007), 77–99.
27. Augustine, *De Trinitate* V, 2, 3; Augustine, *De civitate Dei* XII, 15; Augustine, *Confessiones* XII, 9.
28. Augustine, *Sermo* 1 (PL 38: 66): "Esse est nomen incommutabilitatis."

original forms of things are present in God. All that God has made has a likeness with him. To certain things God has given more perfection, to others less, but all partake in his divine being. We discover in things an order of gradual increasing perfection. Beings in the highest ranks of this hierarchy have a greater resemblance to God.[29] Augustine also contributed to the development of the theory of relations. He was the first theologian to apply the concept of relations in the theology of the Holy Trinity.[30]

In Augustine's writings Thomas read the argument that man has a certain knowledge of God in so far as all men pursue happiness.[31] Regarding the proofs of the existence of God, the Christian apologists and authors of the first centuries did not hesitate to use the arguments which they found in the writings of pagan authors. These proofs often showed the influence of Stoic thought. Augustine himself formulated a proof which was based on the Neoplatonist ontology: since the objects of our knowledge are in our intellect and are always true, there is in our intellect an eternal truth, which is a participation in and a reflection of God's truth. If there is truth, God exists.[32] In another argument Augustine writes that whatever is changing, does not exist by itself, but by some other being.[33] He also knows the argument based on the degrees of perfection found in created things, which demonstrates that there exist a pure truth and pure beauty.[34] Thomas uses it in the Fourth Way, concluding from the limited perfections in our world to a Being which exists in the highest degree of perfection. Augustine also mentions the teleological argument (Thomas's Fifth Way).[35] Augustine is convinced of the fact that our knowledge of God is negative: there is no true science of God in us except when we acknowledge that we do not know Him.[36] Concerning the divine attributes Augustine stresses the simplicity of God: "there is no distinction between his essence and his properties."[37] Thomas fully agrees, but when,

---

29. Augustine, *De civitate Dei* XII, 2.
30. Augustine, *De Trinitate* V, 4.
31. Augustine, *Confessiones* I, 20, 29.
32. Augustine, *De libero arbitrio*, II, 3–16.
33. Augustine, *Confessiones*, XI, 4–6.
34. Augustine, *De civitate Dei* VIII, 6.
35. Augustine, *Sermo* 141, 2 (PL 38: 776–77).
36. Augustine, *De ordine*, II, 16, 44 (PL 32: 977–1020). Translated by Robert P. Russell as *Divine Providence and the Problem of Evil*, in *The Happy Life; Answer to Sceptics; Divine Providence and the Problem of Evil, Soliloquies*, Fathers of the Church 5 (Washington, D.C.: The Catholic University of America Press, 1948), 239–332.
37. Augustine, *De civitate Dei* XI, 10. Cf. Augustine, *De Trinitate* VI, 4, 6: "Simplex multiplicitas, multiplex simplicitas."

influenced by Plotinus, Augustine writes that God is the cause of his own wisdom,[38] Thomas rejects this expression.

In his youth, when he sympathized with Manicheism, Augustine conceived the world as an enormous sponge floating in the infinite sea of the divine being, but later he understood that God cannot be infinite in the manner of a body and grasped the bond between infinity and immateriality.[39] Augustine stresses the presence of God in created beings. Thomas joins Augustine when he speaks of this innermost presence of God, "more intimate in us than we are in ourselves."[40] Augustine also stresses the immutability of God: the human being becomes weaker and perishes because of a lack of being. We must overcome this weakening by anchoring our being in God, who is immutable:[41] "*Quando solidabor in Te?*" God is being itself which remains always the same. In a text where he speaks of the creation, Augustine expresses beautifully the difference between the emanation of the hypostases from the One in Neoplatonism and the Christian doctrine of creation: All things proceed from God, but they are not of his substance ("*ab illo sed non de illo*").[42] When Thomas confirms the uninterrupted dependence of all things on the First Cause, he quotes Augustine: If God interrupts the flow of his causality, all things return to nothingness.[43]

Augustine the Theologian and Thomas

The Presence of Augustine in the Biblical Commentaries

In this section some of the main theological doctrines of Augustine will be examined, as appreciated and quoted by Thomas in his biblical commentaries.[44]

In the *Commentary on the Gospel according to Matthew*, Augustine is quoted more than 250 times, but contrary to what he does in the *Summa theologiae* Thomas mentions there only nineteen works of the great

---

38. Augustine, *Liber de 83 quaestionibus*, qq. 15 and 16.
39. Augustine, *Confessiones* VII, 14, 2: "Evigilavi et vidi te esse infinitum aliter."
40. Ibid., VII, 1, 2: "... intimior intimo meo."
41. Augustine, *De Trinitate* VII, 5, 10.
42. Augustine, *De natura boni*, 1.
43. Augustine, *De Gen. ad litt.*, 4, 12.
44. One could extend this search of references to Thomas's earlier works, such as the *Scriptum super libros Sententiarum* and the *Quaestiones disputatae de veritate*, but the texts quoted below indicate the definite positions of Augustine and of Aquinas.

Church Father from which he takes his quotations. The references concern mainly Christian life. Some examples: about the efficacy of prayer Thomas mentions this commentary of Augustine who says that "the Lord is so good that often he does not give us what we have asked for in order to give us what we want more."[45] At the end of Christ's Evangelical Discourse, Augustine has this comment: "All that Jesus tells us in this sermon comes down to the doctrine of the seven gifts of the Holy Spirit and our beatitude."[46] Why in our days do missionaries not dispose of the same power to work miracles as the apostles had? The reason is that it is not necessary, says Augustine, since the greatest miracle is that twelve poor fishermen converted the entire world.[47] With regard to the question whether certain types of food are impure, Augustine says that nothing is impure by its nature, but that something can become so because of a special signification attached to it. Before the coming of Christ, the Jewish people were living in a time when many things were given a figurative meaning, because the Truth had not yet appeared in full evidence.[48] On the story of the wealthy young man (Mt 19:21), Augustine comments: "When charity increases, avidity and desire become weaker and the perfection of love is found where there no more is any cupidity."

In the *Commentary on the Gospel according to John*, which dates to his second stay in Paris, Thomas closely follows the treatises of Augustine on this gospel. References to Augustine there are more than twice the number of those to John Chrysostom. This is understandable because of his profound theological knowledge and his prominent place in Western Christianity. Already in his proem Thomas invites Augustine to draw attention to the superb meditation on John, who transcended all creatures to arrive at the Creator. Augustine ascribes a mystical sense to many passages of the Gospel and notes that God is the cause which maintains all creatures in being.[49] Thomas adds that in creating things and keeping them in existence God does not use secondary agents. When Jesus says that he does nothing by himself, Augustine comments that these words indicate the eternal birth of the Divine Word. Although the Son is equal to the Father in every respect, it is from the Father that he receives what he is and what he has. After the miracle of the loaves (Jn 6), Jesus told his

---

45. *Super evang. Matth.*, chap. 7, lesson 1, no. 644.
46. Ibid., no. 679.
47. Ibid., chap. 10, lesson 1, no. 811.
48. Ibid., chap. 15, lesson 1, no. 1300.
49. *Super evang. Ioan.*, chap. 5, lesson 17.

disciples: "Work for food that endures to eternal life." Thomas quotes a beautiful text of Augustine on these words: "Eat and you will be transformed into me."[50]

When at the grave of Lazarus Jesus said "Take the stone away" and Martha replied "Lord, by now he will smell; this is the fourth day," Augustine comments that the four days signify a quadruple death: the first day means the death resulting from original sin; the following three days signify the death caused by actual sins, since each mortal sin signifies a certain death: the death caused by despising natural law; next the death caused by transgressing the laws of the country where one is living; and finally the death caused by scorning the evangelical law and the order of grace.[51] When Jesus says: "If anyone loves me he will keep my word … my Father will love him and we shall come to him and make our home with him" (Jn 14:23), Augustine explains that there are three ways in which God comes to us and we go to him: when God produces in us his effects and we accept them; by enlightening us during our meditation; and by helping us when we obey him.[52] When Mary Magdalene recognized Jesus after his resurrection and wanted to embrace his feet, Jesus said: "Do not cling to me" (Jn 20:17). Augustine comments that the meaning of these words is that Mary represented the Christians who come from pagan countries and could not yet embrace the gospel until after the ascension of the Lord.

With regard to the presence of Augustine in the commentaries of Aquinas on the letters of St. Paul, he is quoted more than sixty times regarding the Letter to the Romans. Augustine explains why Paul changed his name, says that this letter was written at Athens, and notes that in the first sentences of the text Paul refutes the heresies of Arius and Sabellius.[53] Thomas repeatedly quotes Augustine's words: *"Nullus credit nisi volens."* To find the correct interpretation of difficult texts Augustine helps us, says Thomas, for when we do not understand certain words, we should look at "what the saints do to see the meaning of those texts of Holy Scripture."[54] Whatever happens, even when it is bad, turns into some good for us.[55] God acts in the interior of men and inclines their

---

50. Ibid., chap. 6, no. 895.
51. Ibid., chap. 11, no. 1507.
52. Ibid., chap. 14, no. 1945.
53. *Super Romanos*, chap. 1, lesson 2.
54. Ibid., chap. 1, lesson 5.
55. Ibid., chap. 8, lesson 6.

hearts in the direction he wants.[56] In his commentary on chapter 12, Thomas quotes Augustine's famous definition of a sacrifice: a visible sacrifice that one offers outside oneself is the sign of an invisible sacrifice by which one offers oneself in submission to God.[57] Augustine recalls that the entire life of the Jewish people had a figurative meaning.[58] We may also quote here Augustine's words mentioned by Thomas: "We must find our joy in the things which will bring us our beatitude."[59]

In his commentaries on the other letters of Paul, Thomas quotes several striking sentences of Augustine. In defense of the literary and philosophical culture which Paul seems to discredit by calling it the wisdom of this world, Augustine says that there are Christians who have formulated their explanations of God's greatness not only with wisdom but also in beautiful language.[60] In his commentary on the Letter to the Galatians, Thomas mentions the divergence of opinion between Augustine and Jerome. Jerome thought that Peter, when he was with Jews, pretended to observe the *legalia* (prescriptions of the Old Law), but Augustine denies it. In Thomas's exposition we encounter this striking formula on the difference between the Old and the New Testaments: fear and love.[61] In the *Commentary on the Letter to the Hebrews*, there are some forty references to the writings of Augustine, for instance: "People turn into nothingness when they sin;" "Perfect love is present, when there no longer is any cupidity;"[62] "Contemplation is the reward of faith." In his famous commentary on the Book of Job Thomas quotes Augustine to warn us against the influence of the devil and tells us that whoever lives outside the right order is already for himself a punishment.

Augustine in the *Summa theologiae*

In the theology of Thomas, the greatest of the Church Fathers holds a special place. One can even say that from the very beginning of the *Summa theologiae* until its end Augustine accompanies and supports the efforts and reflections of Thomas. As our analysis of the relevant texts will

---

56. Ibid., chap. 9, lesson 3: "interius operatur in cordibus hominum ad inclinandas eorum voluntates quocumque voluerit."
57. Ibid., chap. 12, lesson 1. (See Augustine, *De civitate Dei* X, 5.)
58. Ibid., chap. 14, lesson 1.
59. Ibid., chap. 15, lesson 3.
60. *Super 1 Cor.*, chap. 1, lesson 3, no. 43 (Augustine, *De doct. christ.*, II, 40).
61. Gal 6:1: "Parva differentia est veteris legis et novae: timor et amor." Thomas quotes this phrase also in other works.
62. *Super Hebr.*, chap. 5, lesson 2.

show, Augustine's presence in certain questions is more imposing than in others. Already in the very first question, where Thomas examines whether theology is a science, the affirmative *sed contra* argument, which posits the foundation of the entire treatise, is borrowed from Augustine.

To underpin that in sacred theology the literal sense of the Bible is fundamental, Thomas appeals again to Augustine. In the questions on divine simplicity and goodness, Augustine intervenes repeatedly and occupies the place of honor. Augustine, the Platonist, is quoted to demonstrate the identity of goodness and being in God and to explain that goodness consists *in modo, specie et ordine*.[63] The sense of certain affirmations is more precisely explained by Thomas: We can say that all things are good by divine goodness in this sense: that God is their efficient and exemplary cause, but he is not their formal cause. Ever since his youth Augustine had been struck by the mutability of whatever there is in our material world. It is very fitting, therefore, that Thomas borrowed from Augustine the argument *sed contra* of the article on God's immutability.[64]

The presence of the great foctor is relatively modest in the questions on the entitative attributes of God, but question 12 on whether we can know God and see his essence, has been written in a dialogue with Augustine. Thomas quotes the beautiful text which reminds us that when we come to see God, our thoughts will no longer be voluble moving from one subject to another, but we shall see everything in one glance.[65] In another text Augustine tells us that in our natural knowledge of God, we know him insofar as he causes his effects in time.[66] In the articles on God's science, there are likewise numerous references to the great doctor. A fundamental thesis is that God does not know creatures because they exist, but rather they exist because he knows them.[67] Continuing, question 15 on the divine Ideas concerns a profoundly Augustinian theme, God's knowledge. The arguments *sed contra* of these three articles are taken from Augustine's writings.

In question 16 which studies truth, the numerous references to Augustine are found mainly in the difficulties (objections) raised at the beginning of the articles. Thomas most likely wants to involve Augustine

---

63. Augustine, *De doct. christ.*, I, 32; Augustine, *De natura boni*, 3; Augustine, *De Gen. ad litt.*, 4, 3.
64. Augustine, *De natura boni*, 1: "Solus Deus immutabilis est; quae autem fecit, quia ex nihilo sunt, mutabilia sunt."
65. *ST* I, q. 12, a. 10; Augustine, *De Trinitate* XV, 16.
66. "Deus movet per tempus," a text repeatedly quoted (Augustine, *De Gen. ad litt.*, 8, 20).
67. Augustine, *De Trinitate* XV, 13: "... sed ideo sunt quia novit."

in the study of the theme, but wishes also to suggest that the solutions the latter proposed are insufficient. That Augustine is always present in Thomas's mind is shown in the next question (q. 17) about falsehood, where he provides two arguments *sed contra* and a number of texts scattered in all the articles of this question.

In his treatment of God's will and love (qq. 19 and 20), Thomas relies also on Augustine, who provides the argument *sed contra* in the question whether God's will has a cause. As to the theme of predestination, he quotes an important sentence: "Do not feel free to question why God draws this man and not another one, if you do not want to fall into error."[68]

The treaty on the Holy Trinity allows us to examine from close quarters the place of Augustine in the theology of Thomas. In his *De Trinitate* Augustine wanted to show how the Trinity is the one unique and true God, and in particular to demonstrate the unity and equality of the Father, the Son, and the Holy Spirit.[69] Although Augustine was the first theologian to introduce the concept of relation in Trinitarian theology, he is quoted only once in this particular question to tell us that a real relation must be based on an activity. The reason for this absence could be that according to Thomas Augustine distinguished the relations in God from God's substantial being.[70] On the other hand, he presented remarkable insights on the Divine Persons. Thomas explains the precise value of the comparison of the intra-Trinitarian processions with those of word (concept) and love in the human mind, a comparison elaborated by Augustine in books IX and X of the *De Trinitate*.[71]

Questions 33 to 38 deal with the study of the three Divine Persons and show a very strong presence of texts of the bishop of Hippo. As Augustine did,[72] Thomas also declares that the generation of the Son and the procession of the Holy Spirit are incomprehensible for us.[73] Does the Father engender the divine essence? Augustine seems to affirm it in *De Trinitate* V, 3, but Thomas excludes it.[74]

In questions 44 to 49 which study the creation of the world, Augus-

---

68. *Super evang. Ioan.* chap. 26, lesson 2. Cf. Augustine, *De praedestinatione sanctorum.*

69. Augustine, *De Trinitate* I, 2, 4.

70. Cf. Augustine, *De Trinitate* V, 7: "Non omne quod dicitur in Deo secundum substantiam dicitur."

71. Thomas explained this comparison in *SCG* IV, 11 and 19; and in *ST* I, qq. 27 and 37.

72. Augustine, *De Trinitate* XV, 7, 13.

73. *Super evang. Ioan.*, chap. 1, lesson 18.

74. *ST* I, q. 39, a. 5, ad 1. Cf. Bruce Marshall, "Aquinas the Augustinian? On the Uses of Augustine in Aquinas's Trinitarian Theology," in Dauphinais, David, and Levering, *Aquinas the Augustinian*, 41–61.

tine provides the arguments *sed contra* of two successive articles: God created matter and is the exemplary cause of all things;[75] And a vestige of the Holy Trinity appears in creatures.[76] In question 48 on evil, two important theses are borrowed from the great Church Father: evil is present in what is good as in its subject; evil cannot totally corrupt the good.[77]

We now enter the treatise on the angels. An attentive reading of the text of *Confessions* XII, chapter 7, does not allow us to conclude that according to Augustine the faculties of the intellect and will in the angels are identical with their essence. It is nevertheless worth noting that Thomas quotes Augustine in an objection against the thesis that the faculties of the soul and its essence are distinct. Another question is whether there is sense knowledge in the angels. Augustine seems to confirm it,[78] as also do Isidore and Dionysius. But this is not right. We must therefore understand their texts in this way, that they speak according to the opinion of those who say that the angels have a body, or that they express themselves in likenesses.[79] Augustine also introduced the distinction between the matinal and vesperal (morning and evening) knowledge of the angels,[80] the meaning of which was clarified by Thomas. A text of Augustine becomes the basis of the *sed contra* argument in favor of the presence of the faculty of the will in the angels. In questions 61 and 62 on the creation of the angels, Thomas conducts a dialogue with Augustine and follows the latter's view in numerous problems. He bases himself on *De civitate Dei*, XIII, chapter 9, to say that it is more probable that the angels have been created in a state of supernatural grace. He continues this dialogue in his treatment of the sin of the angels. In the difficult question whether the intellect of the fallen angels has been obscured, Thomas turns five times to Augustine.

After the study of the angels follows the treatise about material creatures. Thomas is sometimes of a different opinion and says that Augustine *in hoc sequitur opinionem Platonis*.[81] As for the question whether animals and plants have been created directly by God, or developed from some simple forms, Thomas writes that other doctors affirm the immedi-

---

75. Augustine, *Confessiones* XII, 7; and Augustine, *Liber de 83 quaestionibus*, q. 46.
76. *ST* I, q. 45, a. 7; Augustine, *De Trinitate* VI, 10.
77. Augustine, *Enchiridion*, 14.
78. Augustine, *De civitate Dei* VIII, 6.
79. *ST* I, q. 54, a. 5.
80. *ST* I, q. 58, aa. 6 and 7; Augustine, *De Gen. ad litt.*, 4, 22–26.
81. *ST* I, q. 66, a. 2, ad 1; Augustine, *Confessiones* XII, 12.

ate creation (of the different species), but that Augustine is of the opinion that God has given the earth the power to produce the different species of living beings. Thomas himself seems to prefer the latter theory,[82] but shows deep respect for the solutions advanced by other Fathers.

Question 75 begins the treatment of man. Thomas studies first the nature of the soul. Augustine is quoted repeatedly and tells us that the soul is not the body;[83] it is a substance, but by itself it is not man; man is neither his soul alone, nor his body alone.[84] Thomas must have thought it important to ground the fundamental thesis of his anthropology on texts of the Platonist Augustine. In the following question on the union of the soul and the body, there are no quotations from Augustine, except in two objections and in the argument *sed contra* of the last article, which explains that the soul in its totality is in each part of the body. With regard to the delicate problem of the difference between the soul and its faculties, the position of Augustine, as we have seen above, is not very clear. Thomas mentions some texts where both are identified with one another.[85] Thomas explains Augustine's theological language as discussing knowledge and love in so far as these refer to the soul as being the known object which it loves. When Augustine seems to subscribe to the opinion that these faculties are identical with the soul itself, Thomas comments that one must take into account that in many questions which belong to philosophy, Augustine uses the opinions of Plato, not to affirm them, but only to mention them.[86]

In question 82 Thomas studies man's will. Augustine provides the arguments *sed contra* of the two first articles: the will has a natural inclination to happiness, but it does not will whatever it wants by a natural necessity. Another important problem is whether our soul knows material beings. This question was of great importance in those intellectual circles where Platonism was predominant. Augustine's position is realistic: we come to know material things through our senses.[87] In this connection Thomas recalls that Augustine, although saturated with Plato's theories

---

82. *ST* I, q. 69, a. 2; Augustine, *De Gen. ad litt.*, 5, 4.
83. *ST* I, q. 75, a. 1; Augustine, *De Trinitate* VI, 6; *ST* I, q. 72, a. 2; *De Trinitate* X, 7.
84. *ST* I, q. 74, a. 4; Augustine, *De civitate Dei* XIX, 3: "hominem nec animam solam nec solum corpus esse."
85. *ST* I, q. 75, a. 4; Augustine, *De Trinitate* IX, 4: "Mens, notitia et amor sunt substantialiter in anima."
86. *ST* I, q. 77, a. 5, ad 3; a. 8, ad 6: "Augustinus ibi loquitur inquirendo, non asserendo. Unde quaedam ibi dicta retractat."
87. Augustine, *De Trinitate* IX, 3: "Mens corporearum rerum notitias per sensus corporis colligit."

("*doctrinis platonicorum imbutus fuit*"), did not accept the theory that we know those things only by participating in the Ideas,[88] but thought that corporeal beings can really give us knowledge of the truth.[89] On the other hand Augustine remains close to the doctrine of the Platonists ("... *et hanc opinionem tangere videtur Augustinus*") in so far as he thinks that it is not the body which has sensation, but the soul which uses the body, "*quo velut nuntio utitur ad formandum in seipso quod extrinsecus nuntiatur.*"[90] Despite his different theory of knowledge, Augustine is invited to provide the argument *sed contra* of article 8 of this question: judgment is obstructed when the senses are tied down.[91]

How does the soul know itself?[92] Augustine writes that it knows itself because it is incorporeal.[93] Further on in this question Thomas quotes two more remarks by Augustine: "*Intelligo me intelligere*" and "*intelligo me velle.*"[94] Can we know the things which are above us? Contrary to what Augustine says, the answer of Thomas is rather negative: the natural light of our mind is not the First Truth, but a certain impression of it. As to the knowledge of the separated soul an important text of Augustine is quoted: our intellect acquires the knowledge of immaterial things by itself. The soul, therefore, knows the other spiritual substances through itself.[95] But the separated soul does not possess a natural knowledge of what happens on the earth, but the souls of the blessed receive it from God, Thomas writes, differing here from what Augustine believes.[96]

With regard to the question of the origin of the soul, Augustine thinks that the soul of Adam was created before his body, simultaneously with the angels. His view is understandable since the Platonists taught that the human soul by itself is complete.[97] In question 93, where Thomas examines in which sense man is an image of God, we find many references to Augustine.[98] Did the first man possess immortality? God had given him so powerful a soul that from its beatitude a fullness of gifts flowed to

---

88. Thomas refers to questions 83 and 46.
89. Augustine, *Liber de 83 quaestionibus*, q. 46. Cf. *ST* I, q. 84, a. 6; Augustine, *De Gen. ad litt.*, 12, 16: "non est putandum facere aliquid corpus in spiritum."
90. Augustine, *De Gen. ad litt.*, 12, 24.
91. Ibid., 12, 15.
92. *ST* I, q. 87.
93. Augustine, *De Trinitate* IX, 3.
94. *ST* I, q. 87, aa. 3 and 4.
95. *ST* I, q. 80, a. 2; Augustine, *De Trinitate* IX, 3.
96. *ST* I, q. 89, a. 8; Augustine, *De cura pro mortuis agenda*, 13.
97. *ST* I, q. 90, a. 1; Augustine, *De origine animae*, 13.
98. Thomas took them from Augustine's *De Trinitate*, *Liber de 83 quaestionibus*, *De Gen. ad litt.*, and the *De civitate Dei*.

the body.⁹⁹ Do we have to understand the story of Paradise in its literal sense, or is it better to prefer a symbolic interpretation? A beautiful text of Augustine suggests a spiritual and a literal interpretation.¹⁰⁰

In the last questions of the *prima pars* God's government of the world is examined. Augustine gives a very clear testimony: God takes care not only of the heavens and the earth, but also of the smallest of living beings: he occupies himself directly with all things.¹⁰¹ If the causal influence of God were to be interrupted, all beings would disappear.¹⁰² Augustine says also that human beings are protected by the angels, but, contrary to what Augustine says, Thomas declares that angels cannot work miracles.¹⁰³ The last questions of the *prima pars* examine the action of physical bodies. The problem of the *rationes seminales* is also studied: according to Augustine all things which come into being, were already present in a hidden way, as seeds in the fields.¹⁰⁴ Then, there is also the question of the influence of the celestial bodies on processes on the earth, an influence which Augustine seems to acknowledge. In the article devoted to the question of destiny, Augustine explains the meaning of the word *fatum*.¹⁰⁵

In the second part of the *Summa theologiae* human actions are studied as directed to man's last end. The discussion opens with a series of questions on beatitude. Augustine is asked to provide the most important statements, such as: are several last ends possible? Do all men have the same last end? In what does happiness consist? In order to explain that the beatitude of man is in God, the authority of Augustine is invoked.¹⁰⁶ Augustine also explains that beatitude is not something uncreated but an act of the intellect, "*gaudium de veritate*."¹⁰⁷ The primacy of knowledge in beatitude is stressed: "We love only what we know."¹⁰⁸ Augustine is also quoted to tell us that the soul can be happy essentially without being united to the body, although for complete happiness this union is required.

In the treatise on human actions, Augustine's authority imposes itself

---

99. *ST* I, q. 97, a. 1; Augustine, *Epistulae* 118, 3.
100. *ST* I, q. 102, a. 1; Augustine, *De Gen. ad litt.*, 8, 4.
101. Augustine, *De civitate Dei* V, 11.
102. *ST* I, q. 103, a. 6; Augustine, *De Trinitate* III, 4.
103. *ST* I, q. 110, a. 4.
104. *ST* I, q. 115, a. 2; Augustine, *De Trinitate* III, 8.
105. *ST* I, q. 116, a. 1; Augustine, *De civitate Dei* V, 1 ff.
106. *ST* I-II, q. 2, a. 7; Augustine, *De doct. christ.* 22; Augustine, *De civitate Dei* XIX, 26.
107. Augustine, *De doct. christ.* I, 3; Augustine, *Confessiones* X, 23.
108. Augustine, *Confessiones* X, 23; Augustine, *De Trinitate* X, 1.

in the questions on the moral goodness or badness of what we do. Whether our actions are good depends on the end we intend to reach and is mainly located in the inner act of the will. An important statement tells us that certain acts can never become good, but are bad by what they are.[109]

In the questions on the passions, Augustine is not present in those articles which examine the philosophical aspects of the subject, but he is the great authority in question 24 on the goodness or malice one may find in the passions. Among all the passions love has the first place.[110] When Augustine calls the passions forms of love, the reason is that all passions are caused by love, Thomas says.[111] In the study of the different passions, Thomas draws attention to the human and Christian experience of Augustine. This is very noticeable in questions 35 to 39.

Although Augustine is almost absent from the treatise of the habitus, he is a primary witness in that of the virtues. His well-known definition of a virtue is quoted by Thomas.[112] But he draws attention to Augustine's tendency to stress the intellectual aspect of virtues, a position which risks losing sight of the distinction between intellectual and moral virtues. This position, Thomas thinks, is a remnant of Socrates's thought.[113] In question 59 we find a long text of the *De civitate Dei* IX, 4, on the theory of the Stoics and Peripatetics on the virtues. In the questions on the cardinal virtues, Gregory the Great, Ambrose, and Cicero provide information, but a profound text of Augustine instructs us on the workings of charity in us.[114]

In his treatment of the theological virtues, Thomas reminds us that they belong to the *ordo amoris*.[115] A very beautiful text answers the question whether the moral virtues remain in the soul separated from the body.[116] As for the order of the gifts of the Holy Spirit, Thomas follows

---

109. Augustine, *Confessiones* IX, 26; Augustine, *Retractationes* 1, 9.

110. Augustine, *De Trinitate* VIII, 3.

111. *ST* I-II, q. 25, a. 2; Augustine, *De civitate Dei* XIV. Thomas stresses that love is complacency in the good.

112. Augustine, *De lib. arb.* 2, 19: "Virtus est bona qualitas mentis qua recte vivitur, qua nullus male utitur."

113. *ST* I-II, q. 58, a. 2, ad 2.

114. *ST* I-II, q. 61, a. 5, ad 3; Augustine, *De civitate Dei* XIX, 19: "Otium sanctum quaerit caritas veritatis; negotium iustum suscepit necessitas caritatis. Quam sarcinam si nullus imponit, percipiendae atque intuendae vacandum est veritati; si autem imponitur, suscipienda est propter caritatis necessitatem."

115. *ST* I-II, q. 62, a. 2, obj. 3; Augustine, *De moribus ecclesiae* 15 (PL 32:1309–78).

116. *ST* I-II, q. 67, a. 1: Augustine, *De Trinitate* XIV, 9: "Prudentia ibi erit sine ullo periculo erroris, fortitudo sine molestia tolerandorum malorum, temperantia sine repugnatione libidinum."

Augustine.[117] The treatise on the vices and sins also has numerous quotations from the works of the great Church Father. Here we may also recall his well-known description of sin.[118] In question 74, on sin, several texts of Augustine are presented explaining his statement *"voluntas est qua peccatur."*[119]

A reader may be surprised at the absence of our Church Father in the question which examines the way in which the sin of Adam passes to us. The reason for this absence probably is that Augustine did not explain very well how this sin can pass to us. The answer of Thomas is that we receive a defective human nature, so that our spiritual soul made by God adapts itself to it and so incurs the privation which is original sin.[120]

In his treatise on law Thomas invites Augustine to argue in favor of the existence of eternal law and of human laws. Although Augustine hardly mentions natural law as distinct from the eternal law, Thomas nevertheless refers to him in the arguments *sed contra* of the first and last articles of question 94, as if he wanted Augustine to collaborate in the redaction of the treatise. The last text which Thomas quotes runs: *"Lex tua scripta est in cordibus hominum quam nec ulla quidem delet iniquitas."*[121] Regarding civil law Thomas quotes a very wise text on the question whether the civil law must repress all vices.[122]

The New Law is nothing else but the presence of the Holy Spirit in the hearts of the faithful. On this point the thought of Thomas and that of Augustine are in total agreement. The New Law is the law of freedom. Questions 109 to 114 on grace are marked by the massive presence of quotations from Augustine's works. Without the help of divine grace, man cannot live in conformity with his duties.[123]

In the *secunda secundae* of the *Summa theologiae*, Augustine provides some well-known definitions, such as that of the act of the virtue of faith: *"Credere est cum assensu cogitare."* In question 10, article 8, the question is examined if non-believing persons must be obliged to accept the faith.

---

117. *ST* I-II, q. 67, a. 1; Augustine, *De sermone Domini in monte*, 1, 4.
118. Augustine, *De duabus animabus*, 11: "Peccatum est voluntas retinendi vel consequendi quod iustitia vetat;" Augustine, *De lib. arb.* 1, 11: "Peccare nihil est aliud quam neglectis rebus aeternis, temporalia sectari;" Augustine, *Liber de 83 quaestionibus*, q. 30: "omnis humana perversitas est uti fruendis et frui utendis."
119. Augustine, *Retractationes*, I, 9.
120. *ST* I-II, q. 81.
121. *ST* I-II, q. 94, a. 6; Augustine, *Confessiones* II, 4.
122. *ST* I-II, q. 96, a. 2, ad 3; Augustine, *De lib. arb.*, I, 5.
123. Augustine, *De natura et gratia*, 26.

The bishop of Hippo avows that on this point he has modified his former opinion.[124] In the discussion of heresy, Thomas benefits from the experience of Augustine, who describes the heretic as a person who, to his personal advantage and above all to become known and to draw the attention of the others, conceives or follows new opinions.[125]

Questions 17 to 22 examine the virtue of hope, and questions 23 to 46 the virtue of charity. Augustine defines charity as a movement of the soul to find its joy in God because of God himself.[126] In question 26 on the object of the virtue of charity, Augustine is quoted some ten times. The main act of charity is considered in *ST* II-II, question 27, article 3: "*Frui est amore inhaerere alicui propter seipsum.*"[127] But Thomas introduces slight modifications. When Augustine writes that desire is love, Thomas says that it is the cause of love, and that love is joy in the good. Thomas also introduces a new aspect in that he explains that charity is a friendship.[128] As for considering peace as the effect of love, Thomas completes the famous definition "*pax hominum est ordinata concordia.*"[129]

Questions 34 to 43 examine the vices opposed to charity, of which Augustine gives a good description.[130] He declares that the schismatics do not lose the powers which the sacrament of Holy Orders has given. For the study of the theme of war, Augustine is quoted eight times in four articles. Thomas fully agrees with the pastoral wisdom of the bishop of Hippo who rejects an exaggerated pacifism.[131]

Prudence is studied in questions 47–56.[132] Although Thomas often refers to Gregory the Great in this section, he nevertheless quotes some beautiful texts of Augustine, such as the sentence that prudence is the knowledge of what one should seek and of what one should avoid. At the beginning of the long treatise on justice, Thomas quotes Augustine's definition of this virtue. He also cites the sentence that as the Creator has very wisely ordered, the life and the death of plants and animals are sub-

---

124. Augustine, *Epistulae* 93, 5.
125. *ST* II-II, q. 11, q. 1; Augustine, *De utilitate credendi*, 1.
126. Augustine, *De doct. christ.* 3, 10.
127. *ST* II-II, q. 27, a. 3.
128. *ST* II-II, q. 23, a. 1. See Michael S. Sherwin, "Aquinas, Augustine and the Medieval Scholastic Crisis concerning Charity," in Dauphinais, David, and Levering, *Aquinas the Augustinian*, 203.
129. *ST* II-II, q. 28, a. 1, obj. 1; Augustine, *De civitate Dei* XIX, 12 and 13.
130. Augustine, *Contra Faustum* 20, 3: "Schisma est eadem opinantem atque eodem ritu colentem quo ceteri, solo congregationis delectari dissidio."
131. *ST* II-II, q. 40, a. 3; Augustine, *Quaestiones in Heptateuchum* VI, 14 (PL 34: 547–824).
132. *ST* II-II, q. 47, a. 1; Augustine, *Liber de 83 quaestionibus*, q. 60.

ordinated to our needs.¹³³ Thomas also brings forth the famous text of Augustine on imperialism: without justice the great empires are nothing else but organized robberies (*latrocinia*).¹³⁴ Although it is not forbidden to make some profit, it is a vice to sell one's merchandise for the highest price possible.¹³⁵ In the treatise on the virtue of religion we read the famous description of a sacrifice: *Sacrificium visibile invisibilis sacrificii sacramentum, id est sacrum signum est.*¹³⁶ In his commentary on the Our Father, Thomas follows Augustine giving long quotations from his *De sermone Domini in monte.* Is it allowed to sing in cult services? Thomas borrows the sentence from Augustine: we sing during the service in order that through the pleasure which their ears experience, the mind of the weak may be filled with feelings of piety.¹³⁷

In the treatises on superstition, idolatry, and divination there are also numerous quotations from the works of Augustine. In question 101 he is invited to describe precisely the meaning of the terms "piety" and "veneration" (*cultus*). In the examination of the problem of lying, the Augustinian treatise *Contra mendacium* is quoted several times. At the beginning of the question on fortitude, Augustine explains why fortitude is a virtue. He defines it as the love which supports everything with facility out of love of God.¹³⁸ In the study of patience Augustine occupies a key position. Thomas quotes some beautiful descriptions of what this virtue is and that what it makes us do.¹³⁹

Questions 140–70 deal with the virtue of temperance. Temperance concerns concupiscence which makes us desire things that turn us away from the law of God. Its rule and its measure are necessary in our present life.¹⁴⁰ Chastity is studied in question 151, where the numerous quotations show that in this field Thomas attributes a special authority to Augustine. Thomas even brings in some texts which to certain of our contemporaries might seem to express a pessimistic view of sexuality.¹⁴¹ Next virginity is considered. In this question there is also a remarkable presence of Augustine, since in three of the five articles the arguments

---

133. *ST* II-II, q. 64, a. 1; Augustine, *De civitate Dei* I, 20.
134. *ST* II-II, q. 66, a. 8; Augustine, *De civitate Dei* IV, 4.
135. *ST* II-II, q. 77, aa. 1 and 4; Augustine, *De Trinitate* XIII, 3; Augustine, *Enarr. in Ps.* 70, 15.
136. Augustine, *De civitate Dei* X, 5.
137. *ST* II-II, q. 91, a. 2; Augustine, *Confessiones* X, 33; and IX, 6.
138. Augustine, *De moribus ecclesiae*, 1, 15.
139. Augustine, *De patientia*, 1.
140. Augustine, *De moribus ecclesiae*, 1, 21.
141. Augustine, *Soliloquia* 1, 9.

sed contra rest on his authority, and stress the spiritual character of this virtue. Augustine is also very much present in the questions on luxury, pride, and the sin of the first men.

Questions 171–78 study prophecy and bring some fine texts of Augustine: what is essential in prophecy is not the vision of the imagination of the prophet, but what the latter understands intellectually.[142] Augustine thinks that Paul did see the essence of God.[143] Notwithstanding the great number of profoundly beautiful texts in this section, we must be aware of the fact that in general in the analysis of the problems and the elaboration of the solution the text of Thomas marks much progress.

In his description of contemplation, Thomas refers to the well-known text of *The City of God* XII, 30: "[In heaven] we shall be free and we shall see; we shall see and we shall love; we shall love and we shall praise. There we shall see without end, we shall love without boredom, and we shall praise without getting tired." In question 182, article 1, when Thomas compares the active with the contemplative life, he quotes several texts from Augustine: "Listen to why it is better: because it will not be taken away from Mary. But from you, Martha, the task to carry out all the things to be done in this life will be taken away, but the suavity of the truth is eternal."[144]

The last questions of the *secunda secundae* study the different states of life. Is religious life more perfect than that of the prelates? Thomas refers to a text of Augustine who affirms that the just life does not consist in abstinence nor in the fact of eating, but in the patient toleration of hardship and privation.[145] Is it permissible to seek the episcopacy? The argument sed contra is by Augustine: "The love of the truth brings us to seek a holy freedom from charges, but the necessary demands charity puts on us, make that we charge ourselves with the required tasks."[146]

Thomas has Augustine intervene also in the debate about religious life and the duties of the monks, which in his time in Paris was the subject a fierce debate between some secular masters and the mendicant orders. One of the last texts of this part of the *Summa theologiae* is a long quote from *Confessions* VIII, chapter 11: "You say that you cannot do what he or she has done? Throw yourself in his arms ... ; he will welcome and heal

---

142. *ST* II-II, q. 173, a. 2; Augustine, *De Gen. ad litt.* XII, 9.
143. *ST* II-II, q. 175, a. 3; Augustine, *Epistulae* 147, 13.
144. Augustine, *Sermo* 103, 2; Augustine, *De civitate Dei* XIX, 19.
145. Augustine, *Quaestionum Evangeliorum libri duo*, 2, 11.
146. *ST* II-II, q. 185, a. 1; Augustine, *De civitate Dei* XIX, 19.

you." It is by this text of Augustine that Thomas wants to end the second part of the *Summa theologiae*, in which man's return to God is studied.

This return is accomplished in Christ who revealed to us the road of the truth, by which we can arrive at eternal life. In the first question, article 1, of the third part of the *Summa theologiae*, Augustine enters the scene to point out the enormity of the mystery of the Incarnation of God: God communicates himself out of goodness, so that he himself and a human nature are united in a Divine Person, without, however, God's infinite greatness suffering by it. The "fittingness" of the Incarnation is treated in the second article, a masterpiece constructed with texts from Augustine: there was no more suitable way to heal our misery than the Incarnation: "it increased our hope, awakened our love, invites us to act rightly, and will give us beatitude in heaven." To a series of quotations taken from six works of Augustine, two texts of Leo the Great are joined to support a splendid theological synthesis in full conformity with the tradition of the Church. His prodigious memory made it easy for Thomas to use so many texts and in this way to insert his article into the great tradition of the Church Fathers.

Would God have become man if our first ancestors had not sinned? For Thomas the authority of Augustine and his understanding of Holy Scripture are so great that he follows him on this point. We do moreover find this negative answer in the most authentic tradition of the Fathers. With respect to the time of the Incarnation, Augustine proposes a solution which transcends the difficulties insisting as it does on divine prescience. In this way the first question of part three is a dialogue with Augustine with whom Thomas is in perfect doctrinal agreement. In question 5 the human nature adopted by the Son of God is examined: the body of Christ has been taken up through the mediation of his soul, and the latter through that of the intellect, Augustine says.[147] These considerations, however, must not lead us to Neoplatonist conceptions, Thomas warns: the Divine Word has taken up the different parts of the human nature of Christ through the mediation of the whole.[148]

There are no references to Augustine in questions 9–13, but in question 15 (on the "defects" of the soul of Christ) the situation changes: there were passions in Christ, but these feelings were in him entirely subject to his will. In the following questions there are relatively few quotations

---

147. Augustine, *Epistulae* 137, 2.
148. *ST* III, q. 6, a. 5.

from Augustine. Questions 27–30 contain the essential theses of the Mariology of Thomas, where Augustine is the main authority. A well-known text of his says: "With regard to the holy Virgin Mary, when there is question of sin, I absolutely do not want to hear about it."[149] The virginity of Mary holds a meaning for the entire Church. As to the question whether the matter of the body of Jesus had to be taken from a woman, Thomas borrows texts from six different works of Augustine to resolve it. Thomas next attempts to determine with Augustine how, on the one hand, the body of Jesus descended from Adam, while, on the other, he did not contract the consequence of Adam's sin. Question 48 considers the way in which Christ's passion brought about our salvation. Augustine, again, provides several answers. Two passages explain the way in which the death of Christ is a sacrifice.[150] Numerous quotations concern the descent into the underworld. Augustine explains the resurrection of Christ by the glory of his soul which flowed from his soul to Jesus' body. Thomas proposes seven texts of Augustine on the ascension of Christ, who at the end of the treatise of Christology is also invited to speak about the judiciary power of Christ.

The treatise of the sacraments opens with the Augustinian definition of a sacrament: "*Sacrificium visibile invisibilis sacrificii sacramentum, id est sacrum signum est.*"[151] His description of the way a sacrament works is also well known: "Words are added to the matter, and so the sacrament becomes to be."[152] A well-known sentence of Augustine, reproduced several times by Thomas, is the following: "From where comes the great power of the water that it touches the body and washes the heart, unless through the working of the words, not because they are said, but because one believes."[153] Augustine also provides three arguments *sed contra* in the articles on the necessity of the sacraments, and is quoted by Thomas in the question on the effects of the sacraments. Thomas obviously considers Augustine a great authority on the theology of the sacraments.

Augustine's presence in the treatise on the Eucharist deserves to be stressed. Certain heretics had understood wrongly what Augustine writes about the real presence of Christ in this sacrament, but basing himself on certain texts Thomas shows that according to Augustine the

---

149. *ST* III, q. 27, a. 4; Augustine, *De natura et gratia*, 36.
150. *ST* III, q. 46, a. 2; Augustine, *De civitate Dei* X, 6; Augustine, *De Trinitate* IV, 14.
151. *ST* III, q. 60, a. 1; Augustine, *De civitate Dei* X, 5.
152. *ST* III, q. 60, a. 3; Augustine, *In Ioannis Evangelium*, tract. 80; Augustine, *De doct. crist.* 2, 1.
153. *ST* III, q. 60, a. 6; Augustine, *In Ioannis Evangelium*, tract. 80.

body and blood of Christ are present in this sacrament.¹⁵⁴ There are practically no texts of Augustine on the way in which Christ is present in the Blessed Sacrament (qq. 76–78), but he is quoted several times in the next question on the effect of the sacrament of the Eucharist: "*O sacramentum pietatis, o signum unitatis, o vinculum caritatis.*"¹⁵⁵ In question 80 he reminds us that we must eat Christ spiritually, approaching the altar in innocence.¹⁵⁶ Two more texts deserve to be mentioned on the Eucharist as a sacrifice and on its daily celebration. "In himself Christ has been immolated once and nevertheless he is immolated every day in the sacrament;" "In the East the Greeks follow the custom of receiving him (in the sacrament) once a year. Receive daily what is good for you."¹⁵⁷

We must still consider some quotations from Augustine in the treaty on penance (qq. 84–90). If Christ has given the keys of his kingdom, it is neither foolish nor difficult to believe in the efficacy of the absolution.¹⁵⁸ "Should the absolution be given to one who sins again?" In some beautiful texts Augustine recalls that Christ has repeatedly healed the blind and the sick. Christ calls himself a healer, but which doctor does not heal a sick person several times?¹⁵⁹ There is in the Church a form of penance which one accomplishes every day for one's venial sins.¹⁶⁰ By penance man is restored to his former dignity.

Conclusion

From the above survey the conclusion imposes itself that the *Summa theologiae* was written in an uninterrupted dialogue with Augustine. Thomas has so well meditated on the writings of the great doctor that he could present a chrestomathy of his most profound texts. The reader is struck by the vast extent of Thomas's reading, for he cites not only the generally known works of Augustine but also his sermons, letters, and treatises,

---

154. *ST* III, q. 75, a. 2, ad 2: "Verbum illud Augustini ('corpus enim in quo resurrexit uno in loco esse oportet; veritas autem eius abique diffusa est') et omnia similia sunt intelligenda de corpore Christis secundum quo videtur in proprai specia."

155. *ST* III, q. 79, a. 1; Augustine, *In Ioannis Evangelium*, tract. 26.

156. Augustine, *In Ioannis Evangelium*, tract. 62.

157. *ST* III, q. 83, aa. 1 and 2; Augustine, *Epistulae* 98; Augustine, *Sermo sup.*, 84. Fr. John Hardon mentions Ambrose, *De sacramentis*, 5, 24 (PL 16, 452), as the source for part of the quote (*American Religious Life in Historical Perspective* [Chicago: n.d.], chap. 6).

158. *ST* III, q. 84, a. 3, ad 5; Augustine, *De coniugiis adulterinis*, 2, 9.

159. *ST* III, q. 84, a. 10.

160. *ST* III, q. 87, a. 1; Augustine, *Epistulae* 265.

works which today are almost forgotten. With regard to a certain number of problems in anthropology, he corrects some affirmations of Augustine, and on the other hand he attributes a special authority to him in certain theological themes and sees him as the undisputed master for the interpretation of the New Testament and a witness to man's inner life. Above all, he is the good shepherd who guides us safely in the most difficult questions of the moral life. Lastly, Thomas regards him he as an important source for knowledge of Plato, the Stoics, and other authors of antiquity. Doubtless the most important result of our study is the discovery of a communion of minds between Augustine and Thomas not only on the level of the Christian faith and charity, but also in the search for truth which was the hallmark of both their lives.[161]

161. Cf. Augustine, *Confessiones* VI, 1, and the exclamation *"Beatus qui te novit"*; and Charles Boyer, *L'idée de vérité dans la philosophie de saint Augustin* (Paris: Gabriel Beauchesne, 1920). As for Thomas one may mention his propensity to study and his choice to enter the order of the Dominicans, which made study the means of the apostolate. For a more complete treatment of the presence of Augustine in Thomas's works, cf. Leo Elders, "Les citations de saint Augustin dans la *Somme théologique* de saint Thomas d'Aquin," *Doctor Communis* 40 (1987): 115–67.

7 ~ SAINT JEROME

As has been shown in the previous chapter Thomas ascribed much importance to the thought of the Fathers of the Church, who are the foremost authorities for the interpretation of Holy Scripture: the same Holy Spirit who has inspired the authors of the Bible, assisted and guided also the Fathers. While several studies examined the relation between Augustine and Thomas, it is difficult to find publications which study the significance of Saint Jerome for Thomas. In the following pages an attempt is made to fill this void on the basis of the analysis of some twenty-seven hundred references to Jerome in the works of Aquinas.

In order better to show the importance for Thomas of the theology and the biblical science of this Father of the Church the references and quotations have been ordered in a number of rubrics. Several hundreds of these quotations are found in the objections raised at the beginning of the articles which deal with doctrinal questions. It is not unlikely that a good deal of these texts were put forward by opponents or participants in the disputed questions or that they were mentioned in the doxographies or lists of texts in use at the University of Paris. A considerable number has been taken from the glosses. Some of these quotations come back several times in the works of Aquinas. They are taken from Jerome's letters, his commentaries on Isaiah, Jeremiah and Hosea, and on the Gospel according to Matthew, as well as from the prologues to his translations of different books of the Bible.

This chapter was originally published as "Présence de saint Jérôme dans les oeuvres de Thomas d'Aquin," *Nova et Vetera* 80 (2005): 33–61.

The Authority of Jerome

On the question of authority in theology, the basic principle is, Thomas says, that we must be guided by the doctrine of the Church rather than by what Augustine, Jerome, or any other doctor tells us. Moreover, the authority of none of these theologians prevails over that of the supreme pontiff.[1] But in regard of the study and the interpretation of biblical texts, Jerome enjoyed a great authority in the Middle Ages. To determine the precise meaning of several biblical texts and terms and to illustrate the Palestinian background of the stories and of the usages, Thomas appeals to him. In his lessons on the Psalms, he refers regularly to the translation from the Hebrew which Jerome had made. He mentions the titles of the individual psalms as Jerome had presented them. In his proem to the commentary on the first fifty-four psalms, Thomas recalls the condemnation by the fifth Church council (the Second Council of Constantinople) of a theory of Theodore of Mopsuestia, in which he asserts that in the Old Testament nothing is said explicitly of Christ. Now Jerome has given us a rule, Thomas says, which we observe in the study of the Psalms: we must interpret a text which describes what one did or what occurred at that time, in such a way that it announces something about Christ, because Paul tells us in 1 Corinthians 10 that all those events happened to the Israelites in order to be a prefiguration of the realities of the messianic age.

Jerome is also considered an authority in questions concerning monastic life, evangelical poverty, and chastity. In his *Contra impugnantes* as well as in other works, Thomas leans on Jerome to defend the religious life.[2] He notes that the illustrious doctor Jerome has forcefully refuted the arguments which are advanced against the poverty and the celibate life of the religious.[3] Jerome is also an authority in the fight against heresies. There are many doctors, Thomas writes, who have defended the orthodox faith against the attacks of the heretics, such as Gregory of Nazianzus, Jerome, and Bernard. In his *De perfectione vitae spiritualis*, chapter 23, a sentence from a letter of Augustine is quoted: the episcopacy of Augustine is superior to the presbyterate of Jerome, but in many things Augustine is inferior to Jerome. Thomas recalls that Jerome was a disciple of Gregory of Nazianzus, a Church Father for whom he himself had the highest esteem.[4]

1. *ST* II-II, q. 10, a. 12; *Quodl.* II, q. 4, a. 2.
2. *Contra impugnantes*, part 2, chap. 5.
3. *Contra doctrinam retrahentium*, chap. 1.
4. *De substantiis separatis*, chap. 18.

Jerome and the Profane Culture

In an avowal, quoted a few times by Thomas, Jerome accuses himself of having let himself be fascinated by the works of such profane authors as Cicero, whom he admired too much.[5] At any rate he had learned from them that art of writing which embellishes his works. Thomas also mentions a passage of a letter of Jerome to Eustochium, in which the holy doctor writes that in a dream he heard that a punishment would be inflicted on him for having liked the writings of Cicero too much.[6] In his youth he had indeed fallen in love with Roman literature, since at that time he had less appreciation for the *sermo incultus* of Holy Scripture.[7]

On the other hand Jerome acknowledges, in his Letter 70 addressed to the Great Orator of Rome, that certain ecclesiastical authors have borrowed so much from the doctrines of the philosophers that one hardly knows what to admire more, their literary erudition or their theological science.[8] On this point Thomas observes that profane wisdom remains outside sacred theology. Jerome, however, goes to the point of writing that everywhere in Sacred Scripture one finds texts or ideas borrowed from pagan authors and, in a letter to Rusticus, we read: "You must study a long time in order to be able to teach later."[9] Jerome himself practices a beautiful style. In a letter to Paulinus, chapter 6, he explains why he did not write a long letter, *"neque enim epistolaris angustia longius evagari patiebatur."*[10] Jerome approves indeed resorting to profane wisdom. In a letter to the monk Pammachius, he says that one can study the *sapientia saecularis* provided one removes whatever is reprehensible.[11] Jerome is even quoted by Thomas when he writes that intellectual curiosity in not reprehensible, since Daniel and his friends studied the wisdom of the Babylonians. But in this same article of the *Summa theologiae* a warning of Jerome is quoted: one enters into darkness and indulges in vanity if one occupies oneself day and night with dialectic, physics, or astronomy.[12] Thomas makes a distinction: when the desire for these studies is disor-

---

5. *In II Sent.*, d. 35, q. 3, a. 3, s.c. 1. In Milan Jerome had been the disciple of the grammarian Donatus.
6. *In Boetii De Trin.*, q. 2, a. 3.
7. Ibid., ad 4.
8. *ST* I, q. 1, a 5, obj. 2; *In Boetii De Trin.*, q. 2, a. 3, s.c. 2.
9. *Contra impugnantes*, part 3, chap. 4.
10. *Super Hebr.* 11, 32.
11. Ibid.
12. *ST* II-II, q. 167, a. 1, obj. 3.

derly, or when one engages oneself in the study of things without value, such a conduct is reprehensible. Jerome gives the example of priests who devote themselves to reading comedies. When Paul admonishes us not to use specious discourses, Thomas notes that it is not prohibited to use a literary and refined language, as did Ambrose, Jerome, and Pope Leo the Great.[13]

On the other hand Jerome writes in the spirit of a certain evangelical absolutism as follows about the debates of the philosophers: "*Philosophorum enim dogmata cum creverint nihil mordax, nihil vitale demonstrant; totum flaccidum marcidumque ebullit in olera et in herbas quae cito arescunt et corruunt,*" whereas the preaching of the gospel, which at first was like a small grain, has become a tree.[14]

Striking Sentences of Jerome

One of the advantages Jerome acquired from the years of his literary formation is his command of the Latin language and his capacity to express himself in striking formulae. Many of these sentences are mentioned by Aquinas. Some of the most remarkable are quoted here:

- "*Qui Deum dicit praecipere impossibilia, anathema sit*" (Who says that God commands the impossible, he be anathema).[15]
- "*Cum haereticis nec nomina debemus habere communia*" (We should not even have names in common with heretics).[16]
- "*Poenitentia est secunda tabula post naufragium*" (The sacrament of penance is a wooden board after a shipwreck).[17]
- "*Jejunio sanatur pestes corporis, oratione pestes mentis*" (Fasting heals the diseases of the body, prayer those of the mind).[18]
- "*De rapina holocaustum offert qui vel ciborum nimia egestate vel manducandi vel somnii penuria immoderate corpus affligit*" (To deprive oneself from nourishment or sleep to the point of causing harm to one's health is as making a sacrifice of what one has stolen).[19]

---

13. *Super Col.*, 2, 4.
14. *Catena in Matth.* 13, 31.
15. *In II Sent.*, d. 28, q. 1, a. 3; *In III Sent.*, d. 36, q. 1, a. 1, s.c.; *In IV Sent.*, d. 15, q. 1, a. 2, s.c., etc.
16. *In III Sent.*, d. 4, q. 2, a. 2, ad 5.
17. *In IV Sent.*, d. 14, q. 1, a. 2 D *et passim*.
18. *In IV Sent.*, d. 15, q. 2, a. 1 A, arg. 2.
19. *In IV Sent.*, d. 15, q. 3, a. 1 B. Cf. *Quodl.* V, q. 9, a. 2: "You cheat yourself if by fasting you weaken yourself too much or if you prefer fasting to charity."

- "*Non sanat oculum quod sanat calcarem*" (What is good for one's foot is not necessarily good for the eye).[20]
- "*Discamus in terris quorum scientia nobis perseveret in caelo*" (Let us learn during our life on earth the science which will remain in heaven).[21]
- "*Sine Cenere et Baccho, friget Venus*" (Without bread and wine, sexual lust is extinguished).[22]
- "*Nugae in ore laici nugae sont, in ore autem sacedotis blasphemia*" (Fun in the mouth of a lay person is joking, but in the mouth of a priest a blasphemy).[23]
- "*Qui subiacet uni vitio, omnibus subiacet*" (Whoever has one vice, is exposed to all of them).[24]
- "*Irasci est hominis, non inferre imiuriam christiani*" (Getting angry is proper to man, but not hurting others is proper to Christians).[25]
- "*Semper aliud operis facito ut te diabolus inveniat occupatum*" (Be always occupied with some work, so that the devil does not find you idling).[26]
- "*Numquam de manu et oculis tuis recedat liber*" (You must always have a book at hand and under your eyes).[27]
- "*Non vincor in eo quod fugio, sed ideo fugio ne vincor. Nulla securitas est vicino serpenti dormire*" (I am not defeated by what I flee from, but I am fleeing in order not to be defeated. One is not safe when sleeping next to a snake).[28]
- "*Ama studia scripturarum et carnis vitia non amabis*" (Love the study of Holy Scripture, and you will not love the vices of the flesh).[29]
- "*Quem Sodoma non vincit, vina vicerunt*" (Noah, who had not succumbed to temptations, was vanquished by wine).[30]

20. *In IV Sent.*, d. 17, q. 2, a. 2.
21. *ST* I, q. 89, a. 5.
22. *ST* II-II, q. 147, a. 1.
23. *QD de malo*, q. 2, a. 8, arg. 5.
24. *QD de malo*, q. 12, a. 2, arg. 8.
25. *QD de malo*, q. 12, a. 2, arg. 8.
26. *Quodl.* VII, q. 7, a. 1.
27. *Contra impugnantes*, part 3, chap. 4; see also part 2, chap. 1, s.c. 2.
28. *De perfectione vitae spiritualis*, chap. 12.
29. *De duabus praeceptis*, a. 12.
30. *Super Eph.*, chap. 5, lesson 7.

Rigidness and Temperament in Jerome

Jerome was not always pleasant company, as Rufinus, Augustine, and others experienced. With regard to marriage and sexual intercourse, Jerome even shows a certain severity. We have already noticed it in his remark that the Holy Spirit does not touch the heart of a prophet during the matrimonial act.[31] Elsewhere Jerome writes that those who had intercourse with their wives should not approach the Holy Table. Thomas comments that this is not necessary and that the pleasure which married persons experience is not by itself bad.[32] Is it better to correct fraternally one who is wrong, when the correction would produce the inverse effect? We must correct a brother between four eyes (i.e., between him and you) in order that he does not persist in his sin having lost all feeling of shame when he was reprimanded in front of other persons.[33] Jerome is of the opinion that about what he calls the *veritas vitae* (the most important truths) we should not keep silence, but Thomas thinks that one may renounce reprimanding others if there is no hope of improvement.[34]

With regard to Jephthah, killing his own daughter as a sacrifice, Jerome writes that it was stupid of Jephthah to take a similar vow.[35] As for singing in the church, Jerome thinks that we should sing with our heart rather than with our voice. Thomas notes that the meaning of these words is that the church is not a theater and that we should not sing because it is so pleasant.[36]

In a sentence quoted several times, Jerome writes that it is better to sin openly than to commit sins while making people believe that one is a saint, but Thomas notes that the reason why one simulates also plays a role.[37] According to Jerome clothes of little value are a sign of a sincere person, and a worn coat means that one scorns the things of this world.[38] Who wants to enter in a monastery should do so right away without hesitating. Instead of veering out the cable, one should cut it.[39]

On certain customs of the life of the clergy or the monks, Jerome is

---

31. *In IV Sent.*, d. 9, q. 1, a. 3, qc. 5, arg. 1 *et passim*.
32. *ST* III, q. 80, a. 7, ad 2; cf. I-II, q. 34, a. 1, obj. 1.
33. *QD de virtutibus*, q. 3, a. 2.
34. *ST* II-II, q. 33, a. 6.
35. *ST* II-II, q. 88, a. 2, ad 2.
36. *ST* II-II, q. 91, a. 2, ad 2.
37. *ST* II-II, q. 111, a. 4, ad 4.
38. *ST* II-II, q. 187, a. 6.
39. *ST* II-II, q. 189, a. 10.

also quite severe. "You, priest, who speaks with Christ, you chatter with women."⁴⁰ If a priest has, sinned, he should abstain from celebrating the liturgy.⁴¹ Can priests who have sinned, return to their former position? Jerome denies it, but Thomas observes that it is difficult, but not impossible.⁴² Jerome can also be sarcastic: sinners will at least have the comfort of having their enemies as companions in their sufferings.⁴³

Thomas Corrects Certain Statements of Jerome

In the difficulties and objections put forward at the beginning of many articles of the *Quaestiones disputatae* and the *Summa theologiae*, texts of Jerome are quite often quoted, while in the answers to the difficulties Thomas indicates their meaning. The theological language of Jerome is not yet so precise as that of the theologians of the time of Thomas. It is far from Thomas to present a somewhat pedantic criticism of the great Church Father in his remarks and corrections. He rather wants to associate Jerome in the elaboration of the doctrine of the faith and to sharpen the thought of his readers by helping them to formulate a correct expression of the faith. In the following lines one will find some examples of this way of proceeding.

On the question of the procession of the Holy Spirit, Jerome writes that the third Divine Person is *ingenerate*, a term, Thomas says, which in this case can have a good meaning, provided one does not understand it as excluding all forthcoming from the Father and the Son.⁴⁴ Jerome says that we deserved all we had suffered and have to suffer because of our sins, but Thomas notes that by *sins* we must also understand original sin.⁴⁵ We must not impose any limits on God, says Jerome: if the devil can move from place to place and show his presence everywhere, would then the souls of the martyrs remain enclosed somewhere? Thomas answers (concerning the souls of the saints) that Jerome speaks of what ex-

---

40. *ST* III, q. 80, a. 5, obj. 2.
41. *ST* III, q. 82, a. 5. Thomas notes that a mass celebrated by an unworthy priest is valid.
42. *ST* III, q. 89, a. 3.
43. *Quodl.* III, q. 10, a. 2.
44. *In I Sent.*, d. 13, q. 1, a. 4. In his *Contra errores Graecorum*, 1, chap. 8, Thomas notes that Gregory of Nazianzus also uses the term.
45. *In IV Sent.*, d. 46, q. 1, a. 2, qc. 3, arg. 1.

ceptionally by divine grace may happen, not of what conforms to their natural state.[46] According to Jerome persons who lead a chaste life, undergo martyrdom, but, Thomas notes, Jerome expresses himself in a figurative way.[47] In Letter 21, addressed to Pope Damasus, Jerome seems to exclude free will from God, because God cannot sin. Thomas answers that the fact of being able to sin does not affect the freedom of the will, except in so far as it can turn to what is evil.[48]

When Jerome writes that (in God) the one who sends is separate from the one he sends, Thomas observes that this does not mean that the Son is separated from the Father, since this kind of separation is not found in God, who is omnipresent.[49] According to Jerome the angels have been created before the material world. This is the opinion of the Greek Fathers, Thomas says.[50] Contrary to what Jerome suggests, the differentiation of the appetite into the concupiscible and the irascible appetites is not found in the intellectual appetite.[51] In another text Saint Jerome seems to encourage feelings of envy in adolescents, but it is clear that he means emulation or zeal.[52] Jerome praises the conduct of the Hebrew midwives, who lied in order to protect the life of the male babies: they deserved a heavenly reward. Thomas expresses a certain reserve, since there is in their conduct the deformity of lying. If they deserved heavenly bliss, then it was not because of their lie.[53] A somewhat similar case is that of Jehu, who used deception to kill the followers of the cult of Baal. Jerome speaks of a *utilis simulatio*, but, Thomas says, this is using the expression in a broad sense.[54]

In the question which discusses the morality of anger, Jerome is very much present. When he writes that it is bad to get angry, Thomas agrees with regard to that anger which seeks to inflict evil on another person. According to Jerome it is natural for man to become angry. Thomas adds: "Yes, as long as this anger conforms to reason." According to Jerome anger is contrary to charity, and is, therefore, a mortal sin, but this is not always true, says Thomas, for anger against sin is praiseworthy.[55]

---

46. *In IV Sent.*, d. 45, q. 1, a. 1.
47. *In IV Sent.*, d. 49, q. 5, a. 3, arg. 1.
48. *ST* I, q. 19, a. 10.
49. *ST* I, q. 43, a. 1.
50. *ST* I, q. 61, a. 3: "... secundum opinionem doctorum graecorum."
51. *ST* I, q. 82, a. 5.
52. *ST* II-II, q. 36, a. 2. Cf. *De perfectione vitae spiritualis*, chap. 26: "antequam diaboli instinctu studia in religione fierent," where *studia* has the meaning of strife and dissent.
53. *ST* II-II, q. 110, a. 4, ad 1.
54. *ST* II-II, q. 111, a. 1, ad 2.
55. *ST* II-II, q. 158, aa. 1–3; *QD de malo*, q. 12, a. 1, ad 1.

More difficult is the question of when precisely did the angels learn about the mystery of the Incarnation? According to Jerome they would have learned it from the preaching of the apostles, but Thomas notes that we should not understand this as meaning that the angels would have received their knowledge from human beings, but that they better understood this mystery when the Church was born and the Gospel was announced.[56] As for Jerome's words that joking and small talk in the mouth of a priest are blasphemous, Thomas writes that this remark is exaggerated.[57]

When Jerome says that the wealthy young man of Matthew 20:16 is lying when he declares to have observed all the commandments, since by keeping his possessions he did not love his fellow men as himself, Thomas adds a nuance: the young man had not observed them perfectly.[58] Thomas also disagrees with Jerome who blames clergymen who while enjoying the possessions of their families, accept nevertheless an honorarium for their work; they should rather give it to the poor.[59] When Jerome insists that one should give away one's possessions to the poor and follow Christ, Thomas notes that the perfection of Christian life does not consist in giving away one's possessions. This is only the beginning on the road to perfection.[60] According to Jerome in the primitive Church the order of priests and that of bishops were the same. Thomas explains that Jerome does not want to say that initially episcopacy and priesthood were identical, but that at first the meaning of the word episcopacy was ambiguous.[61]

When Jerome writes that the heretics take over their errors from the philosophers, Thomas observes that the philosophical disciplines as such are different from the faith. Abusing them may lead to error, but this is not a sufficient reason to avoid them.[62] Jerome distinguishes a triple truth: *veritas vitae, veritas iustitiae,* and *veritas doctrinae.* Thomas clarifies the meaning of this text: *veritas vitae* means that a thing has reached its rule; the *veritas iustitiae* may signify that one keeps the right rule in one's dealings with other persons and that one knows what one should do. The *veritas doctrinae* means the manifestation of a certain doctrine.[63]

56. *QD de veritate*, q. 8, a. 9, ad 2.
57. *QD de malo*, q. 10, a. 1, ad 11.
58. *Quodl.* IV, q. 12, a. 2, ad 1; II-II, q. 189, a. 1, ad 1.
59. *Contra impugnantes*, part 2, chap. 6.
60. *De perfectione vitae spiritualis*, chap. 7.
61. Ibid. chap. 23.
62. *In Boetii De Trin.*, part 2, a. 3, ad 6.
63. *ST* II-II, q. 109, a. 3, ad 3.

Doctrinal Questions

Jerome's contribution to the development of theology is modest, at least in so far as the observations go which are mentioned by Thomas. He is seldom quoted in doctrinal questions. With regard to his doctrine about God, his saying that God does not command the impossible is often quoted. God cannot make it such that the past has not been.[64] Thomas also mentions the words of the great doctor that there is no difference in degree between the Divine Persons[65] and that in God there is nothing which is subordinated or of lower rank.[66] Jerome is reluctant to use the term *hypostasis*: "*In hoc nomine hypostasis venenum latet sub mello.*"[67] In fact the word began to be used by Athanasius to indicate the Divine Persons only after much hesitation.

Christology

In Thomas's treatises of Christology, Jerome is referred to quite often, in particular to explain some episodes of Christ's public life, but less in strictly theological questions on the Incarnation. The most important texts will be mentioned here. When before leaving the earth Jesus declares that all authority has been given to him, he says so, according to Jerome, in so far as he is a man. Thomas agrees explaining that this power came to Jesus through the grace of the hypostatical union.[68] As to the question whether there were passions in Christ, Jerome answers affirmatively: Jesus was really sad, but his sadness was a "pro-passion," that remained under the control of reason, an answer appreciated by Thomas.[69] When speaking of Jesus' baptism, Jerome writes that this baptism is a prefiguration of that of us. Since we have been baptized in the name of the Father, the Son, and the Holy Spirit, the Trinity must manifest itself during the baptism of Jesus. If on the banks of the river Jordan the heavens opened themselves, this was not a fracture of the sky, but a vision of the eye of the spirit.[70]

---

64. *In I Sent.*, d. 42, q. 2, a. 2; *ST* I, q. 25, a. 4; *QD de potentia*, q. 1, a. 3 (God cannot make it such that a virgin who was violated, has not been violated).
65. *In I Sent.*, d. 31, q. 3, a. 2.
66. *QD de potentia*, q. 2, a. 5, arg. 9.
67. *ST* I, q. 29, a. 3, obj. 3.
68. *ST* III, q. 13, a. 2, ad 1.
69. *ST* III, q. 15, a. 4.
70. *ST* III, q. 39, a. 8; and a. 5, ad 2.

Jesus ate with publicans to give confidence to the people. It is in fact through Christ that we have access to God.[71] Why must Peter look for a coin in the mouth of a fish? To make clear that Jesus wanted to be poor and that people should not follow him in order to get rich. The episode is an instruction on evangelical poverty.[72] Religious may nevertheless accept gifts as Jesus himself accepted them from certain pious women (Lk 8:1–3). This was also a custom among the Jews, but Paul does not ask for this sort of support, to avoid giving the impression of seeking money from people.

As to the meaning of the temptations of Jesus, Jerome notices that it was Jesus' intention to defeat the devil by humility.[73] When Jesus says that he had been sent to the lost sheep of Israel, this did not mean that his mission did not extend to the pagan nations, but that he must first preach the gospel to Israel.[74] The splendor of Jesus' divinity was so great that it could be seen on his human face and attracted the people. This splendor explains also how a single person was able to chase so many merchants and dealers from the temple.[75] Jesus gave back health to the sick completely and at once, except in the case of a blind man, because of a lack of faith in this man.[76]

In the commentary on the transfiguration of Jesus, Jerome tells us that we should not think that he lost the form and the face he had before, but that a new splendor enveloped him. He showed himself to the apostles, as he will appear during the Last Judgement.[77] According to Jerome the parable of the wicked husbandmen, shows that the Jews knew that Jesus was the heir of the promises and that they had him killed out of envy.[78] Thomas also quoted Jerome's explanation of the darkening of the sun during the passion of Christ: it happened so that his enemies could not see him or so that they would be deprived of light.[79] We owe Christ the more since he suffered for us in a humiliating way.[80] Thomas quotes a text of Jerome in which he stresses the causality of Jesus' burial: by his

---

71. *ST* III, q. 40, a. 1.
72. *ST* III, q. 40, a. 3.
73. *ST* III, q. 41, a. 4.
74. *ST* III, q. 42, a. 1.
75. *ST* III, q. 44, a. 3, ad 2.
76. *ST* III, q. 44, a. 3, ad 2.
77. *ST* III, q. 45, a. 2. Cf. *In III Sent.*, d. 16, q. 2, a. 1, arg. 4: the clarity on the face of Christ was not of a sensible nature. It manifested itself in the interior of the imagination of the three apostles.
78. *ST* III, q. 47, a. 5.
79. *ST* III, q. 44, a. 2, ad 2.
80. *In IV Sent.*, d. 30, q. 2, a. 3.

burial we also shall rise, an idea which Thomas appreciated.[81] According to Jerome the form of the tomb of Jesus and the fact that it was new also have a significance. Jerome seems to have thought that the dead which appeared in Jerusalem after the death of Jesus really were risen, but that they would have to die again.[82] Jesus' words "even the Son does not know the day" apply to the Body of Christ, the Church.[83] With regard to the prayer of Jesus for his disciples during the Last Supper, a prayer which was not entirely fulfilled, Thomas recalls a distinction introduced by Jerome: it was fulfilled in so far as it concerned the predestined.[84]

The Holy Virgin

Jerome's love of the Blessed Virgin is very remarkable. Jerome is the advocate of her virginity which he defends against contrary opinions. He also confirms the virginity of Joseph.[85] The phrase "before they came to live together" (Mt 1:18) does not mean that later Mary and Joseph had marital relations. Joseph is the protector of Mary and Jesus, rather than being the husband of Mary. But Thomas explains that one can only say that Joseph is not the husband of Mary when one understands by "husband" one who has sexual intercourse with his wife.[86] Joseph had no suspicions with regard to the pregnancy of Mary, because he knew her purity (*sciens illius castitatem*). Mary had to be married so as to avoid the suspicion of having committed adultery, and also in order to be protected, and finally, so that the mystery of the birth of Jesus would be hidden from the devil.[87] As for the role of the Holy Spirit in the conception of Jesus, Jerome rejects any physical interpretation.[88] It was appropriate that an angel announced the Incarnation to Mary, since virginity is related to the nature of the angels.[89] The angel greets Mary with the words "full of grace." As a matter of fact, says Jerome, she received the entire plenitude of grace in one in-

---

81. *ST* III, q. 51, a. 1, ad 2.
82. *ST* III, q. 53, a. 3, ad 2.
83. *In Boetii De Trin.*, part 2, q. 3, a. 4, ad 6.
84. *In III Sent.*, d. 17, q. 1, a. 3, qc. 4, ad 2.
85. *In IV Sent.*, d. 30, q. 2, a. 3, s.c. 2. The *Summa theologiae* presents a series of quotations from the works of Jerome in defense of the virginity of Mary.
86. *ST* III, q. 28, a. 3.
87. *Super evang. Matth.*
88. *ST* III, q. 30, a. 2.
89. *ST* III q. 30, a. 2. Cf. *In III Sent.*, d. 8, q. 3, a. 2, qc. 1: "Angelis cognata est virginitas."

stant.⁹⁰ This is why the Blessed Virgin has been elevated above the choirs of the angels.⁹¹ Jerome calls her mother, virgin, and martyr all at once.⁹²

The Angels

Jerome follows the Greek doctors, says Thomas, in their view that the angels were created before the creation of the material world. Augustine, however, thinks that they were made simultaneously with the remainder of the universe. Thomas himself follows this last view, but writes that it is permitted to have a different opinion on this point, since it is not necessarily connected with the faith.⁹³ The human soul has such a value and dignity that from his birth everyone has a guardian angel,⁹⁴ but also an evil angel to put him on trial.⁹⁵ Following Origen, Jerome seems to think that every celestial body also has a soul.⁹⁶

In Ephesians 3:10, Paul speaks of the mystery from centuries hidden in God and which is now preached to the pagans that they may from now on have knowledge, through the mediation of the Church, of God's infinite wisdom and the measures taken by God in the eternal plan which he has conceived in Christ Jesus, our Lord. Jerome understands this text as saying that the angels only learned about the mystery of the Incarnation through the mediation of men, an opinion which Augustine does not share.⁹⁷ The angels of an inferior order would even have been less informed, Jerome says, basing his view on Isaiah 63:1: "Who is this coming from Edom, from Bozrah in garments stained with crimson?"⁹⁸ Thomas notes that the angels did not learn the mystery of the Incarnation from the apostles, but knew it *praesentialiter*, that is, they saw it as present in a view embracing what happen in history and which at the moment of the Incarnation became a clear knowledge.⁹⁹

90. *ST* III, q. 27, a. 5, s.c.
91. *In I Sent.*, d. 44, q. 1, a. 3, arg. 4.
92. *In IV Sent.*, d. 49, q. 5, a. 3 B. Cf. *ST* II-II, q. 124, a. 4, obj. 1.
93. *In II Sent.*, d. 2, q. 1, a. 3; *ST* I, q. 61, a. 3; *QD de potentia*, q. 3, a. 18, arg. 7.
94. *ST* I, q. 113, a. 2. To confirm the theory that we have a guardian angel, Thomas appeals to Jerome.
95. *In II Sent.*, d. 3, q. 1, a. 3, s.c. 1; *QD de veritate*, q. 5, a. 8, arg 6; in q. 11, a. 2, Jerome's interpretation of a text of Daniel is mentioned, according to which each nation has also its angel.
96. *ST* I, q. 70, a. 3.
97. *In II Sent.*, d. 11, q. 2, a. 4. Cf. *QD de veritate*, q. 8, a. 4, s.c 1.
98. *In III Sent.*, d. 3, q. 3, a. 2, qc. 2, arg. 2.
99. *Contra errores Graecorum*, 1, chap. 26. Cf. *ST* I, q. 117, a. 2, ad 1.

In Daniel 10:13, the prophet recounts the apparition of an angel who tells him that his prayer has been granted. The prince of the kingdom of the Persians had resisted him, he says, but Michael came to help him and to confront this prince. Jerome is convinced that this prince is an evil spirit, but Gregory the Great, approved by Thomas, thinks that it is a good spirit, an interpretation very well possible says Thomas, if one allows for differences of opinion among the angels.[100] Jerome thinks that the demons can harass human beings, but that they cannot choose idols as their domicile. Thomas notes that they cannot be in the idols in the way the soul is in the body.[101]

The Sacraments

Thomas refers only a few times to Jerome in his treatises on the sacraments. The texts concern baptism, the Eucharist, penance, priesthood, and marriage. The baptism of Jesus prefigured our baptism which is administered in the name of the Father and the Son and the Holy Spirit. This is also the reason why the Divine Persons manifested themselves during the baptism of Jesus.[102] Baptism frees man from such serious sins as bigamy.[103] A sentence which is quoted repeatedly says that during the Last Supper Jesus is the host and also the food. He eats with his disciples and gives himself to be eaten.[104] When the figure of Christ appears miraculously in a consecrated host, it is not allowed to consume it, since then it is the body of Christ as a victim on the cross.[105]

In a text repeatedly quoted in the works of Thomas, Jerome calls the sacrament of penance a life buoy (*secunda tabula*) after a shipwreck. If one has lost the integrity of Christian life, one can cling to the sacrament of penance.[106] Jerome is critical of a way of saying that it is the priest who absolves the one who is guilty. When he absolves from sins, he does not absolve the persons who want to persevere in their sins, but he absolves those who have decided to leave behind them the sins of the past.[107] The

---

100. *ST* I, q. 113, a. 8.
101. *QD de malo*, q. 16, a. 11, arg. 11.
102. *ST* III, q. 93, a. 8.
103. *In IV Sent.*, d. 27, q. 3, a. 2.
104. *In IV Sent.*, d. 11, q. 3, a. 1, s.c.; *Catena in Matth.*, chap. 26, lesson 27; *ST* III, q. 81, a. 1.
105. *ST* III, q. 82, a. 4, ad 3.
106. *ST* III, q. 84, a. 2.
107. *De forma absolutionis*, chap. 2.

canons of the Church do not determine the amount of penance for each crime, but leaves a margin to the appreciation of the priest.[108]

As to the priesthood, Jerome insists on the fact that every priest must render his life in conformity to that of Christ. It is not enough to celebrate with solemnity the liturgy, but his life must be conformed to the sacrament of which he is a minister. Thomas notes that even when a priest is in a state of great sin, the sacrament he administers is nevertheless valid.[109] Jerome observes that men, married once, can become priests, and when before his baptism a candidate had two wives, he can still receive the sacrament of Orders, but Ambrose and Augustine are opposed to it.[110] According to Jerome not only bishops but also priests are in the state of perfection.[111]

Eschatology

In the writings of Thomas, there are quite a number of references to what Jerome says on eschatology. Owing to the grace which they have received, the saints in heaven can go anywhere they want. This explains why they can help us and intervene for us.[112] A different problem is that of whether all men will die at the end of the world. Jerome thinks that those who are still alive when Christ comes at the end of time, will not die, but Thomas writes that it is better to say that all must die.[113] Jerome mentions four signs which will precede the last judgment. Thomas thinks that here Jerome reproduces what he has found in the Jewish Annals. The sinner in hell will suffer several evils which are connected with his sin. The punishment of Arius has not yet been definitively fixed because his heresy continues to cause damage.[114] On Matthew 24:29 "the sun will be darkened, the moon will lose its brightness," Jerome notes that these words do not mean that the sun will lose its brightness, but that compared to the true light of Christ, the rest will seem obscure.[115]

108. *In IV Sent.*, d. 18, q. 1, a. 3, qc. 4.
109. *ST* III, q. 82, a. 5, obj. 1.
110. *Super Titum*, chap. 1, 8; *Super I Tim.*, chap. 3.
111. *ST* II-II, q, 184, a. 6, obj. 1: "Noverint episcopi se magis consuetudine quam dispensationis dominicae veritate presbyteris esse maiores."
112. *In IV Sent.*, d. 45, q. 1, a. 1, qc. 3.
113. *In II Sent.*, d. 31, q. 1, a. 2, arg. 2; *ST* I-II, q. 81, a. 3, ad 1; *QD de malo*, q. 4, a. 6, arg. 1; *Compendium theologiae*, chap. 243; *Super 1 Thess.*, chap. 4, lesson 2.
114. *In IV Sent.*, d. 17, q. 2, a. 2, qc. 4, arg. 2 and ad 2.
115. *Responsio ad magistrum Ioannem de Vercellis de 43 articulis*, a. 42.

The Observance of the Jewish Law

In the early days of Christianity, the observance of the many precepts of the Jewish law caused problems and had even been the occasion of a conflict between Peter and Paul. According to Jerome observing the obligations of the Ancient Law after the death and resurrection of Christ is sinful and even becomes an act of idolatry.[116] Peter would have feigned that he still observed them, but Augustine in his Letter 82, addressed to Jerome, is of the opinion that before the gospel message had spread in the world these laws could still be observed, provided that converts from Judaism no longer put their hope in them. Texts from the New Testament have led Jerome to say that the apostles gave the appearance of observing these laws and customs.[117] To resolve this disputed question Thomas makes a distinction with regard to Galatians 5:18: "If you are led by the Spirit, no law can touch you": one can observe some of these laws, without placing one's hope in them. Being under the law means that one puts one's hope in the works of the law, as was the case with some of the first Christians. Concerning the decision of the Council of Jerusalem (Acts 15:28), Jerome says that this ruling was given to repress gluttony, but Thomas points out that these rules were meant to facilitate the union of the Jews and the converts from paganism.[118]

Prophecy

According to Jerome the presence of prophecies is a sign of the foreknowledge of God.[119] If the prophets accomplish extraordinary things, they do not do so by their own force but by invoking Christ.[120] In their prophecies the prophets use knowledge they acquired before.[121] Thomas uses a division of prophecy given by Jerome: for certain future events predicted by them, these had been decided by God; in respect of other events, the prophet received foreknowledge, which also takes into account the free will of man. Finally there are also threatening prophe-

---

116. *Super Galatas*, chap. 5, lesson 1; *In IV Sent.*, d. 1, q. 2, a. 5, qc. 3; *ST* II-II, q. 94, a. 3, arg. 5.
117. *ST* II-II, q. 103, a. 4, ad 1; *Super Galatas*, chap. 2, 12 ff.
118. *ST* I-II, q. 103, a. 4.
119. *ST* II-II, q. 171, a. 6.
120. *ST* II-II, q. 172, a. 4, ad 1.
121. *ST* II-II, q. 173, a. 2, arg. 1.

cies.¹²² The line of prophets who announced the coming of Christ came to an end with John the Baptist.¹²³

Human Nature and the Moral Life according to Jerome

Human Nature

In the works of Thomas, one finds few texts of Jerome concerning human nature. In the *Commentary on the Sentences* Jerome tells us that we must understand human nature, the soul, and the body, as parts of a whole.¹²⁴ What is immaterial cannot be seen by the eyes of the body.¹²⁵ Jerome rejects the opinion of those who say that our souls were in heaven before entering our bodies.¹²⁶ Jerome confirms the presence of free will and declares that all men always have the power to sin or not to sin.¹²⁷ Contrary to what Jerome says, Thomas notes that different acts can proceed from one faculty or habit (the so-called synderesis).¹²⁸ Jerome thinks that the most important organ in our bodies is not the brain but the heart.¹²⁹ With regard to the physical world, Jerome seems to think that the sun is ensouled, a view denied by John Damascene.¹³⁰ The celestial bodies would also have souls, but Thomas thinks that we cannot assign a determined place to the heavenly spirits.¹³¹

The Moral Life

Several texts of Jerome, quoted by Thomas, concern questions of our moral life. According to Jerome virtue consists in love which makes us love God and our neighbor.¹³² Thomas approves the distinction Jerome makes between sins in our thought, sins in our words, and sins in what we do,¹³³ but he does not follow him in his division of the commandments.

---

122. *ST* II-II, q. 174, a. 1, s.c.
123. *ST* II-II, q. 174, a. 6, ad 3.
124. *In III Sent.*, d. 2, q. 1, *proemium*.
125. *In IV Sent.*, d. 49, q. 2, a. 2, s.c. 3.
126. *QD de potentia*, q. 3, a. 10, s.c. 3.
127. *QD de veritate*, q. 24, a. 12, s.c. 1.
128. *ST* I, q. 79, a. 1, ad 1.
129. *QD de spir. creat.*, a. 4, arg. 8.
130. *QD de veritate*, q. 5, a. 9, ad 14; *Quodl.* XII, q. 6, a. 2.
131. *QD de potentia*, q. 6, a. 6.
132. *QD de virtutibus*, q. 2, a. 5, arg. 1.
133. *ST* I-II, q. 72, a. 7, s.c.

Jerome divides the first commandment in two: I am your God; you will not have other gods, but leaves out the precept of the sanctification of the Sabbath.[134] The "sins against the Holy Spirit" are understood by Athanasius, Hilarius, Ambrose, Jerome, and Chrysostom as a blasphemy which one pronounces against the Holy Spirit, but Augustine, followed by Thomas, gives a different explanation.[135] Jerome reminds us that charity is not a friendship based on some practical use, but a real friendship based on the fear of God and love of the Scriptures. Thomas expresses it more precisely: because of God one can even love those who are not virtuous.[136] The order to follow in love is: God, our father and our mother.[137] Differences of opinion, such as those between Barnabas and Paul, Jerome and Augustine, are compatible with Christian charity.[138] Jerome observes that discord makes the greatest enterprises stagger. Thomas adds that it happens that we have a different opinion, but that by pride or vanity people defend their opinion in a disorderly way.[139]

Several texts of Jerome are quoted in the question about scandal. Thomas invites him to tell us, what scandal does consist in: giving others the occasion to sin by what one says or what one does. Jerome explains the meaning of Matthew 16:23 where Jesus reprimands Peter quite rudely, and notes that elderly persons are hardly influenced by scandals. The millstone at the neck, of which Jesus speaks, is an expression which was used in Palestine. Except our obligations in the field of the virtues, the Christian doctrine, and our duties in the field of justice, we should not do things which might become an occasion of scandal. Thomas adds that sometimes following the evangelical counsels can be necessary, even if it causes scandal.[140]

Is it permitted to be worried about one's daily life? Jerome says that we must work and not think too much about the future and not worry about the next day,[141] but Thomas thinks that it is legitimate to have a

---

134. *ST* I-II, q. 104, a. 4.
135. *ST* II-II, q. 14, a. 1; *QD de malo*, q. 3, a. 14; *Super Romanos*, chap. 2, lesson 1.
136. *ST* II-II, q. 23, a. 1, arg. 3, and ad 3.
137. *ST* II-II, q. 26, a. 10.
138. *ST* II-II, q. 29, a. 3, ad 2.
139. *ST* II-II, q. 37, a. 2. In q. 33, a. 3, ad 1, Thomas explains that a text of Jerome quoted in arg. 1 does not mean that fraternal correction is reserved to priests.
140. *ST* III, q. 43, aa. 1–7. Jerome takes the words of Jesus that it may be preferable to enter into life crippled or lame or with one eye than to have two eyes and to be thrown into the fire of hell, as referring to one's relations with one's family and friends (*Catena in Matth.*, 18, 5).
141. *ST* II-II, q. 188, a. 7, ad 2: "Sufficit nobis praesentis temporis cogitatio. Futura quae incerta sunt Deo relinquamus."

moderate solicitude. The text of Matthew 6:34 ("Do not worry about tomorrow") refers to the future.[142] Is it permissible to swear? According to Jerome the Lord had not forbidden taking an oath with God as witness, but did not allow swearing by the heavens, as did the Jews. The reason for this prohibition is that the one who swears respects or loves the person by whom he swears. One should not give this honor to creatures. If one takes an oath contrary to the truth, right judgment, or justice, he commits perjury.[143]

In several other questions of this second part of the *Summa theologiae*, there are references to Jerome. For instance, giving something to the prophets for their daily life is not simony. Nothing corrupts so easily one's character as flattery. Intemperance is not to be generalized as a vice, since children do not stay angry when they have been offended and do not feel a desire when they see a beautiful woman.[144] According to Jerome our conscience functions through the synderesis, which even in Cain was not extinguished.[145] When one is a prisoner of one vice, one is also of all vices.[146] There is a type of pride which is good, and another form which is bad. Ingratitude is also a form of pride.[147] Nothing is so dangerous for a man as the desire for glory.[148] The desire for food ties the soul (to the things from below).[149] Jerome gives general advice: everyone must work for the salvation of his soul.[150] To bring out better the distinction between what one must do and what one may do in addition (*ad melius*). Thomas quotes Jerome, who tells us that the commandments are observed by the virtue of justice, the (evangelical) counsels by charity.[151] Our charity must extend to those who share our faith, but we must also help Jews and Samaritans. Those who receive spiritual goods from their masters, must give them temporal things in return.[152]

---

142. *ST* II-II, q. 55, aa. 6 and 7.
143. *ST* II-II, q. 89, aa. 2–3; q. 98, a. 1, ad 1.
144. *ST* II-II, q. 100, a. 3; q. 115, a. 2, obj. 1; q. 142, a. 2, obj. 1.
145. *QD de veritate*, q. 16, aa. 1–3.
146. *QD de malo*, q. 2, a. 9, arg. 1.
147. Ibid., q. 8, a. 2, arg. 17; q. 9, a. 2, arg. 4.
148. Ibid., q. 9, a. 2, arg 4.
149. Ibid., q. 14, a. 2, arg 7.
150. *Quodl.* VII, q. 7, a. 1.
151. *ST* I-II, q. 99, a. 5.
152. *Contra impugnantes*, part 2, chap. 6.

Jerome and the Religious Life

The ideal of Christian life, says Jerome, is to learn on earth the science which will remain with us in heaven.[153] Jerome himself had chosen to follow the evangelical counsels, and so his writings contain many texts on the quest for Christian perfection and the religious life. Jerome is somewhat terse and rude when he admonishes his readers, but wise and firmly decided to defend *the only necessary thing*. In general Thomas agrees with him and refers to him hundreds of times on the life according to the evangelical counsels. Not all understand Jesus' invitation to follow him closely, but only those to whom this has been given. This calling is not a question of chance or destiny, but is given by God to those who asked him for it, who wanted it, and who worked to receive it.[154]

Jerome seems to think that the different monasteries practice one form of religious life, as also there is only one form of episcopal ministry, but Thomas observes that there is a great variety of works of charity and of asceticism, and that therefore several forms of religious life are possible.[155] The ideal for Jerome is that of a monastic life far from densely populated areas ("If you want to be a monk, you have nothing to look for in the city"). Thomas defends the possibility of leading a devoted life in a city, so that one can also devote oneself to the active life.[156] Jerome is all in favor of theological studies, of which the science will remain in heaven. If one objects that the apostles did not study, the answer is that they received the knowledge they needed from the Holy Spirit.[157] To walk on the road towards perfection, is it better to live in a community than to live alone? Jerome recalls the advantages of a common life, both for learning and for repressing evil inclinations, thanks to the example of others, but a perfect solitary life is superior to the life in a community.[158]

By all things the body desires, the soul is hampered in putting itself energetically on the road towards the supreme good.[159] Piety towards our parents should not keep us back from consecrating our life to God. If necessary we should act against the opposition of our parents.[160] The

---

153. *ST* I, q. 89, a. 5, s.c.
154. *Super evang. Matth.*, 19, 11.
155. *ST* II-II q. 188, a. 1.
156. *ST* II-II, q. 188, a, 2.
157. *ST* II-II, q. 188, aa. 1, 2, 5, and 7.
158. *ST* II-II, q. 188, a. 8.
159. *In IV Sent.*, d. 49, q. 1, a. 4.
160. *ST* II-II, q. 101, a. 4: "... per calcatum perge patrem, per calcatam perge matrem, ad

texts of Jerome betray a certain radicalism with respect to the observance of poverty and the detachment from one's possessions. It is about following Christ in his poverty,[161] who did not have a roof he could call his own.[162] In a text repeatedly quoted by Thomas, Jerome says that to give one's possessions is not enough, one has to follow Christ.[163] Thomas also refers to Jerome's letter to Jovinianus, who placed marriage and a consecrated life on the same level and argued that it would be better to distribute one's belongings little by little than at once. Jerome refutes him quoting Jesus words: "Sell whatever you have."[164] In his letters to Lucius, Heliodorus, and Paulinus, Jerome encourages his correspondents to give up all their belongings and to do as the apostles. As long as we are engaged in the things of this world and our mind is occupied with pursuing wealth, we do not have free time to occupy ourselves with Christ. The ideal is that, after having given away our possessions, we give ourselves to Christ. In a *Letter to Marcus*, quoted by Thomas, Jerome says that he has taken nothing from others, never received anything without working, and gained everyday his life with his hands and by the sweat of his face. Thomas comments: Jerome never asked for things which were not necessary. In a letter to Oceanus, Jerome notes that Rome celebrates the memory of Alexius, who went begging for his food.[165] He thinks that poor and worn clothes are a sign of a pure spirit.[166]

Is it allowed for the religious to live on alms, even if their monastery has possessions? Jerome thinks that in such a case the gifts received should be given to the poor, and concludes with a striking sentence: "Be careful that you are not collecting the possessions from other people, while the Lord himself is begging."[167] Thomas explains under which conditions a monastery can receive gifts.[168] When Jerome complains that certain monasteries have become too rich, Thomas notes that evangelical poverty

---

crucem evola" (Jerome, *Epistula* 14, PL 22: 248). Cf. also a phrase quoted in *De duobus praeceptis*, chap. 6): "Solum pietatis genus in hac re est esse crudelem." Cf. *In IV Sent.*, d. 38, q. 2, a. 4, qc. 2: "To follow Christ we must sometimes stand up to the opposition of our family." Cf. also *Contra doctrinam retrahentium*, chap. 9.

161. *ST* II-II, qq. 185–86.
162. *Contra doctrinam retrahentium*, chap. 15.
163. *ST* II-II, q. 184, a. 3, ad 1; *Quodl.* I, q. 9, a. 2, ad 2.
164. *De perfectione vitae spiritualis*, chap. 12, where Thomas writes: "Blessed Jerome also refutes the error of Jovanianus who places marriage on the same level as virginity."
165. *Contra impugnantes*, part 2, chap. 5.
166. Ibid., part 3, chap. 1.
167. *ST* II-II, q. 187, a. 5.
168. *ST* II-II, q. 187, a. 4.

does not consist essentially in destitution, but in the imitation of Christ.[169]

With regard to obedience Jerome says that in a monastery one submits one's own will. We do not do what we would like to do ourselves, we eat what is put before us, we have what we receive, we put on the clothes which are given to us, we do our part of the work, we are still sleepy when we get up, and we get up before having slept sufficiently. Out of love for God, one does things which as such one does not want to do.[170]

In one of his letters, Jerome writes that it is not the vocation of a monk to teach, but to do penance.[171] Gerald of Abbeville and others of his group tried to prove with the help of some texts that monks should not teach, but Thomas shows that Jerome does not exclude teaching. He himself taught, and he gave lessons to Paulinus. Thomas adds that it is evident that priests must instruct the faithful who have been entrusted to their care, although in this case there is no question of a theological magisterium, but of the explanation of the Good News.[172] A monk has no right to have a teaching position, but it would be senseless to say that a monk cannot teach because he is trying to lead a holy life.[173] In a letter to Rusticus, Jerome writes that a monk must always have a book in his hands.[174] Study and work are the weapons with which to sanctify oneself. People who do not want to work should not be admitted to a monastery. In a letter to Vigilantius, Jerome defends in strong words the right of monks to receive alms, who recite the divine office and study. A monk works in the vineyard of the Lord and cuts and cleans the vines. Jerome recommends manual work and study to fight laziness.[175]

With regard to fasting Jerome writes that fasting is not just abstaining from food, but from everything which may lead us into temptation.[176] As such fasting is praiseworthy at any time.[177] When one is fasting the measure of one's fast should be the conservation of one's personal being.[178] To deprive oneself from food to the point of causing damage to one's health

---

169. *ST* II-II, q. 188, a. 7.

170. *De perfectione vitae spiritualis*, chap. 12: "Non facias quod vis, comedas quod iuberis, habeas quantum acceperis, vestiaris quod datur, operis tui pensam persolvas, ambulansque dormites et necdum expleto somno surgere compellaris."

171. *Contra impugnantes*, part 2, chap. 1.

172. Ibid.

173. *ST* II-II, q. 187, a. 1, obj. 1.

174. *Contra impugnantes*, 2, chap. 1, s.c. 2.

175. Ibid., part 2, chap. 4.

176. *In IV Sent.*, d. 15, q. 3, a. 1, qc. 1, arg. 2; *ST* II-II, q. 147, a. 1, ad 2.

177. *ST* II-II, q. 147, a. 5, ad 3.

178. *In IV Sent.*, d. 17, q. 2, a. 3, qc. 2.

is as it were to offer a sacrifice from what one has stolen.[179] Jerome adds this remark: It does not make a difference whether one kills oneself in a short time or during a protracted period. Fasting is not the act of perfect virtue, but the basis of the other virtues.[180] Fasting heals the diseases of the body, prayer those of the mind.[181]

Thomas also quotes the criticism which Jerome addressed to Vigilantius, who was against priests becoming monks, with the pretext that there would not remain a sufficient number of priests for the ministry. Jerome answers that there is no danger, since few are so virtuous: *"Rara est virtus nec a pluribus appetitur."*[182] Thomas agrees with Jerome: not allowing the clergy to become monks would be like a refusal to draw water from a river for fear that it would dry up. In another place he writes that religious life is so difficult that only a few Christians embrace it.[183] In his *Contra Jovinianum* Jerome praises virginity so much that he seems to depreciate marriage.[184]

Jerome and the Heretics

In the age of Jerome, the young Christian Church was afflicted by numerous heresies. Although Jerome has not written theological treatises to refute them, he was very much aware of the danger of those heresies for the Church, and in his biblical commentaries and letters he formulates refutations and criticisms, without however entering into dogmatic details. He most likely thought that it was better to propose the Word of God in its most authentic form in faithful translations and so to bring the faithful to open their minds to divine revelation. He insists on the duty of vigilance: words spoken lightly without taking into account the doctrine of the faith, may lead to heresy.[185] It is possible to fall into heresy if one understands a passage of the Bible wrongly. Thomas notes that this happens when one opposes oneself to divine revelation. For Jerome, to fall into

---

179. *In IV Sent.*, d. 15, q. 3, a. 1, qc. 2. Cf. *Quodl.* V, q. 9, a. 2: "One makes a mistake if by fasting, one weakens oneself too much or if one prefers fasting to charity."
180. Ibid., d. 15, q. 3, a. 1, qc. 1, arg. 2.
181. *In IV Sent.*, d. 15, q. 2, a. 1, qc. 1, arg. 2.
182. *ST* II-II, q. 189, a. 7, ad 2.
183. *Quodl.* III, q. 5, a. 2, ad 2.
184. *Contra doctrinam retrahentium*, chap. 2.
185. *In IV Sent.*, d. 13, q. 2, a. 1, arg. 1, and ad 5: "Verba inordinate prolata sunt occasio et causa erroris."

heresy is rather a question of the will.[186] A heretic is a person who attaches himself stubbornly to a sect he has chosen.[187] The difference between heresy and schism is that between a genus and its species. Thomas notes that certain people begin by sinning against charity and fall later into a heresy.[188] Separating oneself from the Church brings with it mostly deviations in doctrine.[189] Jerome considers certain philosophical systems dangerous. When commenting on the words "Provide yourselves with no gold or silver," Jerome writes that we must keep what the Lord has given us and not take over anything from the perverse doctrines of the heretics and philosophers.[190]

In his Commentary on the Letter to the Galatians 5:10 ("Anybody who troubles you in future will be condemned"), Jerome writes that the rotten parts of the body must be excised and the bad sheep driven out of the fold, in order that the rest of the sheep are not contaminated. In Alexandria (the heretic) Arius was only a spark, but because he was not reduced to silence right away he set the whole world on fire.[191] We should not even have the same names in common with the heretics nor converse with them.[192] Nevertheless Jerome writes that we should not drive out too soon a brother from the community, because he can easily change his mind the next day.[193] Should we always forgive heretics and receive them? Thomas quotes Matthew 18:21 and concludes that we must always forgive the one who sinned against us, but that it is not up to us to forgive the one who sinned against God or our neighbors.[194]

In the parable of the sower the heresiarch Valentinus read the theory of the three natures, spiritual, animal, and terrestrial.[195] On Jesus' words "No one knows the Father except the Son" etc., Jerome comments that Eunomius should be ashamed of claiming to have the knowledge which the Father and the Son have of each other.[196] While the centurion at the foot of the cross exclaims that Jesus is the Son of God, Arius preaches

---

186. *ST* II-II, q. 11, a. 1, obj. 1 and 2.
187. *Super Titum*, 3, 10.
188. *In IV Sent.*, d. 13, q. 2, a. 1, ad 2.
189. *ST* II-II., q. 39, a. 1, ad 3.
190. *Catena in Matth.*, 13, 2.
191. *ST* II-II, q. 11, a. 3.
192. *In Boetii de Trin.*, part 1, q. 2, a. 3, ad 6.
193. *Catena in Matth.*, 13, 21.
194. *ST* II-II, q. 11, a. 4, ad 2.
195. *Catena in Matth.*, 13, 4.
196. Ibid., 11, 27.

that he is a man.¹⁹⁷ The blind man in the gospel cries "Jesus, Son of David, have mercy on us," Marcion and the Manichees should pay attention and notice that the Savior is called Son of David.¹⁹⁸

Jerome applies the passage of the unclean spirit who returns with seven others to the heretics who decorate their houses with an appearance of virtue, but who are living in a state much worse than that of the gentiles. For the gentiles there is the hope that one day they will have the faith, but with regard to the heretics it is strife and discord.¹⁹⁹ Jerome thinks that all heretics are anti-christs,²⁰⁰ who build their theories on sand, so that they are bound to collapse.²⁰¹

Jerome and Holy Scripture

For the medieval theologians Saint Jerome was the great doctor of the interpretation of the Bible, the specialist of the Greek and Hebrew languages, who had made excellent translations of the inspired texts and who by his evangelical life was thought to be very close to the spirit of the Word of God. This is the reason why Thomas consults him frequently for the explanation of difficult passages and for information on the Palestinian and Jewish background of the Bible. Having overcome his initial disgust at the sober style of the biblical texts, Jerome took a lively interest in Sacred Scripture. He makes a sustained effort to come as close as possible to the original texts. His different translations, in particular of the Old Testament, his knowledge of the Hexapla and the homilies of Origen, and his commentaries made a profound impression on his contemporaries and the medieval masters. Through his efforts to make translations as close as possible to the original texts, Jerome was a forerunner of modern biblical studies. But this work was not without difficulties: sometimes the Christian communities remained attached to a particular version which was in use among them and hesitated to adopt a new translation. Augustine preferred the authority of the Septuagint, which had been used by the authors of the New Testament, whereas Jerome tried to find the *veritas hebraica*. This difference gave rise to fierce exchanges in which at last

---
197. Ibid., 27, 54.
198. Ibid., 9, 29.
199. Ibid. 12, 41.
200. Ibid. 24, 5.
201. Ibid. 7, 24.

the mansuetude and charity of the bishop of Hippo succeeded in reconciling the monk of Bethlehem.

For a certain number of questions, Jerome has been an authority who could not be neglected. Thomas recalls that Jerome divides the Old Testament into three groups of writings: the law, the prophets, and the hagiographers.[202] Thomas also stresses that Jerome, the great specialist of the literal sense of the text, insisted on the figurative sense of different passages. The Holy Spirit is the main author of Holy Scripture who, in only one word, can manifest much more than its obvious literal meaning.[203] For example, the prophets spoke of the events of their time in such a way that they also indicated what was going to happen in the future. With regard to the Book of Revelation Jerome observes that under the words of the text different senses are hidden.[204]

As has been mentioned above Thomas reminds us that the fifth council condemned the theory of Theodore of Mopsuestia, according to which the Old Testament does not explicitly say anything about Christ, an opinion rejected by Jerome. In *Quodlibetum* VII, question 6, which studies the different senses of the texts of Holy Scripture, Jerome is quoted in the argument *sed contra* of the first article, next to a text from Daniel 12:4 ("*Pertransibunt plurimi et multiplex erit scientia*"), to establish an argument based on authority to confirm that the Bible has several senses. We must, however, notice that for the theory of the four senses Thomas bases his exposition on Augustine and Bede.[205]

In the prologue of his commentary on the Book of Job, Thomas writes that according to Jerome a considerable part of the book has been written in hexameters, in the manner of a poem and therefore one must understand many passages as being figurative. In his commentary on Isaiah, he also quotes several observations of Jerome and reproduces in detail the description the latter had given of the style of the text. To give an example, with regard to the verse "An offshoot comes out of the root of Jesse," Thomas notes that Jerome and all the holy doctors understood the text in a figurative sense. Jerome defends against the Hebrews that it is not possible to understand everything in a literal sense.[206]

The style of the text of the gospels shows four categories: command-

202. *Principium biblicum*.
203. *Quodl.* VII, q. 6, a. 1, ad 5.
204. Ibid., s.c. 2.
205. Jerome is also not quoted in *ST* I, q. 1, a. 10.
206. *Super Isaiam*, chap. 11.

ments, counsels or recommendations, testimonies, and examples.[207] As was to be expected, we encounter a great number of references to Jerome in the *Catena aurea in Matthaeum*, 848 to be precise. Thomas often quotes Jerome first before several other Fathers, with regard to the meaning of a text, but in his own commentary on this gospel Thomas bases himself more on Ambrose, Augustine, and Chrysostom. To see better what the exegesis of Jerome meant for Thomas, one may compare the following numbers: Jerome is quoted in the *Catena* 848 times, Augustine 700, and Chrysostom 1,287. If the number of references to Jerome in the works of Thomas is greater than that to Dionysius and Ambrose, references to Chrysostom there are still more numerous, namely, 3,687, as also those to Augustine (over 11,000).

Jerome is consulted on the question of the genealogy of Joseph, and a great number of his comments on the text of the first Gospel have been taken over by Thomas. When at his baptism Jesus said to John "Leave it like this for the time being" (Mt 3:15), the evangelist refers these words to indicate that Jesus must be baptized with water, but that John would be baptized spiritually. With regard to the Beatitudes, Jerome writes that it is not enough to want justice, but that one must be hungry for it. The peaceful are called blessed because they first make peace in their own heart, and next among brothers who are involved in conflicts. The truth of the gospel message does not allow us to take oaths, since for a faithful one his word is equivalent to the truth. As for the beauty of the lilies growing in the fields, Jerome exclaims: "In all truth, which silk, which royal purple, which dying of tissues can compete with the flowers! What has a red color like a rose, or is white like a lily!"

All through the *Catena* Thomas quotes striking sentences of Jerome. On Matthew 7:24 Jerome notes: "Sand is fluid, one cannot put all of it in a container. In the same way the theories of the heretics are built on sand and do not have any consistency." The scribe of Matthew. 8:19 did not see in Jesus more than one master among others. The man was only a grammarian, says Jerome, and not a *spiritualis auditor*. The calming of the storm shows that all creatures obey the majesty of their creator. Commenting on the resurrection of the daughter of Jairus Jerome says that the event signifies Israel lying dead in the house of God. The verse "The Good News is proclaimed to the poor" (Mt 11:5) means that the preaching of the gospel does not differentiate between the wealthy and the poor,

---

207. *Quodl.* IV, q. 12, a. 2, arg. 7.

aristocrats and ordinary people; this shows the truth of what the Master says: from now on every one who can be saved is in a position of equality. In Matthew 20:20 the mother of Zebedee's sons requests a special favor for her sons. Jerome comments: *"Aviditate feminea praesentia cupit, immemor futurorum."* In Matthew 21:2 Jesus tells the apostles: "You will find a donkey and a colt ... bring them to me." Jerome notes that the story seems impossible; what was Jesus going to do with two donkeys? We must seek the spiritual meaning of the text: the cloak which the apostles put on the back of the animal signifies the doctrine of the virtues, knowledge of the Scriptures, the dogmas of the Church. For Jerome the expulsion of the dealers from the temple is the greatest of the signs wrought by Jesus. A superterrestrial power radiated from his eyes. Jerome stigmatized also the cupidity of the priests who allowed this kind of business in a sacred place. The parable of the two sons (Mt 21:28) shows that the kingdom of God will be transferred to the heathens.

In his *Super evangelium sancti Matthaei*, Thomas uses the prologue of Jerome who points out the manner of writing of the apostle and explains the structure of the gospel. He comments on the mysteries at the beginning of the gospel, those of Jesus' public life and those at the end, and of Jesus when leaving this earth. Jerome stresses that this gospel shows the human aspects of Christ, so that by passing through Christ as a man, we come to call him God. Thomas adds the remark that among the evangelists Matthew deals mainly with the humanity of Christ. When in the beginning of his commentary Thomas frequently refers to Jerome, further on he quotes Ambrose, Chrysostom, and Augustine. With regard to Jesus' words in Matthew 26:39, "Father, ... if it is possible let this cup pass me by," Jerome reads this meaning: "If it is not possible that the truth goes to the side of the gentiles without the Jews giving up (their way of life), your will be fulfilled."

The sentences of Jerome quoted above are only one choice out of many. Jerome accompanies Thomas in his commentary step by step, but in the *Catena aurea in Marcum* there are noticeably fewer references to the works of Jerome, but those quoted are long and concern the spiritual sense of the passages as well as penance. For example, when one wants a nut the shell must be crushed, and the hope of recovering one's health alleviates the pain of the treatment.[208] According to what we read in the

---

208. *Catena in Marcum*, chap. 1, lesson 6.

Catena, Jerome is very well acquainted with the institutions in Palestine in the days of Jesus, and his commentary, always theologically correct, witnesses to a profound spirituality. He does not miss any occasion to unmask a heresy. John the Baptist is a voice that cries in the wilderness, because the Spirit of God has abandoned the Jews.

In the *Catena aurea in Lucam* Jerome is quoted fourteen times; the quotations are taken from his *Commentary on Isaiah* and his *De viris illustribus*. About the manner of writing of Saint Luke, Jerome says that "his language both in the Gospel and in the Acts is polished and gives evidence of profane eloquence." We also find some beautiful texts about the Virgin Mary, quoted in the section on the Virgin Mary. In the *Catena aurea in Johannem* there are only six references to Jerome, concerning mostly technical questions such as whether Mary the sinner who anointed Jesus is the same as the sister of Lazarus, something denied by Jerome.[209]

Jerome provides some details to Thomas in the *Commentary on the Letter to the Romans*. According to Jerome Paul would have written this letter in Corinth, but Augustine thinks that it was in Athens. Thomas seems to prefer the solution of Jerome, who informs us also about the name Paulus. Saul would have adopted it after having converted the well-known Roman proconsul, Sergius Paulus. Regarding the Letter to the Hebrews Thomas writes that Jerome and other doctors accept it among the writings of Paul. In a comment on chapter 7, verse 1, Jerome writes concerning Melchizedek (Gen 14:17) that Salem cannot be Jerusalem, since its distance from Jerusalem was too great to allow the king to come to meet Abraham.

In his prologue to the *Commentary on the Psalms*, Thomas writes that in the time of Jerome there existed a translation in a bad state because of the many mistakes made by the copyists. Jerome corrected it at the request of Pope Damasus, and this translation was used in Italy. It differed from another made after the text of the Septuagint. At the request of Paula, he made a translation from the Greek which, Thomas says, is now in use in France. Finally at the request of Sophronius, Jerome made a new translation directly from the Hebrew, which was not in use in any church, but Thomas knew of it. In his commentary on the first fifty-four psalms, he notes a few times: "*Littera Hieronymi planior est*"; "*Littera Hieronymi habet*"; "*Hieronymus habet pulchrius.*" This translation of Jerome is often

---

209. *Catena in Matth.*, chap. 26, lesson 3.

close to modern versions. Thomas mentions also the sometimes different titles Jerome placed above each psalm.

According to Jerome the study of the Bible imposes on us a real asceticism. It gives us the science which we shall conserve in the other world. During our present life the study of Holy Scripture turns us away from the vices of the flesh.[210]

---

210. *De perfectione vitae spiritualis,* chap. 9.

8 ~ SAINT JOHN CHRYSOSTOM

Saint John Chrysostom is one of the great Fathers of the Eastern Church whose life and apostolate have been commemorated in numerous biographies and panegyrics.

Born about 350 at Antioch, a brilliant student of letters and theology, he led an ascetic life. Ordained a priest in 368, he was charged with preaching in the cathedral of his native city during some ten years and acquired the reputation of being the greatest of Christian preachers. Against his own wishes he was made bishop of Constantinople. His attempts to reform the clergy hit on several obstacles. He was banished twice and died in exile in 407. His austere way of life and his integrity as well as the quality of his writings gained him the admiration and veneration of later generations. Because of his eloquence he received the surname of Chrysostom (Golden Mouth). Ever since the fifth century, Latin translations were made of his Seven Panegyrics of St. Paul and of several of his homilies on the gospel according to St Matthew, which circulated in the West. In the twelfth century these *Homilies on the Gospel according to Matthew* were translated into Latin by Burgundio of Pisa. His *Homilies on the Gospel according to John* are shorter and not so well known.

Chrysostom tries to determine the literal sense of the texts, but mentions also their spiritual sense and gives some practical applications. His writings are characterized by their rich spiritual and moral doctrine, yet his contribution to dogmatic theology is not very important. Against the Arians he stresses the divinity of Christ and his equality with the Father, but as we shall see, what he says about the Blessed Virgin is incongruous. On the other hand, his observations on the virtues are excellent, and his texts very close to the daily life of the people.

Thomas certainly had at his disposition the homilies on the Gospels

---

This chapter was originally published as "La présence de saint Jean Chrysostome dans les oeuvres de saint Thomas d'Aquin," *Nova et Vetera* 83 (2008): 57–76.

according to Matthew and John, as well as those on Genesis. In the questions of the *Summa theologiae* II-II on the virtues and vices, Chrysostom is very much present and takes part in the discussion. His observations have a considerable authority, and they throw light on the problems or suggest distinctions which help to find a solution. In the third part of the *Summa theologiae*, there are more than 120 references to Chrysostom which help to explain the words of Jesus as well as the events of his public life. They show how much value Thomas attached to the observations of this great Father of the Church. The fact that Thomas had Latin translations of several of his works facilitated this frequent appeal to Chrysostom, who accompanies Thomas in the questions on the life of Jesus.

On the following pages the reader will find a selection of the most important texts of Chrysostom among the more than three thousand quotations in Thomas's works. These are spread over the works of Thomas as follows: 1,281 in the *Catena aurea in Matthaeum*; 204 in the *Catena aurea in Marcum*, 417 in the *Catena aurea in Lucam*, 790 in the *Catena aurea in Joannem*; 184 in the *Expositio super Matthaeum*, and 259 in that on John. For the *Summa theologiae* the numbers are as folllows: twenty in the *prima pars*; eleven in the *prima secundae*; eighty-three in the *secuna secundae*; 126 in the *tertia pars*. From these numbers we learn that Chrysostom especially provides valuable observations on the moral life of Christians as well as on the life and words of Christ.

The frequency of quotations in the *Catena aurea*, as well as in the commentaries on the Gospels according to Matthew and John is explained by the fact that Thomas had access to translations of the homilies of Chrysostom on the gospels. On the other hand there are only about a dozen references in the commentary on the Letter to the Romans, four on 1 Corinthians, and seven in the commentary on the Letter to the Hebrews. We find only one reference in most of Thomas's other biblical commentaries. There are no quotations in purely philosophical texts, nor in the *De substantiis spiritualibus, De unione Verbi, QD de potentia*, etc. With regard to the number of quotations from Chrysostom compared to those from Augustine, Jerome, Origen, and Ambrose, in the *Catena aurea in Matthaeum* they are respectively 1, 281, 848, 705, 332, and 44. For the commentary on the Gospel according to Matthew the numbers are: 184, 260, 174, 94, and 20.

On several occasions Thomas gives successively the explanations of a text by Chrysostom and by Augustine. In general he prefers the latter, but not always. Chrysostom thinks that the stories of Matthew 14:22

and John 6:16 (Christ walks on the water) are different episodes, but Augustine considers them as describing the same event. Thomas prefers Augustine's solution.[1] It also happens that Augustine gives the figurative meaning of a text, while Chrysostom describes the literal sense. Thomas frequently presents the interpretations of different authors without himself taking a position. The quotations from different Fathers and authors propose possible interpretations and remind the reader that the sense of the inspired text is very profound. In his homilies on the gospels, Chrysostom often comments on the different texts with the help of moral examples.

Holy Scripture

Thomas calls Chrysostom, Ambrose, and Augustine *expositores Sacrae Scripturae*.[2] The authority of Chrysostom in matters of Holy Scripture is so great that when he has given an explanation of a text, the Greeks no longer accept another view. This is the reason why they follow him when, as Thomas writes in his prologue to the Gospel of John, he connects the words *quod factum est* with the preceding sentence.[3] The small differences between the stories of the evangelists are a sign that what they write is true.[4] In the following section a limited but illustrative number of explications of the gospel text by Chrysostom will be quoted.

Why does the apostle John mention the testimony of John the Baptist in the prologue of his Gospel? He does that so that we might understand better that by Christ we are introduced into the kingdom of grace, that God offers us his light and wants all to come to know the truth and be saved.[5] Someone might think that the words "and the Word has become flesh" mean that the Word changed itself into a human body. In order to exclude this, the evangelist adds "and he lived among us" in our nature, while he preserved his divine nature. "We saw his glory" indicates the numerous gifts we received, even the privilege of being able to see God.[6] "He comes after me, ranks before me" (*ante me factus*) must be un-

---

1. *Super evang. Ioan.*, chap. 6, lesson 1.
2. *ST* I-II, q. 69, a. 2.
3. Prologue of the Gospel according to John, v. 4. (lesson 2). Thomas sees a reference to all that Christ has done during his life on earth. Thomas reads: "Quod factum est in ipso vita erat."
4. *Catena in Matth.*, preafatio 2.
5. *Super Ioan.*, chap. 1, lesson 3.
6. Ibid., chap. 1, lesson 7.

derstood as showing Christ's priority in dignity.[7] Chrysostom explains the words "grace in return for grace" as the series of revelations that the people of God received under the Old Testament: the uniqueness of God, who is the Creator of the world; the refusal of any form of idolatry.[8] "Among you there is one whom you do not know:" Thomas invites Chrysostom, Gregory the Great, and Augustine to explain that Christ lived among his contemporaries as a man, whose greatness they did not know, that is, his divine nature.[9]

Concerning the wedding at Cana (Jn 2:1–11), one might wonder why the Blessed Virgin, knowing that her Son had this power, did not invite him earlier to work a miracle. The answer of Chrysostom to this question is that Jesus conducted himself as one of the other guests (*unus aliorum*) and the right moment had not yet come. In this way he explains the initial refusal of Jesus, but Mary, full of zeal for the honor of her son, wanted him to work a miracle right away, before the suitable moment had come. Anyway it had not yet been noticed that there was going to be a shortage of wine.[10] Chrysostom does not have a high opinion of Nicodemus in his nightly conversation with Jesus. He should have understood that Jesus was speaking about a spiritual rebirth. The comparison with the wind that Jesus made cannot yet apply to the Holy Spirit, because Nicodemus was still an unbeliever.[11]

In Thomas's commentary on the Gospel according to Matthew, Chrysostom provides numerous details about the daily life of the persons and the circumstances of the events described by the evangelist, details which betray a sharp insight into human psychology. But it also happens that he proposes fantastic explanations, as regarding the Baptist's saying "brood of vipers" (Mt 3:7): just like water heals snake bites, the water of baptism washes away the sins of the Pharisees and Sadducees; the Jews kill their prophets, just as young snakes kill their parents; a snake is beautiful when seen from the outside, but in its innermost being it is full of poison.[12] The commandments of Moses are easy to observe, and therefore the reward for keeping them faithfully is modest, but their transgression constitutes a serious sin. Those of Christ, such as not getting angry,

---

7. Ibid., chap. 1, lesson 9.
8. Ibid., lesson 10.
9. Ibid., lesson 13.
10. Ibid., chap. 2, lesson 2.
11. Ibid., chap. 3, lessons 1 and 3.
12. *Super evang. Matth.*, chap. 3, no. 264.

are difficult to observe in daily life, but observing them carries a great reward, while transgressing them is a lesser sin.[13]

The commentary of Chrysostom of Romans 9:3 ("I would willingly be condemned and be cut off from Christ ...") is quoted several times in the works of Thomas.[14] This text does not mean that Paul loves his fellowmen more than God. On Matthew 19:12, Chrysostom notes that one must not maim oneself to avoid sinning, but repress sinful thoughts.[15] Jesus's advice to his disciples not to take money with them (Mt 10:8) applies to the situation in the Palestine of those days.[16]

Regarding the text "As for that day, nobody knows, neither the angels nor the Son" (Mk 13:22), Chrysostom says that if Christ must judge, he also knows the moment of the judgement.[17] "'My Father, if it is possible let this cup pass me by' is the prayer of a man who with his natural will refuses his death."[18]

During the reign of the kings of Judea, even if they were bad, God sent prophets. But now that an iniquitous king was in power, Christ was born. The reason is that a serious disease without hope of recovery needs a more capable physician.[19] Thomas mentions two opinions about the star which appeared to the Magi: According to Chrysostom and Augustine, the star would have appeared to them two years before the birth of Christ, while others think that it appeared after the birth of Christ.[20]

Chrysostom, who in his youth had impaired his health by an ascetical life, was surprised to see so much austerity in the life of John the Baptist. He thinks that through his baptism John wanted to prepare the people for Christian baptism. God permitted the death of John, in order that the favor of the people would be transferred to Christ.[21] In question 39 which deals with the baptism of Jesus, there are numerous quotations from Chrysostom. After the baptism of Jesus, the Old Law ceased to be in force. Christ received baptism at the age of thirty, after having observed the Law. This means that no one could say that he made the Law disappear because its observation was above his power.[22]

---

13. Ibid., chap. 5, no. 471.
14. *ST* II-II, q. 27, a. 8, ad 1; *Super Romanos*, chap. 9, lesson 1.
15. *ST* III, q. 10, a. 2, ad 1.
16. *ST* II-II, q. 185, a. 6, ad 2.
17. *ST* III, q. 10, a. 2, ad 1.
18. Ibid., q. 21, a. 4, ad 1.
19. Ibid., q. 35, a. 8, ad 2.
20. Ibid., q. 36, a. 6, ad 3.
21. Ibid., q. 38, aa. 1–6.
22. Ibid., q. 39, a. 3.

When Jesus was baptized, the heavens opened for those with a spiritual eye, but during his passion the sky was totally obscured.[23] After mentioning Chrysostom's restrictive interpretation of the words: "The devil showed him all the kingdoms of the world." Thomas quotes him again when he says that Jesus has worked an ocean of miraculous healings and has shown that his power was equal to that of the Father.[24] Christ died on a wooden cross, raised high to clean the air, while the earth was cleansed by his blood which trickled down; his arms were stretched out in order to attract with one hand the people of Israel, and with the other those who must come from the four corners of the world.[25]

The Jews wanted Jesus to be condemned, not so much because for transgressing their law, but for being supposedly a revolutionary and public enemy.[26] The parable of the wicked husbandmen shows that the chiefs of the Jewish people did not surrender Jesus out of ignorance, but had him crucified out of hatred. They knew that he was the Son of God.[27] According to Chrysostom, Matthew divided the genealogy of Joseph into three sections, to show that neither before nor after the exile the people of Israel converted.[28] Chrysostom's attitude in respect of the Jews is quite hard.[29] The Christians no longer observed the *legalia* of the Jews. Chrysostom gives the following reason: when a treaty or a promise has been fulfilled, one no longer observes the regulations, of which the finality was to secure its accomplishment.[30]

Thomas seeks advice from Chrysostom as well as from the other Fathers and doctors on difficult or ambiguous passages such as the injunction not to speak of a miraculous cure, the question whether the centurion (Mt 8:5) presented himself in person to Jesus or did so through the mediation of some priests, that of whether the daughter of Jairus was already dead or whether she was dying when her father addressed himself to Jesus (Mt, 9:18), what is the precise meaning of John's question "Are you the one to come?" (Mt 11:3), and while at the baptism of Jesus John hinted that he knew that Jesus was the Messiah.[31]

23. Ibid., q. 39, a. 5, ad 3.
24. Ibid., q. 43, a. 3.
25. Ibid., q. 46, a. 4.
26. Ibid., q. 47, a. 4, ad 3.
27. *Super evang. Matth.*, chap. 21.
28. *Catena in Matth.*, chap. 2, lesson 2.
29. It is explained in part by his own experience of their powerful community in Antioch. See *Super evang. Matth.*, chap. 1, lesson. 8.
30. *Super Galatas*, chap. 2, lesson 1.
31. *Super evang. Matth.*, chap. 11.

Why did Jesus speak to the crowds in parables (Mt 13:13: "that they see without seeing?") According to Chrysostom it was the malice of the people that prevented them from understanding. Thomas prefers the more theological explanation of Augustine.[32] As for the parable of the fig tree (Mt 24:32) Chrysostom notes that when God wants to explain something he always resorts to a comparison with what happens in nature. When the tares are weeded out, the wheat might be pulled up with them, and so they should be allowed to grow: Chrysostom considers this an order not to kill the heretics and thus avoid even greater evils. Augustine, however, writes that he has learned by experience that by force one succeeds in converting some of them.[33] In the parable of the ten bridesmaids, Jesus means those who keep their vow of celibacy.[34]

After having given the order to execute John the Baptist, King Herod was sad. Chrysostom sees in it the sign of a certain honesty, which one sometimes finds even in bad people, but according to Jerome the evangelist attributes to Herod the feelings which he should have felt as a human being.[35] Peter's suggestion at the transfiguration to make three tents was motivated by his desire to make Jesus stay on that mountain, protected by Moses and Elijah, far from the dangers which threatened him in Judea, but other Fathers see in this suggestion a sign of Peter's devotion. At any rate Peter was mistaken when he thought that Christ could obtain the glory without the cross.[36] When Jesus said that it is easier for a camel to pass through the eye of a needle than for a rich man to enter the kingdom of heaven, Chrysostom suggests that by the camel are meant the heathens, who crumble under the weight of idolatry; the rich signify the Jews, the needle Christ, and the eye of it is the Passion.[37] In the same line of explanation, he says that the vine of which Jesus speaks means justice, which produces the virtues.[38] According to him we can read the sentence "the last will be first" in two ways: there will either be a perfect equality for all or the last will really be the first.[39]

The Sadducees had agreed with the Pharisees to corner Jesus with their question on the resurrection of the dead. In his answer Jesus first

---

32. Ibid., chap. 13, no. 1112.
33. Ibid., chap. 3, no. 1151.
34. Ibid., chap. 25, no. 2012.
35. Ibid., chap. 14, no. 1229.
36. Ibid., chap. 17, no. 1430.
37. Ibid., chap. 19, no. 1602.
38. Ibid., chap. 20, no. 1623.
39. Ibid., no. 1648.

refers to the Bible, and then to reason. This is what we must do when our adversaries raise their questions with malevolence. If, however, a question is asked out of ignorance, we must first give the reasons, then quote the authority.[40]

With regard to the prediction of approaching catastrophes in Matthew 24, Chrysostom thinks that they are those of the time before the destruction of Jerusalem by the Romans. According to him Matthew and Luke wrote their gospels before this destruction, but John after it happened.[41] The words of Jesus "I shall go before you to Galilee" (Mt 26:32) signify the transmigration from this mortal existence to immortal life.[42]

In his exposition of the chapters of the Gospel according to John on the public life of Jesus, Thomas often mentions observations of Chrysostom on details of the text. When in John 5:17 Jesus says "My Father goes on working," he wants to show his conformity with his Father.[43] With regard to John 5:32, "Another witness speaks on my behalf," Chrysostom says that this other is the Baptist. When in John 6:30 the Jews ask: "What work will you do?" Chrysostom considers this a ridiculous question, since Jesus had wrought so many miracles. Augustine, on the other hand, sees a criticism in the sentence, because by his words that he would give nourishment for eternal life Jesus seemed to surpass Moses.[44] Jesus's words "Whoever comes to me, I shall not turn him away" means that Jesus does the will of the Father, who wants that all be saved.[45] "They will all be taught by God" (Jn 6:45). Chrysostom says that here "all" means many. Thomas explains: in so far as it depends on God, all may be instructed, but not in so far as it depends on the people.[46] We can understand the words of Jesus about his flesh being real nourishment: what is real nourishment is the nourishment of the mind, for it is the mind which gives life.[47] When Jesus says that one of his disciples was a demon (v. 70), Chrysostom wonders whether he made a mistake when he selected his disciples, and answers that Judas was chosen on the basis of what he was at that moment. His election did not take away his free will. With regard to John 7:2 ("his brothers said to him: 'why not leave this place and go to

40. Ibid., chap. 22, no. 1791.
41. Ibid., chap. 24, nos. 1914 and 1936.
42. Ibid., chap. 26, no. 2210.
43. *Super evang. Ioan.*, chap. 5, lesson 3.
44. Ibid., chap. 6, lesson 3.
45. Ibid., chap. 6, lesson 4.
46. Ibid., chap. 6, lesson 5.
47. Ibid., chap. 6, lesson 8.

Judea?'"), Thomas first quotes the explanation of Augustine (they tried to become famous), to present next what Chrysostom writes: His brothers had conspired with the Jews.[48] All through this chapter Thomas places besides the comments of Augustine, who gives the spiritual meaning of the texts, the observations of Chrysostom who has an open eye for the concrete situation.

Why did Jesus, who first said that he did not want to go to the feast of the Tabernacles, nevertheless go up to Jerusalem? In order not to show his divinity too much, and so reduce faith in his human nature.[49] The prediction "You will look for me and not find me" (v. 36) has mainly been fulfilled during the siege of Jerusalem. According to Chrysostom, before the resurrection, the Holy Spirit had not yet been given to the apostles with the gifts of prophecy and working miracles, but Thomas puts the remark aside, referring to Luke 11:19 and to Augustine.[50]

In John 8:32, Jesus promises to those who will remain in the truth of his words, that the truth will make them free. Nevertheless the Jews told Jesus that they descended from Abraham and therefore were free. Chrysostom understands this passage in the sense that Moses and the ceremonies of the Old Testament could not really liberate the Jews from sin, an explanation which Thomas does not make his own ("*Chrysostomus hoc aliter introduxit*"):[51] Jesus answers the Jews that they cannot be liberated by the observation of the Law, but only by the Son of God. The Jewish leaders asked Jesus if he was greater than their father Abraham (8:53) Chrysostom comments on this question as follows: In their materialist way of thinking the Jews reason that "Abraham who observed the commandments has died and you say that those who keep your words, will never know the taste of death."[52]

About the cure of the man born blind, Chrysostom writes that Jesus used his spittle, putting it on the eyes of the man, to show that power went out from him. Augustine, however, insists on the mystical meaning of the event: the spittle which comes from the head, signifies the Word who comes from the Father; the mud the Word made flesh.[53] But in chapter ten Chrysostom indicates the mystical meaning of the sheep-

---

48. Ibid., chap. 7, lesson 1.
49. Ibid., chap. 7, lesson 1.
50. Ibid., chap. 7, lesson 5, no. 1093.
51. Ibid., chap. 8, lesson 4, no. 1210.
52. Ibid., chap. 8, lesson 8, no. 1275.
53. Ibid., chap. 9, lesson 1, nos. 1310–11.

fold: the door is Holy Scripture which gives us access to God. Since Jesus calls himself the shepherd, he cannot at the same time be the gate of the sheepfold.

Passing to chapter eleven we notice that Chrysostom, with Origen and Jerome, thinks that Mary of Bethany is not the same person as the prostitute of Luke 7:37, while Augustine and Gregory the Great confirm that the two Marys are the same woman. When in John 11:4 Jesus was informed of the illness of Lazarus, Jesus said that this sickness would not end in death (*ad mortem*). Chrysostom thinks that the sickness must follow its natural course and end in death, and Jesus used it to work the resurrection of Lazarus. Thomas corrects Chrysostom: on the natural level one can say that the illness would pursue its course and that Lazarus would die, but since all things are subject to divine providence, this illness was from the very beginning ordered to the glorification of God.[54]

Jesus says "are there not twelve hours in the day?" Chrysostom explains these words as follows: While initially the leaders of the people wanted to kill Jesus, this may no longer have been their intention later on.[55] About Martha's words "I believe that you are the Christ, the son of God," Chrysostom observes that this woman did not understand the profound words of Jesus, but admitted that he was the Messiah.[56] In front of the tomb of Lazarus, Jesus wept so as to show, Chrysostom says, the truth of his human nature. He told them to take the stone away which closed the opening, so that the bystanders would witness what he was going to do. According to Augustine the removal of the stone signified the removal of the weight of the legal obligations.[57]

Mary of Bethany anointed the feet of Jesus. Chrysostom says that if she would have asked Jesus beforehand, he might have answered that it would be better to give the money to the poor. The high priest and his counsel decided to kill Jesus and also Lazarus. Why not the man born blind, asks Chrysostom. He answers that Lazarus was a highly placed person and the people might have gone to Bethany (to see Lazarus) instead of assisting at the coming festivities in Jerusalem.

"If anyone hears my words and does not keep them faithfully, it is not I who shall condemn him" (Jn 12:47). Chrysostom gives a simple expla-

---

54. Ibid., chap. 11, lesson 1, no. 1478.
55. Ibid., chap. 11, lesson 2.
56. Ibid., chap. 11, lesson 4, no. 1519.
57. Ibid., chap. 11, lesson 6.

nation of these words: then I am not the cause of his condemnation.[58] As to John 13:10, "You too are clean," Chrysostom says that nevertheless the disciples had not yet been freed from original sin. Why did Peter tell John to ask who the traitor was among them instead of doing it himself? Chrysostom gives three reasons: Peter had just been reprimanded; he did not want Jesus to answer openly; he let himself be instructed by John, as the active life is instructed by the contemplative[59] Philip said, "Lord, let us see the Father." According to Chrysostom he thought that he could see God with his bodily eyes. Why does Jesus, in John 14:10, speak first of "the words he said" and then mention his works? Doctrine comes first, works follow.[60] In the sentence "Everything I have learnt from my Father I have made known to you" (15:15), "everything" means all that the disciples could understand.[61] "None of you has asked, 'Where are you going?'" (16:5). Jesus' question is explained by the fact that the apostles, under the impression that their life was going to be threatened (16:2) were thinking about their own future rather than about what would happen to Jesus.[62] About Jesus' words "When that day comes you will not ask me any questions," Augustine says that taken in its literal sense the sentence is not quite true, since after the resurrection the disciples are still questioning Jesus. Thomas prefers the explanation of Chrysostom: "that day" means the time when the Holy Spirit will teach them.[63] Why does Jesus use the past tense in his priestly prayer, "they have accepted that I came from you?" The reason is that the past tense of the verb expresses greater certitude. Moreover in the course of time the faith of the apostles became more perfect.[64] Verses 10 to 12, "All you have is mine," encourage the apostles: Jesus is equal to the Father. "The glory you have given to me" as a man, I have given to them, partly with regard to doctrine, partly as for the power to work miracles, and I shall share even more of it with them.[65]

Why did the armed men sent by the chief priests shrink and fall to the ground when Jesus spoke to them? In order that the faithful could know that Jesus surrendered himself freely and that by this sign the Jews had

---

58. Ibid., chap. 12, lesson 8, no. 1724: "Chrysostomus haec omnia exponit planius."
59. Ibid., chap. 13, lesson 4, no. 1806.
60. Ibid., chap. 14, lessons 2 and 3.
61. Ibid., chap. 15, lesson 3.
62. Ibid., chap. 16, lesson 2.
63. Ibid., chap. 16, lesson 6.
64. Ibid., chap. 17, lesson 2.
65. Ibid., chap. 17, lesson 5.

an opportunity to convert themselves.⁶⁶ According to Chrysostom, Peter, the fervent disciple, had to such a point been affected by his negation of Jesus (18:25) that he no longer seemed interested in what happened to his master. But Thomas notes that this explanation does not hold up (*stare non potest*) since in that case the second and third denials would have been pronounced during the absence of Christ.⁶⁷

About John 18:31 Chrysostom writes that the Jews did not have the right to execute someone for crimes committed against the republic. Chrysostom understands the words "My kingdom is not of this world" as meaning "my power."⁶⁸ Chrysostom thinks that Adam died on Calvary.⁶⁹ The evangelist gives a very precise description of the burial of Jesus in order to exclude false rumors spread by the Jews that the body of Jesus had been secretly taken away. Just so, the cloth that had been over his head would not have been there if the body had been taken away.⁷⁰ About the women who went to the grave, Chrysostom writes that if it is true that sadness and pain make us avoid the places where we have been together with a deceased friend, one can nevertheless go there to find some solace.⁷¹ Regarding the appearance of Jesus on the shore of Lake Tiberias, Chrysostom says that this episode shows the difference between Peter and John: Peter is more fervent, but John has a greater understanding.⁷²

Theological Questions

In *In I Sent.* a text of Chrysostom explains why, when thinking about the essence of God, we use different concepts: each of the different choirs of angels praises a different perfection of God.⁷³ To indicate the relation between the Father and the Son, Chrysostom uses the term "cause," where he should have said "principle."⁷⁴ In *In IV Sent.*, distinction 49, question 2, article 1, Chrysostom wonders how a creature can see one who is uncre-

---

66. Ibid., chap. 18, lesson 1.
67. Ibid., chap. 18, lesson 4, no. 2325.
68. Ibid., chap. 18, lesson 6.
69. Ibid., chap. 19, lesson 3, no. 2416.
70. Ibid., chap. 20, lesson 1.
71. Ibid., chap. 20, lesson 2.
72. Ibid., chap. 21, lesson 2.
73. *In I Sent.*, d. 2, q. 1, a. 3.
74. *In I Sent.*, d. 29, q. 1, a. 1, ad 2. Cf. *In II Sent.*, d. 13, q. 1, a. 5: *causa* when speaking of God: "Hic communiter et improprie Chrysostomus loquitur." Cf. *In III Sent.*, d. 11, q. 1, a. 1, arg 5: "Filius habet causam sui esse."

ated. Thomas comments that he is speaking here of the full vision of God which is out of reach for every created intellect. The question if one can see God in this life is mentioned by Thomas in his *Commentary on Isaiah*, chapter 6, lesson 1.

Chrysostom raises two questions concerning the prologue of the Gospel of John: Why does the evangelist begin by mentioning the Son, without speaking of the Father? The answer: all knew the Father because of the Old Testament. In the second place we are brought to the knowledge of the Father through the Son. Why does he speak of the Word instead of saying the Son? John wanted to avoid that some readers might think of a biological generation. He writes: "In the beginning was the Word" to bring out at the very beginning of his gospel the divine nature of the Son of God. The words "and the Word was with God" express that the Son is subsistent in the divine nature.[75] Contrary to what Arius says, the Son is co-eternal with the Father. In this connection Thomas quotes Chrysostom to inform his readers about the Platonist doctrine of the three hypostases.[76] For Chrysostom the words "Through him all things came to being" show the equality of the Son to the Father, while for Hilary they are a confirmation of the eternity of the Son, and for Augustine, of his consubstantiality with the Father. In the story of the creation, Moses lists successively all that God created, but John writes only that all things have been made by him in order to lead us directly to the knowledge of God himself. The evangelist adds the words "not a thing had its being but through him" and connects "all that came to be" with the preceding sentence. "All that came to be had life in him" indicates not only creation though the Word, but also the inextinguishable flux of divine causality to creatures as well as his government of the world. These words also indicate that the Divine Word does not make things by natural necessity, but by intellect and will.[77]

Like Basil and Ambrose, Chrysostom thinks that at the moment of the creation of the world, unformed matter (*informitas materiae*) preceded in time the formation of things.[78] Moses did not mention the creation of the angels because of a lack of understanding of the people in his day.[79] To be deprived of the vision of God is a greater punishment for the damned than to suffer from the flames of hell.[80] According to Chrysostom the cre-

75. *Super evang. Ioan.*, prologue.
76. The text says: "et alii etiam platonici," a reference to Middle and Neoplatonism.
77. *Super evang. Ioan.*, chap. 1, lesson 2.
78. *ST* I, q. 66, a. 1.
79. *ST* I, q. 67, a. 4.
80. *In II Sent.*, d. 33, q. 2, a. 2, arg. 1.

ation of the celestial bodies is said to have taken place of the fourth day—a certain reduction of their value—to remove Israel from the danger of idolatry. The fact that the Son of Man has the power to forgive sins shows that in Christ God's power is indissolubly united to human nature.[81]

The souls of sinners are not transformed into demons, but can suffer the punishments set aside for the evil spirits.[82] According to Chrysostom judiciary power does not belong to Christ in so far as he is a man, but in so far as he is God. Thomas corrects these words: Christ has this power in so far as he is the head of redeemed humanity.[83] The words "that they may be one in us, as you are in me and I am in you" (Jn 17:21) signify the distinction between the Divine Persons (against Sabellius) and at the same time their unity (against Arius).[84]

Thomas mentions some texts of Chrysostom about demons and the belief of some people that the souls of the dead become demons.[85] He also mentions the common conviction of the faithful that there are good and evil spirits.[86] On several occasions Thomas quotes Chrysostom's view on the diffusion of the gospel message at the end of the apostolic era (Mt 24:34): "Before this generation has passed away...." The meaning is the diffusion of certain knowledge about Christ, but not of the foundation of Christian communities in all the countries of the world. Thomas prefers this explanation to that of Augustine who writes that there are peoples who have never heard of Christ.[87]

Chrysostom also speaks of Peter's authority with regard to the question of who is the greatest in the kingdom. The disciples could not bear that Peter had been preferred to them. The Son had given the power of the Father and of himself over all there is in heaven and on earth to a mortal man. Peter is called the master and doctor of the universe.[88] Indeed Thomas presents Chrysostom as a vigorous defender of the primacy of Peter. In his *Homilies on the Acts of the Apostles* he says that Peter is the summit of the very holy choir of the apostles.[89] In his *Super evang.*

---

81. *ST* III, q. 16, a. 11, ad 2.
82. *ST* I, q. 108, a. 8, ad 3.
83. *ST* III, q. 59, a. 2.
84. *Super evang. Ioan.*, chap. 17, lesson 5.
85. *QD de malo*, q. 16, a. 1.
86. *De substantiis separatis*, chap. 20.
87. *ST* I-II, q. 106, a. 4, ad 4; *Super Romanos*, chap. 10, lesson 3; *Super evang. Matth.*, chap. 24, no. 1921.
88. *Contra errores Graecorum*, 2, 32 and 33.
89. Ibid., 2, 37.

Ioan., chapter 21, lesson 2, Thomas quotes Chrysostom: Peter is the most excellent of the apostles, the spokesman and chief of their group. John recounts the episode of the special vocation of Peter in order to emphasize that Peter was fully reinstated in his former position. Peter, for his part, rather wanted to know which position was going to be assigned to John, whom he liked very much.

The Holy Virgin as Chrysostom Sees Her

When Mary was engaged to Joseph she already lived in his house.[90] Chrysostom expressed some reservations as to the virtues of Mary, whereas he clearly stated her virginity. With regard to the phrase "The mother and the brothers of Jesus were looking for him" (Mt 12:48), he writes that his mother wanted to become more famous and was showing a certain ambition, something which seems to indicate that she had not been preserved from all sins. Thomas comments that "*in verbis illis Chrysostomus excessit,*" but smooths over the expression,[91] an attempt in which he did not much believe himself.[92]

With regard to Jesus' words in Matthew 12:48 ("who is my mother; who are my brothers?") Chrysostom says two things: one is right, the other not, Thomas says. Jesus' mother and his brothers felt a human emotion when they heard Jesus preach and saw the crowds following him wild with enthusiasm, and wanted also to become famous themselves. This interpretation is partly correct in respect of the brothers. See John 7:5: "Not even his brothers in fact had faith in him," but it is wrong regarding the mother of the Lord, because according to the Catholic faith she has never sinned, neither serious sins, nor venial sins.[93]

In Matthew 23:35, Jesus speaks of a certain Zechariah who was killed between the sanctuary and the altar. Chrysostom thinks that he was the father of John the Baptist who would have defended the Virgin Mary when the Jews wanted to chase her from the room (in the temple) where virgins could take their place. But Thomas quotes the more likely explanation of Jerome.[94]

---

90. *ST* III, q. 29, a. 2, ad 3.
91. "Possunt tamen exponi."
92. *ST* III, q. 27, a. 4, ad 3.
93. *Super evang. Matth.*, chap. 12, no. 1073.
94. Ibid., chap. 23, no. 1894.

The Sacraments

The blood which flowed from the side of Jesus is the beginning of the sacraments.[95] Baptism is performed by immersion to show that the power of the Father, the Son, and the Holy Spirit fills the person who receives baptism.[96] The immersion is like a burial.[97] It is not just the water alone which purifies us, but also the grace of the Holy Spirit.[98] During his public life Jesus himself did not baptize, contrary to what his disciples did. Moreover, before the passion of Jesus, these baptisms did not give the Holy Spirit.[99] Thomas introduced a correction: the Holy Spirit was not given visibly, but in the innermost being of those who believed in Jesus.

With regard to access to the sacraments, one must have the right age, and the required qualities and sex, but access to Christ is free for all.[100] Chrysostom mentions that according to certain authors Christ would not have given the Holy Spirit (Jn 20:22), but he himself is convinced that Jesus gave the Holy Spirit in view of forgiving sins.[101]

In his treatise on the Eucharist, Thomas quotes the following beautiful text of Chrysostom: Christ gives himself to us, to touch him, to eat him, to embrace him. When we come back from the holy table we are like lions exhaling fire and have become terrifying for the devil.[102] Chrysostom does not go into speculative questions, as we see in his commentary on the text of the institution of the Eucharist in Matthew 26:26–29. Thomas does not quote him here.

"Every saint is a priest" is a formula which Thomas corrects.[103] Thomas also rectifies the expression that it is better to function well as a priest, than as a monk: he says that Chrysostom speaks here of bishops.[104]

"Moses allowed the *libellum* of repudiation in order to avoid a greater evil. He takes away the fault, but the moral disorder remains."[105] Those

---

95. *ST* III, q. 79, a. 1.
96. *In IV Sent.*, d. 3, q. 1, a. 4, qc. 2, s.c. 2.
97. *ST* III, q. 66, a. 7.
98. *ST* III, q. 73, a. 1, ad 2.
99. *Super evang. Ioan.*, chap. 4, lesson 1.
100. *ST* III, q. 72, a. 8, ad 3.
101. *Super evang. Ioan.*, chap. 20, lesson 4.
102. *ST* III, q. 79, aa. 1 and 6.
103. *In IV Sent.*, d. 13, q. 1, a. 1, qc. 2, ad 5.
104. *Quodl.* III, q. 6, a. 3.
105. *In IV Sent.*, d. 33, q. 2, a. 2, qc. 2, ad 5: "A peccato abstulit peccati culpam." Cf. *Super evang. Matth.*, chap. 19, no. 1557.

who speak with pleasure about (their) divorce are immoral.[106] Why does God not let males and females be born together, if they are destined to form one flesh? If he had done that, marriage would be necessary. At present everyone is free and can also not marry.[107] When Chrysostom writes that contracting a second marriage after the death of a spouse is fornication, Thomas says that he is speaking of what sometimes incites people to marry again,[108] for elsewhere he considers such a second wedding legitimate.[109]

The Moral Life

"Sin only exists in the act of the will."[110] Penance makes us bear everything, Chrysostom says; and one should not say that a poor fellow who complains and sighs is being deceptive.[111] Thomas comments that in a spirit of penance, one bears what one has chosen freely, but that the virtue of patience lets us tolerate what comes from the outside.[112] The devil cannot tempt us as much as he would like to do, but only so much as God allows him.[113] In respect of our contacts with non-Christians, Chrysostom writes that one can accept an invitation from them to dinner.[114]

In several of his works Thomas mentions the opinion of Athanasius, Hilary, Ambrose, and Chrysostom on the meaning of the expression "sins against the Holy Spirit," namely to blaspheme God. But Thomas himself prefers the solution Augustine gives of this difficult text: the sin against the Holy Spirit is to persevere obstinately in one's sin.[115]

Chrysostom seems to hold that the exterior act adds nothing to the goodness or badness of the inner act.[116] The different beatitudes proclaimed by Jesus in the Evangelical Discourse would come down to the same thing.[117] For the Jews death was the absolute evil, because they con-

---

106. Ibid., no. 1547.
107. Ibid., chap. 19, no. 1550.
108. *In IV Sent.*, d. 42, q. 3, a. 1, arg. 1.
109. *Super Romanos*, chap. 7, lesson 1.
110. *QD de malo*, q. 2, a. 2, arg. 4.
111. *In IV Sent.*, d. 15, q. 2, a. 1, qc. 4, ad 4.
112. *In IV Sent.*, d. 14, q. 1, a. 1, qc. 5.
113. *ST* I, q. 14, a. 5.
114. *ST* II-II, q. 10, a. 9, arg. 1.
115. *ST*. II-II, q. 14, a. 1; *QD de malo*, q. 3, a. 15, ad 1; *Super Romanos*, chap. 2, lesson 1.
116. *ST* I-II, q. 20, a. 4, arg. 1.
117. *ST* I-II, q. 69, a. 4, ad 1.

centrated themselves entirely on the present life.[118] Do not judge, Jesus tells us. This does not forbid us to criticize others with benevolence, but when we are proud of our own justice we cannot condemn others because of some suspicion.[119] To curse someone comes close to homicide.[120]

We should learn to bear insults magnanimously, but we must not tolerate that God be insulted.[121] Is it allowed to wear a necklace made of biblical texts? Chrysostom insists on the fact that one should not indulge in superstitious customs. It is better to keep those texts in our heart.[122] When he writes that nothing is a better friend of the devil than drunkenness, Thomas observes that this is not the greatest of sins, although it is more natural to us because of concupiscence.[123] As for the commandment of love Chrysostom writes that there are two things in love: one is its principle, the second its effect. Now its principle is double: either passion or a decision of our reason. To love with all one's heart refers to one's feelings, with all one's soul and mind to reason.

When dealing with the capital sins in the *Quaestiones disputatae De malo*, Thomas quotes some texts of Chrysostom which illustrate the most frequent faults such as vanity, which sneaks in secretly and corrupts everything inside ourselves. One even finds it in the disciples of Jesus.[124] Getting angry without reason is also a fault, but never to become angry is not good either. This can promote vices in others, or bring them to become negligent and to do what is wrong.[125] About anger Chrysostom says that nothing promotes a sinful state so much as anger. It takes root in us, destroys love, and leads to error.[126]

According to Matthew 26:8 ("Why this waste?") the disciples criticize the anointing of Jesus' head, while Jesus himself defends what the woman did. Chrysostom suggests that if this woman had talked with Jesus before carrying out her plan, Jesus might have told her to give the money to the poor. It happens, he says, that when we later reflect on something we did that was good, we tell ourselves that it would have been better, not to do it.[127]

---

118. *ST* I-II, q. 105, a. 4, ad 7.
119. *ST* II-II, q. 60, a. 3.
120. *ST* II-II, q. 76, a. 4.
121. *Quodl.* V, q. 13, a. 1.
122. *ST* II-II, q. 96, a. 4.
123. *ST* II-II, q. 150, a. 3.
124. *ST* II-II, q. 9, a. 2.
125. *ST* II-II, q. 9, a. 2.
126. *Super evang. Matth.*, chap. 5, no. 483.
127. Ibid., chap. 26, no. 2136.

The Spiritual Life

In a beautiful text Chrysostom tells us: "Consider the pleasure that came to you and how great is the privilege you received of being able to converse with God in your prayers, to have a conversation with Christ and to ask him all you want and desire."[128]

"To pray for oneself is necessary but fraternal charity encourages us to pray also for others. In God's eyes it is not the prayer that we address to God in need which is most pleasing, but the prayer to which fraternal love induces us."[129] "God never refuses his gifts to him who prays, since in his goodness he moves him not to stop praying."[130]

Jesus fasted to show us what a great good fasting is as a means against the devil.[131] Fasting is sad for naïve persons but a joy for those who seek wisdom.[132] Jesus was led by the Spirit out into the desert. Chrysostom observes that all the children of God are also led there. They are not satisfied to remain behind doing nothing, but the Spirit moves them to do something important, to be in the desert, a place where the devil is absent, because there is none of the injustice there in which the devil finds its delight. Every good work we do is like the desert with respect to the flesh and the world.[133]

If you do not allow children to come close to God, who would be worthy?[134] Christ leaves us free to follow him, he does not impose this choice.[135] A monk does not have as much value as one who occupies himself with other people.[136] We must praise the apostles Peter and Andrew for having given up their business and followed Christ. Nothing is so important as to occupy oneself with celestial things and to answer without hesitation to the voice of Christ.[137] The disciples of Christ must entrust themselves to divine providence without being worried about the next day.[138]

When we pray "Our Father, who art in heaven" we do not enclose

---

128. *ST* II-II, q. 83, a. 2, ad 3.
129. *ST* II-II, q. 83, a. 7.
130. *ST* II-II, q. 83, a. 15.
131. *ST* III, q. 40, a. 2, ad 3.
132. *De perfectione vitae spiritualis*, chap. 9.
133. In *ST* III, q. 41, a, 2, ad 2 Thomas writes that by "going to the desert" Chrysostom means that one leaves behind those things which may lead into temptation.
134. *Quodl.*, IV, q. 12, a. 1.
135. *De perfectione vitae spiritualis*, chap. 10.
136. Ibid., chap. 20.
137. *Contra doctrinam retrahentium*, chap. 9.
138. Ibid., chap. 15.

God in heaven, but we lift up our mind above this earth. "Hallowed be thy name" is a petition placed at the beginning of our prayer, since it is becoming that before everything else we seek the glory of God.[139] In his lessons on chapter 6 of the Gospel according to Matthew, Thomas quotes several remarks of Chrysostom: when praying one must not wish to be seen nor speak to God in a loud voice, but recollect oneself in the evening after the many distractions of the day. By saying "Our Father" we express in only one word the pardon of our sins, the annulment of punishment, justification, sanctification, and liberation, adoption as God's children, having God himself as our heritage, and the gifts of the Holy Spirit.[140] By the words "Hallowed be Thy name," we ask that God may help us to accomplish such works that he is glorified.

Chrysostom seems to consider the active life of a priest as superior to that of a monk. Thomas suggests that in this case he is speaking of the office of a bishop.[141] With regard to Matthew 5:42 "From one who wants to borrow, do not turn away," Chrysostom writes that to lend at exorbitant rates is like the bite of a serpent. At first it may seem handy, but later on this poison spreads through everything one does.[142] In the words "For to everyone who has will be given more" (Mt. 25:29), Jesus is speaking of doctrine, Chrysostom says: whoever is capable of teaching, but does not teach, loses this faculty. Another who is less talented, but who practices, acquires it and can become a master.[143]

Striking Sentences

Chrysostom uses several touching formulae, which are quoted by Thomas. Some examples:

- "Nothing can resist the ardor of a great love."[144]
- "Small differences in the accounts of witnesses make them more truthful."[145]

---

139. *Compendium theologiae*, 2, chap. 8.
140. Ibid., chap. 6, 581.
141. *ST* II-II, q. 184, a. 8, ad 1.
142. *Super evang. Matth.*, chap. 5, no. 550.
143. Ibid., chap. 25, no. 2074.
144. *In III Sent.*, d. 27, q. 1, a. 3, s.c. 4.
145. *ST* II-II, q. 70, a. 2, ad 2.

- "Those who watch lascivious or cruel spectacles are people without shame or decency."[146]
- "What is bad is not that one is poor, but the fact that one does not want to be poor."[147]
- "The wealthy must creep before princes in order to keep their wealth."[148]
- "The more possessions one has, the more one seeks to increase them."[149]
- "Attempting to do a good job is excellent, but seeking honors is vanity."[150]
- "We pray for ourselves because it is necessary, we pray for others out of charity."[151]
- "A woman has spoken only once and subverted the whole world."[152]
- "It is admirable that a poor person like Paul orders a rich man to receive a servant kindly."[153]
- "Who can compete with the Good News? God on earth, man in heaven, the friendship of God with our nature, the struggle finished with the aggressive enemy, the devil confused, death overcome, paradise opened."[154]
- "For a person of corrupt morals, a famous pedigree is of no use."[155]
- "Both good people and bad have possessions. To the bad they are detrimental, to the good they are useful."[156]
- "I do not want to hear you talk about great undertakings, if you accomplish very little of what you say."[157]

---

146. *ST* II-II, q. 167, a. 2, ad 2.
147. *Contra impugnantes*, 2, chap. 5, ad 1.
148. Ibid., 2, chap. 6, ad 6.
149. *De perfectione vitae spiritualis*, chap. 7.
150. Ibid., chap. 19.
151. *Compendium theologiae*, 2, chap. 5.
152. *Super 1 Cor.*, chap. 14, lesson 7.
153. *Super Philemon*.
154. *Catena in Matth.*, praefatio, 2.
155. *Super evang. Matth.*, chap. 3, no. 268. This was an answer to the Hebrews who boasted of having Abraham as their Father.
156. Ibid., chap. 6, no. 595.
157. Ibid., chap. 23, no. 1840.

9   THE COMMENTARIES ON TWO TREATISES OF BOETHIUS

An examination of Thomas's relation to Boethius is called for not only because of the fact that Thomas commented on two treatises of Boethius, but also because of the latter's influence on the study of the liberal arts in the Latin West. Born about 480 Boethius became consul at Rome in 510, at that time a mainly honorary function. Apparently the emperor Theodoric wanted to gain the support of the group of senators of which Boethius was the leader, in order to promote a greater cultural union between Rome, the Germanic regions, and Byzantium. Gifted with an enormous capacity for work, Boethius dedicated himself to the task of rendering the wisdom and science of Plato and Aristotle accessible to students in the Latin part of the empire and so to save the spiritual heritage of Greece, threatened with disappearance in his age when the Romans no longer read Greek. But he could finish only a small part of this enormous undertaking of translating the works of Plato and Aristotle. The emperor, who suspected Boethius of organizing a conspiracy, had him arrested and imprisoned at Ravenna, where Boethius wrote his famous *De consolatione philosophiae*. He was executed at Pavia in 525. Boethius also did not carry out his project to write a study on the harmony between the thought of Plato and that of Aristotle.[1] His translations and commentaries on the *Categories*, the *De interpretatione*, and the *Analytics* of Aristotle, and the *Isagoge* of Porphyre, as well as his treatises on music, astronomy, arithmetic, and geometry, determined the program of studies in the schools and faculties of the liberal arts in the West until the enormous stream of

---

1. See *De Interpretatione*, PL 64: 433CD. This project tells us about the thought of Boethius. He follows Aristotle in questions about logic, but turns to Plato and Neoplatonism in metaphysics and theology. Among the Greek commentators of Aristotle, Porphyry has exercised a profound influence on him. He also used certain ideas of Themistius and Ammonius. Cf. Pierre Courcelle, *Les lettres grecques en occident de Macrobe à Cassiodore* (Paris: E. de Boccard, 1948), 265.

translations from the Greeks and Arabs reached the West in the twelfth century and the *logica nova* entered the scene.

With regard to the study of the arts and philosophy prior to the thirteenth century, historians speak of the *Aetas Boetiana*, because his translations, commentaries, and treatises provided a mass of notions and doctrines to the dialecticians, philosophers, and theologians. They were like the framework in which the intellectuals moved. The language of Boethius is that of an intermediary stage between Cicero and the Latin of the medieval schools. He formulated definitions, proposed a method in scientific studies, and set an example of the art of writing commentaries. He also developed the theory of abstraction, and some of his definitions became widely used, such as that of man's free choice: *liberum de voluntate iudicium*; of the concept of eternity: *interminabilis vitae tota simul et perfecta possessio*; and of beatitude: *beatitudo est status omnium bonorum congregatione perfectus*. We find traces of them in the works of Aquinas.

In addition to this general presence of the works of Boethius in the writings of Thomas, the latter has written commentaries on two of the five theological treatises of Boethius, namely, the *De Trinitate* and the *De Hebdomadibus*. The *De Trinitate* is the first of these five treatises and is addressed to his father-in-law Symmachus. Remarkable in the *De Trinitate* is that, contrary to what Augustine and Hilary did, Boethius does not refer to Holy Scripture, because, as he writes at the end of this work, he wanted to present some arguments in favor of a doctrine which itself is firmly established on the solid foundation of the faith. It is possible that the discussion which arose in 519 concerning the formula *unus ex Trinitate carne passus* led him to write this work.[2]

During the twelfth century at least some twenty commentaries were written on the *De Trinitate*, in particular by masters of the school of Chartres, as, for example, Gilbert de la Porrée. At that time schools had become better organized and the rational style of the text appealed to the masters, but during the thirteenth century Thomas seems to have been the only one to comment on it. In his commentary, however, there are no traces of the works of his predecessors.[3]

This makes one wonder why Thomas undertook to comment on this treatise, alone among the masters of the thirteenth century. When we

2. Cf. Viktor Schurr, *Die Trinitäts Lehre des Boethius im Lichte der skytischen Kontroversen* (Paderborn, Germany: F. Schöningh, 1935), 96.

3. Cf. Leo Elders, *Faith and Science: An Introduction to St. Thomas'* Expositio in Boethii De Trinitate (Rome: Herder, 1974), 12–15.

consider the beautifully elaborated doctrine of the sciences and theology which Thomas sets forth in his exposition, some historians have placed its redaction in a later period of his life. Nowadays a date before 1260 is considered most likely.[4] S. Neumann draws attention to the fact that Thomas, having obtained the position of master in sacred theology at Paris, could not take up teaching right away because of the opposition of some professors. For this reason Thomas may have taught some months in the *studium* of the Dominicans at Paris and chosen the treatise *De Trinitate* as the subject of his classes. This allowed him to examine the status of theology as a science, as well as that of the philosophical sciences and to consider the methods to be used in their study. When toward the end of 1256 Thomas could finally start teaching as a *magister in sacra pagina*, he chose a book of Holy Scripture for his classes and directed the disputed questions on the *De veritate*.[5] But he did not continue the work at the *De Trinitate* of Boethius, perhaps thinking that he had accomplished the most important part of the task, that is, the clarification of the scientific status of theology and of the speculative sciences and exposed the different methods to be used. Moreover the theological contents of Boethius's treatise may not have seemed very important in the thirteenth century.

The Commentary of Thomas

Thomas proceeds as follows in his exposition: he chooses a short section of the text and formulates two problems related to what Boethius says in the passage. Thomas studies these problems, formulating two questions; the subject of each is subdivided, analyzed, and discussed in four articles. The method to study a problem by means of a question and by presenting contrary arguments and replies to them had been developed by Peter of Poitiers.[6] It began to be widely used in academic teaching and is prominent in the *Expositio in Boetii de Trinitate*, but Thomas uses also the *expositio*. The choice of two methods, in particular that of the second, allowed Thomas to leave the text of Boethius's treatise entire, rendering pos-

---

4. Martin Grabmann, *Die Werke des hl. Thomas von Aquin*, 3rd ed. (Münster: Aschendorff, 1949), 312. Hannibaldus de Hannibaldis quotes the text in his commentary on the *Sententiae*, 1261–62.

5. Siegfried Neumann, *Gegenstand und Methode der theoretischen Wissenschaften nach Thomas von Aquin, auf Grund der Expositio super librum Boethii De Trinitate* (Münster: Aschendorff, 1965), 7 ff.

6. Martin Grabmann, *Die Geschichte der scholastischen methode* (Graz: Akademische Druck und Verlagsanstalt, 1957), 2: 523–24.

sible at the same time an independent discussion of important themes. Considering the regularity of the construction of Thomas's treatise it is tempting to conclude that it is not a reproduction of academic disputes. The choice of the themes of the four articles which deal with the contents of each question is inspired by texts of Boethius. To give an example, the third question has as its subject faith. One would expect a discussion of the growth of faith, a theme treated by Hugh of St. Victor and by Thomas himself in *Summa theologiae* II-II, question 1, article 7, but it is not touched because Boethius himself remains silent on it.

The prologue to the treatise and the *expositiones* are very well written. Thomas uses a Latin of classical beauty, and the sentences are bathed in the light of Scripture. The short commentaries of the text of Boethius, from four to six pages, are so well constructed that they incorporate the words of Boethius himself in a very clear commentary. But the style is more abrupt in the following questions. Often a phrase of Boethius provides the point of departure for a question, as for instance in the first question, the words *lux divina dignata est* with regard to the possibility of the knowledge of God. In this question Thomas examines to what extent God helps us to come to know him.

In his treaty, as reported in question one, Boethius writes that the Holy Trinity is the object of the faith, but he adds that man can nevertheless investigate this mystery. William of Saint-Thierry and Saint Bernard criticized Abelard for his attempts to explain—let us say reduce—this mystery to the level of natural things. Thomas observes that except if there is a divine revelation, man only knows God on the basis of his effects, which proceed from God's operation common to the three Persons and, therefore, do not lead to the knowledge of the Trinity.

In the text of Boethius we read the words which provided Thomas with the themes of the different questions and articles. To give an example, the subjects of the four articles of the second question have as their point of departure some short sentences of the proem of Boethius: "... *investigatam diutissime quaestionem* ... ; *formatam rationibus ex intimis sumpta philosophiae disciplinis, ... novorum verborum significationibus velo.*" During the lifetime of Thomas the nature and the status of theology was a very lively discussed theme. The doctrinal development given by Thomas goes way beyond the few vague suggestions one finds in the text of Boethius. In a masterly way Thomas explains the different aspects of the question.

In his prologue Boethius says that he does not want what he writes to be misunderstood or scorned by some readers who have difficulty understanding or have malicious intentions, and that for this reason he presents a very concise text. These lines provided Thomas with the opportunity of treating the theme of the literary expression of the science of theology. Scientific theology as it was developed in the thirteenth century differed indeed in form from monastic theology.[7]

How to Explain the Plurality of Beings

The themes discussed in the four articles of the third question have their point of departure in the first lines of the first chapter of the text. The last of these four articles intends to give a very precise formulation of faith in Holy Trinity and lays the foundation for the commentary on the following chapters of the *Expositio super librum Boethii De trinitate* which, however, Thomas never wrote.

In the fourth question Thomas examines a theme of central importance for the study of the Holy Trinity, and which is also fundamental in Platonism and regards the second principle introduced by Plotinus, otherness (*alteritas*). This *alteritas* is described as movement. Thomas takes as his point of departure the following proposition: "*Principium enim pluralitatis alteritas est; praeter alteritatem enim nec pluralitas quid sit intelligi potest*," a phrase which we find at the beginning of the first chapter of Boethius. Ever since Parmenides had proposed his theory of the total unity of being, the problem of the origin of the difference between things had been discussed continually by the Greek philosophers. In order to explain the differences between the Ideas, Plato introduced the form of otherness,[8] which passes through all the Ideas. In his school the second principle was called the indeterminate dyad, or the other, as Aristotle writes in *Metaphysics*, 1087b26: "Others oppose the different and the other to the One and others oppose plurality to the One. But if, as they claim, things consist of contraries, and to the One either there is nothing contrary, or if there is to be anything, it is plurality..."[9] Plotinus introduced alternateness as the factor that distinguishes the νοῦς from the

---

7. For further details see Elders, *Faith and Science*, 50.
8. Plato, *Sophistes*, 255 C.
9. Aristotle, *Metaphysics*, trans. W. D. Ross (Oxford: Oxford University Press, 1924).

One. And this alternateness is described in terms of motion. By its nature it is the primordial movement and the source of all motions. Through the translation of Plato's *Timaeus* by Chalcidius as well as through Augustine, Dionysius the Areopagite, and the works of Proclus and Avicenna, this traditional doctrine of Plato spread in the Latin West.

In his answer to the question of the cause of plurality, Thomas stresses that we must first make a distinction between simple things and composite beings. He discusses the cause of the difference between the first: these things simply differ from each other by what they are, that is to say, in a being is included that it is not another one. Thomas then examines the question of the difference between God and his creatures. While he rejects the Neoplatonic doctrine of a serial emanation from a supreme principle, he shows that creatures do not differ from God or from each other by an intermediate factor, which would be derived from the first principle: all created beings have an immediate relation with God. To be different signifies that each thing has its own being which differs from that of other things.

In the second article Thomas explains the principle of individuation. On this point Boethius is ambiguous, since he hesitates between the conception of Aristotle and a different position which considers individuation as dependent from the accidents of things. Thomas interprets Boethius as if he had said that quantity is an instrumental cause of the individuality of material things,[10] a thesis which is Thomas's own position: because of its divisibility and owing to its potential dimensions, quantity functions as a demand, to which the substantial form answers by constituting the individual thing.

In the next article of this fourth question, a text of Boethius serves as the point of departure: "*Tamen locus cunctis diversus est, quam unum fingere nullo modo possumus,*" a sentence which one finds at the end of the first chapter of the treatise of Boethius. It provided Thomas with the opportunity to examine if two bodies can simultaneously be in the same place. Thomas gives his solution: each body by the very fact of having extension, is measured by place, since "place is the relation of distance or proximity of a body with what is surrounding it." This means that two bodies cannot be in the same place, but in his answer to the first objection Thomas adds that this is not a metaphysical impossibility.

---

10. Boethius may perhaps have come closer to this solution in certain of his comments in certain texts of his commentary on the *Categoriae*.

The Theory of the Theoretical Sciences

A short phrase of Boethius at the beginning of the second chapter of his treatise becomes for Thomas the starting point of the fifth question, which is devoted to the theoretical sciences: *"nam cum tres sint speculativae partes."* It is followed by a short description of physics, mathematics, and theology.[11] This tripartition of the sciences by Aristotle in *Metaphysics* E, as explained by Boethius and Cassiodorus,[12] imposed itself, although certain authors upheld the Stoic division of the sciences and the arts in physics, ethics, and logic. In his commentary on the *De Trinitate* of Boethius, question 5, article 1, Thomas writes that the division in the seven liberal arts is inadequate, as a division of theoretical philosophy, of which he vindicates the independence. With regard to the distinction between the theoretical sciences, he writes, contrary to a widespread opinion, that it is not necessarily consecutive in the different degrees of ontological perfection: the science which studies plants is of the same nature as that which studies animal life, although animals are more perfect. According to Thomas, the subject of a science as such is constituted by the intellectual activity of man. The subject is not the thing as such, but the thing in so far as it is seized in the act of the intellect. The conclusion is that theoretical philosophy is divided into three sciences, namely, physics which studies material things in the universal, mathematics which abstracts quantity with its relation to substances from the concrete extended bodies, and first philosophy which examines being as such.

The second article deals with a difficult question: how can one have a scientific and necessary knowledge of things which are subject to incessant changes? Porphyry hesitates; and Boethius, in his first commentary on the *Isagoge*, 19 C, prefers the solution of Plato, while in his second commentary he seems inclined to accept the solution of Aristotle. This led Godfrey of St. Victor to express this hesitation in verse form:

> Assidet Boethius stupens de hac lite
> audiens quid hic et hic asserit perite
> et quid cui faveat non discernit rite
> non praesumit solvere litem definite.[13]

---

11. Boethius takes up the division which Aristotle had given in *Metaphysics* E, chap. 1.
12. *De artibus ac disciplinis liberalium literarum*, PL 70: 1167.
13. Quoted in Hugh Fraser Stewart, *Boethius: An Essay* (London: W. Blackwood and Sons, 1891), 254.

> Boethius sits there amazed by this quarrel,
> listens to what both competently affirm
> and does not well discern which side to prefer.
> He does not arrogate to give a definite solution.

The medieval commentaries on the *De Trinitate* witness to this incertitude. The solution of Thomas is to make a distinction between the form of a thing and the concrete whole (*totum integrum*). The form is not a reality distinct from the whole, but on the other hand it is not totally identical with it. The form is as the more profound reality, which remains connected with a transcendental source. The process of becoming always concerns the concrete whole.[14]

In the third article of the question, Thomas examines how the different operations of the intellect constitute the intelligibility characteristic of the subjects of the theoretical sciences. The subject of the mathematical sciences provides the model. This subject is constituted by an abstraction, Aristotle says.[15] Thomas makes the theory of Aristotle his own: the mathematical sciences study quantity, the sensible qualities of which have been left out. What is new in Thomas's exposition, is that he indicates the conditions that we must observe in order that no error creeps into this process of abstraction: 1) what is abstracted must not depend for its intelligibility on other elements, from which it is separated by the intellect; 2) the aspect which is considered separately does not exist outside the thing and its other properties with which it is united. Thomas adds that among the accidents quantity occupies the first place but does not contain in itself the other sensible accidents such as qualities.[16]

In this third article Thomas formulates the theory of the *separatio*, namely, the fact that not every being is necessarily material. By this negative judgment which is based on the immateriality of our thought, we free being from a necessary connection with material things. In this way the speculation of being qua being lies open before us, and we enter into metaphysics. This is the first time a philosopher made clear the nature of metaphysics.

In the last article of this question, Thomas examines the nature of

---

14. Cf. Thomas, *In VII Metaph.*, lesson 15: "Generatur domus particularis, non autem ipsa species domus."

15. *Nicomachean Ethics*, 1142a17: τὰ μὲν δι'ἀφαιρέσεως ἐστιν.

16. In *II Phys.*, chap. 3, no. 161, he adds that the quantity in order to be conceived by the intellect must depend from the substance.

theology. In chapter II of his treatise, Boethius describes the subject of theology as being without motion, abstracted (from material things) and separable, because God's substance has no matter and movement. Boethius's summary corresponds to the description Aristotle gives of the theoretical sciences in Book E of the *Metaphysics*. Contrary to this position which makes God the subject of metaphysics, Thomas follows Avicenna: God cannot be the subject of first philosophy. On the other hand, he is the subject of the theological knowledge which depends on revelation. In metaphysics God is studied in so far as he is the principle of beings. In the following part of his exposition, he explains the different ways in which a being can be the principle of other beings, and concludes that all beings are caused by and depend on a First Being, which is being in the highest degree (*maxime ens*) and pure actuality. By investigating the causes of being, the philosopher can reach God, the First Cause.

The Method to Be Used in the Theoretical Sciences

In the fifth question Thomas laid the foundation for the division of the theoretical sciences, but we are still left with the thorny problem of the methods to be used in the different sciences. Thomas examines this theme in the sixth and last question of his work. Although Aristotle himself did not compose a special treatise on this theme, he was very much aware of it: the method to be used, he writes, varies according to the subject which is studied.[17] Moreover we find in his different works scattered observations on the way we must proceed in the sciences.

The point of departure for Thomas is a short and obscure sentence of Boethius in the second chapter: *In naturalibus igitur rationaliter, in mathematicis disciplinaliter, in divinis intellectualiter versari oportet*. Boethius probably found these terms when he was writing his commentary on the *Isagoge* of Porphyry. The terms seem to refer to a conception of three powers of the soul which apprehend three sectors of reality. Thomas's treatment of the problems of the methods to be employed is different and admirable in its riches and precision.

Aristotle has not given a complete and clear treatment of the meth-

---

17. Aristotle, *Nicomachean Ethics*, 1094b22–27.

od to be followed in *Physics*. Thomas mentions three views in this regard, and then gives next his own theory. He notes that the word *rationalis* expresses best the natural activity of the intellect which moves from what is best known (sensible things) to the understanding of their intelligible essence. In the natural sciences the mind goes from the knowledge of one thing to that of another and concludes from the effects that their causes exist and vice versa.

Boethius uses the term *disciplinaliter* to characterize the method to be used in the mathematical sciences. In his time the term *disciplina* was the translation of the Greek word ἐπιστήμη, but *doctrina* was also used. Cassiodorus, for instance, says that the mathematical sciences are doctrinal sciences.[18] In the twelfth century several authors commented on the term *disciplinaliter*.[19] Surprisingly a certain ambiguity shows in the meaning given to the term, while the Greek authors were usually very clear in the way they determined the character of the mathematical sciences. These sciences had, indeed, a primary importance as a model for studies. Thomas follows Aristotle in the analysis which he proposes in the *Posterior Analytics*, I, chapter 27, 87a31–37. The mathematical sciences study what is not connected with certain physical things. For instance, they abstract from movement and from qualities, and their objects are less complex. These sciences also reach a high degree of certitude.

What does Thomas say about the method to be used in metaphysics? Boethius qualifies it as *intellectualiter procedere*. By these terms he means a mode of knowledge in which the mind uses neither images nor impressions drawn from the senses.[20] The distinction between the understanding of the intellect and reasoning had already been used by Plato,[21] but it became more important in the works of Plotinus, who stated it as the difference between νοῦς and λογος. Man can transcend the realm of material things, turn to God, and partake in his simplicity. In his treatise on Boethius's text, Thomas does not examine the question whether intellect and reason (*ratio*) are the same cognitive faculty, but he considers them only is so far as they signify activities of the mind. He points out that the relation of *ratio* to the intellect is that of multiplicity to unity, referring to *De consolatione philosophiae*, IV, 6. In his later works Thomas prefers to use the verbs *movere* and *discurrere* to describe the activity of our reason

18. Cassiodorus, De artibus ac disciplinis liberalium litterarum, PL 70: 1168 D.
19. See Elders, *Faith and Science*, 127 ff.
20. Cf. Boethius, *De consolatione philosophiae*, V, 4.
21. Plato, *Phaedo* 65e–66a.

(*ratio*), while he says that the intellect rests in that what it has learned. Thomas points out that first philosophy, as the supreme science of being and as theology, is most intellectual.

The words of Boethius "*in divinis intellectualiter versari oportet neque deduci ad imaginationes sed potius inspicere ipsam formam*" have given Thomas the themes for his second and third articles, where he explains in greater detail the way in which man can know God in theology: he must purify his cognitive life, push aside the crude phantasies about the gods of the poets, and ascend from hypotheses to the absolute principle of all things. In Middle Platonism the supreme activity in philosophy—the ἐποπτικόν—was thought to be the perception of the simple and radiating truth.[22] For Plotinus it is also essential to turn away from material things. Augustine says, in his turn, that in order to reach the supreme wisdom, man must leave behind the things which are external to him as well as their images.[23] From the time of Proclus, philosophers conceived the world as a series of successive layers which, the further removed from their source they are, lose their clarity as an εἰκών of the supreme reality. The phrase of Boethius should be read in this context.

Thomas shows how complex the question is: Holy Scripture, when speaking of God, uses images all the time, and philosophy tells us that man cannot think without resorting to representations of his imagination. On the other hand, the theology of the spiritual life tells us that man should lift up his heart and dedicate himself to the study of God. In view of this difficulty, Thomas proposes a distinction between the *apprehensio* of something and the judgement about it. This distinction which Thomas will use to determine prophetical knowledge[24] is found in a few lines of Aristotle's *De anima*, III, 3. Aristotle says that there is a certain resemblance between sensitive knowledge and thought, since both have in common an activity which is distinguishing and judging, since the senses may also, besides apprehending objects, analyze them, taking one aspect and forming in this way a certain judgment. The higher the cognitive faculty is, the more explicit this function of judging becomes. Thomas describes the collaboration of sense knowledge with the intellect in the natural sciences and mathematics. In metaphysics, which studies

---

22. Pierre Hadot, "La métaphysique de Porphyre," in *Porphyre*, ed. Heinrich Dörrie (Geneva: Vandœuvres, 1965), 125.

23. Cf. Augustine, *De Trinitate* XII, 15, 25; Augustine, *De vera religione*, chap. 24; chap. 35: "incorporaliter Deo inhaerere."

24. See *ST* II-II, q. 173, a. 2.

the universal and immaterial, the senses seize material objects while the intellect discovers the need for a transcendent cause. In this way images of the senses can become a preparation for the higher activity of the intellect concerning God.

The *De Hebdomadibus* and the Doctrine of Participation

Thomas also wrote a commentary on a second very short treatise of Boethius titled *De Hebdomadibus*.[25] The meaning of the title is not immediately clear, but what Boethius writes in the text presents a good starting point for the treatment of certain questions such as the meaning of the goodness of things. A well-known sentence of the text says: *diversum est esse et id quod est*. Boethius also raises the question whether things are good in and by their substance. Thomas writes that Boethius is not very clear in what he says about the question of being. In simple things (such as immaterial beings), what they are and their being differ for us, since we think them separate, but in composite thing they differ in reality. Among these simple beings only God does not participate in being (*esse*), but subsists by himself. God cannot but be unique. The other simple beings are not being itself, but participate in it.[26] Thomas comments that with certain restrictions one may read in this treatise of Boethius a preparation of the doctrine of the real distinction in created things between their essence and the act of being.

But what Boethius really intended to say is different, as Pierre Hadot has pointed out: certain Neoplatonist philosophers taught that there is a real distinction between being and "that which is," according to which being corresponds to the first hypostasis, and "that which is" to the second. In this view "that which is" is later. When Boethius speaks of existing things, instead of the second hypostasis he has modified this theory and from this point of view, his theory differs from that of the Neoplatonists. His distinction between being itself and "that which is" had a considerable importance for the medieval authors.[27]

25. Boethius, *De Hebdomadibus*, PL 64: 1311–14.
26. Ibid., no. 34 ff.
27. Pierre Hadot, "La distinction de l'être et de l'étant dans le *De Hebdomadibus* de Boèce," in *Die Metaphysik im Mittelalter: ihr Ursprung und ihre Bedeutung*, ed. Paul Wilpert (Berlin: De Gruyter, 1963), 147–53.

In his second lesson of the commentary, Thomas discusses the second chapter of the text. Thomas saw in it a sketch of a study of the principles, since Boethius deals with being, unity and the good. He first explains what he considers to be the sense of Boethius's phrase "*ipsum enim esse nondum est.*" When Boethius writes that being itself (the *ipsum esse*) does not yet exist, that is true, Thomas says, if you consider it in abstraction from concrete existence. That which is, says Boethius, can participate, whereas being itself does not. Thomas uses this statement to present a summary of his doctrine of participation. Participating is like taking part (of something), and this can be in different ways according to the mode of participation. (a) One may speak of participation in a general way when something receives and possesses partially what belongs to another. In this way one can say that man participates in animal, since he does not have "animality" in its full extension. For the same reason we say that Socrates participates in human nature, and (b) that a subject (substance) participates in an accident or matter in a form, since the form is common by what it is, but becomes determinate when applied to a being and is given to a precise subject. (c) One can also say that an effect participates in its cause, especially when it does not acquire the equivalent of what its cause possesses. An example is the way in which the air participates in sunlight.

If we leave aside this participation of the effect in its cause, it is impossible that being itself (*esse*) participates in something. It cannot participate in something in the manner in which matter or the subject receives a form or an accident. Likewise being cannot participate in something like an individual being participates in the universal. But "that which is" participates in being. Thomas uses the principle that "that which belongs essentially to a thing, is the cause of what is said of this perfection by participation" to apply it to the relation of creatures to God. "God is a being (*ens*) by his essence, since he is being (*esse*) itself. All other things are beings by participation."

In this survey of three modes of participation, we notice that Thomas also mentions Plato's well-known theory of participation, which was resolutely rejected by Aristotle and which is deficient in that Socrates does not participate in the idea of man, since he does not have a *part* of human nature, but possesses it essentially. A further particularity is that here Thomas mentions some typically Aristotelian doctrines such as the relation of matter to its form and that of accidents to their substance, as modes of participation. By mentioning these—let us say—defective ways of participation, Thomas prepares the way for what for him is true participation, namely, that of an effect in its cause, and of creatures in divine being.

Boethius adds some summary remarks on being. Concerning this text Thomas explains that at first we simply notice that something exists—this is the apprehension of a being as our first concept (something which is)—to apprehend next that this being is *something*, for instance a stone, a tree. A thing exists because it participates in being itself, and when existing it participates in some contents so as to be something.[28] Among propositions the best known are those of which the terms are among the first concepts apprehended by us, such as being, thing, one, good.[29] This leads to a discussion of the one and the good in the second lesson. The text about the One examines both composed and simple beings. In composed things being (*esse*) differs from that which is (*id quod est*). Since being is simple, composite things are not their being. Boethius notes that simple things are their being, but Thomas observes: a thing may be simple from one point of view but not from another standpoint. If there are forms without matter, they are simple in so far as they are not material and have no extension, but not necessarily under other aspects. What is really simple and subsists can only be one; the only really one being cannot be other than God.[30]

Boethius mentions next "good" as that which all strive to attain. Thomas notes two ways in which the good is related to the appetite: 1) every diversity dissociates, but the appetite must aspire (to reach) resemblance, since the appetite is satiated by that which is equal to what it desires; 2) from this it follows also that when one aspires to something according to an acquired habitus which is not conformed to our nature, there will be a dissociation.[31]

This discussion is continued in the third lesson: the good is the proper object of the appetite. Considering that all things seek the good, we may say that the good belongs to them, in other words, that all things are good.[32] If so, the question presents itself of whether things are good by their essence or by participation. Thomas answers that they are not good

---

28. In Boetii De Hebdomadibus, lesson 2, no. 24.
29. Ibid., no. 20.
30. Ibid., no. 34 ff.
31. Ibid., nos. 36–38.
32. Ibid., no. 41.

by the essence of goodness, since each of them has its own essence which is different from that of the other things, such as men and animals. Thomas concludes that the goodness of creatures is twofold: (a) by their relation with the Primary Good; their being and whatever they are proceeds from the First Good; (b) everything is called good in so far as it is perfect in its being and its operations.[33] For Boethius, however, the goodness of things is not given with what they are, but signifies their dependence on God and is not intrinsically present in them.

In this chapter the numerous points of contact between the writings of Boethius and the thought of Aquinas have been stressed. It would seem that in reality Thomas has taken very little from this learned author from the end of Antiquity, but that what Boethius wrote in the field of the liberal arts has undoubtedly been an important factor in the formation of the young Thomas.[34]

---

33. Ibid., no. 62 ff.
34. For more details, see Ralph McInerny, *Boethius and Aquinas* (Washington, D.C.: The Catholic University of America Press, 1990); and Henry Chadwick, *Boethius: The Consolations of Music, Logic, Theology and Philosophy* (Oxford: Clarendon Press, 1981).

10 ~ SAINT GREGORY THE GREAT

During the Middle Ages Gregory the Great enjoyed an undisputed authority, especially in questions concerning the life of the Church, moral theology, and the allegorical sense of texts of Holy Scripture. His presence in the writings of Thomas is massive. There are in fact more than twenty-five hundred references and quotations, more than those to Jerome or Ambrose, but fewer than to Chrysostom and to Augustine. This study of the place of Gregory the Great in the works of Thomas is not a first. Professor Enzo Portalupi has the merit of having examined exhaustively the presence of Gregory in the *Quaestiones disputatae de veritate*[1] as well as those in the *Quaestiones disputatae de malo*.[2] Our essay does not have the pretension of being a complete study of the patristic sources of Aquinas, nor is it meant to be an examination of the works of Saint Gregory. The aim is to show what Thomas has seen as important in these works and in which subdivisions of theology he has quoted him.

Gregory is a source of doctrine and spirituality of great value. Thomas reminds us that a single doctor does not excel in all matters in the study of theology, but blessed Gregory, he writes, was an excellent specialist of moral theology, Saint Augustine was a genius in solving difficult theological questions, while Blessed Ambrose was admirable in giving allegorical interpretations.[3]

One of the writings of Gregory which Thomas used is the *Liber moralium*, a commentary on the forty-two chapters of the Book of Job, which

This chapter was originally published as "La présence de Grégoire le Grand dans les œuvres de saint Thomas d'Aquin," *Nova et Vetera* 86 (2011): 155–80.

1. Enzo Portalupi, "Gregorio Magno nelle 'Quaestiones disputatae de veritate' di Tommaso d'Aquino," *Rivista di filosofia neo-scolastica* 77 (1985): 556–98.
2. Enzo Portalupi, *Studi sulla presenza di Gregorio Magno in Tommaso d'Aquino*, (Freiburg, Switzerland: Universitätsverlag, 1991).
3. *Sermo* 1, 3: "Gregorius optime scivit moralitates, beatus Auguistinus quaestiones solvere et beatus Ambrosius optime allegorizavit."

193

the pope composed over a rather long period. He revised the text several times. The definitive redaction dates to about 600. Its text is not a systematic study of the Book of Job, but rather the fruit of meditations on the biblical text which aim at counseling monks, the clergy, and also lay Christians in order to help them in their search of the perfection of Christian life.

Another not less important source for Thomas is the *Two Books of Homilies on the prophet Ezekiel*, which Gregory began to write in 593. He has, however, not commented on the whole text. At the beginning of the second book of his *Homilies*, he excuses himself for not having found the time to study the text of the prophet thoroughly (*perscrutari*), because of his pastoral and pontifical tasks, as well as because of the fears caused by the approaching king of the Lombards who had begun to move toward Rome.[4] In this work as well as in his treatise on the Book of Job Gregory tries to show the spiritual sense of the text.[5]

Thomas repeatedly quotes another great work of Gregory: his *Forty Homilies on the Gospels*, divided into two books, printed in the Latin Patrology of Migne after the *Homilies on Ezekiel*, although certain of these homilies may be anterior to 593. The homilies present instructions on our moral life, but are also an exposition of dogmas of the faith and a refutation of heresies.

On a few occasions Thomas refers to the *Liber Regulae pastoralis*, which goes back to 590–91 and explains which qualities one must possess in order to be an appropriate candidate for the seat of bishop, and how a bishop must face the problems of the moment. For a considerable part, Gregory writes, a bishop's life must be devoted to meditation. Gregory also mentions the tension which may arise between pastoral work and a life of prayer and contemplation.

Finally there is, among the writings of Gregory the Great, the *Dialogues*, a hagiographic book of an outspoken moralizing character, where many miraculous events in the life of saints, as well as visions and prophecies, are related. Thomas refers twenty-five times to it, nine of these are in the *Quaestiones disputatae de veritate*, but there is only one reference in the *Summa theologiae*. The interest Gregory shows in stories about the saints seems to be due to his conviction that they help us understand Holy Scripture.[6]

---

4. Gregory the Great, *Hom. in Ezech.* II, preface (PL 76: 934).

5. Ibid., *Hom.* 1 (PL 76: 956).

6. Gregory, *Hom. in Ezech.*, 10 (PL 76: 901): "In sanctorum vita cognoscimus quid in scriptura intelligere debemus" (*In IV Sent.*, d. 1, q. 2, a. 2, qc. 3, arg. 2).

Several letters of Pope Gregory are also quoted in the works of Thomas, in particular with regard to practical questions, such as the administration of the sacraments and problems of the moral life. The *Epistularium* of the pope has been published in Migne, *Patrologia Latina* 77. It is quoted by Thomas under the title of *Registrum*. There are in his works sixteen references to this *Registrum*,[7] as for instance to the famous letter to Bishops Virgil of Arles and Theodore of Marseille, in which the pope declares that Jews should not be forced to embrace the Christian faith,[8] a decision which became the law and the fundamental text with regard to the attitude to adopt with respect to the Jews.[9] There is also the well-known letter to Augustine, missionary and bishop in England, and a missive to Archbishop Boniface.[10]

To facilitate consulting the references to these works in the writings of Thomas the quotations have been divided into some rubrics.

The Presence of St. Gregory in the Biblical Commentaries of Aquinas

At the beginning of the *Summa theologiae*, Thomas quotes a fundamental text of Gregory concerning the riches of doctrine contained in Holy Scripture, riches which surpass all the sciences in the way Scripture expresses itself, since by means of the same words it describes what happened and it shows the mystery hidden under the veil of these events.[11] In another important statement Gregory notes that Holy Scripture presents spiritual realities by means of corporeal images, so that we lift ourselves up from what we know in this life to the desire of what is yet unknown to us.[12] The New Testament is contained in the Old as a wheel in another wheel.[13]

There is a massive presence of Gregory in the *Catena aurea* on the

---

7. It contains some letters of the pope concerning the government of the Church. See *Catena in Matth.*, chap. 26, l, 7.
8. PL 77: 509: *ST* II-II, q. 189, a. 2.
9. *ST* II-II, q. 10, a. 11, s.c.
10. *In IV Sent.*, d. 40, q. 1 (intro.); d. 45, q. 2, a. 3, qc. 3.
11. Gregory, *Moralia* 20, 1 (PL 76: 135); *ST* I, q. 1, a. 10, s.c.: "Sacra Scriptura omnes scientias ipso locutionis suae more transcendit: quia uno eodemque sermone, dum narrat gestum, prodit mysterium" (text modified by Thomas).
12. Cf. Gregory, *Hom. in Evang.* 2, 11 (PL 76: 1114); *ST* I-II, q. 3, a. 7.
13. Gregory, *Hom. in Ezech.*, 1, 6 (PL 76: 834); *ST* I-II, q. 107, a. 3.

four gospels. He is quoted 184 times in the exposition on the gospel of Matthew, 60 times in that on Marc, more than 300 times in that on the gospel according to Luke, and 182 times in that on the gospel of John.

In his prologue Thomas quotes the explanation of Gregory of the vision of Ezekiel about the figures which symbolize the four evangelists. In chapter 2, lesson 6, we read the beautiful commentary of Gregory on the Three Magi: "They took another road back; after we have come to know Jesus, we can no longer travel along the road by which we came to him." Very much attached to the singing of the psalms, Gregory writes that when we sing the psalms with our heart, we open ourselves to God, that he may give us the understanding of the mysteries of which we sing and the grace of remorse.[14] Gregory sees in the apostle John who arrived first at the tomb of Christ, a symbol of the Synagogue and in Peter a symbol of the Church of the Gentiles.[15]

St. Gregory and the Allegorical Sense of the Bible

In his Commentary on the Book of Job in which he explains the literal sense of the text, Thomas refers to Gregory only twice. At the beginning of his exposition he writes that the blessed Pope Gregory helped us to understand the text and explained to us its mystical sense (*mysteria*) in a very subtle way and with great eloquence, so that there is nothing left for us to add to it. The only other reference to Gregory is in chapter 17, where he says that anger, because of the envy which comes with it, prevents us from judging correctly.

Among the Fathers of the Latin West, Gregory is the incontestable master of the allegorical sense of biblical texts. He explains his intention in the *First Homily*, book 2, on Ezekiel: the literal sense is that of the historical facts and of things which can be understood, while one can also discover a spiritual meaning in it concerning the mysteries of the faith, if one understands the texts allegorically.[16]

Allegorical interpretations are frequent. "The axe laid to the roots of the trees" (Mt 3:10) signifies Christ the Redeemer, his human nature is

---

14. Thomas, *In Psalmum* 1; Gregory, *Hom. in Ezech.* 1, 1 (PL 76: 793).

15. *Catena in Ioan.*, chap. 20, lesson 1.

16. Gregory, *Hom. in Ezech.* 2, 1 (PL 76: 956): "Scriptura autem sacra et ea quae accipi secundum litteram possunt, plerumque spiritualiter intelligenda sunt, ut fides habeatur in veritate historiae et spiritualis intelligentia capiatur de mysteriis allegoriae."

the handle, his divinity the knife. With regard to the miracles wrought by the disciples of Jesus (Mt 10), Gregory notes that the holy Church does every day spiritually what the apostles did physically. Jesus comforts those who bend under a burden. Gregory comments: it is a hard yoke and a great weight to be subject to temporal things, to seek the things of this earth, to support what is staggering, and to look for what is passing without wanting to disappear with it.[17] On Jesus words "Who is my mother?" Gregory says that one may become the mother of Christ by preaching the gospel (*mater efficitur praedicando*). To explain the parables of the treasure hidden in a field and of the pearl (Mt 13:44), Thomas quotes several texts of the pope. In another parable a faithful servant receives in recompense five talents (Mt 25:14 ff), Gregory sees in the talents a symbol of the five external senses. Hiding the talent one has received in the ground means to dissipate the knowledge and gifts one has received in this-worldly occupations. Gregory writes that many Christians take this servant as their model. They are uncertain and hesitate as to a better way they should choose and persevere in their laziness. It is obvious that the allegorical explanations of Gregory are sometimes farfetched, as in his explanation of the parable of the two talents, which are supposed to symbolize the intellect and activity. But we admire the ingenuity of the great pope, with which Thomas puts us in contact by his numerous quotations.

Let us consider some allegorical explanations which are found in the *Catena aurea* on the gospel according to Mark. Jesus sent the disciples out in pairs (Mk 6:7), because there are two commandments, to love God and to love one's neighbor.[18] The disciples gathered the people together in squares of hundreds and fifties, a sentence in which Gregory also sees a symbolic meaning. On Mark 9:42 where Jesus speaks of scandal, Gregory adds a comment which is repeatedly quoted by Thomas in his works: "We must try not to scandalize our fellow men, but when sometimes people are scandalized by what we preach, it is better to let this feeling appear than to abandon the truth."[19] The millstone around the neck of the one who scandalizes the little ones signifies the preoccupations and the burden of life in the world.[20]

The woman whose sins were forgiven (Lk 7:36) represents the gentiles who converted. To kiss the feet of Jesus means to venerate the mys-

17. Gregory, *Moralia*, 11, 10.
18. *Catena in Marcum*, chap. 6, lesson 2.
19. Gregory, *Hom. in Ezech.*, 1, 7 (PL 76: 842).
20. *Catena in Marcum*, chap. 9, lesson 42: "... saecularis vitae circuitus ac labor exprimitur."

tery of the Incarnation. Gregory also sees a spiritual meaning in the return of the master (Lk 12:35), either during the first watch (adolescence), the second watch (mature age), or during the third watch (old age). In this connection Gregory speaks of the sluggishness and the languor of our mind: we must be fervent, else we shall not survive in the turbulent sea of this world (Lk 13:34). He considers, in fact, the life of Christians to be a perpetual struggle (Lk 14:24) and applies the scene of the expulsion of the dealers from the temple as typical of what also happens in the Church: certain men have become priests, but transform their sacred ministry into a business (Lk 19:45).

John writes that on the Feast of Dedication, when Jesus declared that he was the Son of God, it was winter. Gregory sees in it a symbol of the cold-hearted attitude and animosity of the Jews.[21] When after his resurrection Jesus remained standing on the shore of Lake Tiberias, whereas during his public life he walked on the water of the lake, this has a spiritual meaning: the sea is the world with its commotion, while the mainland signifies the tranquility of eternity.[22]

In the commentaries of Thomas on the Letters of St. Paul, there are only a few references to the writings of Gregory. While in his exposition of the literal sense of the Book of Job Thomas avoids quoting Gregory, in his *Scriptum super Libros Sententiarum*, he mentions occasionally the allegorical meaning which Gregory reads in expressions of the text of Job such as "the clouds disperse the light" (Job 36:28), namely, Christian doctrine is disseminated by the preachers;[23] "Has your arm the strength of God?" (Job 40:4) signifies Christ.[24] On a few occasions Thomas reminds us that Gregory sees in the seven daughters of Job symbols of the three theological and the four capital moral virtues, and in the five talents of the Gospel parable, the five external senses. Pope Gregory resorts, in fact, everywhere to allegories.

Faith and Theology

In the course of time the knowledge which the Fathers of the Old Testament had of the mystery of man's salvation became more profound,

---

21. *Super evang. Ioan.*, chap. 10, lesson 5.
22. *Catena in Ioan.*, chap. 21, lesson 1; Gregory, *Hom. in Evang.* 2, 24 (PL 76: 1184).
23. *In I Sent.*, d. 16, q. 1, a. 3.
24. *In III Sent.*, d. 1, q. 2, a. 2, ad 2.

and the closer they were to the coming of the Savior, the better they understood the sacrament of salvation.[25] In a *Homily on the Octave of Easter*, Gregory comments as follows on the words of Jesus (Jn 20:21): "As the Father sent me, so I am sending you": "*Eo mittitur Filius quo generatur.*" Thomas gives several interpretations of this sentence and stresses its importance.[26] A statement repeated several times by Thomas is that all things will return to nothing, if the hand of the Creator does not keep them in existence.[27]

In the following section we study texts of Gregory while we follow the order of the questions in the *Summa theologiae*. In *Summa theologiae* I, question 107, article 1, which deals with the language (*locutio*) of the angels, Thomas quotes Gregory three times: when our mind will go beyond the material world of communication, it will dedicate itself to sublime and as yet unknown ways of communication.[28] Since our body blocks the possibility of looking inside the mind of others, we use the remedy of language. An angel does not know this obstacle: he can communicate something to others as fast as he wants.

In his treatise on prophecy, *Summa theologiae* II-II, questions 171–74, Thomas uses some profound intuitions of Gregory: the gift of prophecy is not always at the disposition of the prophet; while a prophet speaks of the present or of the past he predicts the future. Prophecies concern things which are far away from what we know. A prophet himself does not always understand well what he is announcing, and there are different degrees in how far his message is removed from what we know.[29] In a text referred to several times by Thomas, Gregory says that "our knowledge of God has increased over the course of time."[30] We must understand this text, Thomas says, as referring to the time before the coming of Christ.[31] In addition to his profound reflections on prophecy, Gregory is also an important witness on charisms.

In the third part of the *Summa theologiae*, there are more than ninety

---

25. This text, taken from Gregory, *Hom. in Evang.* 2, 16 (PL 76: 980), is quoted a dozen times by Aquinas.

26. *In I Sent.*, d. 15, q. 4, a. 3.

27. Gregory, *Moralia*, 16, 36 (PL 75: 1143).

28. Gregory, *Moralia*, 2, 7 (PL 75: 559).

29. The main text of Pope Gregory on prophecy is found in *Hom. in Ezech.* 1 (PL 76: 980), and is quoted some ten times by Thomas.

30. Gregory, *Hom. in Ezech.* 2, 4 (PL 75: 980): "Per successiones temporum crevit divinae cognitionis augmentum."

31. *ST* II-II, q. 174, a. 6, ad 1.

references to what Gregory says about the life of Christ, as it is described by the evangelists. Another observation is that Pope Gregory is in favor of a certain liberty with regard to the form which in different countries is given to the divine cult.[32] If, in questions of dogmatic theology, Gregory's contribution is minimal, except in angelology, he offers very valuable remarks on our moral life. He sees the pastoral aspect of questions, and by means of short but very eloquent sentences, he explains strikingly the meaning of what the Bible says. Thomas reproduces several of them: "At the annunciation of the angel and the descent of the Spirit the Word comes to the womb, and then the Word becomes flesh" (*Angelo nuntiante et Spiritu adveniente mox Verbum in utero, mox intra uterum Verbum caro*).[33]

By taking on human nature Jesus was born, so to say, in a foreign country (*Per humanitatem assumptam quasi in alieno nascebatur*).[34] A difficulty: could Jesus as a child learn doctrine from the side of men? Gregory answers that at the age of twelve Jesus listened and interrogated the doctors in the temple, but that he did not teach, since exposing doctrinal questions is not given to man, except in adult age (*doctrinae sermo non suppetit nisi in aetate perfecta*).[35] Christ fasted for forty days, since the power of the Ten Commandments was fulfilled by the four gospels.[36] Sometimes Thomas corrects or completes the explications of Gregory who, with regard to the resurrection of Christ, said that Jesus had a real human body which one could touch, but that it was a body full of glory and incorruptible.[37]

In the questions about the sacraments the quotations from the works of Gregory concern mainly the practical aspects of their administration. Here are some examples: the necessity of the triple immersion for baptism; is faith necessary on the part the one receiving the sacrament?[38] As for the question whether priests can confer the sacrament of confirmation, Gregory's answer is affirmative, especially if the sacrament is administered together with baptism. Thomas sees in it a concession made by the

---

32. Gregory, *Registrum*, epist. 64 (PL 77: 1187; ST II-II, q. 93, a. 1, arg. 3).
33. Gregory, *Moralia* 18, 27 (PL 76: 90; ST III, q. 33, a. 1, s.c.).
34. Gregory, *Hom. in Evang.* 1, 8 (PL 76: 1104).
35. Gregory, *Hom. in Ezech.*, 1, 2 (PL 76: 769; ST III, q. 12, a. 3, ad 3; Thomas notes that Jesus did everything as it is appropriate to man's nature).
36. Gregory, *Hom. in Ezech.* 1, 16 (PL 76: 1137; ST III, q. 40, a. 2, ad 3).
37. Gregory, *Hom. in Evang.* 2, 23 (PL 76: 1182; ST III q. 55, a. 6).
38. Gregory, *Registrum*, epist. 43 (PL 77: 498; ST III, q. 66, a. 8); Gregory, *Registrum*, epist. 67: (PL 77: 1205).

pope in the fullness of his powers.[39] In the treatise on the Eucharist there are several references to texts of Gregory. This sacrament confers grace, since "the love of God does not know any rest;" one should not abstain from receiving Holy Communion out of humility.[40] With regard to the sacrament of penance, Gregory notes that in order to receive it one must have the intention of committing the sins one confesses no more, but one may nevertheless receive it if one has sinned again. If we do not forgive our neighbors, do our own already forgiven sins come back?[41] In his answers to these questions, which are mostly of a practical nature, Thomas sometimes indicates a wrong source, for instance, Gregory instead of Isidore or Ambrose, when he quotes by memory or when his sources contained an error.

The Angels

In some of the difficulties brought forward at the beginning of the articles of the *Summa theologiae* or the *Quaestiones disputatae* is mentioned that Gregory calls the angels rational animals.[42] Thomas corrects the expression. One can use it if by rational one means to say that the angels have no sensitive knowledge and that in them there is no distinction between intellect and reason, but as such the expression is a metaphor. As Augustine had taught before him, Gregory affirms that the angels were created simultaneously with the material world.[43] Their number surpasses very much that of material things and is infinite, and all the angels enjoy the contemplation of God.[44] Holy Scripture says of the angels that they assist before the throne of God. It means that they do not perform material tasks in the world and, above all, that they enjoy the intimate contemplation of God.[45] According to Gregory the angels who administer material things are more numerous that those who are before the throne of God.[46]

---

39. Gregory, *Registrum*, epist. 26 (PL 77: 696; ST III, q. 72, a. 11).

40. Gregory, *Hom. in Evang.* 2, 30 (PL 76: 1221; ST III, q. 79, a. 1, ad 2); *Reg. past.* 1, 6 (PL 77: 19).

41. Gregory, *Hom. in Evang.* 2, 34 (PL 76: 1256; ST III, q. 84, a. 10, arg. 4); *Dialogues* 16, 60 (PL 77: 128; ST III, q. 88, a. 2).

42. Gregory, *Hom. in Evang.* 10, ("*in die Epiphaniae*"; PL 76: 1110): "Animal rationale nominatur" (*In II Sent.*, d. 3, q. 1, a. 6, arg. 2; ST I, q. 51, a. 1, arg. 2).

43. Gregory, *Moralia* 32, 12 (PL 76: 6442): (*In I Sent.*, d. 2, q. 1, a. 3; ST I, q. 119, a. 1; cf. QD de potentia, q. 6, a. 4, s.c. 1).

44. Gregory, *Hom. in Evang.* 34 (PL 76: 1251; *In I Sent.*, d. 2, q. 1, a. 3; ST I, q. 112, a. 4).

45. *In IV Sent.*, d. 49, q. 2, a. 6. The biblical text referred to is Job 1:11.

46. Gregory, *Moralia*, 17, 13: PL 76: 20 (ST I, q. 112, a. 4).

In a text quoted by Thomas in his commentary on Isaiah, we read that the angels do not possess anything individually,[47] which means that the angels of the higher orders possess in their way what is proper to the lower hierarchies, and vice versa.

A general rule formulated by Gregory is that corporeal things are administered by spiritual beings.[48] If this is so, how do we explain that Holy Scripture only speaks of a ministry of certain angels? For Gregory the text of Hebrews 1:14 ("They are all spirits whose work is service, to help those who will be the heirs of salvation") caused a difficulty, since according to him only the angels of lower orders are sent on a mission. Thomas resolves the difficulty by suggesting that the angels of a lower order accomplish their missions moved by or subordinated to the angels of the higher orders.[49] But the angels perform their ministry in such a way that they do not interrupt their contemplation of God.[50] With regard to the fallen angels, Gregory thinks that Lucifer was the first, the most gifted among the angels.[51] In comparison with the other angels, he was more illustrious.[52] The fallen angels conserve their nature.[53]

The intellect of the angels is of a superior nature to the intellect of human beings.[54] If the nature of the angels in more subtle, the image of God is more pronounced in them.[55] Compared with human beings angels are spiritual substances, but compared to God, the limitless spirit, they are like bodies.[56] Their knowledge is without error.[57] Do the angels know the thoughts of man? Gregory seems to affirm it.[58]

In a sentence which comes back a few times, we read that man has sense knowledge in common with the animals, and thought with the an-

---

47. *Super Isaiam*, chap. 37: Gregory, *Hom. in Evang.* 2, 34 (PL 76: 1255).
48. Gregory, *Dialogues* 4, chap. 5 (PL 77: 329; *In II Sent.* d. 14, q. 1, a. 3; *ST* I, q. 110, a. 1).
49. *ST* I, q. 112, a. 4, ad 1.
50. *In II Sent.* d. 10, q. 1, a. 4, s.c. 1.
51. Gregory, *Moralia* 32, 23, 47, after *Quodl*. V, q. 4, a. 1, ad 1.
52. Gregory, *Hom. in Ezech.* 28, 13 (acc. to *De substantiis separatis*, chap. 20.).
53. Gregory, *Moralia* 2, 3 (PL 75: 557; *ST* I, q. 112, a. 3).
54. Gregory, *Hom. in Evang.* 34 ("*de centum ovibus*"; PL 76: 1247; *In II Sent.* d. 23, q. 2, a. 1, ad 2).
55. Gregory, *Hom. in Evang.* 34 (PL 76: 1250; *In III Sent.*, d. 2, q. 1, a. 1, qc. 2).
56. Gregory, *Moralia*, 2, 3 (PL 75: 557; *QD de malo*, q. 16, a. 1, arg. 7). Thomas corrects in an elegant way what Gregory writes about a certain corporeity of the angels ("*in comparatione cum Deo sunt compositi*"). When Gregory calls the devils animals, he wants to say "*beings endowed with reason*" (*QD de potentia*, q. 6, a. 6, ad 1).
57. Gregory, *Dialogues* 4, chap. 26 (PL 77: 357). Thomas notes that Gregory is speaking of the elevation of the soul by divine grace; the light of grace excludes all errors (*QD de malo* q. 16, a. 6, ad 8).
58. Gregory, *Moralia* 22 (PL 34: 388), but Thomas writes that by a decision of our will we can keep secret our intimate thoughts.

gels.⁵⁹ The angels have a universal mission with regard to man and the material world. In a text repeatedly quoted by Thomas, Gregory says that in this visible world nothing gets its proper place unless through the invisible creatures.⁶⁰

With regard to the role of the angels in the life of Christ, Thomas quotes Gregory: in the visible mission of the Son among men, all of what happens in the interior of people is an immediate effect of Christ as a Divine Person, but as to what happens on the outside and is visible, the angels can be intermediaries.⁶¹

Can the angels who are called "powers" work miracles? Gregory affirms it, but Thomas notes that a miracle is something which lies beyond the natural order; only God can do miracles.⁶² An interesting question is whether the angels who are sent to man, stay close to God. In the text quoted above, Gregory says that they see God always, but elsewhere he writes that those angels who do not leave to be at the service of man, stay close to God. The angels which administer the creation are more numerous than those who stay with God.⁶³

The Order of the Immaterial Beings

Gregory is the most important witness concerning the theology of the hierarchies of the angels. In *In II Sent.*, d. 9, q. 1, a. 4, ad 2, Thomas writes that the name "angel" signifies a spiritual being charged with a task, but that here Gregory does not enter into details about the nature of the angels (*"est nomen officii, non naturae, ut dicit Gregorius"*). This takes us to the question of the hierarchy of the angels. Dionysius bases his exposition on the order of spiritual perfections, while Gregory considers their different ministries.⁶⁴ To give an example, he explains the name "Dominations" by the fact that these angels direct others, who are subordinate to them.⁶⁵ In

---

59. Gregory, *Hom. in Evang.* 29 ("*in Ascensione Domini*"; PL 76: 1214). "Homo sentit cum pecoribus, intelligit cum angelis."

60. *Responso ad lectorem Venetum de articulis XXXVI.* Gregory says so in *Dialogues* 4, chap. 1 (PL 76: 448–51): "... quod in hoc mundo visibili nihil nisi per creaturam invisibilem disponi potest."

61. *In I Sent.*, d. 16, q. 1, a. 4. Thomas refers to Gregory, *Moralia* 28, 1.

62. Gregory, *Hom. in Evang.*, 34 (PL 76: 1251; *ST* I, q. 110, a. 4).

63. Gregory, *Moralia* 2, 4 (PL 76: 20).

64. *ST* I, q. 108, a. 5; Gregory, *Dialogues* 1, 4 (PL 77: 330).

65. Gregory, *Hom. in Evang.* 34, no. 10 (PL 76: 1251).

several of his works Thomas discusses the question of the hierarchy of the angels, according to the expositions of Dionysius and Gregory. Thomas himself formulates the following principle: there must be order and a hierarchy in the ranks of the pure spirits, as there is among material things. To determine this order Thomas rather follows Dionysius, but with regard to their ministry in favor of men, he consults Gregory above all.

In the *Summa contra Gentiles*,[66] using texts of both Dionysius and Gregory, he distinguishes nine choirs: in the first hierarchy there are the Seraphim, the Cherubim, and the Thrones; in the following the Dominations, the Powers, and the Forces. Then, finally, he distinguishes between the Principalities, Archangels, and Angels. According to Gregory the angels are charged with less important tasks, the archangels with more important ones.[67] Thomas is reserved regarding the attribution of missions to the different classes of the angels.[68] He has, for instance, a broader view of the task of the archangels who can also carry a message to one person, but who are useful for all. All what concerns the propagation of the faith, the divine cult, etc. is also of their resort. Thomas presents, moreover, a systematic consideration: the superior beings have a more universal power and receive a greater causal influence from God. This influence also reaches the spirits on lower levels through the mediation of the superior orders.

Gregory places the Principalities in the group of angels who are in the middle, after the Dominations. The Powers find their place after the Dominations. The Forces after the Powers. The different names used by the Apostle to describe the angels is a function of their different tasks.[69] The Cherubim, the Seraphim, and Thrones are not sent out on missions. If so, how to explain that a seraphim purified the lips of Isaiah? Thomas notes that Gregory does not have an answer.[70] In a gloss on Exodus 3, Gregory says that the angel who appeared to Moses is called lord and then also an-

---

66. *SCG* III, 80.

67. Gregory, *Hom. in Evang.* 34, no. 10 (PL 76: 1251).

68. *Super. Col.*, chap. 1, lesson 6: "Videtur mihi quod superiores quatuor numquam mittuntur, sed inferiores mittuntur, quod patet ex eorum nominibus." The Powers are engaged where miracles are wrought, the Forces where enemy powers must be confronted, the Principalities are involved in the government of cities and states. Thomas draws attention to the complementarity of the enumeration of the classes of angels which Paul gives in Col 1:16 and Eph 1:21. Gregory rather follows Eph 1:21, but he also knows the enumeration of Col 1. He thinks that a particular order of angels assists when miracles are worked (*SCG* III, 103).

69. Gregory, *Hom. in Evang.* 34, no. 8 (PL 76: 1249): "Novem vero angelorum ordines diximus, quia videlicet, testante sacro eloquio, scimus angelos, archangelos, virtutes, potestates, principatus, dominationes, thronos, cherubim et seraphim."

70. *Super Isaiam*, chap. 6, lesson 1: "Gregorius istam quaestionem in quadam homilia de centum ovibus dimittit sub dubio."

gel, because he helped him on the outside and gave orders to Moses himself, giving him the faculty of speech.[71]

Christian Moral Life

In the second part of the *Summa theologiae*, we find texts of St. Gregory in numerous questions. Thomas quotes him 479 times. His view of the moral life and of the necessity of the practice of the virtues shows in this sentence pronounced by the pope in a homily: "It is worthless to assist at feasts organized by man, if you are not invited to assist at those of the angels."[72] In the questions on human acts, Nemesius is frequently quoted, while Gregory is absent, but he is present in the questions on the goodness and malice of our acts. He supports the argument of Thomas which says that there are no individually indifferent acts: if a word spoken vainly (*verbum otiosum*) is bad, it is evident that every act in which right reason or usefulness is lacking is also bad.[73]

Gregory is often quoted as a source of information in the study of the passions, such as sadness, or the different degrees and the effects of anger.[74] He gives in fact a detailed description of these effects: palpitations of the heart, trembling, difficulties uttering words, fiery looks, etc., in a text reproduced by Thomas. If someone remains silent and shuts his anger up in his heart, it becomes even more fierce.[75] Gregory also says that anger has a blinding effect, something which did not happen to Christ when he chased the vendors from the temple. To explain this difference Thomas makes a distinction which sheds light on the text of Gregory: anger shows itself in two ways: it precedes the deliberation of our reason and so it influences it unfavorably, or it is consecutive to the thought of reason.[76] The virtue of fortitude helps us to face dangers and renders dangerous situations less frightening.[77]

In what Pope Gregory preaches and writes, a pastoral intention dominates everywhere, that is, the promotion of a life according to the virtues.

---

71. Ibid.
72. Gregory, *Hom. in Evang.* 2, 26 (PL 76: 1202; quoted in *ST* I-II, q. 3, a. 1. arg. 1).
73. Gregory, *Hom. in Evang.* 1, 6 (PL 76: 1098; *ST* I-II, q. 18, a. 9).
74. *ST* I-II, q. 48, aa. 2 and 3. The texts are found in Gregory, *Moralia* 5, 45–46 (PL 75: 724).
75. Gregory, *Moralia*, 5, 45 (PL 75: 725; *ST* I-II, q. 48, a. 4).
76. Gregory, *Moralia*, 5, 45 (PL 75: 726; *ST* III, q. 15, a. 9).
77. Gregory, *Hom. in Evang.* 2, 35 (PL 76: 312).

An example: Jesus did not want the miracles he accomplished to be widely known in order to recall to his disciples that they should never boast of their apostolate.[78] In connection with a text of Aristotle in the *Nicomachean Ethics*, Thomas raises the question whether the habits of the theoretical intellect may be called virtues. In a restricted sense, he writes, this can be done, since they direct the intellect to carry out correctly its activity, but these habits as such do not make us act in view of the good. The virtues of the appetite, on the other hand, such as justice or charity, let us use well these habits of the theoretical intellect. A quotation from Gregory confirms it: the contemplative life is more meritorious than the active life: "*contemplativa est maioris meriti quam activa.*"[79] Numerous texts of Gregory elucidate the nature of the theological virtues, symbolically designated by the three daughters of Job.[80] Gregory says about charity that if our love of God does not produce good works, it is no longer present.[81]

As for the moral virtues, the central role of prudence is stressed. Gregory notes that if the other virtues do not act prudently in what they try to reach, they are no virtues at all.[82] The entire complex of the cardinal virtues becomes visible in our good works.[83] These four virtues are so much interconnected that they seem to be one virtue. One does not really possess prudence if one is not just, courageous, and moderate. A virtue without the other virtues is nothing or is imperfect.[84] Like the branches of a tree come from only one trunk, virtues proceed from charity.[85] In another text Gregory calls the virtues forms of justice. Thomas adds a remark to make the wording more correct: Gregory speaks of the virtues according to what they are in general: every virtue which makes that what we do is right can be called justice. One could also speak of a certain overflowing of the virtues: a person who masters his passions will also be courageous.[86] Temperance is one of the main virtues: if one does not master gluttony, all the virtues crumble.[87]

---

78. Gregory, *Moralia*, 19, 23 (PL 76: 120).
79. Gregory, *Moralia* 6, 37 (PL 75: 764).
80. Gregory, *Moralia* 1, 27 (PL 75: 544; *ST* II-II, q. 17, a. 1).
81. Gregory, *Hom. in Evang.* 2, 30 (PL 76: 1221; *ST* II-II, q. 25, a. 9).
82. Gregory, *Moralia* 22, 1 (PL 76: 212; *ST* I-II, q. 58, a. 4).
83. Gregory, *Moralia* 22, 49 (PL 75: 592; *ST* I-II, q. 61, a. 2).
84. Gregory, *Moralia* 22, 1 (PL 76: 212; *ST* I-II, q. 65, a. 1): "Virtutes si sunt disiunctae non possunt esse perfectae, quia nec prudentia vera est quae iusta, temperans et fortis non est."
85. *Super evan. Ioan.*, chap. 15, lesson 2.
86. *ST* I-II, q. 61, a. 4, ad 1.
87. Gregory, *Moralia* 30, 18 (PL 76: 558).

The authors on spiritual theology insist on the importance of humility, but is humility really more important than the four cardinal virtues? Several authors give a positive answer. Gregory writes that the humility of God himself has become the demonstration of our redemption;[88] if one wants to practice the other virtues without humility, he works in vain.[89] A reader is impressed with seeing how Thomas resolves the question of the place to assign to humility: it is the most important virtue after the theological virtues and justice.[90]

According to Gregory obedience is not so much just one virtue as the mother of all virtues. Mainly in difficult circumstances and with regard to disagreeable tasks, obedience shows its true greatness.[91] By obedience we offer our will to God in order to bind ourselves ever more to him. In the respective question 104 of the second part of the *Summa theologiae* where Thomas studies obedience, Gregory is very much present. Patience is also one of the primary virtues. Real patience makes us support serenely the evil which others inflict on us.[92] Gregory calls it the root and the guardian of all other virtues.[93] The virtue of piety lets us wear out ourselves in works of charity.[94] But without discretion piety loses its usefulness. On the other hand, detailed knowledge is worthless if it is not based on piety.[95] True justice knows no disdain, but has compassion.[96] As it is sometimes worse to love a sin than to commit it, it is worse to hate justice than not to act with justice.[97]

Vices and Sins

As for sins and vices in general, Gregory thinks that one sin is the child of another, since it disposes one to commit other sins.[98] Sometimes a sin

---

88. Gregory, *Reg. past.* 3, chap. 17 (PL 77: 78 ff.; *ST* II-II, q. 161, a. 5, arg. 4): "Argumentum redemptionis nostrae inventum est humilitas Dei."
89. Gregory, *Hom. in Evang.* 1, 7 (PL 76: 103): "Qui ceteras virtutes sine humilitate congregat quasi paleas in ventum portat."
90. *ST* II-II, q. 161, a. 5.
91. Gregory, *Moralia* 35, 14 (PL 76; *In II Sent.*, d. 44, q. 2, a. 1, arg. 6).
92. Gregory, *Hom. in Evang.* 2, 35 (PL 76: 1261; *In III Sent.* d. 33, q. 3, a. 3, qc. 1, ad 3).
93. Gregory, *Hom. in Evang.* 2, 35 (*ST* II-II, q. 136, a. 2).
94. Gregory, *Moralia* 1, 32 (PL 75: 547).
95. Gregory, *Moralia* 1, 31, 45 (PL 76: 621).
96. Gregory, *Hom. in Evang*, 2, 34 (PL 76: 1246; *ST* II-II, q. 30, a. 1, ad 1).
97. Gregory, *Moralia* 25, 11 (PL 76: 339).
98. Gregory, *Moralia* 25, 9 (PL 76: 334).

one commits is the punishment of a former sin.⁹⁹ Gregory distinguished the sins according to their causes rather than by their objects.¹⁰⁰ For Gregory the capital sins are like the leaders of an army.¹⁰¹ He does not consider pride a special sin, but rather the source and base of all sins. "Pride is the mother of all vices."¹⁰² Pride seems to reside in the irascible appetite.¹⁰³ Concerning the division of pride into four kinds, Thomas simply writes that the authority of Gregory suffices to confirm it.¹⁰⁴

For the treatise on the vices in the *Summa theologiae*, Gregory is the most important source. This is also the case for the *Disputed Questions on Evil*, questions 8–15,¹⁰⁵ so that in this field Gregory the Great is considered one of the foremost authorities among the Fathers, if not the most important. His authority is sufficient to brush away objections against the division of pride into four kinds.¹⁰⁶

Of the seven capital vices, five relate to our spiritual life, two concern our bodily existence.¹⁰⁷ The latter are less serious, but more infamous.¹⁰⁸ According to Gregory the first vices which enter in man are like guides which persuade him to give in to them. Afterwards we do not even reason about whether to give in or not. Thomas writes that Gregory describes what often happens although not always.¹⁰⁹

With regard to the vice of acedia, Thomas follows Gregory, who also calls it sadness, when one is sad because of the goods God gives us.¹¹⁰ Against those who say that acedia is not a capital sin, Thomas writes that this opinion collapses when confronted with the authority of Gregory in this matter.¹¹¹ Thomas also quotes some instructive texts on the vices of envy and anger.¹¹² Envy leads to hatred, gossip to pleasure in the bad luck

---

99. Gregory, *Hom. in Ezech.* 1, 11 (PL 76: 915).
100. Gregory, *Moralia* 30, 45 (PL 76: 621).
101. Ibid., 30, 45, 61.
102. Gregory, *Moralia* 31, 45 (PL 76: 621; *ST* II-II, q. 158, a. 7).
103. Gregory, *Moralia*, 2, 16 (PL 75: 593; *ST* II-II, q. 162, a. 3).
104. *QD de malo*, q. 8, a, 4; Gregory, *Moralia* 23, 6 (PL 76: 258).
105. In these disputed questions there are more than eighty references to texts of Gregory.
106. *ST* II-II, q. 61, a. 4.
107. Gregory, *Moralia* 31, 45 (PL 76: 625). Gregory speaks of these vices as if they are an army which threatens us.
108. Gregory, *Moralia* 33, 12 (PL 76: 628).
109. Ibid., 33, 61 (*In II Sent.* d. 43, q. 1, a. 5, ad 2).
110. Cf. *ST* II-II, q. 35, a. 4; Gregory, *Moralia* 31, 45. For what Thomas writes on acedia, see Leo Elders, "L'acédie, un vice capital," *Nova et Vetera* 69 (1994): 175–84.
111. *QD de malo*, q. 11, a. 4, s.c. ("contra est auctoritas Gregorii").
112. Cf. Gregory, *Moralia* 5, 46 (PL 75: 728), on the effects of envy: "Color quippe pallore afficitur, oculi deprimumntur, mens accenditur, membra frigescunt, fit in cogitatione rabies."

of the other person. Envy poisons the entire soul.[113] As for avarice Gregory writes that its object can also be good positions, when one desires them immoderately.[114] Unchastity is also a capital sin.[115] Regarding the question whether the use of beauty products is allowed, several authors—and also to some extent Gregory—declared themselves in favor of a prohibition, whereas Thomas writes that moderate beauty care is licit.[116]

To conclude this summary of observations of Gregory on sins and vices, one may recall the following beautiful text: A vice frequently found in people is to sin covertly, to deny that they have committed this particular sin or, once when they have been designated as having committed it, to aggravate their case by defending themselves.[117]

The Gifts of the Holy Spirit

Before the thirteenth century theologians did not always have a clear idea of the nature of the gifts of the Holy Spirit. In the questions about these gifts, Thomas frequently quotes Gregory. The Holy Pope, in fact, often speaks of the presence of the Holy Spirit in us. He sees the seven gifts symbolized in the seven daughters of Job[118] and notes that the virtues alone are not sufficient to let us act well. The gifts protect us against errors, make us understand what to do, help us to avoid impetuosity, strengthen us against fear, give knowledge against ignorance, piety and the fear of God against hardness of the heart and pride.[119] The gifts are conferred to all the faithful, but the Holy Spirit is not always with the prophets. The distinction between the charisms *gratis data* and the seven gifts of the Holy Spirit helps to solve difficulties. The gifts are necessary to arrive at eternal salvation.[120]

A text of Gregory seems to indicate that some of the gifts may be possessed without the other ones, but Thomas recalls the beautiful text of the Book of Job, where we read that the sons and daughters of Job nour-

---

113. Gregory, *Moralia* 31, 45 (PL 76: 622; *ST* II-II, q. 36, a. 4).
114. Gregory, *Hom. in Evang.* 1, 16 (PL 76: 1136).
115. Gregory, *Moralia* 31, 45 (PL 76: 621; *ST* II-II, q. 153, a. 4, s.c.).
116. Gregory, *Hom. in Evang.* 2, 40 (PL 76: 1303; *ST* II-II, q. 169, a. 1).
117. Gregory, *Moralia*, 22, 13 (PL 76: 230; *ST* II-II, q. 69, a. 1, ad 3).
118. Gregory, *Moralia* 1, 27 (PL 75: 544).
119. Gregory, *Moralia* 2, 49 (PL 75: 592; *ST* I-II q. 68, a. 5).
120. Gregory, *Moralia* 2, 56 (PL 75: 598).

ished themselves mutually.[121] Moreover, Thomas observes that the texts of Pope Gregory on the gifts are not always very clear, and that he sometimes speaks of the gifts as if these are only meant to help us in our activities during life on earth.

Eschatology

The parable of the vineyard laborers sent to the vineyard at different hours of the day provides Gregory with an opportunity to distinguish between five periods in the history of mankind: those beginning at day break signify the period from Adam to Noah; the third hour, the time from Noah to Abraham; those at the sixth hour, the centuries from Abraham to Moses; the period of the workers of the ninth hour, that from Moses until the arrival of Christ; and the last ones at the eleventh hour, the time from Christ until the end of the world.[122]

In the questions where Thomas studies the judgment after our death, heavenly beatitude, the resurrection of the body, and eternal suffering by fire Gregory is often consulted.

The Soul after Death and the Quality of the Resurrected Body

In the *Scriptum super libros Sententiarum*, book 4, distinctions 44 and 45, there are several references to the *Dialogues* of Pope Gregory. He recounts that according to several heretics the bodies of the Christians resurrected would become subtle and intangible, similar to the air,[123] but Christ has shown that his risen body is real and palpable, although glorified. Thomas quoted Gregory on the qualities of the glorified body. It resembles gold because of its clarity and crystal because of its transparence.[124] Somewhat further on in his text Thomas speaks of the fire of hell. Gregory thinks that there is only one kind of fire in hell, but that not all the condemned are punished in the same way.[125] This fire is not a fire

---

121. Gregory, *Moralia* 2, 32 (PL 75: 547; ST I-II, q. 68, a. 5).
122. *Catena in Matth.*, chap. 20, lesson 1; Gregory, *Hom. in Evang.* 19 (PL 76: 154).
123. Gregory, *Moralia* 14, 56 (PL 75: 1378).
124. *In IV Sent.*, d. 44, q. 2, a. 2.
125. Gregory, *Dialogues* 4, chap. 39 (PL 77: 393).

lit by man and does not need combustibles; it is inextinguishable;[126] it does not produce light, because the condemned are sent into the darkness.[127] Gregory says nothing about a place where hell would be located. In these texts Thomas corrects the insufficient explanations of the pope. The fire of hell is as an instrument of divine justice and retains the souls which are so to say tied by it. In this way the souls see the fire as harmful to them.[128] When Gregory writes that the soul sees itself on fire, Thomas notes courteously that this does not seem an adequate explanation ("*hoc iterum non videtut sufficere*"), since in that case the pain of the soul would be apparent and not real. God gives the fire the power to retain the soul in one place only.

Gregory mentions several apparitions of the dead to the living. Thomas is embarrassed to explain the relation of the souls with a place. He suggests that there may be a certain congruity of them with place, in the way pure spirits can be in a place.[129]

The Active Life and The Contemplative Life

In the works of Thomas there are many quotations from the writings of Gregory, but in the four questions about the active and the contemplative life, *Summa theologiae* II-II, questions 179–82, they are of surprising density and total fifty-two texts. Thomas wrote his text while he had the *Moralia* and the *Homilies on Ezekiel* before his eyes. In thirteen of the eighteen articles of these four questions, the arguments *sed contra* are borrowed from Gregory. It is true that Gregory is not Thomas's only source: Augustine and Aristotle are also present. We also see some texts of the great pope in the objections which oblige to give a more precise answer to the question raised at the beginning.

The most important doctrines concern the two genera of Christian life, about which God himself has instructed us through his word, namely, the active and contemplative lives,[130] an exhaustive division, clearly taught by Luke.[131] Augustine mentions a third way of life, *ex utroque*

---

126. "Gehennae ignis cum sit corporeus et in se missos corporaliter exurat, non nutritur, sed creatus semel inextinguibilis durat."
127. *In IV Sent.*, d. 50, q. 2, a. 3, qc. 4.
128. Ibid., d. 44, q. 3, a. 3, qc. 3.
129. Ibid., d. 45, q. 1, a. 1, qc. 1: "eo modo quo corporalia in loco esse possunt."
130. Gregory, *Hom. in Ezech.*, 2, 2 (PL 76: 952).
131. Gregory, *Moralia* 6, 37 (PL 75: 764).

compositus,[132] but this third way can be reduced to the two fundamental ways. A fundamental text of Gregory helps Thomas to determine what contemplative life is. This consists not just in the activity of the intellect, but also in loving God and our neighbors; one keeps God present in one's mind.[133] The one who chooses the contemplative life, sets aside, in so far as it is feasible, external activities.[134] However, the love of one's neighbor remains present. Thomas explains that the moral virtues belong to the contemplative life as dispositions, and that as far as affects go love of one's neighbors is present in it.[135]

The work of the active life ends with the death of the body.[136] In the third book of the *Scriptum super libros Sententiarum*, there are numerous references to Gregory in the question which examines the active and the contemplative life, borrowed from the *Homilies on Ezekiel*. In several of these texts Gregory praises the value of contemplative life, which consists in the love of God and of one's neighbor.

"When one applies oneself with all one's power to the love of God and one's fellowmen and when one rests from bodily work and efforts in such a way, that one no longer feels the desire to undertake something but by treading on all preoccupations, one is inflamed by the desire to see God."[137] "The contemplative life is of a higher quality than the active life, because in the active life one engages oneself in what is useful for our duties on earth, while in the contemplative life one enjoys already an inner foretaste of our future rest."[138] Gregory has nevertheless a very positive conception of the active life, taken over by Thomas: "The active life consists in giving bread to the hungry and in instructing the ignorant by words of wisdom."[139] Contemplative life consists in meditating on divine truth.[140] But knowing what belongs to the study of things has little importance for the practice of the moral virtues. Practicing these virtues, as well as the consideration of what God has done, can prepare us for contemplation. To the question whether in this life man can see the essence

---

132. Augustine, *De civitate Dei* XIX, 2, 3.
133. Gregory, *Hom. in Ezech.*, 2, 2 (PL 76: 764).
134. Gregory, *Hom. in Ezech.*, 2, 2 (PL 75: 953; *ST* II-II, q. 180, a. 2, s.c.: "... ab exteriori actione quiescere").
135. *ST* II-II, q. 180, a. 2.
136. Gregory, *Moralia* 6, 37 (PL 75: 764; *ST* I-II, q. 67, a. 1).
137. Gregory, *Hom. in Ezech.*, 1, 2, 2, 8 (PL 76: 963; *In III Sent.*, d. 35, q. 1, a. 2, qc. 3).
138. Gregory, *Hom. in Ezech.*, l., 1; Hom. 3, 9 (PL 76: 808; *In IV Sent.*, d. 35, q. 1, a. 4, qc. 2).
139. Gregory, *Hom. in Ezech.*, l, 2, Hom. 3, 8 (PL 76: 953; *In IV Sent.*, d. 35, q. 1, a. 3).
140. Gregory, *Moralia* 6, 37 (PL 75: 764; *ST* II-II, q. 180, a. 4).

of God, Gregory gives a negative answer,[141] although he mentions certain very holy persons who set aside all images and who lift themselves up above material things. Concerning rather technical details, such as the description of the way to proceed in the act of contemplation, Gregory yields his place to Dionysius, Richard of St. Victor, and Aristotle. But as for the joy which contemplation gives us, Gregory is quoted again: the contemplative life is very attractive and sweet, because when one considers the one whom we love, we lose interest in the things of this world and our love becomes more intense.[142]

Does teaching belong to the active or to the contemplative life? On this point Gregory is not very clear. On the one hand he writes that the masters of the spiritual life make the realities of heaven which they have contemplated known to their brothers, but he also says that it is proper to those who conduct an active life to instruct the ignorant with words of wisdom.[143] Thomas solves the difficulty by a distinction: if the knowledge one possesses is ordered to external activities, teaching this knowledge belongs to the active life, but when one meditates with joy on the truth, one is in the contemplative life. Expressing what one is thinking in words is an act of the active life. On other points Thomas also renders Gregory's texts more precise.

Does the active life have a greater value than the contemplative? A superior must distinguish himself by his actions in directing the community, but he must nevertheless remain attached to contemplation. We may call the active life a servitude, and contemplative life freedom.[144] Another question is that concerning the merits of the active and the contemplative life. Gregory seems to choose, on this point, the side of the contemplative life, but Thomas observes that when one engages oneself with greater love in one's work, one's merits are also greater.[145]

Gregory is the authority who helps to resolve the following question: is the contemplative life rendered more difficult by being engaged in practical work? Three texts of Gregory are quoted on this problem, but Thomas solves the difficulty by a distinction: we cannot do two things at the same time, but the active life can help the contemplative by reducing the disorder of the passions.[146]

---

141. Gregory, *Hom. in Ezech.*, 2, 2 (PL 76: 953; *ST* II-II, q. 180, a. 5).
142. Gregory, *Hom. in Ezech.*, 2, 2, (PL 76: 956).
143. Gregory, *Hom. in Ezech.*, 1, 5 (PL 76: 527).
144. Gregory, *Reg. past.*, 2, chap. 1 (PL 77: 26–27; *ST* II-II, q. 182, a. 1).
145. Gregory, *Moralia* 6, 37 (PL 75: 764; *ST* II-II, q. 182, a. 2).
146. Gregory, *Moralia* 6, 37 (PL 75: 746; *ST* II-II, q. 182, a. 3).

At the end of question 182, Thomas refers the reader again to Gregory and points out that the two ways of life must help each other.[147] The central texts of Gregory on the active and the contemplative life return in other works of Aquinas, sometimes even more than once, as is the case with the beautiful text of the second homily of the commentary on Ezekiel, quoted in this note.[148] In his homilies Gregory also used the story of Martha and Mary of the gospel according to Luke. Mary who listens to the words of the Lord symbolizes the contemplative life, Martha who busies herself with household tasks, the active.[149] Just like Jacob after having embraced Lia came to love Rachel, those who seek to reach perfection first do things which are useful, but surrender themselves later to the rest of the contemplative life.[150]

The Religious Life

In questions 183–85 of the second part of the *Summa theologiae*, Thomas studies the different stages of our spiritual life, and distinguishes, as Gregory does,[151] between beginners, those who made progress, and those who reached perfection, but he seems to doubt the possibility of becoming perfect in this life.[152] Thomas presents a subtle variation of this answer in his analysis based on Matthew 5:48: it is possible, even in an active life, to reach the perfection of love which excludes every desire which might prohibit our mind from turning entirely to God. Is the state of life of the religious more perfect than that of bishops? Gregory seems to say so in one of his texts, but Thomas writes that the one who gives the perfection of the life of grace to others is more perfect than the person who is trying to reach it in religious life.[153] Actually, in two other texts quoted by Thomas, Gregory seems to accept this solution.

Is seeking to become a bishop allowed, or refusing it when it is of-

---

147. Gregory, *Moralia* 6, 37 (PL 75: 764).
148. Gregory, *Moralia* 6, 37 (PL 76: 753): "Contemplativa vita est caritatem Dei et proximi tota vita retinere, ab exteriori actione quiescere, soli desiderio creatoris inhaerere ... sed calcatis curis omnibus ad videndam faciem Creatoris exardescit." We find this text in *Quodl.* VII, q. 7, a. 2; *Contra doctrinam retrahentium*, 2, chap. 4; *Contra impugnantes*, 2, chap. 1, etc.
149. *Catena in Lucam*, 10, 28.
150. Gregory, *Moralia* 6, 61 (PL 75: 764).
151. Gregory, *Moralia* 1, 24, 11 (PL 76: 302); *ST* II-II, q. 183, a. 4).
152. Gregory, *Hom. in Ezech.*, 2, 2 (PL 76: 954).
153. Gregory, *Reg. past.*, 1, 7 (PL 77: 20; *ST* II-II, q. 184, a. 7).

fered? Gregory thinks that it is praiseworthy to aspire to the episcopate, if in doing so one seeks more difficulties and greater pains. Thomas makes a distinction between what one wants oneself and what one wants to do because others ask us to do it. The desire to be useful to one's neighbor is praiseworthy.[154] When one is asked to become a bishop, one must not persist in one's refusal when one's superiors exert pressure on one. Gregory refers to the example of Isaiah who in his desire to help his contemporaries, sought the mission of a preacher.[155] Life in a religious order may be called a state of perfection in so far as the religious devote themselves totally to the service of God.[156]

Thomas quotes several texts of Gregory about giving up one's belongings and about obedience. If one gives all one has and one's entire life to the eternal God, one can really speak of a holocaust.[157] On the question whether the religious are allowed to teach and to preach, Gregory hesitates. He writes that one cannot engage a monk for an ecclesiastical function, while he must at the same time observe the obligations of his religious life. Nevertheless he allows monks engaged in the apostolate to preach and to baptize.[158] Are there different forms of religious life? Pope Gregory did not yet make this distinction,[159] but Thomas explains that there are different ways of devoting oneself to a life of charity. Gregory himself also writes that no sacrifice is more agreeable to God than zeal for the salvation of souls.[160] In summary we can say that the teachings of Pope Gregory on the religious life do not go into details but are inspired by a profound devotion.

Striking Formulae

In Aquinas's works we find a good number of striking formulae of Gregory which occur sometimes two or three times. Certain of these formulae may have been taken from collections of texts which masters and students of theology had at their disposal. These sentences distinguish themselves

---

154. Gregory, *Reg. past.*, 1, 8 (PL 77: 21; *ST* II-II, q. 185, a. 1).
155. Gregory, *Reg. past.*, 1, 7; *ST* II-II, q. 180, a. 2.
156. Gregory, *Hom. in Ezech.*, 2, 8 (PL 76: 1037; *ST* II-II, q. 186, a. 1).
157. Gregory, *Hom. in Ezech.*, 2, 8.
158. Gregory, *Reg. past*, 1, 5, 13 (PL 77: 722).
159. Gregory, *Hom. in Ezech.* 2, 18 (PL 76: 1037).
160. Gregory, *Hom. in Ezech.* 1, 12 (PL 76: 1037).

by their concision and expressiveness. In the following, a number of these formulae are quoted which Thomas seems to have appreciated:

- What do the saints in heaven ignore, who see the One who sees everything? ("*Quid est quod non videant ubi videntem omnia vident*").[161]
- Faith has no merits when human reason provides direct knowledge ("*Fides non habet meritum cui humana ratio praebet experimentum*").[162]
- We begin on the earth with the contemplative life in order that it become perfect in the heavenly fatherland ("*Contemplativa vita hic incipitur, ut in caelesti patria perficiatur*").[163]
- In the succeeding periods of history and with the progress of time, our knowledge of God has grown ("*Per successiones et incrementa temporis crevit divinae cognitionis augmentum*").[164]
- A sin which is not expiated by penance soon leads by its weight to another sin ("*Peccatum quod per paenitentiam non deletur, mox suo pondere ad aliud trahit*").[165]
- The contemplative life is to love God and one's neighbor ("*Vita contemplativa est Deum et proximum diligere*").[166]
- If the other virtues do not proceed with prudence in what they seek to attain, they cannot be virtues ("*Nisi virtutes reliquae ea quae appetumt prudenter agunt, virtutes esse nequaquam possunt*").[167]
- No one becomes suddenly the greatest, but living an honest life, he begins with small things in order to arrive at great things (*Nemo repente fit summus, sed in bona conversatione a minimis quis inchoat, ut ad magna perveniat*).[168]
- If our first parents had not been corrupted by the depravation of sin, they would not beget children for hell ("*Si parentem primum nulla putredo peccati corrumperet, nequanquam ex se filios gehennae generaret*").[169]
- The proof of love is that one shows what one has done ("*Probatio ergo dilectionis exhibitio est operis*").[170]

---

161. Gregory, *Dialogues* 4, 33 (PL 77: 376).
162. Gregory, *Hom. in Evang.* 26 (PL 76: 1197).
163. Gregory, *Hom. in Ezech.*, 1, 2, 2 (PL 76: 956).
164. Gregory, *Hom. in Ezech.* 2, 4 (PL 67: 89).
165. Gregory, *Hom. in Ezech.*, 1, 11 (PL 76: 915).
166. Gregory, *Hom. in Ezech.* 2, 2 (PL 76: 915).
167. Gregory, *Moralia* 2, 46 (PL 75: 588).
168. Gregory, *Hom. in Ezech.* 2, 3 (PL 76: 929).
169. Gregory, *Moralia* 4, 31 (PL 75: 671).
170. Gregory, *Hom. in Evang.* 30, 1 (PL 76: 1220). This text is quoted about ten times by Thomas.

- Our love of God is never idle. If it is there, it accomplishes great things. If it stops being active, it is not love ("*Numquaam est Dei amor otiosus. Operatur enim magna, si est; si vero operari renuit, amor non est*").[171]
- No sacrifice is more agreeable to God than zeal for the souls ("*Nullum sacrificium est Deo magis acceptum quam zelus animarum*").[172]
- The fire of love kindled here on earth, will burn more strongly when we see the One we love ("*Amoris ignis qui hic ardere inchoat, cum ipsum quem amat viderit, in amore ipsius amplius ardescit*").[173]
- If the same spiritual attitude is not present in the heart of the one who listens, the master teaches in vain ("*Nisi idem spiritus cordi adsit audientis, otiosus est sermo doctoris*").[174]
- (Man) has being in common with stones, life with trees, sense knowledge with animals, thought with angels ("*Esse cum lapidibus, vivere com arboribus, sentire cum animalibus, intelligere cum angelis*").[175]
- Sins of the flesh are less serious, but bring more shame ("*Peccata carnalia sunt minoris culpae et maioris infamiae*").[176]
- Those who imprudently look around themselves, often become victims of sins and a prey of desires which at first they did not want ("*Quisquis incaute exterius respicit plerumque in delectatione peccati cadit atque obligatus desideriis incipit velle quod noluit*").[177]
- One gets oneself the more away from the supreme love, the lower the pleasures are in which one finds one's delight ("*Tanto autem quisque a supremo amore disiungitur quanto inferius delectatur*").[178]
- One who in times of peace (for the Church) does not give his coat because of God, how is he going to give his life during a persecution? ("*Qui vero tranquilitatis tempore non dat pro Deo tunicam suam, qualiter in persecutione daturus est animam suam?*").[179]

---

171. This sentence is cited by Thomas in the introduction to his treatise *De duobus praeceptis charitatis*.
172. Gregory, *Hom. in Ezech.* 2, 12 (PL 76: 932).
173. Gregory, *Hom. in Ezech.* 2, 9 (PL 76: 1049).
174. *Catena in Ioan.*, chap. 14, lesson 7.
175. Gregory, *Moralia* 8, 48 (PL 75: 855).
176. Gregory, *Moralia* 33, 12 (PL 76: 688).
177. *Catena in Matth.*, chap. 5, l, 16.
178. *Catena in Ioan.* 14, lesson 7.
179. *Catena in Ioan.* 15, lesson 4.

- Who made the world by himself, governs it also by himself (*"Mundum quippe per seipsum regit qui per seipsum condidit"*).[180]
- The harassment of our life by perverse people is in fact an approval of it (*"Perversorum derogatio vitae nostrae approbatio est"*).[181]
- If people despise the life of a preacher, his preaching will also be scorned (*"Cuius vita despicitur, necesse est ut eius praedicatio contemnatur"*).[182]
- The strength of one's love multiplies one's zeal in seeking (*"Vis amoris studium multiplicat inquisitionis"*).[183]
- A preacher works in vain with his words outside himself, if the power of the Redeemer is not at work in his interior (*"Frustra laborat extra lingua praedicatoris, si intus non operatur virtus redemptoris"*).[184]
- We see by faith, we find strength by hope, and are united by love (*"Videt quidem per fidem, erigitur per spem, unitur per charitatem"*).[185]
- The evils which afflict us here on the earth, force us to turn to God (*"Mala quae nos his premunt ad Deum ire compellunt"*).[186]
- There are three degrees in a temptation: suggestion, pleasure, consent (*"Triplex tentationis gradus, per suggestionem, delectationem et consensum"*).[187]
- If we keep the passion of Christ in mind, nothing is so difficult that it cannot be supported with patience (*"Si passio Christi ad memoriam revocatur, nihil adeo durum est, quod non aequanimiter toleratur"*).[188]
- Words or acts without basis (Mt 12:26) have no good reason and are without usefulness for a neighbor (*"Quod caret iusta necessitate et pia utilitate, otiosum reputatur"*).[189]
- To be forgiven too easily is an incentive for sinning again (*"Facilitas veniae incentivum praebet delinquendi"*).[190]

---

180. Gregory, *Moralia* 24, 20 (PL 76: 876).
181. Gregory, *Hom. in Ezech.*, I, 9 (PL 76: 876).
182. *Breve principium*, chap. 2.
183. *In Psalm.* 26, 3.
184. *In Psalm* 37, 2.
185. *In Psalm* 44, 7.
186. *In Psalm* 55, 5.
187. *Super evang. Matth.*, chap. 4, lesson 1.
188. *Super Hebr.*, chap. 12, lesson 1. No source is indicated.
189. Gregory, *Reg. past.* 3, chap. 14 (PL 77: 74; QD *de malo*, q. 2, a. 5).
190. *In IV Sent.*, d. 6, q. 3, a. 1. The text is from St. Ambrose.

Conclusion

Gregory the Great is often quoted in the difficulties put forward at the beginning of the articles in the *Summa theologiae* or of the *Quaestiones disputatae*. This seems to show that in Thomas's time the writings of Gregory were quite present in the study of theology and in the academic disputes, if not in their integrity, at least in collections of important texts. What surprises in the pope's writings is the facility with which he finds applications of biblical texts in the field of morals, his inventiveness of allegories, his interest in contemplative life, but also a certain pessimism with regard to human nature. Several times he complains that a number of Christians not only do not conduct themselves well, but also criticize the good others do,[191] or even persecute the faithful.[192] Job complains about those who address reproaches to him. Gregory applies it to the Christians who make things hard for those in the Church who are useful to many others.[193] He warns prelates: they must know that they deserve as many deaths as they have given bad examples to the faithful entrusted to them.[194]

---

191. Gregory, *Hom.* 11, 2.
192. Cf. Thomas, *Super evang. Ioan.*, chap. 15, lesson 5.
193. Gregory, *Moralia* 13, 2 (PL 75: 1018).
194. According to Thomas, *Super Hebr.*, chap. 13, lesson 3.

11 ❧ THE PLATONISM OF PSEUDO-DIONYSIUS

In his *La philosophie au Moyen-Âge*, Étienne Gilson introduces the chapter on Dionysius as follows: one of the most important sources of medieval thought are the writings of an author who calls himself Dionysius the Areopagite. The name is a reference to Acts 17:22 ff. where Luke describes Paul's speech before the council of the Areopagus in Athens. Some believed what Paul said, and among them, Dionysius the Areopagite. His writings, at least those which reached us, are *The Celestial Hierarchy*, *The Ecclesiastical Hierarchy*, *On the Divine Names*, *The Mystical Theology*, and some ten letters. These works appeared for the first time in Byzantium in 533. They arrived in the West in the ninth century as a gift of the emperor Michael the Stutterer to Louis the Pious. The French king gave the manuscripts to Hilduinus, the abbot of Saint-Denis, near Paris. Hilduinus had them translated into Latin, a translation revised by John Scotus Eriugena. John Sarracenus revised the texts in turn, and it is this translation which Thomas used in his exposition on the *De divinis nominibus*.

While in the Middle Ages the legend that Dionysius, the author of these writings, was a disciple of Paul was generally accepted, serious problems arose when, later, certain passages appeared to have been borrowed from authors of the fifth century and correspondences were found with the theology of Greek authors of the fourth century and the declarations of the Council of Chalcedon (451). Very striking are several sentences borrowed from the *De malorum subsistentia* of the Neoplatonist author Proclus,[1] who died in 485. But as did his contemporaries, Thomas accepts the dating of the *De divinis nominibus* to the first century.

Thomas came to know this book when he was a student and assistant of Albert the Great at Cologne, where he transcribed the text of Albert

---

1. Cf. Josef Stiglmayr, "Der Neuplatoniker Proklos als Vorlage des sog. Dionysius Areopagita in der Lehre vom Übel," *Historisches Jahrbuch* 16 (1895): 253–73, 717–48.

on the treatise. During his stay in Italy between 1259 and 1268, he himself wrote a commentary titled *In librum beati Dionysii De divinis nominibus expositio*, when he resided in Orvieto and/or in Rome. He was well aware of the Platonic character of this text and of its obscure style. Thomas suggests that the author wanted perhaps to withdraw the dogmas of the faith from the mockeries of the pagans, who ridiculed the conference of Paul before the Areopagus. Dionysius uses the way of writing of the Platonists which in the time of Thomas was less used in the schools.[2] In his *Scriptum super libros Sententiarum*, book II, d. 14, q. 1, a. 2, Thomas writes that Dionysius follows Aristotle in almost all questions, but later in the *Disputed Questions on Evil*, question 16, article 1, ad 3, he corrects this, saying that in the greater part of his works Dionysius accepts the doctrines of Platonism.[3]

This places us before the question of why Thomas wrote his commentary. As we shall see when examining his text, Thomas reformulates, corrects, and completes the text, in order to place it in the framework of his own philosophy of being. Undoubtedly he wanted to put it at the disposition of his students and to show its treasures, but in a form which agrees with the terminology and the principles drawn from reality, and which excludes a reduction of the faith to the categories of Platonism. The works of Dionysius have exercised a profound influence on medieval theology and spirituality: they offer a brilliant view of a creation, bathing in light, order, and beauty. According to certain historians Dionysius would even have given some color to the dry and impersonal Aristotelianism of Thomas, but this view is perhaps not quite correct.

In a first book, *The Foundations of Theology*, the text of which has not reached us, Dionysius explains that God goes beyond all we can think and all our concepts. Hence we must speak about God in a negative way: God is not wise, God is not good, etc. God is entirely incomprehensible. This is called the recourse to negative theology, characteristic of the doctrine of the *De divinis nominibus*. God is the super-divine divinity (*hyperdea divinitas*); he is above substance, that is, *supersubstantialis*.[4] However,

---

2. See the *proem* to his *In De divinis nominibus*.
3. For an overview of Christian Platonism, Pseudo-Dionysius, and the reaction against this Platonism, see I. P. Sheldon-Williams, "The Greek Platonist Tradition from the Cappadocians to Maximus and Eriugena," in *The Cambridge History of Later Greek and Early Medieval Philosophy*, ed. A. H. Armstrong (Cambridge: Cambridge University Press, 1970), 425–537.
4. Pseudo-Dionysius, *De div. nom.*, II, chap. 42; Pseudo-Dionysius, *De mystica theologia*, I, 2; Pseudo-Dionysius, *De div. nom.*, V, 4. On negative theology, see Leo Elders, *The Philosophical Theology of St. Thomas Aquinas* (Leiden: Brill, 1990), 141–43.

in order to help us. Holy Scripture applies certain names to God, such as one, almighty, good, etc., and goes to the point of saying that he is our friend. But whatever we say of God, remains far below of what he is in reality—transcendent being.

God in the Theology of Dionysius

In his *De divinis nominibus* Dionysius describes a middle road with regard to our knowledge of God: God presents himself as the Good—we think here of Plato's *Republic*—which is as a shining sun radiating on the different classes of beings and so divides its light over the world. Dionysius represents this causality of the first principle as a stream of light which descends from its origin and passes through successive different degrees of being, descending from the nobler beings to the lower ones. The degree of ontological value of a being depends on the place it holds in this hierarchy. The causal influence of God passes through intermediaries and shows the characteristics of a cascade which grows larger as we descend in this hierarchy. Dionysius is not very explicit with regard to the important question if the procession of creatures results from the divine essence, as is the case with the hypostases in Neoplatonism, or is the effect of a free decision by God.

Dionysius uses the image of illumination, but the causal stream which flows from God is also an ontological emanation. The world becomes a theophany which lets us know its author. The emanation provokes a movement of love in creatures, which makes them go beyond themselves and aspire to God. This love of what is superior to us is an ecstatic love.

Dionysius coined the term "thearchy" (θεαρχία) to signify God who is at the same time the supreme principle above everything and the foundation (ὑπόστασις) of beings. He calls God also the One, a name which Proclus gave to his first principle. God is separate from all things and remains in himself (V, 284); he is without substance (οὐσία; IV, 11), or, better expressed, he is an ὑπερούσιος οὐσία). According to Christian theology God is independent of his creatures and exists in a Trinity of Divine Persons. For Dionysius God is being: his other properties are like participations in his divine being, but he considers the One, still better the super-one,[5] as the best name we can give to God, because the One exists without multi-

---

5. Pseudo-Dionysius, *De div. nom.*, chap. 2, 11; chap. 13.

plicity.[6] Thomas corrects this view and writes that being (*esse*) is the first qualification of God and encompasses all God's perfections.

Dionysius acknowledges that God is above everything, but influenced as he is by Neoplatonism pays little attention to the question whether God is a person, whereas in his commentary Thomas stresses the personal nature of God. God is not a neutral source of being and light, but acts through his intellect and will (*per intellectum et voluntatem*). Thomas also underlines God's independence from the creation (lesson 14). The radiance of light and being which Dionysius ascribes to God, is not a necessary process, as the radiation of the sun. In this way Thomas transforms the God-thearchy of the *De divinis nominibus* into the doctrine of the personal God of the Bible in the manner in which he elaborated his own natural theology.

In his theology, influenced as it was by Neoplatonism, Dionysius expresses himself sometimes in terms which suggest that God is the supersubstantial being of all things[7] and the being of all that exists (*Ipse est esse existentium*). Thierry of Chartres and other theologians also used expressions which, when understood literally, are pantheistic. Thomas lets us see what is involved in this way of speaking: God would no longer be transcendent, and would be caught in becoming. In Thomas's third lesson of the first chapter, Dionysius affirms that God knows everything, including that which is inferior to him. Thomas explains that God's science is a causal knowledge (no. 77). When Dionysius says that God is the substance of all things, Thomas corrects this, saying that he is the principle of the existence of things (*principium subsistendi*) (nos. 100–101).

In the second and third lessons of Chapter 2, where Dionysius mentions the Divine Persons, Thomas renders the text more precise and reformulates it in order to give it a clear and theologically acceptable sense. He points out that the distinction between the Divine Persons is made according to the processions (no. 157). All through the passage on the production of the creatures, Thomas transposes what Dionysius writes in a sober and very clear language. In another example of this re-formulating of sentences, Dionysius's words that Christ has really become a substance intend to say that he is a Divine Person (hypostasis) which has a human nature.[8]

---

6. For the Neoplatonists multiplicity is a factor of division and therefore a cause of imperfection.

7. Pseudo-Dionysius, *De div. nom.*, V, 4.

8. *In De divinis nominibus*, chap. 2, lesson 5, no. 207.

The Divine Names

In the third chapter of his book Dionysius begins to study the theme of the names of God. He examines them in so far as they manifest the procession of creatures from God. Since God is the Good, he is also a cause, because the good communicates itself. It is perfect, and so God wants to make things which resemble him (no. 227). Thomas mentions in passing that the Platonists did not make a distinction between matter and privation: "matter was for them a not-being" and causality did not extend to it, except the causality of the Good, inasmuch as matter aspires to the good (no. 226)

Chapter IV is the central part of the book, where Dionysius begins his exposition of the divine names. Thomas comments on this chapter in twenty-three lessons, and proposes first a division of the following parts of the book according to this scheme: in Chapters IV to VIII Dionysius shows that all things proceed from divine goodness (chap. 4), both as regards their being (chap. 5) and regarding life (chap. 6), and likewise also in respect of intellectual life (*sapientia*) (chap. 7) and the virtues (*iustitia*) (chap. 8). He explains next how everything proceeds from God by comparing things one to another, according to their equality or their diversity (chap. 9); he mentions the external relations between things (chap. 10) and the resulting peace (chap. 11). Finally he explains how all things are ordered to the end (chap. 12) and at the end considers this end to which all things are directed (chap. 13).

The Good is present on the different levels of the creation: among the angels, in man, and in perishable beings. In the first lesson of chapter IV, Thomas, starting from a few words of the text, draws a sketch of the angels which Dionysius calls intelligible and *intellectualia*, a distinction of the Platonists: the *intellectualia* are the superior angels, the intelligible ones the angels of lower rank. With regard to the causality of the sun, which illustrates how things proceed from the good, Dionysius writes that the sun does not reason and does not choose, words which he does not repeat when he speaks of divine causality, since when God acts, he does so with his intellect and his will (no. 271). In the second lesson Thomas comments on Dionysius's text about the creation of the beings which are deprived of reason. He speaks about matter in the way the Platonists do. It is true that the Platonists distinguish forms and matter, but confuse matter with privation and call it a not-being (no. 295), although he stated that matter desires the form (no. 296) but is responsible for the absence of a form. But he also writes that God does not have a form because of the excess of his substance (no. 297).

In the third lesson of Chapter IV, Thomas recalls the beautiful description of the activity of the sun, which is the source of sensible light and an image of the universal causality of God. In his next lesson Thomas refers to Dionysius's words about the intelligible light of which God is the source, which, says Thomas, is nothing else but the knowledge of the truth. He adds a few lines on the effect of spiritual darkness: the ignorance of the truth, errors, and bad habits which render the soul indolent so that it no longer knows what its true destination is. They shut people up in themselves, so that their heart is no longer open to the good. In the fifth lesson of Chapter IV, Thomas comments on Dionysius's doctrine of God's beauty. In this connection Thomas first recalls what constitutes beauty: harmony and clarity. God is the cause of all harmony, since according to the doctrine of the Platonists, the higher beings are present in those of a lower level because of the latter's participation, and the beings of lower levels are in the higher ones because of the excellence of the latter. This is the well-known maxim of Proclus: all things are in all. Thomas adds that every form is a participation in the clarity of the divine being. Beauty adds to the good a relation to our cognitive faculties. In the next lesson, the sixth, Thomas comments on the causality of the beautiful. According to Dionysius the different parts of the universe are caused by beauty. Thomas agrees in so far as the form of things proceeds from the radiance of clarity, which is the cause of their beauty. The order of things and their ordination to the end constitute harmony which is the other element of beauty. In this way even movement and rest can be seen as marked by beauty.

The Activities of the Intelligences and Love

In his seventh lesson Thomas examines Dionysius's theory of "motions," that is, of the activities of the immaterial beings. As an introduction he mentions first the different movements of the material beings, in respect of quantity, qualities, and place; then, at a different level, there are the operations of the sense faculties, the intellect, and the will. Dionysius describes the operation of the intellect in the terms of a circular motion, but

Thomas corrects this way of seeing it: the circular movement of the human soul differs from that of the angels. An angel receives his intellectual knowledge from God and returns to the contemplation of God. This is different for man who receives the contents of his thought from the things around him, which are different. At best one can speak of a circular movement when man leaves the consideration of the outside things to turn to the study of the angels and to ascend at last to God himself (no. 375).

In lesson eight of this fourth chapter, Dionysius explains that the goodness and beauty of God are not only the causes which set things in movement, but they also keep things in being and are the final causes in view of which all things move and act. All that exists and that becomes in whatever way, exists and becomes because of the good and the beautiful as its exemplary causes, and is moved by them as the causes of its movements and, finally, exists and acts for their sake.

Love is the theme of the ninth lesson. Since the good and beauty are the end of all things, they are loved and desired. Thus love is a central force in things. To help us understand better what Dionysius writes about love, Thomas explains first in the next two pages what love and what its object are: love is the relation (*habitudo*) and adaptation (*coaptatio*) of the appetite to a thing as to its good. In a certain sense the person who loves has the object of his love present in him and as united with him (no. 401). There are as many forms of love as the different things can be goods for us: for instance, our personal good; all which is related to it as, for instance, the love of our parents; or the love of what is a part of this good, as for instance the hand of our body; there is also the love with which a part loves the whole (no. 406).

In lesson ten Dionysius speaks of ecstasy. Thomas gives a beautiful explanation: when one turns to something, not in order to have it but concentrating on what the thing is in itself, he leaves himself behind to lose himself, so to say, in what he loves. We must love God in such a way that there is nothing left in us which is not ordered to God. But Dionysius goes beyond this and ascribes this ecstatic love also to God, who leaves himself behind, puts down in a sense his greatness (*deponitur quodammodo a sua excellentia*). Thomas corrects this way of saying: God does not leave himself behind, but in his goodness he occupies himself (*ingerit*) with his creatures (no. 437) without abandoning anything of his being (no. 437). The term *deponitur* used by Dionysius must not be understood as if God lays down part of himself.

In lesson eleven some questions connected with the theme of love are treated. How is God himself love? He is the cause of the love which he bestows and provokes (*inmittit et generat*). By his entire being and essentially he is loveable; he is his love. As for the effects of love Thomas notes that love moves us to action: it directs what we do for the sake of the beloved, and it shows itself by certain signs. As properties of love one may mention the union of the lover and the beloved; love makes one tends toward the beloved; love is a simple act, whereas, for example, a passion such as anger is not. Love is the first act of the appetite and is itself active.

In the section of Chapter IV examined by Thomas in his twelfth lesson, Dionysius gives some excerpts of what Hierotheus had written to him about love.[9] He probably is speaking of some short passages of a commentary on The Song of Songs. The contents agree with what Dionysius had written in the first part of the chapter. Thomas gives a summary: Hierotheus distinguishes five forms of love, which range from God's love to the natural appetite. What is common to all these forms is their unifying power and the correspondence between the one who loves and the beloved, at least in a certain way. Thomas explains what these forms of love have in common, and how one may reduce them to God's love (no. 460).

In lesson 13 certain questions with regard to evil are mentioned: if the Good is the source of all things, where does evil come from? Is not the Good the source of everything? Thomas distinguishes four questions with respect to the devils: how must we explain that the devils do not desire the good and the beautiful? Thomas answers that they have lost the uniformity of desire characteristic of the angels. Another question is how to explain the great number of demons. Have they all been made by the Good, that is, by God? A following question is how a thing which was good by its nature, deteriorated. What has rendered the devils evil?

The Metaphysics of Evil. The Demons

At this point of the text of Chapter Four Dionysius raises four questions about evil in general: What is evil? From which principle does it proceed? In which being is it found? How can a thing abandon the desire of the

9. In the course of the treatise the name of Hierotheus is mentioned repeatedly by Dionysius as his beloved master. In the *Hierarchia Ecclesiastica* he appears under the name of Hierarcha. The name is symbolic as the person himself may be. Others, however, speak of a school of St. Basil, St. Gregory, etc. in which Hierotheus would have been a master.

good and seek what is evil? The answer to these questions is given in the following pages. As we have already pointed out, in the writings of Dionysius there are a number of passages which he borrowed from Proclus; in particular, the questions on evil follow Proclus's *On the Subsistence of Evils*.

In lesson 14 Thomas comments on the text and summarizes its contents in an admirable way. When Dionysius writes that the Good is not the cause of evil, Thomas says that it is not the cause *per se*, but a cause *per accidens*, while he adds that this correction is not against the thought of Dionysius (no. 476). Evil has no essence and exists in a subject which as such is good, but which misses something. Dionysius speaks about evil as if it were a thing. But evil is not a thing, and, on the other hand, also not entirely non-existing (no. 480).

After showing that evil does not have an essence, he now shows that it is not a cause and also is not the product of a cause. Dionysius then asks from where it comes (lesson 15). Evil is real and can contribute to the good—we see this in the corruption of a thing, which can be the way toward the generation of something, and in this way contribute to the perfection of the universe. When Dionysius writes that we must not think that something less good is the opposite of a greater good, Thomas notes that according to Aristotle something less warm can be the contrary of what is warmer (no. 488). What Dionysius writes corresponds with the doctrine of Proclus.

In the following section of his treatise[10] Dionysius affirms that evil as such does not corrupt. It is only *per accidens* that it can exercise a certain activity, owing to the good connected with it and which is its subject (lesson 16, no. 495). When Dionysius writes that things participate in the good according to their capacity, Thomas observes that the reason for the diversity of the goods which they receive depends either on natural causes or on a cause which operates by its will. In this last case the end sought by the cause is the determining factor (no. 502). As Dionysius observes there are great differences between things: some beings are without life, others which are alive, are deprived of reason, he goes to the point of saying that God himself is without essence (substance, οὐσία). Thomas says that God is above all substances. At any rate every form of evil inheres in a subject, and pure evil does not exist (no. 509).

But here again the question of the origin of evil presses (lesson 17).

10. PG 3: 717 B ff.

Evil cannot be caused by what is good and is also not produced at the same time as a good effect is. We must not say, either, that both the good and evil come forth from the same principle. The First Principle does not have any contraries in itself. There is no evil in God nor in a supposed second principle opposed to God. God is good by his essence, does not separate himself from the good. The conclusion imposes itself: evil is not a being (no. 519).

In the following part of his exposition Dionysius reaffirms that there is no evil, neither in God nor in the angels. Thomas adds, in the *good* angels (lesson 18). The angels are like an image or a mirror of God (no. 524). Nothing in the angels is opposed to the clarity of their intellectual nature. Thomas says that the angels do not receive God's beauty in its totality, but possess a likeness of it. According to Dionysius the angels *make* a reflection of the divine form, Thomas notes that "make" should not be understood in an active, but in a disposing sense (no. 526).

The demons are not evil by their nature but because of a defect in the good they have, namely, in their will (lesson 19). The good of the immaterial beings consists in their obeying the will of God. When they turn away from it, they are going bad. Thomas concludes his clarifying exposition of the text of Dionysius by saying that the fallen angels wanted what was above their state (no. 537). Dionysius does not say that the demons have a corporeal nature, although he mentions this opinion. They are not evil, unless in the sense that some good is missing in them. They wanted a certain good without observing the due order (no. 540).

How is evil present in souls? It is not in them as something positive, but as a defect, a privation. Passions which are bad in human beings, are not bad in animals (lesson 20). With regard to the evil found in natural things (lesson 21), Dionysius writes that in a universal nature there cannot be any evil: all processes depend on the universal nature of things and cannot counteract it. The evil in nature appears when a thing cannot reach what belongs to its nature (no. 552). Thomas reminds his readers that for Dionysius matter as such is not evil (nos. 559–68).

Is evil caused by what is good or derived from it, or is it produced by a different cause (lesson 22)? There is no evil first principle which would be the cause of all evils. These rather result from a multiplicity of different causes. Why does divine providence permit that there is evil if the evil is not sought nor willed by God (lesson 23). Dionysius answers that an evil from which one suffers or which one commits turns later into an advantage for him or becomes useful for others and society (no. 595). It is not the intention of divine providence, which wants to preserve things according to their nature, to impede creatures endowed with a free will from exercising this freedom of choice (no. 596). In his commentary Thomas shows that to sin by desire or in one's thought is a weakness: one does not see which is our real good, or one does not have the will to accomplish it (no. 602), Nevertheless God's help is not lacking, and those who do not accomplish it are responsible (no. 604). What Dionysius writes in Chapter IV is rendered much more precise and clear in the commentary Thomas gives of it.

The Models of the Beings and Divine Causality

After this long fourth chapter in which Dionysius discusses the good, light, beauty, love, ecstasy, and evil, the fifth chapter examines a philosophical question, the exemplarity of the models according to which the beings of our world have been made. In this chapter Dionysius wants to treat the divine names in so far as they explain how God's providence attributes the various perfections to things (lesson 1). Thomas reinterprets what Dionysius writes (no. 611). Some Platonists introduced numerous intermediary entities between the First Principle and our world, but Dionysius rejects these: there are no other first principles: being, life, wisdom are nothing else but God (no. 613).

The angels are closer to the Good than other beings who have less intelligence. They participate more in the One himself, who is, Thomas adds, God himself (no. 617). The Platonists, Dionysius writes, placed the "existent" above the first created intellect. In order to go beyond this opinion, which reminds one of the Neoplatonist doctrine of the hypostases, Dionysius writes that God is the cause of the first "existent" and of the mind (νοῦς). Thomas presents the arguments of Dionysius very clearly. Obscure sayings are reproduced by him in an intelligible way, in the general framework of the philosophy of being (no. 625). When God is said to be the being of existing things (*esse existentibus*), Thomas comments that this is an expression of the Platonists. It does not mean that God is the formal being of existing things, but we must understand these words in a causal meaning (no. 630). Somewhat further on Thomas writes again that the Platonists, whom Dionysius often follows (*utatur*) in this book, accepted Ideas of man, of living beings, etc., saying that these Ideas differ from each other and from the First Principle. Dionysius was in partial agreement with this theory, but he placed the Ideas in God (no. 634). Whatever exists is a being, and God who made all things is the main Being (no. 636).

In the second lesson of his commentary on Chapter V, Thomas explains that God is the cause of individual things in so far as they exist in their own nature, Thomas reminds us that God is not contained in the concept of common being. This depends on God and is in God as contained in him. In the third lesson, the question of the models of things (*exemplaria*—παραδείγματα) is discussed. According to Plato the forms as models are causes which determine the things with their properties in our world, but Thomas adds, that God is also the cause of what is proper to each thing and contains in himself the model of all that can be made. Thomas concedes that one can speak of the beings above us as models for us, not in the sense that they would be the end which we would aspire to, but that when considering them we tend to God (no. 668). God is the cause of everything because he contains everything in himself in the unity of his being (no. 672).

In Chapter VI of the *De divinis nominibus*, Dionysius examines God's universal causality with regard to life and to what is proper to the life of the angels. Having treated of being he now considers the procession of life. Life is less common than being. He gives first a definition: all things which have movement as originating in themselves are living beings. The divine life is the supreme cause of all forms of life. God gives to life as such,[11] that it is life, and does that also for each particular form of life. So he gives life to the angels and to the demons. The life of these immaterial beings is the supreme form of life (no. 683). In the second lesson human life and inferior forms of life are discussed. In a certain way man's life is similar to that of the angels, but considered from another point of view, it is different. Dionysius mentions next, but very briefly, the glorification of human life in the resurrection, as a superior form of life. God is the cause of all forms of life (no. 692).

---

11. Dionysius speaks of "life as such," "*ipsius per se vitae.*" Thomas translates "id est vitae communis" (no. 680).

Wisdom, Truth and Faith. Justice and Liberation

After considering the different forms of life and God as their source, Dionysius now studies wisdom, the mind, reason, truth, and faith. Thomas comments on this Chapter VII in five lessons. A general principle put forward by Thomas says that things on a lower level and which come later are always found in those things which are earlier than them (no. 697). Now at the level of causality (final causality is meant here), the good is earlier than being, for it extends its causality even to not-being. On the other hand, being extends to more things than life, and life to more things than wisdom. In the concept of life the presence of goodness is presupposed. Compared to divine wisdom our human wisdom seems deficient. God's wisdom is above everything. The world of God is above and beyond us, and we must leave ourselves to come to know God and to love him.

In the second lesson of Thomas's commentary, we read that God's wisdom is the cause of all forms of wisdom and that in it we find all the treasures of knowledge and science. What we know is derived from God's wisdom (no. 715). Dionysius speaks of a circle in the process of knowledge: thanks to the properties of the things which surround their essence, we come to know their essence; one perceives several properties and ends by grasping their unity in this essence (no. 713). Thomas summarizes as follows: "*In processu rationis ab uno incipiens, per multa procedens ad unum terminatur*" (In the operations of reason one starts from one thing, one proceeds coming to know several, to end at only one).

How does God know things in his wisdom? (third lesson). In his commentary Thomas renders clear what Dionysius writes with regard to God's wisdom. God would not be able to know everything if things were not present in him as in their cause. By knowing himself God knows everything (no. 723). The extent to which we know God is the theme of the fourth lesson. The difficulty is that we do not know the divine essence which transcends everything. At this point the three ways in which we know God are introduced:[12] the way of negation; the way of excess, which concludes that God is above everything we can say of him; and the way of affirmation, which ascribes attributes to God such as wisdom, simplicity, and good. Thomas seems to agree with Dionysius over the whole

---

12. These three ways have been elaborated in Middle Platonism.

line of the section, and concludes with the following words: to know God consists in that we know that we do not know what he is (no. 731).

In the last part of Chapter VII, Dionysius explains what comes with divine wisdom, that is, reason, truth, and faith. God is called *ratio* (reason or λόγος), because of his cognitive power, and also since he is a cause and contains all things in himself and possesses the explanation of everything.[13] God's reason is as the simple truth of all that exists and by faith the faithful are in the truth. Through the gift of faith God places all of us in the truth and helps us to remain in it. The faithful have a simple knowledge of the truth, free from doubts and without concerns. For this reason Paul speaks of *substance* when he defines faith (no. 737). The comments of Thomas elucidate the text of Dionysius.

The title of Chapter VIII surprises: on strength (*virtus*), justice, salvation, liberation, and also on inequality. In the first lesson we read that God is the source of all power and that all that creatures can do is due to God. God's power transcends all that we can conceive, and in him everything preexists. His power does not become weaker when he acts. Next Dionysius passes to the theme of the infinity of the divine power. We do not attribute infinity to God in the sense of a limitless extent or magnitude, but by way of a negation: God's power has no limits, since it is not restricted to one effect only, and it is above all other powers; it is not bound by the number of creatures which God has already made, and, if God would make more creatures, his power would not become less. His power is beyond what our intellect can conceive (no. 750). At the end of his commentary, Thomas stresses that every being has some power. When Dionysius notes that being itself has a power which makes it exist, Thomas comments: one cannot say in the strict sense of the word that being exists, but that through being something exists (no. 751).

In the second lesson of this chapter, the central question is how God's power is communicated to the different beings. First comes the transmission to the angels. Their being is unchangeable, and their intellectual activity never stops, nor is their desire for the infinite good ever satiated. God's power is at work in all things bestowing on them union with God in friendship, as well as a certain communion with Him. Dionysius mentions next the effects of divine power on the different groups; it preserves the angels from all corruption; God's power keeps in being also

---

13. In this context Thomas mentions the meaning of *ratio*, namely, "the explanation of all things" (no. 735).

the celestial bodies and the order of their movements; he determines the different periods of time by the revolution of the celestial beings. Thomas points out that the circular trajectory which they follow, lets them return to their point of departure; God gives an almost irrepressible force to the elements such as fire and the tides. We also see this power of God at work in living beings, such as plants. At last Dionysius mentions the divine power in the field of grace: its effect is the deification of man, that is to say, his participation in the divine life. Everything in the universe is kept together by the power of God. Whatever possesses nothing of this force does not belong to the universe.

Why are certain things excluded from the divine power (lesson 3)? The answer is that God cannot deny himself and so cannot not be true, existing, or powerful, so much so that contradictions do not fall within his power. Lesson four studies divine justice, the only moral virtue which can be attributed to God in the strict sense of the term. It is proper to God in its three functions: divine justice maintains the diversity between the creatures without there being any confusion between them; the third act of divine justice is that it lets everything do the work which is fitting to it (nos. 775–77). Certain critical authors say that God should take away from people the possibility to sin (no. 780), but God deals with all things according to their nature (no. 781). What to think of suffering and the death of the just? If they desire spiritual goods, they will be content that finally they can obtain them. The afflictions in our earthly life make us turn to spiritual things. Thomas gives here a good commentary which clarifies and completes the arguments of Dionysius. If people fight for justice, God does not let them alone, but helps them, gives them strength, and does not weaken them by too much prosperity (no. 783).

In lesson five, Thomas comments upon what Dionysius writes of the effects of divine justice—salvation, redemption, and inequality, that is, the differences between things and their divergent destinations. We must notice, however, that the exposition of Dionysius on salvation is closer to a treatise of philosophical theology than to a study of what God has revealed. Essential to salvation is that things are preserved in what is proper to them. What comes first is the conservation of things in the good, something which is done in different ways: God does not allow feeble beings to be put to the test above their strength. He allows that certain beings are hurt and tempted, but gives them the power to resist. The reproach has been addressed to Dionysius that he interprets man's supernatural salvation in ontological terms and forgets what Paul says about the justification of man through faith. But in his *De divinis nominibus*, Dionysius does not speak about justification by the faith. This subject is treated in the *De ecclesiastica hierarchia*, Thomas was very much of aware of it, because in this lesson, at the beginning of his commentary, he writes that the salvation of which Dionysius speaks consists in the fact that God preserves things in being and in the order in which he placed them and also gives them in their own operations (no. 786). We should also notice that the numerous intermediate powers which the Neoplatonists placed between the supreme principle and man are not mentioned by Dionysius.

How Holy Scripture Speaks of God. The Divine Attributes

Chapter IX deals with the attributes and contrary properties adjudged to God in the Bible, such as great and small, different and similar, resting and in movement. What does the Bible mean when it calls God great (lesson 1)? Can we ascribe to God sameness and otherness? (lesson 2). Thomas explains that being the same is attributed to God because of his immutability. He does not change in his being. He notes that Dionysius successively excludes from God local motion, alteration, increase, and diminution. His text is formulated in the climate of Platonism, but Thomas explains its contents in terms of the philosophy of being and the principle of act and potency. According to Dionysius the word "other" is also said of God: all things participate in God and are in Him in the variety of their different beings. There is not a single perfection in things which is not in one way or another a resemblance to God (no. 823). The theme of the third lesson is how to use the terms "similar" and "dissimilar." The lesson 4, the last of the chapter, examines in which way the immobile God is said to move. Thomas gives an impressive explanation of the way in which the Bible or authors of spiritual theology speak of different movements of God.

What is the meaning of the term "omnipotent," and what do names like the Eternal and the Ancient (of Days) mean when said of God (Dan 7:9)? With surprising ease Thomas explains the meaning of these attributes. To give an example, in Chapter X Dionysius writes:

The Hierarchy is almighty, because it exercises its power over all things and does not share its authority with those over which it governs; and all things tend toward it with a movement of loving desire. It also is so since it imposes yokes on all things—with their consent—and it lets grow in all hearts the amiable sweetness of a divine desire, almighty and indissoluble, the object of which is its proper beauty.

Thomas explains this poetical text in terms of the natural love of the good which things have. From this love of the end is born the desire of what is adjusted to it and becoming. Since our last end is God's goodness, all other particular ends to which things move by their particular nature, are subordinated to it. All things love God necessarily in the goods which they strive to attain. One may speak of this natural order to the good as natural laws (*naturales leges*) and a kind of giving birth (*partus*) to agreeable (*dulces*) effects, by which one comes to love the divine goodness. Dionysius speaks of divine love as something which keeps all things together. It is indefectible since it is necessary (no. 858).

In the second lesson Thomas comments on the text of the vision of Daniel (Dan 7:9), in which God is described as the Ancient of Days, by explaining God's relation with time: a person may be called ancient because of old age—God contains all periods of time (*praehabet omnium durationem*), and he is before all of them. God is old, but always young. Ancient can also mean distinguished and principal. In the last section of the chapter, Dionysius speaks of a perpetual duration (*aevum*) and of time (lesson 3). Thomas explains the different senses of the word *aevum*: what is common to them is that it does not change, that it is ancient and is experienced in its totality, whereas time has its parts. The duration of the existence of the angels must, however, be distinguished from the divine eternity (no. 875).

Peace

Peace is the theme of Chapter XI. Dionysius says about the peace that "it is that which unites all things and which produces the consent of all and their cohesion." Thomas gives the following commentary on this text. Because the word "peace" is often used by men, its meaning becomes clear when we consider the relations between them. Men are at peace when they agree on the common good which they must realize. Therefore, the notion of peace implies that things are united, have the same views and attitude in respect of a particular end or question. From this point of view one may also speak of the peace which reigns among natural things. The words of Dionysius's text get a meaning in the comments of Thomas, who adds the following thought: even if certain persons or things are in disagreement with regard to their own ends, they nevertheless agree in their desire of the last end (no. 885). The sentence "their divisible multitude is reduced to unity" signifies that the peace of God is the final cause of all things and is desired by what is natural in all things. By division a thing becomes defective (no. 886).

The greatness and the causality of the divine peace, surpass everything. In God there is no diversity at all, while our participation in divine peace is imperfect (lesson 2). How can one say that all things desire peace (lesson 3)? This is a central question in Neoplatonism: why does the principle of unity not impose itself more, and why are there so many conflicts? Many things rather seem to enjoy their otherness. Thomas explains that nothing is totally deprived of the search for unity, because all things seek what is fitting to them and so do not escape from this common trend. Those things which seek otherness do not do so according to their natural appetite (no. 932). Thomas adds that there were no real proofs of the existence (of the different) Ideas, but that the Platonists of the first generation and those who came after them were led into error by mistaken considerations (no. 933).

The Government of the World. The Unity of All Things

In Chapter XII Dionysius examines the names which signify the government of the world by God: divine providence, God's wisdom in governing the world, its achievement, and its effects. Thomas adds a beautiful commentary on the name "King of kings" and on the term "domination."

The theme of Chapter XIII, the last chapter of the treatise, is the Perfect and the One. Dionysius wants to show the end to which divine providence leads us by pointing out that all things are reduced to unity. What is found divided and in succession in creatures is united in God. Whatever we can say of God is summarized in the terms "perfect" and "one." Created things do not have their perfections from themselves but from

God. God's perfection is limitless, and his power extends to all things.

From the consideration of divine perfection, Dionysius passes to that of God's unity. The entire creation is in fact united in God, who conserves his unity. Unity is, indeed, the cause of all. Things participate in God by being unified in a same "form," namely, the universe. Thomas notes that the Platonists place God—the supreme being—above being, life, and intellect, but not above the Good. Dionysius, however, says that even the word "good" is not adequate, but that we nevertheless use it to designate the ineffable greatness of God (no. 994). At the end of this section he returns to the way of negation and stresses the inadequacy of all we say about God and excuses himself for the defects of his exposition.

The Celestial and the Ecclesiastical Hierarchies

Thomas did not write a commentary on the *De Coelesti Hierarchia* of Dionysius, but used this treatise to establish the order which reigns among the angels and their hierarchy. Holy Scripture and the liturgy of the Church tell us that there is an immense number of these immaterial beings. But an immense number without any order does not conform to the requirements of reason. In the *Summa theologiae* I, question 108, Thomas is guided by chapter VI of this treatise of Dionysius. His point of departure is the fact that human beings acquire their knowledge from the sensible things which they perceive by their senses. The angels, however, receive their knowledge from God. We may distinguish three degrees in this process: the superior angels have a more universal knowledge than those of a lower level. We can say this because the thought of wise men is more complete and universal than that of those who live from very numerous, always changing impressions.

The intelligible contents of things (Thomas speaks of *rationes rerum*) can be considered in three ways: (a) In so far as they proceed immediately from God. This is why the first hierarchy of the angels is so to say suspended from God and sticking to Him. They live, as Dionysius writes, in the vestibule of God. (b) Other angels receive this knowledge in dependence on created universal causes. This is the second hierarchy. (c) The angels of the third hierarchy consider these intelligible contents in so far as they are applied to individual beings. This division, however, is rather that from Thomas himself than from Dionysius. In the following articles of question 108, Thomas distinguishes different orders within each of these three hierarchies.

With regard to the *Ecclesiastic Hierarchy* Thomas quotes this interesting text on a few occasions in his *Scriptum super libros Sententiarum*. In *Summa theologiae* I, question 1, article 10, he refers to a sentence of Dionysius saying that the New Law (of the gospel) is the prefiguration of the future glory. In *Summa theologiae* I, question 108, article 2, argument 3, a phrase from the *Ecclesiastic Hierarchy*, chapter 5, is quoted: "The order of deacons purifies, that of the priests instructs, and that of the bishops gives perfection." In his *Contra impugnantes* 2, chapter 3, ad 28, Thomas insists on the right of the mendicants to exercise ministries and to teach, quoting Dionysius: whoever is of inferior rank can also exercise these functions. Inspired by texts of Dionysius and Gregory the Great, Thomas elaborated his doctrine of the classes of the angels, in which he tries to put the different orders of angels, mentioned in the Bible and in the liturgy, in systematic order.

In the *Ecclesiastic Hierarchy* we also find the following sentence: "negations with regard to God are true, but affirmations incongruous," a phrase often quoted by the Scholastics.[14] Dionysius does not say that it is impossible to formulate affirmative sentences about God—God is the cause of all things and Holy Scripture uses these affirmations—but on a higher level of knowledge we must deny what we have affirmed about God, since God is above everything.[15] In his commentary on this text, Thomas analyzes what an affirmative proposition is about: a being which in reality is one ("this man is white") can be distinguished by our reason as having components. The composition which we state in our judgement expresses the identity of two different forms in a subject. Our intellect grasps the simple forms in the manner of composite things, in which there is a subject to which a predicate is attached. But it knows that God is not composed and for this reason the attribution of a predicate to God in an affirmative proposition can be true.[16] Dionysius, says Thomas,

---

14. Pseudo-Dionysius, *De Coelesti Hierarchia* 2, 3 (PG 3: 141 A): "Negationes de divinis vero incompactae." "Incompactae" is the translation by John Scotus Eriugena of the Greek term ἀναρμόστος.

15. Pseudo-Dionysius, *De mystica theologia* 1, 2 (PG 3: 1000 B). Cf. Henri-Charles Puech, "La ténèbre mystique chez le Pseudo-Denys l'Aréopagite et dans la tradition patristique," *Études carmélitaines* 23, no. 2 (1938): 33–53.

16. *ST* I, q. 13, a. 12.

wants to say that no name can be said of God in the mode of signification it has in God, because the being of God transcends our thought. In the disputed questions on power, question 7, article 5, ad 2, Thomas explains that affirmations can be made about God with regard to the thing signified, but that they must be denied for their mode of signifying. The realities affirmed of Him, belong to Him in a more sublime way.[17]

Thomas concludes his exposition of the *De divinis nominibus* of Dionysius with the words that his explications remain much below the profound reflections of Dionysius and that the reader may correct or complete what he would have less well explained.

---

17. On the negative theology, cf. Leo Elders, *La théologie philosophique de saint Thomas d'Aquin* (Paris: Téqui, 1995), 225–29.

12 ∽ THE METAPHYSICS OF THE LIBER DE CAUSIS

Since the Second World War several studies have been devoted to the rather short treatise called *Liber de causis*, which until the time of Thomas was attributed to Aristotle. The work occupied an important place in the academic studies at the Faculty of Arts in Paris. The student of the *De causis* has now at his disposition the well-documented edition of the text by Father Pera together with the text of Thomas's commentary and the semi-critical edition of the *De causis* by H. D. Saffrey.[1] Vansteenkiste published the Latin translation by Van Moerbeke of the *Elementatio* of Proclus, an important source of the *De causis*.[2] There are also editions of some medieval commentaries, for instance, one attributed to Siger of Brabant. Several studies on the Arabic text of the *De causis*, as well as on other pseudo-Aristotelian treatises, have also been published. But the precise attitude of Thomas with regard to the treatise has been much less studied. This explains why we find ourselves before conflicting judgments. Otto Bardenhewer thinks that the treatise would have exercised a decisive influence on Thomas,[3] while Karl Prantl writes that Thomas corrupted Aristotelianism by the mysticism of the *De causis*.[4] More recently Christina D'Ancona Costa has given an Italian translation with important and valuable notes.[5]

This chapter was originally published as "Saint Thomas d'Aquin et la métaphysique du Liber de causis," *Revue Thomiste* 89 (1989): 427–42.

1. Thomas Aquinas, *In Librum de causis expositio: Cura et studio Ceslai Pera*, ed. Ceslas Pera (Taurini: Marietti, 1955). We indicate the paragraph numbers of the text of Fr. Pera to facilitate consultation. See also *Sancti Thomae de Aquino super Librum de causis Expositio*, ed. Henri-Dominique Saffrey (Fribourg: Société Philosophique, 1954).

2. "Procli elementatio theologica translata a Guilelmo de Moerbeke (Textus ineditus)," *Tijdschrift voor Philosophie* 13 (1951): 263–302, and 491–531. See also the very useful study of Clemens Vansteenkiste, "Il Liber de Causis negli scritti di San Tommaso," *Angelicum* 35 (1958): 325–74.

3. Bardenhewer, *Die pseudo-aristotelische Schrift über das reine Gute*.

4. Karl Prantl, *Geschichte der Logik im Abendlande*, vol. 3 (Leipzig: Verlag von S. Hirzel, 1870), 114.

5. Thomas Aquinas, *Commento al Libro delle Cause*, ed. Christina D'Ancona Costa (Milan: Rusconi, 1986).

By the middle of the thirteenth century, the *De causis* was considered an important work on metaphysics which by its theses and explications on the First Cause and immaterial beings was a very welcome completion of the twelfth book of Aristotle's *Metaphysics*. Several titles were used to designate this book, such as *De intelligentiis*, *De esse*, and *De essentia purae bonitatis*, but the name *Liber de causis* prevailed. About 1160 the book was translated from the Arabic by Gerard of Cremona. This translation has possibly been revised by Gundisalvi. Albert the Great writes that a learned Spanish Jew, Abraham Ibn Daud (Avendauth), a collaborator of Gundisalvi, was its author. A. Pattin accepted this attribution,[6] but it is perhaps more likely that Avendauth was connected with the book for another reason. He may have brought the text with him when he established himself in Toledo.

Certain characteristics of the Arabic vocabulary of the work suggest that it belongs to a group of translations from Greek originals completed in Bagdad about 850. Thus far, however, no explanation has been found why four great Arab philosophers, Al Kindi, Al Farabi, Avicenna, and Averroes do not mention the *De causis*.[7] But an Arab author of the tenth century, Abu Hasan Muhammad Ibn Yusuf al-Amiri seems to know the work.

The treatise was welcomed in the Latin West as a supplement to the theology of Aristotle. The same role may have been assigned to it in Bagdad in the ninth century. As soon as it became known in the West, it inspired attempts to introduce a new method in theology.[8]

Widespread study of the work was nevertheless slowed by the interdiction of the use of certain books of Aristotle. After 1230 this interdiction was no longer applied and so the *De causis* came to be used more widely. A *Guide for Students* written between 1230 and 1240 mentions the *De causis* as one of the texts to be studied in metaphysics. The *Charta* of the University of Paris prescribed its reading This explains why the trea-

---

6. See Adriaan Pattin, "Over de schrijver en de vertaler van het *Liber de causis*," *Tijdschrift voor Filosofie* 23, no. 2 (1961): 323–33, and *Tijdschrift voor Filosofie* 23, no. 3 (1961): 503–36. See also the study published by Cristina D'Ancona Costa, *Recherches sur le Liber de Causis* (Paris: J. Vrin, 1995).

7. See Richard C. Taylor, "*The Kalam Fi Mahd Al-Khair (Liber de causis)* in the Islamic Philosophical Milieu," in *Pseudo-Aristotle in the Middle Ages: The Theology and Other Texts*, ed. Jill Kraye, W. F. Ryan, and Charles B. Schmitt (London: Warburg Institute, University of London, 1986), 37–46. Taylor refers to the study by Everett Rowson in *Encyclopedia of Islam*, 2nd ed., suppl. 1–2 (Leiden: Brill, 1980), 72–73.

8. See the *Maximae theologiae* or *Regula de sacra theologia* of Alain of Lille.

tise, ascribed to Aristotle, was widely diffused. Pattin lists one hundred codices with its Latin translation. R. C. Taylor even speaks of 237 manuscripts containing this text.[9] Great theologians of the first half of the thirteenth century refer to it: William of Auxerre, Philip the Chancellor, William of Auvergne, Alexander of Hales, Roland of Cremona, and Adam de Bocfeld wrote commentaries; Roger Bacon, Henry of Ghent, and Siger of Brabant each composed a series of questions on the treatise.[10] R. C. Taylor mentions more than twenty texts by medieval authors on the *De causis*. Albert the Great published a study under the title *De causis et processu universitatis*.[11]

In his different works Thomas quotes or refers to the *De causis* some 230 times.[12] These quotations are frequent in the earlier works, such as the *Scriptum super Libros Sententiarum*, but very few in the *Summa contra Gentiles*. Throughout his references to the *De causis*, Thomas draws attention to the Platonic character of this treatise and corrects some of its doctrines, such as, the theory that our cognitive faculty comes to the soul by the action of the separate intelligent beings.[13] Thomas also points to a correspondence of what *De causis* says with certain views of Dionysius.[14] In his investigation of the doctrinal roots of the treatise and his rejection of what is irreconcilable with the Christian faith, Thomas is much more precise than his contemporaries.

The Commentary of Aquinas on the *Liber De causis*

Thomas wrote his commentary toward the end of his second stay in Paris, that is to say, after William of Moerbeke had finished his Latin translation of the *Elementatio* of Proclus and after Book XII of the *Metaphysics*

---

9. Richard C. Taylor, "The Liber de causis: A Preliminary List of Extant MSS," *Bulletin de philosophie médiévale* 25 (1983): 63–84.

10. See Saffrey, Introduction to *Sancti Thomae de Aquino super Librum de causis Expositio*, xviii.

11. The second part of this work, composed between 1260 and 1268, contains a paraphrase and a doctrinal exegesis of the *De causis*.

12. See Vansteenkiste, "Il Liber de Causis negli scritti di San Tommaso."

13. *In II Sent.*, d. 18, q. 2, a. 2, ad 5.

14. Cf. D'Ancona Costa, *Recherches sur le Liber de Causis*, 78. The author speaks of a substantial sympathy with the fundamental theories of the treatise. Cf. D'Ancona Costa, "Saint Thomas, lecteur du Liber de causis," *Revue thomiste* 92, no. 4 (1992): 785–817.

had begun to be called Book *Lambda* (Λ).[15] To determine more precisely the date of composition of the *Expositio* of Thomas, it has been suggested that Thomas had to finish his commentary on the twelve last propositions of the *De causis* in haste because of his imminent departure for Naples (Easter 1272). This would be the reason why this part of his commentary is more concise.

The *Expositio* is characterized by very precise explanations of the text, a comparison of its different theses with the respective propositions of Proclus, and frequent notes on Platonism. It also draws attention to correspondences with theories of Dionysius, and, finally, it sheds light on the text itself of the *De causis*. If we ask why Thomas wrote his commentary, there are the following reasons:

- in order to carry out the task he undertook of adapting philosophical texts for their use at the university and to provide the necessary tools for a thorough study of the philosophy of being;
- to retrieve from the *De causis* whatever was true and to render more complete the *Metaphysics* of Aristotle. Aquinas mentions this purpose himself in his preface which connects the *De causis* with the *Corpus aristotelicum*. He notes that the highest happiness, accessible to man in this life, comes to him through the study of the *optimum intelligible*;
- to draw attention to certain errors which an inconsiderate use of the treatise helped to diffuse;
- a final reason may have been the challenge of determining the place of a somewhat mysterious text which was ordinarily attributed to Aristotle.

The central thesis of the commentary of Thomas is that whatever doctrine is proposed in the *De causis*, it is found more elaborated in the *Elementatio* of Proclus. In this work, which was very important for Neoplatonists, and was given second rank by them immediately after the *Enneads* of Plotinus, Proclus tries to establish the fundamental laws which govern all beings: all things proceed from the One in a process of serial causality. The central problem is that of explaining the plurality of beings. According to Proclus the universe is organized in such a way that the effects are always less perfect than their causes. In his system these causes are formal causes. The effects have a resemblance with their caus-

---

15. After the introduction of Book K as Book XI in 1270.

es, in which they participate. They are really continuous with them, although less perfect and therefore different.

Proclus tries to give a comprehensive scheme of all of reality which he conceives as a pyramid of beings. In the process of emanation, the unity of the supreme Principle is split. The beings at a lower level are characterized by multiplicity and mobility. Nevertheless the particular effect preserves a dynamic relation with its cause; it remains within its cause and returns to it. In this way there is a cyclical process. What is universal is prior and more active; being is prior to life, which in its turn is prior to the intellect.

As a Platonist Proclus affirms the existence of subsistent forms. In this way the attributes and even relations become subsistent entities. Another characteristic of Proclus's system is its monism: the divine is diffused in the universe; there is no creation in the proper sense of the term. In the works of Proclus one encounters more or less veiled attacks on Christianity.[16] Some Christian authors did not let the opportunity pass to criticize Proclus. In the twelfth century Bishop Nicholas of Methone criticized the *Elementatio* for certain theories which according to him were irreconcilable with revealed truth.[17]

The philosophy of Proclus is the result of 250 years' reflection by the Neoplatonists. According to Dodds, to whom we owe the masterly edition of the Greek text of the *Elementatio*, the work of Proclus is characterized by two tendencies: (a) the desire to elaborate a common Hellenistic philosophy and to marginalize the different sects; (b) a religious desire to construct a bridge between God and the soul and to create a scheme of redemption which could enter into competition with Christianity.[18]

The Main Theses of the Treatise

Returning to the commentary of Thomas we notice that he used a text with thirty-two propositions, whereas modern editions have thirty-one.[19]

16. See Henri-Dominique Saffrey, "Allusions antichrétiennes chez Proclus: le diadoque platonicien," *Revue des Sciences Philosophiques et Théologiques* 59, no. 4 (1975): 553–63.

17. See Athanasios Angelou, *Nicholas of Methone: Refutation of Proclus' Elements of Theology: A Critical Edition with an Introduction on Nicholas' Life and Works* (Leiden: Brill, 1984).

18. See Proclus, *The Elements of Theology*, trans. E. R. Dodds, 2nd ed. (Oxford: Clarendon Press, 1963).

19. In most manuscripts propositions 4 and 5, as Thomas mentions them, are a single proposition.

Thomas proposes the following division of the text: the first proposition is the basis of the entire text. It deals with the causality of the First Principle. Propositions 2 to 15 concern the question of the distinction between the primary causes—that is, God, the intelligences, the souls (2 to 5)—and explain what is proper of each of these causes (6 to 15). Propositions 16 to 32 examine the relations between these beings: they show that beings at a lower level are dependent on what is on a higher level and receive, in different ways, a causal influence from the higher levels. The fundamental axiom of this system is that every first cause exercises a greater causal influence on its effects than the secondary universal cause (prop. 1) At first sight Proclus seems to agree with a metaphysics of creation, but Thomas notes that the text is speaking of formal causality and not of efficient causality. He nevertheless thinks that Proclus's axiom may be transposed to the order of generation and corruption, and even suggests that this is perhaps what the author wants to say.[20]

When he examines the axiom which affirms that the First Cause has a greater causal influence than the second, Thomas refers to the *Elementatio* of Proclus. Proclus, Thomas says, explains this point better (*expressius*).[21] The axiom concerns primarily efficient causes and is valid for causes per se. But this interpretation seems to go beyond the text of this impenitent Platonist which Proclus was. The axiom *Causa prima plus influit in effectum quam causa secunda* is mentioned several times in Thomas's works, but does not carry precisely the same meaning as it does for Proclus, who sees in it a law of formal causality.

In the second lesson we have another example of the way in which Aquinas comments on the *De causis*. Examining the second proposition "The higher beings are either before eternity or after eternity, but they are above time," he refers in his commentary to proposition 88 of the *Elementatio* and notes that Proclus formulated this thesis in line with the assumptions of the Platonists, who affirm, in fact, that the more universal and abstract a being is, the greater is its priority. Now being (*esse*) is more abstract and universal than eternity. So it is prior. Where the author of the *De causis* speaks of *esse* alone, Thomas, who does not admit abstract subsistent forms, adds the adjective *separatum*, apparently in order to identify it with divine being which is subsistent per se. God's be-

---

20. Number 20 of the edition of Pera. We must nevertheless add after "*corruptionis*" the words "alicuius individui. Et hoc est eius intentio."

21. *In De causis*, no. 24.

ing is prior to the eternal being of the intelligent beings. Finally Thomas observes that the author of the *De causis* is closer to the positions of Plato and Aristotle than to the doctrine of Proclus, since he connects "that which is with eternity" with the intelligent beings. In accordance with this change, the author associates "that which is after eternity" with the order of real things and not with abstractions as Proclus did.

In this second proposition the author starts from the hypothesis that the celestial bodies have souls. Thomas notes that Dionysius agrees in general with the text, but that he does not admit the presence of souls in the celestial bodies, a refusal which has a foundation in the Christian faith.[22] A sentence of this text is repeatedly quoted by Thomas: "*Anima est in confinio aeternitatis et temporis.*"

The third proposition introduces the *anima nobilis*, that is, the highest soul which exercises its causality through the entire cosmos. It participates in the knowledge of the divine intellect which is above it. According to this text this soul has a threefold operation, namely, it exercises a general causality (under the direction of the First Cause) with regard to the world; it has an intellectual activity, which it receives from the intellect which belongs to a higher order; in the third place, it has an operation by which it moves the world. The *De causis* corrects thesis 201 of Proclus, by adding that the First Cause creates the being of the soul, even if it does so through the mediation of the intelligent being. The author seems to affirm here that creation takes place with the help and by the mediation of secondary causes.[23]

On this topic Thomas first give a summary of the doctrine of Plato in general: the highest Idea, the One or the Good, does not participate in anything, while all things participate in it.[24] Dionysius has corrected this position by showing that such separate forms as Life, Wisdom, etc. must be identified with the First Cause.[25] Aquinas observes next that creation through intermediaries would not be in agreement with the very essence of Platonism, since according to Plato's doctrine the being of the soul depends on being itself.[26] Now what is valid for the being of the soul, applies also to its essence. We must reject the position of the author of the treatise that the separate intelligent beings confer on the soul its

22. Ibid., 1, 2, no. 62.
23. This is the opinion of Avicenna, as Thomas points out in the *De substantiis separatis*.
24. *In De causis*, lesson 3, no. 65 ff.
25. Ibid., no. 72 ff.
26. Ibid., no. 80.

intelligence. This position contradicts also the doctrine of Aristotle and the truth, since it introduces a multiplicity of forms in the essence of the soul. On the other hand, we can admit that the superior intelligent beings illuminate those of a lower order. In his works Thomas does not use this third proposition, except for the affirmation that the being of things is produced by the First Cause. The commentary informs us also about the position of Thomas with regard to the movers of the celestial bodies. That the latter would be ensouled is rejected as false and contrary to the facts. For argument's sake he mentions the theory as a hypothesis ("*si tamen sint animata*"). This theory of the animation of the celestial bodies is also rejected elsewhere, as in *In II Sent.*, question 8, article 1, and in *In III De anima*, lesson 17, no. 855. In this last text the following argument is put forward: the celestial bodies are immutable; that excludes sensitive knowledge. An ensoulment would therefore be useless. Yet, excluding the presence of a soul does not mean that the celestial bodies cannot be moved by an intellect. Since they contribute to the genesis of life, as well as to the formation of the human bodies, they must be directed by an intellect.[27] One may add that the motion of the celestial bodies does not tend to rest. This means that it does not result from their nature but is caused by an external agent.[28]

The Doctrine of Being of the *De causis*

The fourth proposition states a well-known principle: *Prima rerum creatarum est esse*. In his different works Thomas quotes the maxim repeatedly in order to stress the fundamental place of being in creatures. In his commentary he explains first how the author understands it. For the author of the *De causis* and for the Platonists being is not the primary Good itself. Proclus had in effect divided the second hypostasis of Plotinus into being, life, and intelligence. According to Dodds he was influenced in formulating this tripartition by the following two reasons: (a) the awareness that the real is logically prior to thought; and (b) the conviction that all the intelligibles have a triadic structure. Being comes after the One and presents a certain duality, namely, of the limited and the unlimited. It is noticeable that Proclus does not use the binome matter-form, but that of

27. *SCG* III, 23.
28. Ibid.; *In II Sent.*, d. 14, q. 1, a. 3.

the opposites *substance-potency*. Substance represents the limited, potency the unlimited. A thing is itself, but has at the same time the possibility to become something different.

Returning to the *De causis*, we notice that the author does not make being a subsistent form. For him, however, being does not mean the *esse* of all existing things, a sense it has in the works of Dionysius. In the *De causis* being means the participated being of the things of the first grade of the hierarchy of created things. Their being is above all, is before all other things, and has greater extension; it is more intimately unified. Being is multiplied and is given to the things of the first order in the universe, since it is composed of the limited and the unlimited.

The Intelligences and Their Causality

For the Platonists it is embarrassing to explain how a simple form can be multiplied.[29] The answer to this problem is that the individually or specifically different subject participates in being and that in this way there is multiplication. At this point Thomas goes so far as to attribute to the *De causis* the real distinction between the act of being and the essence. It would be implied in the distinction the author makes between the finite and the infinite.[30] Continuing his commentary Thomas explains how the nature (essences) of the intelligent beings can differ one from another. This difference cannot be a material difference as we find it in the individuals which belong to the same species. In the case of the separated substances, it is a formal distinction: one nature is, by what it, is more perfect (or less perfect) than another. This doctrine, however, is not found explicitly in the *De causis*, but is added by Thomas, who returns to the text of the fourth proposition, when he notes that the more perfect intelligent beings are closer to the One.[31]

According to the *De causis* the intelligent beings are distinguished from each other in so far as the higher ones know by means of more universal species. At first sight this remark seems wrong, since that which is known (the *res intellecta*) is the same for the different intellects. On the basis of this principle, Averroes argued that since the *res intellecta* is the

29. *In De causis*, lesson 4, no. 105.
30. Ibid., no. 106.
31. Ibid., nos. 114–16.

same, there is only one intellect.³² The difficulty is resolved by a distinction: even if it is true that the things known by the different intellects are the same, the intelligible species are adapted to the more or less perfect nature of the intellect in which they are. In this way they are at the origin of a more or less universal knowledge of the known thing.³³

In the last lines of this proposition, the author affirms that the intelligent beings of a higher order influence those at a lower level. Thomas adds the principle which explains this: everywhere in nature we see that a being in act acts on what is in potency. Thus the superior angels illuminate those which are subordinated to them.³⁴ The commentary on this fourth proposition is very remarkable, since it is not only a detailed analysis of the text, but a further development and clarification of it, while Thomas appears to agree fundamentally with the theories expressed.

The fifth proposition of the *De causis* mentions the causality of the intelligent beings in respect of the souls and the differences between them. According to the text the soul is placed (literally: imprinted) in the body by an intelligent being. Thomas notes that this is not exact.³⁵ At best one can admit that these intelligent beings exercise a certain preparatory influence on what is to become a human body. The souls of the animals possibly depend on the celestial bodies, but we must maintain that every human soul has an inviolable free will. An analogous correction is made with regard to the theory of the distinction between the spiritual souls, which is not caused by the celestial bodies, but depends on the adaptation of the souls to their respective bodies. Thomas recalls here a basic principle of hylomorphism.³⁶

The First Cause is above any possibility creatures would have of knowing its being. It can only be known in so far as the secondary causes, which receive their existence from it, represent it. Concerning this question, the *De causis* distinguishes between four levels of knowledge, a division which, in the final analysis, goes back to the passage on the Divided Line in Plato's *Republic*. Thomas comments on this sixth proposition noting that a thing can be known (a) through its cause in so far as it is in its effect; (b) through itself; (c) through the effects it produces.

An affirmation of the text ("the First Cause is not illuminated by oth-

32. Ibid., no. 127.
33. Ibid., no. 124.
34. Ibid., no. 129.
35. Ibid., lesson 5, no. 138.
36. Ibid., no. 147.

er causes") provides Thomas with the opportunity to treat the question of the illumination of the intellect and to develop a beautiful exposé of the metaphysics of light: all things are known by their being in act, which is as a light; to be in act is effected by the cause of this or that being. This is why things are known by their causes. The First Cause is pure actuality. It is the light which makes things be in act. Proclus himself, who totally agrees with this conclusion, writes that all things are incessantly illuminated by the divine light.[37]

Thomas proposes a new formulation of the four levels of knowledge according to the *De causis*: our language follows from the intellect, the intellect follows from reason, and reason follows from meditation (i.e., the knowledge of the internal senses), and this meditation follows the cognition of the external senses. According to Proclus, who on this point is followed by the author of the *De causis*, God does not know, and cannot know himself since he is above being. But Thomas writes that *secundum rei veritatem* God is the infinite being itself and is knowledge of himself. The created intellect has as its object the essences which participate in being. This criticism of a position of Proclus is at the same time a correction of the meaning Proclus gave to the principle that the first created reality is being (*primum creatum est esse*). For Thomas the word *esse* does not have exactly the same sense Proclus gave it, since it can also, in an analogous way, signify divine being.

In its seventh proposition the *De causis* undertakes to establish the nature of spiritual beings. The reasoning as based on the indivisibility of their operation is somewhat confused. Self-knowledge is also introduced here: spiritual beings know themselves, whereas a material being cannot reflect on itself. Thomas acknowledges the validity of this argument: what is merely material cannot have any knowledge of itself, since its different parts are outside of each other.[38] The theme of self-knowledge is mentioned again in proposition 15. In this text Thomas corrects the theory of Proclus who argued that the human soul knows itself.

The eighth proposition concerns the question how the intelligent beings know as well what is above them as the things at a lower level. The Neoplatonists accepted Aristotle's doctrine of the *nous* (νοῦς) which is itself the object of its thought,[39] but contrary to Aristotle they hesitated to

37. Proclus, *Elementatio*, prop. 143.
38. *In De causis*, lesson 6, nos. 168–170.
39. This refers to the doctrine that the Prime Mover contemplates himself (νόησις νοήσεως; *Metaphysics* XII, 1074b34).

exclude from this supreme *nous* the knowledge of what is below it or superior to it. Proclus explained the presence of this knowledge in the *nous* with the principle that "everything is in everything." Beings on a higher level produce or constitute what is lower to them by a formal causality, and so they know it. Thomas rejects this opinion which says that this causality would be the formal cause of knowledge. This is only the case in God. He adds the remark that the intellect knows things according to its own mode of being, but that it knows them nevertheless as they are in themselves.

The dependence of things on the First Goodness is examined in the ninth proposition, which is based on the corresponding thesis 9 of the *Elementatio*. Aquinas explains that the multiplication of a perfection in different beings must be reduced to unity.[40] Thomas then corrects the theory which holds that the intelligent beings would contain in themselves things situated at different levels of being. They do not contain them as things they produce, but as effects which they direct and govern.[41] The reason is that the being and the essence of all things are created by the First Cause. Things can nevertheless acquire additional perfections by the action of the intelligent beings.

According to the tenth proposition each intelligent being is full of forms. In his commentary Thomas first explains what is common to all intelligent beings, to consider next the differences which may occur in their knowledge. This knowledge can in fact be more or less universal. The intellect of the angels is indeed full of forms, as the *De causis* affirms, while at the beginning of his cognitive life man's intellect is like a *tabula rasa*. The knowledge of the intelligent beings of a superior level of the hierarchy of beings is indeed characterized by a broader universality, but this does not mean that the intelligent beings would only know what is universal.

Thomas's commentary on this proposition replaces the thesis which the author of the treatise defends by a coherent doctrine. In this same lesson there are four references to Dionysius. Thomas intends to give an acceptable meaning to the latter's epistemology.

The eleventh proposition has been formulated with the elements of two theses of Proclus. The *De causis* affirms that the intelligent beings produce eternal effects immediately, but that the beings in time do so through the mediation of other things. Certain commentators under-

---

40. Ibid., lesson 9, no. 213.
41. Ibid., nos. 220–22.

stood this sentence as if these intelligent beings know what is corruptible as if it were eternal. Averroes thought that it is impossible for an eternal agent to produce new effects, except in the case when time already exists. Thomas observes that this interpretation is against the faith: it means that God cannot make anything new.[42] Actually time is created simultaneously with the world. God can make things which exist in time. He can conceive immutable beings on the one hand and things subject to time on the other, while he himself does not change at all.

Self-knowledge

An axiom of Proclus affirms that "everything is in everything," but in different ways: In the intellect everything is present in an intelligible way, in living beings everything is there under the form of life, and in beings at large everything is present as being. The *De causis* seems to place being and life within the intelligent beings as two independent forms or even as two intelligent beings. Thomas says that the text of the passage is corrupt or that there is a misunderstanding.[43]

While proposition fourteen exposes the theory of the soul as placed between the intelligent beings on the one hand and sensible things on the other, the following thesis is a development of the doctrine of self-knowledge, already mentioned in the seventh proposition. Thomas refers to six theses of Proclus in order to give a systematic, coherent, doctrinal explanation in as many stages: self-knowledge presupposes immateriality; what returns to itself subsists in itself; returning to oneself at the level of knowledge is accompanied by a return at the level of substance; this conversion to oneself is total and engages the whole being; every soul that knows itself is incorporeal. Thomas adds a remark of his own: self-knowledge is not effected through the mediation of the essence of the soul, but with the help of the cognitive species (*species cognoscitivae*).

Propositions sixteen to twenty-four concern God, his government of the world, and his influence on secondary causes. Differently from what Proclus said, Thomas notes that the *De causis* does not say that power (*potentia*) is a subsistent entity. It places supreme power in the First Cause. The text says that the power of the created, intelligent beings is

42. Ibid., lesson 11, no. 264.
43. Ibid., lesson 12, no. 281.

infinite. Thomas understands this in a sense that the intelligent beings which exist at a less elevated level cannot fully know what is above them.

The eighteenth proposition formulates the principle that in each genus that which comes first is the cause by which is constituted all that is in this genus.[44] The following Proposition considers the order of things in the universe. We shall come back to it later when we must consider the Platonism of the *De causis*.

Propositions twenty to twenty-two examine the question how the higher causes, and in particular the First Cause, exert their influence on the regions of the universe close to its center. How can God create a great variety of effects without being implicated in what is inferior to him? The author answers that God acts through his being and not through a relation added to his being. Thomas seems to admit the doctrine of the *De causis* and that of Proclus on this point, despite its Neoplatonist character: God's causality is conceived as an emanation in a context of an overall monism. At this place Aquinas does not make any objection against this doctrine, but in his commentary on proposition twenty-four he declares that the real cause of the diversity of beings is not a certain differentiation by the recipients of the divine influence, but God himself.[45] The thesis of the *De causis* is quoted in the *Summa theologiae* I, question 3, article 8: "*Causa Prima regit omnes res praeterquam quod commisceatur.*"

The twenty-first proposition explains the self-sufficiency of God. Since God is one and united in the most absolute way, he has no parts on which he would depend: he is without composition. Thomas renders the argument more explicit and goes beyond the text of the *De causis* and that of Proclus by adding that whatever is composed, has a cause which unites its parts and keeps the thing in existence. He adds that different things do not combine to form a unity unless when they are brought together by a cause.[46]

The being of God is entirely complete. This is the central affirmation of proposition twenty-two. Thomas explains that in the world of beings, there are formal determinations on the one hand and the substances to which they belong on the other. Neither the former nor the latter are complete by themselves, whereas God is above all the modes of being of created things.

---

44. See lesson 18, no. 340.
45. Lesson 24, no. 399.
46. Lesson 21, no. 371.

According to proposition twenty-six, each substance which exists by itself is incorruptible. Thomas explains that existing by oneself can mean (a) the form by which something is; or (b) the agent by which it was made; things which are their own form never lose their being by themselves: they are incorruptible. But they have an efficient cause. Only God is entirely independent.[47]

The last propositions of the *De causis* concern the order of things. Aquinas points out that there must be something between the spiritual, incorruptible substances and the sensible and corruptible things. The celestial bodies are this interposed, mediating reality.[48] As regards the human soul, it is above time in its substance, but it is in time with regard to its operation.

Our summary of the text of the *De causis* and of the main themes of Thomas's commentary, and in particular of the corrections he introduced in the doctrinal orientation of the treatise, has shown that Thomas accepts several important positions, but that all through his commentary he corrects certain doctrinal orientations. In several places he completes the contents by elaborating what the text says. In this way the commentary of Thomas presents a coherent metaphysical doctrine. This doctrine, it is true, is inspired by positions of the *De causis* and the *Elementatio*, but nevertheless it is proper to Thomas. Attention has been drawn to the transposition of the maxim *"omnis causa primaria est plus influens."* According to Thomas this maxim does not apply primarily to formal causality, but to the other genera of causality, and in the first place to efficient causality. Thomas also stresses that the human soul receives its existence from God, although cosmic factors may have a certain influence on the material which is to serve in the formation of the human body.[49]

With regard to the problems of knowledge, the commentary on the sixth proposition states that the human intellect is only ordered to those things which have a quiddity (essence) which participates in being. Thomas accepts the doctrine of the treatise according to which the higher the intelligent beings are in the hierarchy of beings, the more their knowledge is universal. Yet their knowledge also extends to particular beings.

In a dense and quite long commentary, Thomas explains why creation at the beginning of time is possible,[50] how the intelligent beings

---
47. Lesson 26, no. 413.
48. Lesson 30, nos. 441–47.
49. Lesson 5.
50. Lesson 11.

know each other[51] and what is the basis of their self-knowledge.[52] With regard to the use of certain doctrines of the treatise by Thomas, the following list enumerates the propositions most frequently quoted in his different works:

On causality:

> *Causa prima plus influit in causatum et plus unitur quam causa secunda.*
> *Causa secunda semper agit in virtute causae primae. Effectus non procedit a causa secunda nisi per operationem causae primae.*
> *Virtus quanto magis est unita, tanto est fortior.*
> *Quanto aliqua causa est altior, tanto ad plures se extendit.*

On metaphysical questions:

> *Prima rerum creatarum est esse.*
> *Quanto aliquid est superius tanto est magis unitum.*
> *Omne quod recipitur in aliquo est in eo per modum recipientis.*
> *Bonum dicitur per informationem*

On God:

> *Deus est supra omne nomen quod nominatur.*
> *Causa prima superior est omni narratione*
> *Deus est ante aeternitatem.*
> *Deus regit omnia praeterquam commisceatur cum eis.*

On the intelligent beings (angels):

> *Intelligentia est substantia quae non dividitur.*
> *Omnis intelligentia est plena formis.*
> *Intelligentia scit quod est supra se et quod est sub se.*
> *Angeli superiores habent formas magis universales.*
> *Substantiae intellectuales redeunt ad essentiam suam reditione completa.*
> *Intellectus, quando scit essentiam suam, scit reliquas res.*
> *Intelligentia est haben formam et esse.*

On man:

> *Anima intellectiva est creata in confinio (horizonte) aeternitatis et temporis.*

---

51. Lesson 12.
52. Lesson 15.

On knowledge:

Cognoscens cognoscit secundum modum substantiae eius.
Omnis sciens qui scit essentiam suam est rediens ad essentiam suam reditione completa.

Thomas accepts the doctrine of the immateriality and the non-temporality of the separate substances. He identifies those intelligent beings with the angels, although on this point Albert the Great hesitated. As for the maxim *"Prima rerum creatarum est esse,"* we must keep in mind that he applies it not only to the being of the superior intelligence but to that of all things. A further observation is that the being of created things is not a subsistent form, but the actuality of the different things themselves.

This list of some axioms quoted repeatedly by Thomas seems to suggest that Thomas attached a great value to the *De causis*. On closer inspection, however, one hesitates to draw this conclusion, since while commenting on the text he expresses very frequently his reservations as to the doctrines and methods presented in this treatise.

What Thomas Has Criticized

An important thesis rejected by Thomas is that our human intellect is given to our soul by the higher intelligent beings. This error, which is characteristic of the *De causis*,[53] is not only contrary to the truth but also to the doctrine of Aristotle.[54] In certain of his works Aquinas also reproaches the author for teaching that human souls are created through the angels as intermediaries,[55] but in his commentary on the respective texts he writes that this interpretation is based on a misunderstanding because this opinion would contradict Plato's theory that all things participate in Being itself.[56]

Already in the first years of his teaching in Paris, Thomas was well aware of the Platonic character of the *De causis*.[57] On several occasions he stresses that it is wrong to consider the different perfections as subsistent forms: they exist in the unity of the divine being. If these perfec-

---

53. See *In II Sent.*, d. 18, q. 2, a. 2.
54. *In De causis*, lesson 3, no. 83.
55. See *QD de potentia*, q. 3, a. 4, ad 10; *De substantiis separatis*, chap. 10.
56. *In De causis*, lesson 3, no. 79.
57. See *In I Sent.* d. 8, q. 1, a. 3; d. 14, q. 2, a. 1.

tions were subsistent forms, they would coexist the one next to the other in the human soul, which would no longer be one being. The commentary on the second proposition draws attention to this: Proclus follows the assumptions of the Platonists, who admit the existence of universal forms, separate from the material world. He thinks that the more abstract and general a form is, the higher is its rank.[58] Thomas draws attention to the fact that the *De causis* does not follow Proclus over the whole line but comes close to the positions of Plato and Aristotle in so far as the treatise affirms that being is the first perfection of the intelligent beings and of the soul. Their degree of perfection depends on their relation with eternity and with time (and so also with movement).[59]

The commentary on the third proposition contains a detailed analysis of the theory of the Ideas and recalls the corrections made by Dionysius: all subsistent forms must be identified with the First Cause.[60] In his exposition of the fourth proposition Thomas continues his examination of the doctrine of Plato and explains why the Platonists place the One and the Good above being and consider them as more universal than being: the One and the Good are said of certain things, as for instance of matter, of which being is not predicated (for they say that matter is a non-being).[61]

All through his commentary Aquinas insists on the efficient causality of the First Cause and corrects in this way the drift of the Neoplatonist theory which considers only formal causality.[62] Thomas makes another correction of their theory of the knowledge of these intelligent beings: contrary to what the Platonists say, these intelligent beings do not receive their cognitive species by a participation in the Ideas, but by the causal influence of God.[63]

Where, according to Proclus, our human soul knows its own essence, Thomas notes that we must understand this in connection with his position which affirms that the intelligent beings of a lower level participate in the knowledge of those which are of a higher order. Thomas notes that the soul receives its cognitive faculty from its essence, but not its cognitive acts. According to Plato the cause of these acts is the participation

---

58. *In De causis*, lesson 2, no. 53.
59. Ibid., lesson 2, no. 56. See also Aquinas, *Commento al Libro delle cause*, 187.
60. Lesson 3, no. 72f.
61. Lesson 4, no. 98.
62. See the commentary on the first proposition.
63. Lesson 10, no, 241.

in the forms or Ideas, but Aristotle explains these acts by the presence of cognitive species (*species intelligibiles*).[64] "In conformity with the theory of Aristotle who on this point is more in agreement with Catholic doctrine, we do not place a great number of forms above the intelligent beings, but only one, which is the First Cause."[65]

The commentary on the sixteenth proposition points out that, contrary to what the Platonists do, the *De causis* does not admit a real difference or diversity between the abstract forms and the ideal forms (the Ideas).[66] Aquinas comes back to this point in the eighteenth lesson: according to the doctrine of the faith and that of Aristotle, "being alive" and "being intelligent" are not produced by different causes, but by one principle. The next lesson mentions the theory of the hierarchy of beings in the universe. Thomas does not criticize it except in so far as he notices that according to the Christian faith there is only one being at the highest level of reality. God is the universal cause. Between the beings on the various levels of reality, there are no abrupt divisions but continuity: the higher beings of a lower level touch the lowest ones of the higher level.[67]

In addition to these doctrinal corrections which concern the Platonism or the Neoplatonism of the treatise, the commentary of Thomas contains also quite a number of critical observations on points of doctrine of the text of the *De causis* itself. Thomas is convinced that without studying the *Elementatio* of Proclus, it is impossible to understand the text well. On several occasions he writes that *"ad huius propositionis intellectum"* it is necessary to consult Proclus. More than ten times Thomas writes that a certain doctrine is not demonstrated—or not demonstrated well—by the author and that the real proof is found in Proclus.[68] Thomas also points out occasionally that the order of a demonstration is not logical.[69] In the eleventh lesson we read a rather severe observation: the author of the *De causis* has combined two propositions of Proclus, but while trying to be brief, he gets lost in obscurity.[70]

In certain sections of his commentary, Thomas quotes so many prop-

64. Lesson 15, no. 313,
65. Lesson 13, no. 289.
66. Lesson 16, nos. 319.
67. Lesson 19, nos. 351–52.
68. Cf. this list of these passages: lesson 6, nos. 174 and 184; lesson 7, nos. 187, 191, and 194; lesson 9, no. 210; lesson 12, no. 277; lesson 13, no. 286; lesson 14, no. 295; lesson 15, no. 302; lesson 20, no. 365; lesson 21, no. 372; lesson 28, no. 425; lesson 29, no. 434; lesson 30, no. 443.
69. Lesson 25, no. 405; lesson 28, no. 432.
70. Number 259.

ositions of Proclus, that he neglects the *De causis*, as if he wanted to say: if you want to know which are the theories of this treatise, just consult the *Elementatio theologica*. Already in his preface Thomas observed that the propositions which an Arab philosopher had taken from Proclus, were more completely formulated in the *Elementatio* where their treatment went into greater detail.

The Presence of Pseudo-Dionysius in Thomas's *Expositio in Librum de causis*

We must also draw attention to the important place which Dionysius occupies in Thomas's commentary. In ten of the thirty-two lessons, Thomas compares the thesis of the *De causis* with the views of Dionysius in order to show correspondences and differences. Some examples will help us understand the purpose of these comparisons. In the second lesson Dionysius is invited to indicate the limits of the theory of the eternity of the intelligent beings and to show that the heavens are not ensouled.[71] Dionysius is also quoted as being in favor of the rejection of Plato's theory of a plurality of subsistent forms at the level of God's being (*Oportet dicere quod omnia ista sunt essentialiter ipsa prima omnium causa*).[72] According to Thomas the opinion of the author of the *De causis* that, on the level of knowledge, the intelligent beings exercise a certain influence on the human soul could in a way be true, for as Dionysius says, the souls receive illuminations through the mediation of the angels.[73] According to Dionysius the essence of the human soul is strictly one.[74] Being is the first perfection of which created things partake.[75]

A quote from Dionysius confirms the thesis that the intellect is united to God as to someone unknown.[76] His noted maxim "*Negationes in*

---

71. Lesson 2, nos. 50 and 62.

72. Lesson 3, no. 73. See also lesson 4, no. 99: "... Dionysius ordinem separatorum abstulit"; lesson 18, no. 344: "Secundum Dionysium primum ens et prima vita et primus intellectus sunt unum et idem, quod est Deus."

73. See lesson 10, no. 255: "Unde Dionysius dicit XV cap. Caelestis Hierarchiae: 'Unaquaeque essentia intellectualis donatam sibi a diviniore uniformem intelligentiam provida virtute dividit et multiplicat ad inferiora ductricem analogiam.'" One may also compare nos. 242, 245, and 246.

74. Lesson 3, nos. 84–85.

75. Lesson 4, no. 99. One may compare with lesson 9, no. 211: "[Deus] per ipsum [suum esse] omnium est existentium causa."

76. Lesson 6, nos. 160, 161, and 171.

divinis sunt verae, affirmationes autem incompactae vel inconvenientes" is mentioned, as is also a passage in which it is affirmed that in the study of God, there is neither *sensus* and *opinio* nor *nomen* and *sermo*. Leaning on a text of Dionysius, Thomas corrects the theory of the *De causis* and of Proclus which said that God cannot be known since he is above being. It is better to affirm that God is the infinite being; what we know of him are finite participations.[77]

On another occasion Dionysius is quoted to confirm that the effects must preexist in their exemplary causes, with which they have a certain likeness.[78] Finally Dionysius confirms with his authority the theory of a gradual transition between the different levels of beings.[79]

If one raises the question why Thomas refers so often to Dionysius, the answer seems to be that he wished to present a group of doctrines inspired by Platonism and admitted by the majority of the theologians of his time, but to transpose them to the level of the philosophy of being. One of the advantages of this way of proceeding was that certain of his readers who sympathized with Augustinianism could in this way be led to accept his conclusions and avoid certain defects of Neoplatonism.

Thomas's commentary is not only a critical study of a Neoplatonist text by a disciple of Aristotle, but more importantly an attempt to recuperate the crumbs of truth present in the *De causis*. The commentary, for that matter, intends also to study the metaphysics of Proclus even more than that of the Arab treatise. As we have seen Thomas does not accept all the theses of the two philosophers. By correcting and completing them, he tries to place these theories in a larger context, that of his philosophy of being. One may also stress that Thomas consulted very carefully the documentation available to him, analyzed the theories proposed with great acuity and honesty, and, because of his knowledge of the philosophical tradition, wrote a masterpiece of philosophical analysis.

77. Lesson 6, no. 176.
78. Lesson 14, no. 297.
79. Lesson 19, no. 352f.

13 ∾ SAINT JOHN DAMASCENE AND SAINT ANSELM OF CANTERBURY

John Damascene

Saint John of Damascus, currently called John Damascene, was born towards 674 at Damascus and died in 749 at the monastery of Saint-Saba in Jerusalem. After a short employment in the service of the caliph, he became a monk, combining his zeal for a holy life with an inextinguishable zeal for study. As the last of the Fathers of the Eastern Church, he was well acquainted with the writings of Aristotle, but his main sources of doctrine were the great Eastern Fathers such as Basil, Gregory of Nazianzus, Gregory of Nyssa, and Cyril of Alexandria. But he does not know Augustine and Latin theology except the letter of Pope Leo the Great to Flavian. Of his important work, *The Source of Knowledge*, the third part, *De fide orthodoxa*, was translated into Latin by John of Bourgogne and was studied by theologians in the West. This is noticeable in the works of Aquinas, where there are more than a thousand references to the *De fide orthodoxa*, a work that was considered a commentary on the Creed of Nicaea.

John Damascene defends the cult of the saints because of their special relation with God as his servants and friends. He puts his great knowledge at the service of this cause and defends the veneration of images of the saints against the attacks of the so-called iconoclasts. Well-known is his *Discourse against Those Who Reject the Holy Images*. He says, of course, that one cannot make an image of God as he is in himself, but we may venerate the images of Christ, of the Virgin Mary, and of the saints. He also shows that what Holy Scripture prohibits is the cult of idols.

Ideas and affirmations of John Damascene recur frequently in the objections or difficulties put forward at the beginning of the articles in the Disputed Questions such as those on truth, and on power, on evil, etc.

These interventions of those who participated in the academic disputes show the relevance of the thought of Damascene in the Latin West in the age of Aquinas. It is also possible that Thomas integrated many of Damascene's texts in order to show that theologians in the West highly appreciated the theological writings of the Eastern Fathers, and so to promote mutual understanding and eventual reunion.

On a few points Damascene deviates from what in the West is considered the orthodox expression of the faith. One may point to his insufficient explanation of the procession of the Holy Spirit, the relation of man's free will to divine providence and predestination, and the reception of the being of Christ into that of the eternal *Word*. In a well-known text he affirms that Christ is the instrument of the Divine Word, a sentence which if not explained may lead to the view that in Christ there are only acts of his divinity.[1]

Our Knowledge of God

At the very beginning of the *Scriptum super Libros Sententiarum*, we read the sentence that all men know by nature that God exists, but Thomas restricts the meaning of this phrase to the knowledge of resemblances of God (*"secundum eius similitudinem et non secundum quod est in sua natura"*).[2] We encounter these famous words of John Damascene at the beginning of the question whether God exists. Thomas answers that we only have a general and confused knowledge of God's existence, but that this does not mean that we know in the proper sense of the word that God exists.

In several texts of his different works, Thomas quotes the sentence that with regard to God we cannot know what he is, but only what he is not.[3] With regard to this question, Thomas explains why this is the case, but he observes that, contrary to what Damascene writes, such names as "infinite" and "eternal" can be said of the divine substance, although they express it imperfectly.[4] Thomas approves of what Damascene says about the name of God, that is, that "the One who is" is the best name we can give to God.[5] Repeatedly the latter calls God "an infinite ocean of being."[6]

When Damascene writes that divine providence is the act of God's

---

1. *QD de unione Verbi*, a. 5, arg. 4, and s.c. 2.
2. *In I Sent.*, d. 3, q. 1, a. 2, ad 1; *ST* I, q. 2, a. 1, arg 1.
3. *QD de veritate*, q. 8, a. 1, arg. 1; *ST* I, q. 2, a. 2, arg. 2; *QD de potentia*, q. 9, a. 7.
4. *ST* I, q. 13, a. 2, arg. 1.
5. *ST* I, q. 13, a. 11.
6. *QD de potentia*, q. 10, a. 1, ad 9.

will, Thomas notes that it includes also God's science.⁷ Damascene seems to limit the divine predestination of man by excluding our free decisions from it in order to preserve our freedom. Neither our good actions nor those that are evil *would be* determined by God.⁸ Thomas gives a benign explanation of this text: John Damascene wants to say that God does not force our will.

Concerning the theology of the Holy Trinity, Thomas appreciates what Damascene writes on the three Divine Persons and on what distinguishes them from each other: this is not a distinction relative to their substance, but according to what is proper to the Father, the Son, and the Holy Spirit.⁹ Damascene explains the terms "not-begotten" and "*Word*," said respectively of the Father and the Son,¹⁰ and stresses that in God everything is one, except that being not-begotten is distinctive of the Father, being begotten characteristic of the Son, and "to proceed from" distinctive of the Holy Spirit. But in the following section, he speaks of a distinction according to reason (*distinctio rationis*), an expression that Thomas corrects by writing "*secundum relationem*."¹¹ The distinction of reason is said of the distinction between the divine attributes, such as wisdom and love, which in reality are identical in the unity of the divine being. But the distinction between the Divine Persons is real. In God everything, indeed, is one and the same reality, except for what is proper to the Divine Persons.¹²

With regard to the procession of the Holy Spirit, Damascene says nowhere that the Holy Spirit proceeds from the Father and the Son, but he nevertheless in one way or another (*in aliquo modo*) mentions a connection between the Son and the Holy Spirit.¹³ As for the fact that Damascene does not see that the Holy Spirit proceeds from the Son, Thomas notes in the *Summa theologiae* that the Nestorians were the first to say that the Holy Spirit does not proceed also from the Son, but regarding Damascene, certain authors say that he does not deny that the Holy Spirit proceeds also from the Son.¹⁴ On the other hand, the word "gift" (*donum*) would not be appropriate to denote the Holy Spirit.¹⁵

---

7. *QD de veritate*, q. 2, a. 1, arg. 9; q. 5, a. 1, ad 1; q. 10, a. 12, etc.
8. *ST* I, q. 23, a. 1, arg. 1.
9. *ST* I, q. 31, a. 1, ad 2.
10. *ST* I, q. 33, a. 4, ad 3; q. 34, aa. 1 and 2.
11. *QD de potentia*, q. 9, a. 5, ad 14.
12. Ibid., q. 7, a. 6, ad 2.
13. Ibid., q. 10, a. 5.
14. *ST* I, q. 32, a. 2, ad 2.
15. *ST* I, q. 38, a. 1, arg 3.

In the third part of the *Summa theologiae*, in which the Incarnation of the Son of God and the sacraments are studied, there are 139 references to Damascene, which shows that it was important for Thomas to have present also the testimony of this great Father of the Eastern Church. At the very beginning of this part of the *Summa theologiae*, Damascene explains the suitableness of the Incarnation: according to a phrase of Saint Paul, the invisible being of God lets itself be seen in the world which he made: by the mystery of the Incarnation, the goodness and wisdom of God as well as his justice and his power are shown.[16] The Council of Chalcedon had resolved the question of the union of the divine nature and the human nature of Christ. Certain theologians had made some less correct statements about this union, and even Damascene said that the human nature of Christ had been deified; but Thomas quotes the definition of the council which declared that there is no union of the human *nature* of Christ with the divine nature.[17] In the next article of the *Summa theologiae*, Damascene explains that the Son of God has not adopted human nature in general or as a universal nature, but as an individual nature,[18] and that the Incarnation is the union of two natures in one person.[19]

It is noteworthy that Thomas prefers to quote the texts of Damascene concerning the central aspects of the doctrine of the Incarnation, as if he wants to confirm the doctrinal unity of the Eastern and the Latin Churches. But certain expressions of this important Church Father must be formulated with greater precision, as Thomas does in question 3, article 6. Thomas quotes yet another testimony of Damascene, where it is expressly stated that the Divine *Word* has united itself to an *individual* human nature.[20] Since the soul of Christ has been adopted in so far as it was capable of knowing God, one can say that the union of the Divine Word with the soul of Christ was effected by its intellect.[21]

A different question is that of the feelings and natural operations of man, such as being hungry and being tired. Did Christ have these natural feelings and states of mind? Damascene writes that all these feeling depended on the will of Christ. Thomas makes the answer more precise: if we limit our reflections to the soul of Christ as such, these experienc-

---

16. *ST* III, q. 1, a. 1, s.c.
17. *ST* III, q. 2, a. 1.
18. *ST* III, q. 2, a. 2, ad 3.
19. *ST* III, q. 2, a. 3, s.c., and a. 4, s.c.
20. *ST* III, q. 4, a. 4, s.c.
21. *ST* III, q. 6, a. 2.

es and feelings arose quite naturally and were not subject to his will, but in so far as his soul is the instrument of the Word of God, all states and movements of Christ's body were under its control.[22] Concerning the limitations and defects inherent in human nature, such as death, Damascene thought that those defects which are incurable were not taken on by Christ, but Thomas notes that Christ did not take on these defects as inevitable consequences of the sin of Adam, but by his own will, as a punishment for our sins in view of our redemption.[23]

Another difficulty results from the fact that what we say of the human nature of Christ, we say of his Divine Person. Some authors wanted to apply that also to his divine nature, but Damascene notes that this is not possible: we cannot attribute to the divine nature what is proper to the human nature.[24] We say, for instance, that the Son has been begotten, but not that his divine nature has been begotten. The difficulties we experience to express ourselves correctly on the mystery of God become man return in question 6, article 7, where in the *sed contra* argument Damascene reminds us that we do not say that man has been made divine, but that God has become man. In the *corpus articuli* Thomas adds some profound remarks in order to make clear how to speak about this mystery and what we should not say, an effort of clarification that is pursued in the following article.

As for the question whether in his human nature Christ exercised the faculty of free choice, Damascene seems to give a negative answer, but Thomas understands his words as saying that in Christ there were no doubts nor any hesitation.[25] There was in Christ only one group of human operations in so far as the processes and movements in his vegetative and animal nature were also governed by his reason and will.[26]

In the following questions of Thomas's treatise about Christ, there are a number of references to Damascene, as for instance to his well-known definition of prayer: "*Oratio est ascensus mentis in Deum*" (q. 21, a. 1, arg. 3); to his saying that the veneration exhibited to an image passes to the one who is represented (q. 25, a. 3); the Holy Spirit purified the Virgin Mary, Damascene says, in order that what she was going to conceive should not be infected by original sin (q. 32, a. 4, ad 1). He reminds us

---

22. *ST* III, q. 13, a. 3.
23. *ST* III, q. 14, a. 4.
24. *ST* III, q. 16, a. 5.
25. *ST* III, q. 18, a. 4.
26. *ST* III, q. 19, a. 2.

that Christ did not suffer because of a lack of knowledge, grace, or virtue, but only because of that which was inflicted on him from the outside. He also stresses that after the death of Jesus his body remained united to his Divine Person.[27]

The Angels

Following the Greek Fathers Damascene writes that the angels were created before the material world.[28] The fallen angels sinned simultaneously and the most important of them were charged with the surveillance of order on earth.[29] Thomas sees here a certain accord with the opinions of the Platonists, who called the inferior angels demons and said they were limited to the sublunar region of the universe. We should not reject this view as contrary to the faith, Thomas says, because God administers all creatures through the mediation of the angels, as Augustine confirms.[30] Philosophers and Christian theologians spoke in different ways about the immaterial substances. He quotes in this question the opinions of Plato, Aristotle, and Avicenna.

As was the case with the Platonists, several Christian authors thought that particular angels were put in charge of the different material beings. Damascene did also and thought that the devil as an angel was put in charge of the order of things on earth.[31]

Compared with man the angels are immaterial, but according to Damascene they are corporeal when compared to God.[32] Thomas suggests that on this point Damascene may be following Origen. Moreover, in this context he may understand "corporeal" to mean "to be composed."[33] Immortality would not belong to their nature, but would be a gift of divine grace. Thomas gives a benign interpretation of this position: Damascene speaks of a perfect immortality, in the sense of the exclusion of any change. Augustine is quoted to confirm this: "Every change is a certain death."[34] The angels cannot be in different places at the same time; when they are in the heaven, they cannot be on earth.[35] Thomas mentions also a striking sen-

27. *ST* III, q. 50, a. 2.
28. *ST* I, q. 61, a. 3, arg. 1.
29. *ST* I, q. 110, a. 1, ad 3.
30. *ST* I, q. 63, a. 7.
31. *ST* I, q. 110, a. 1 ad 3.
32. *QD de malo*, q. 17, a. 1, ad 7. See *QD de spir. creat.*, a. 1, arg. 14.
33. *De subst. spir.*, chap. 19.
34. *ST* I, q. 50, a. 5, ad 1.
35. *ST* I, q. 52, a. 2, s.c.

tence of Damascene: An angel operates there where he is.[36] He adds that the intellect and will of the angels work in total independence from time and space.

Damascene recalls that the angels speak with each other without having recourse to a spoken language.[37] They can also instruct us in a certain way, he says, by illuminating the sense images which are in the imagination, to cause next the intelligible species in the possible intellect, but Thomas does not accept this explanation: it would no longer be man himself who conceives his thoughts.[38] According to Damascene the angels would not have any practical knowledge, but Thomas explains that the distinction between theoretical and practical knowledge applies to man, not to angels who from the very beginning have an infused knowledge.[39] The will of the good angels is confirmed in the good.[40] Against gnostic theories Damascene writes that whoever says that the angels created certain things in our world incurs an *anathema*.[41]

With respect to the devils, Damascene says that they belonged to the group of angels charged with maintaining order on earth. Their influence on the intellect of man is limited: they can suggest images to our sense faculties. Damascene writes that the devils can suggest to human beings any form of malice and sordidness,[42] but Thomas restricts this influence, since the use of our cognitive faculties is subject to our will. The devils can influence man by suggesting through the mediation of his sense faculties what is evil. In this sense one can say that the devil is the *immissor malarum cogitationum*. Are all sins due to the influence of the devil? Damascene seems to affirm it by saying that every malice and all kinds of sordidness are conceived and planned by the devil,[43] but Thomas limits the range of these words: one can say that the devil is the indirect cause of all sins in that he seduced Adam and that, as a result of the fall of Adam, a certain inclination to sin took root in people. The devil, however, is not the direct cause of all sins, since certain sins are the effect of man's free will.

---

36. *ST* I, q. 107, a. 4, arg. 1.
37. *QD de veritate*, q. 9, a. 4, s.c. 3.
38. Ibid., q. 11, a. 3, arg. 12, and ad 12.
39. Ibid., q. 8, a. 9, ad 1.
40. *ST* I, q. 64, a. 2.
41. *QD de potentia*, q. 3, a. 4.
42. *ST* I, q. 111, a. 2. arg. 2.
43. *ST* I, q. 114, a. 3, arg. 1.

Man

Creatures, such as man, have been drawn from nothingness and tend to nothingness.[44] Thomas sees a certain lack of clarity in Damascene's treatment of the different acts of our intellect. He seems to make these acts the product of different faculties, but Thomas points out that these different acts are the work of the same faculty.[45] According to Damascene we can know the immaterial substances, since we can define them, and even philosophers have described them. But according to Thomas this would only be the case if these immaterial beings were the form and the species of material beings, as the Platonists said. We abstract the quiddity of the material things from their matter but that we shall never be able to do this with regard to the immaterial substances. We can only know these beings by way of negation, that is, by removing whatever is material.[46]

An interesting question is whether man is also an image of God with regard to the three Divine Persons. According to Damascene, being an image of God means that man has an intellect and free will.[47] Thomas thinks that in view of God's nature, man having been made in the image of God includes being also an image of the three Divine Persons. Where Damascene writes that man is in the image of God with regard to the intellectual nature of God,[48] Thomas notes that this does not exclude that man is also in the image of the three Divine Persons, since being in the image of God's nature implies that he is also in the image of the three divine Persons.

Life after Death

Damascene argues that no substance is deprived of its natural operation. This means that after our death our souls will continue thinking and will be gifted with knowledge.[49]

Human Free Will and God

Damascene is an important witness to the presence in us of free will, which has its base in the intellect. This means that animals do not have

---

44. *QD de veritate*, q. 5, a. 2, s.c. 5.
45. *ST* I, q. 79, a. 10.
46. *ST* I, q. 88, a. 2, ad 2.
47. *ST* I, q. 93, a. 5, arg. 2.
48. *ST* I, q. 93, a. 5.
49. *QD de veritate*, q. 10, a. 1, s.c. 1.

free will.⁵⁰ Repeatedly he underlines our freedom of choice. But free choice is nothing else but the will itself.⁵¹ Damascene states that a sinful act is against our nature, and Thomas says that this is true, but that a person who commits a sin conceives his act as something good and as conformed to his nature in so far as it pleases the senses or corresponds with one or another sinful habit.⁵²

In this question on what is voluntary and involuntary, Damascene is very present. The question is discussed whether concupiscence makes our acts involuntary. As characteristic of the involuntary Damascene mentions sadness, which always accompanies such an act. Furthermore it calls for pity or asks for our understanding.⁵³ In this connection Thomas quotes a phrase of Damascene who writes, as Aristotle says, that certain forms of involuntary acts are caused by ignorance. Thomas himself explains in greater detail the various ways in which ignorance affects the voluntary character of our acts.

In the question about the circumstances of our human acts, Damascene and Nemesius are quoted, who declare that ignorance of the circumstances causes that actions are not voluntary. According to Damascene the acts of our free will do not directly fall under divine providence, a position which results from his preoccupation to preserve man's free will. In connection with this opinion, he introduces the distinction between God's will preceding the choice of man, and God's will after he has left man the freedom to choose and decide for himself. This is called the *voluntas consequens* of God, which takes into account what a person has decided to do. Certain texts could give a wrong idea of Damascene's concept of our free will. He writes that the fact that man has been created out of nothing explains that he can go in different directions and choose what is evil. But Thomas writes that the real cause of our free will is that we are endowed with reason.⁵⁴ Thomas comments as follows on this position: we should not understand these words in such a way that what pertains to man's free will would be excluded from divine providence, but that man's actions are not determined by God to only one action, as is the case with things which do not have free will.⁵⁵

---

50. *ST* I-II, q. 6, aa. 1 and 2.
51. *ST* I q. 83, aa. 3 and 4.
52. *ST* I-II, q. 6, a. 4, ad 3.
53. *ST* I-II, q. 6, a. 7, s.c.
54. *QD de veritate*, q. 24, a. 2, ad 4.
55. Ibid., q. 5, a. 5 arg. 1, and ad 1.

Moral Life

John Damascene insists on the central place of conscience, which, he says, is for us the law which directs our actions. Thomas explains the functioning of conscience by drawing attention to the role of the first principles of the moral order.[56] Damascene's description of the *synderesis*—the habitus of these first principles—lacks clarity. St. Basil also is not very clear in his exposition of this point.[57] The rational part of man is directed by the will.[58] As Aristotle had done before him, Damascene distinguishes our appetitive faculties from the cognitive. Nemesius and Damascene distinguish between two sensitive appetitive faculties, the concupiscible and the irascible faculties.[59]

With regard to Damascene's doctrine of the will, Thomas notes that in one text he seems to distinguish between the will and the faculty of free choice (θέλω and βούλομαι), but in the *sed contra* argument Thomas quotes a text which states that the faculty of free choice is no other than the will.[60] In questions 6 to 21 of the *prima secundae* of the *Summa theologiae*, we meet several quotations of texts of Damascene, often accompanied by the observation "as Aristotle did, Damascene writes...." In the different stages that lead to a free choice Damascene places consent (*consensus*) in one's agreement with what he has deliberated about. For him consent does not concern the end, but only the possible ways leading to the end.[61] Thomas quotes Damascene also to establish that the command by which we pass to the execution of what we have chosen precedes the execution.[62]

As for the difficult question whether the acts of our reason can be commanded by the will, Damascene gives an affirmative answer, which is elaborated and formulated with greater precision by Thomas. He gives two definitions of a passion, and while he affirms that it has its seat in the sensitive appetite, he explains that it corresponds with a good or bad object present in the imagination. Thomas adds that a passion is accompanied by changes in the organism.[63] With regard to the question of the

---

56. Ibid., q. 17, a. 1.
57. *ST* I, q. 79, a. 13.
58. *ST* I, q. 83, a. 3.
59. *ST* I, q. 81, a. 2.
60. *ST* I, q. 83, a. 4.
61. *ST* I-II, q. 15, a. 3.
62. *ST* I-II, q. 17, a. 3.
63. *ST* I-II, q. 22, a. 3.

morality of the passions, Damascene seems to hold that passions that arise in opposition to the natural movements are morally bad, but Thomas notes that, if it is true that the passions add something to the natural movements of our heart, they do not always deviate from the order of natural reason.[64] Acedia,[65] considered a capital sin by Gregory the Great, is for Damascene a sort of sadness and not a sin.[66]

In a text of the second book, chapter 12, of his *De fide orthodoxa*, Damascene suggests that concupiscence is not a special passion, since it has different passions as its contraries, such as sadness and fear, but Thomas notes that there is a passion directly opposed to the desire (concupiscence) of a good, but that it has no name.[67] Delight or pleasure can also be said of the sensitive appetite, while joy (*gaudium*) is only found in beings gifted with reason. Regarding sadness Damascene distinguishes between four kinds: an evil which one expects causes fear, but an evil that is present, sadness.[68] Thomas corrects the opinion of Damascene that concupiscence would not be a cause of sadness:[69] what one desires is in a certain way already present, but when an obstacle to acquiring it turns up, it saddens us.[70] To the question whether anger is to be distinguished from the other passions, Damascene gives a positive answer. Are there different kinds of anger? On this point opinions of the theologians diverge, but, Thomas says, Damascene and Nemesius distinguish three kinds of anger according to the three factors that provoke it.[71]

An important question in the treatise of the virtues concerns whether we receive the virtues together with our human nature. Damascene affirms it, but Thomas explains that we may speak of our human nature according to what is most formal in it, its rational character, or according to our bodily complexion. In these two senses one may say that there is a certain onset of the virtues in us.[72] Somewhat further on in the treatise, question 94, article 3, Thomas has Damascene affirm again that the virtues are natural and subject to natural law. Are sins against our nature, as Damascene says they are? Thomas adds a precision: the faculty which

---

64. *ST* I-II, q. 24, a. 2, ad 2.
65. Disgust in spiritual things and spiritual activity.
66. *QD de malo*, q. 2, a. 12.
67. *ST* I-II, q. 30, a. 2, ad 3.
68. *ST* I-II, q. 35, a. 8; q. 36, a. 1.
69. *QD de malo*, q. 2, a. 12.
70. *ST* I-II, q. 36, a. 2, ad 2.
71. *ST* I-II, q. 46, a. 8.
72. *ST* I-II, q. 63, a. 1.

produces the sinful act is natural, but in so far as sins are against the moral law, they are against our nature.[73]

In the *secunda secundae* of the *Summa theologiae*, there are some thirty references to texts of Damascene on the virtues and vices. He describes mercy as a sort of sadness, as envy also is.[74] With regard to the virtue of piety Damascene writes that our cult of God must be expressed also in the attitude of our body, since we are composed of soul and body.[75] For Damascene evil is like darkness, a position that has led some to affirm that evil is more than just a privation, that is, a form opposed to the good. Sins would even take away the good of nature, something that happened to the fallen angels.

Supernatural Life

Thomas praises the description that Damascene gives of faith: faith is the foundation of the things we are hoping for and manifests the things which we do not see.[76] Damascene adds that what we hope to receive is in the first place eternal life and then all that we ask from God.

The Celestial Bodies

According to Damascene the celestial bodies are not the cause of what happens on the earth, nor the cause of our actions.[77] He relies on St. Basil for his denial of the ensoulment of these bodies.[78] They do not have a soul nor any sense knowledge. But Thomas notes that God does not want to exclude all causality from the celestial bodies. Their influence, however, remains limited to physical things,[79] and they are not the first cause of the generation and corruption of material things.[80]

Conclusion

All through his works Thomas quotes numerous sentences of St. John Damascene, but quite often he corrects somewhat the way in which they have been formulated so as to prevent wrong conclusions from being

---

73. *ST* I-II, q. 75, a. 2, ad 3; cf. q. 109, a. 7, arg. 3.
74. Ibid., q. 30, a. 1, s.c., and q. 36, a. 1, s.c.
75. *ST* II-II, q. 84, a. 2.
76. *QD de veritate*, q. 14, a. 2.
77. *ST* I-II, q. 9, a. 5.
78. *ST* I, q. 70, a. 3.
79. *QD de veritate*, q. 5, a. 10.
80. *ST* I, q. 115, a. 4, s.c.

drawn from them. In *In I Sent.*, d. 5, q. 1, a. 1, Damascene says that the Father begets the Son by his divine essence, but Thomas comments that one cannot say that the divine essence begets: nature begets through a special faculty or power.[81] We have ascertained that John Damascene is very present in the academic disputes about certain points of doctrine, and consequently also in Thomas's works such as the commentary on the *Sentences*, the *Summa theologiae*, the *Disputed questions on Ttruth, on Power, on Evil*, and *on De spiritualibus creaturis*, but he is practically absent in the *Summa contra gentiles* and the exposition on *De divinis nominibus*.

Anselm of Canterbury and Thomas Aquinas

Saint Anselm was born in 1033 at Aosta in Northern Italy. As a young man he took a great interest in studies and was attracted by the renaissance of the liberal arts studies in France. He spent three years in Burgundy and went from there to Avranches and the abbey of Le Bec in Normandy to meet the monk Lanfranc, who was, like Anselm himself, a native of Lombardy and was considered the most learned person of his time. Anselm became a monk of the abbey at the age of twenty-seven and was later elected prior to succeed Lanfranc, who had been elected abbot of the abbey of St. Stephen in Caen. When in 1078 the abbot Herloinus, founder of the abbey of Le Bec, died, Anselm was elected his successor. Anselm had a special talent for instructing and training the young who came from all over the country to attend his lessons. Already in those years he had to go occasionally to England for the business interests of the abbey, and so he became well-known there. When the episcopal see of Canterbury became vacant in 1093, Anselm was appointed archbishop primate of England. But because of a conflict with the king he had to leave England and go to Rome. He returned after the death of the king and died at Canterbury in 1109.

Anselm is known for his motto *Credo ut intelligam* and has sometimes been considered a dialectician, like the monk Berengar of Tours who wrote his works some years before him. Berengar taught that reason is a source of knowledge superior to faith; by his reason man is an image of

---

81. *In I Sent.*, d. 7, q. 1, a. 1, ad 2.

God. But the position of Anselm is different: the foundation of all reasoning in theology is that one firmly accepts all that the faith teaches us, and that one starts from there to try to understand and to explain it. Author of several monographs, Anselm takes each time a well-defined question and analyzes it to consider its different aspects. The disciples of Anselm asked him to provide them with a rational explication of the existence and the attributes of God, a request that makes one think of the manner in which the dialecticians of that time proceeded, but in reality Anselm's theology is anchored profoundly in the faith.[82]

On the other hand, Anselm does show, against the anti-dialecticians, that we are allowed to study the truths of the faith and try to understand what they tell us. The theologian can use analogies taken from the natural world and the principles of dialectic, notwithstanding the fact that certain theologians were inclined to follow Saint Ambrose's laconic saying that "God had not wanted to save his people through dialectic."[83] Despite his confidence in the power of our reason, Anselm knew that we shall not arrive thereby to an understanding of the mysteries of the faith. Moreover he was not the first theologian of the Latin Church to profess a faith which sought to understand, "*fides quaerens intellectum*." Centuries before him Augustine had taken the text of Isaiah 7:9, "*nisi credideretis, non intelligetis*," as his point of departure in his attempts to develop the doctrine of the faith.[84]

Anselm entered the history of philosophy with his proofs of the existence of God, in particular his so-called ontological argument, in which he takes as a point of departure the presence in our mind of the concept of the greatest—a demonstration which has provoked discussions until our time. We shall show below what Thomas says about it. It is true that it is foreign to our way of thinking and proceeding to argue from the presence in our mind of a concept-idea that what this concept expresses, exists in the real world, but one may recall here the Platonist theory of the emanation of the νοῦς from the One, and reality from the νοῦς, a theory according to which being succeeds to thought. If the *Monologion*, in

---

82. Dialectic was one of the seven liberal arts, but in the eleventh and twelfth centuries its study was contaminated by the controversy over the universals. Some dialecticians professed a rationalism, which led to a denial of certain dogmas of the faith. Berengar of Tours tried to equal Lanfranc but developed heretical views, in particular concerning the Eucharist.

83. Anselm, *De fide ad Gratianum*, I (PL 16: 537): "Non per dialecticam placuit Deo salvum facere populum sum."

84. In particular in his *De vera religione*, Augustine explains how to proceed in the study of the dogmas of the faith.

which Anselm presents his "ontological" proof of the existence of God, and the *Proslogion*, in which he examines the divine attributes, are studies at the level of philosophy, his well-known treatise *Cur Deus homo* has as its point of departure the revealed truth of the Incarnation of the Son of God and is definitely a theological text which indicates some arguments rendering this mystery of the faith more comprehensible.

In the works of Thomas there are more than three hundred references to texts of Anselm. Some of them concern theological questions, such as the Holy Trinity and the generation of the Son of God, while others deal with philosophical issues. A considerable part of these references are found in the objections or difficulties formulated at the beginning of articles in the *Scriptum super libros Sententiarum*, the *Summa theologiae*, and the *Quaestiones disputatae*. This shows that the writings of Anselm were used in university teaching and known by the theologians of Thomas's time. In the following part of this chapter, these references have been ordered according to a number of themes concerning philosophical and theological issues.

The Ontological Argument

Although in his works Anselm does not make a clear distinction between natural theology and the doctrine of the faith, he tries to establish the *existence* of God and the *divine attributes* with the aid of reason alone. In his *Proslogion* he develops his famous argument of the existence of God, while in his *Monologion* he tries to answer the question of what or how God is and presents an entirely reasoned and fairly complete exposition of the divine attributes.

At the beginning of the *Summa theologiae*, Thomas asks whether God's existence is known by itself.[85] Next he presents a version of Anselm's argument: The word "God" signifies a being greater than which we cannot designate any other. But that which exists in reality and in the intellect is greater than what is only in the intellect. Therefore as soon as we have understood the name "God," he exists in the intellect and consequently also in reality. Therefore it is evident that God exists.

Thomas answers that even if the word "God" had this meaning, it would not follow that such a being as one is thinking about, exists in reality. Our true knowledge is drawn from reality; from the existence of a concept, one cannot conclude that its contents exist in reality, unless we

---

85. *ST* I, q. 2, a. 1. One may compare *In I Sent.*, d. 3, q. 1, a. 2 ad 2, where Anselm is mentioned.

have drawn this concept directly or indirectly from reality.[86] In this text of the *Summa theologiae*, Thomas does not mention Anselm by name as the author of this demonstration, although he frequently mentions Anselm elsewhere in his works. The reason for this omission could be that he does not want to quote the great Anselm as the author of an erroneous demonstration or associate the theologian Anselm with an argument that from the Aristotelian point of view is erroneous. On this point of an immediate evidence of the existence of God, Bonaventure has remained a disciple of Anselm.[87]

In the questions on the attributes of God in the *Summa theologiae*, there are hardly any references to Anselm. Thomas quotes nevertheless the sentence that whatever is most perfect must be attributed to God.[88]

Truth

Anselm wrote a special treatise on truth, titled *De veritate*, in the form of a dialogue between a master and his disciple. He examines first what is called logical truth, that is, the truth of our affirmations and negations. If what we say is conformed to reality, our discourse is true. In the seventh chapter of his *De veritate*, Anselm treats of the truth of things.

In his *Quaestiones disputatae de veritate*, Thomas begins his discussion with an analysis of the ontological truth. This truth is the thing itself in so far as it lets itself be known; it is the reality of a being and of its contents. In the second place, Thomas says, the truth is completed when what we think and what we say are conformed to reality. This is confirmed by the definition of Anselm, namely, that truth is rectitude, that is, the conformity of our thought with reality,—a conformity which is perceived only by the mind.[89]

According to Anselm whatever is, is true through the First Truth,[90] in so far as it is determined by divine truth. Thomas adds a distinction: whatever is true is true by the First Truth as by its primary exemplary cause, but it is formally true by the created truth of its own form. According to Anselm the truth of man's predestination is the same as that of a prediction about the future, although the latter has no definite truth, but

---

86. See Wolfgang Bassler, "Die Kritik des Thomas von Aquin am ontologischen Gottesbeweis," *Franziskanische Studien* 55 (1973): 97–190.
87. Étienne Gilson, *La philosophie de Saint Bonaventure* (Paris: J. Vrin, 1953), 110.
88. Anselm, *Monologion*, chap. 14: *QD de potentia*, q. 1, a. 1, arg. 2.
89. *QD de veritate*, q. 1, a. 1; *ST* I, q. 16, a. 1.
90. Ibid., q. 21, a. 4, arg. 5, and ad 5: "Omne verum est verum veritate prima."

Thomas notes that a prediction about the future concerns the future and brings no certainty, whereas the truth of predestination concerns the future as it is present in divine science.[91]

God

Let us consider first the well-known words of the *Proslogion* "God is (that being) greater than which one cannot conceive anything." Thomas examines this sentence in the *Summa theologiae* where the question is studied whether it is evident that God exists. Thomas answers in the negative, as we have seen. But the fact that God's existence is not evident and can be denied by us does not prohibit that he is thought to be the greatest being, greater than whatever we can think.[92] Regarding the perfections of God, Thomas quotes the *Monologion*, chapter 3: all perfections that we find in creatures exist in God in an eminent way.[93]

Thomas quotes a beautiful text of Anselm on the question whether God always acts with justice: "God is righteous when he punishes sinners according to what they have deserved, and he is just when he forgives in accord with his goodness."[94] Anselm confirms that God is omniscient, noting that God does not know what is not, what has not been, and what shall never be.[95]

With regard to the theology of the Holy Trinity, Thomas quotes a sentence from Anselm: if God the Father had adopted a human nature, he would have had two sons, which would have been inconvenient.[96] According to Anselm the slightest inconvenience has no place in God—a phrase from the *De incarnatione Verbi* that is quoted several times by Thomas. The Father begets the Son by expressing himself in his Word, and expressing himself also produces the creatures.[97] Anselm ascribes the verb "to say" not only to the Father but also to the other Divine Persons. Thomas observes that Anselm understands the verb "to say" (*dicere*) in the sense of knowing, but this use of the term is not appropriate.[98] Another correction concerns a sentence of the *Monologion*, chapter 60: "For the supreme Spirit to say [*dicere*] signifies nothing else but to con-

91. Ibid., q. 6, a. 3, ad 6.
92. Ibid., q. 10, a. 12, arg. 2, and ad 2.
93. *In I Sent.*, d. 2, q. 2, a. 3.
94. *ST* I, q. 21, a. 1, ad 3.
95. *QD de veritate*, q. 2, a. 8, arg. 2; Anselm, *Monologion*, chap. 30.
96. *In III Sent.*, d. 1, q. 2, a. 3, arg. 1.
97. *QD de potentia*, q. 2, a. 4, arg. 8; q. 3, a. 15, arg. 13.
98. *ST* I, q. 34, a. 1; *QD de veritate*, q. 4, a. 2, ad 4.

template what one is looking for in one's thought [*cogitat*]."[99] The term *cogitare* is used here to signify the quest for truth, an activity that is not found in God.[100]

The Divine Word

According to Anselm the Word of God knows everything in the act by which God "says" it, an act in which he also says the creatures. Thomas explains the reason. The Word knows the creatures in the acting power of the Father, and what is not in it, is not known.[101] This brings us to the question whether the name "Word" includes a relation with creatures. A text in the *Monologion* seems to deny it, while a text of Anselm in the third *sed contra* argument of the same article affirms that each word implies a relation with what is expressed by it. The question is complex, as Thomas shows: the Divine Word has no real relation with its creatures, but one can say that the Word is related to them in so far as it makes them exist.[102]

In his investigation to understand the reason why the truths of the faith are mysteries, Anselm studies in particular the mystery of the incarnation of the Son of God and stresses the need for giving satisfaction for the sins of mankind. Several references to Anselm's book *Cur Deus homo* point to the importance of the theme: giving satisfaction is to give God the honor due to Him, in consideration of the debt contracted by the sins men have committed.[103] This satisfaction, however, could not be given except by the infinite merits of the Son of God.[104]

With regard to the will of Christ an opponent suggested that just as Damascene distinguishes a dual will, simple willing and deliberate choice, these two types of activity of the will should also be in Christ, but, Thomas writes, as Anselm says, there is only one (human) will in Christ as in other men.[105]

---

99. "Dicere summo spiritui nihil aliud est quam cogitando intueri."
100. *ST* I, q. 34, a. 1; *QD de potentia*, q. 9, a. 9, ad 2; *QD de veritate*, q. 4, a. 4, ad 4.
101. *QD de veritate*, q. 2, a. 8, arg. 4, and ad 4.
102. Ibid., q. 4, a. 5, arg. 2, and ad 2.
103. *In IV Sent.*, d. 15, q. 1, a. 1. This text is quoted three times by Thomas.
104. *QD de veritate*, q. 29, a. 3, arg. 4. Thomas notes that the satisfaction given by Christ as such is not infinite, but that it acquires a certain infinity by the circumstances, Christ being the Son of God.
105. *In III Sent.*, d. 17, q. 1, a. 1, qc. 3, s.c. 2.

The Holy Spirit

In an objection raised in relation with the procession of the Holy Spirit, Thomas quotes a text of Anselm's treatise *De processione Spiritus Sancti*, according to which the procession of the Holy Spirit from the Son (the *Filioque*) would not be necessary to distinguish the Holy Spirit and the Son,[106] since the fact that the Son is begotten and the Holy Spirit proceeds would constitute a sufficient distinction between the two Divine Persons, but Thomas notes that the fact that the Son and the Holy Spirit both have their origin in the Father is not sufficient to distinguish them. We must therefore add that the Holy Spirit proceeds also from the Son.[107] According to Thomas it is the intention of Anselm to mention first the points of doctrine on which we, the Latins, agree with those in the Eastern Church who deny that the Holy Spirit proceeds also from the Son. The sentence quoted above is a contribution to the theological discussion rather than an expression of the truth.[108] Thomas also mentions a text of the treatise *Cur Deus homo*, in which Anselm writes that it was impossible for the three Divine Persons to adopt a human *persona* in a hypostatic union.[109]

The Holy Virgin

In several of his works Thomas quotes a saying of Anselm about the Holy Virgin, in which he declares that she is shining so much in her purity that one cannot find her equal among creatures.[110] In other treatises Thomas also quotes Anselm's eulogy of the Blessed Virgin on the abundance of grace given to her and her preservation from all sins during her life.[111]

Creation, Man, and the Human Will

In God created things are the creative essence of God.[112] This is also the reason why each thing has its truth when it realizes what it is intended to be in the Spirit of God.[113]

---

106. *ST* I, q. 36, a. 2, arg. 7.
107. *ST* I, q. 36, a. 2, ad 7.
108. *QD de potentia*, q. 10, a. 5, ad 2: Anselm accepts what is true in the doctrine of the Orthodox Churches but maintains that the Holy Spirit also proceeds from the Son.
109. *ST* III, q. 3, a. 6.
110. *In I Sent.*, d. 17, q. 2, a. 4, arg. 3.
111. *ST* III, q. 27, a. 2, arg. 2; *Quodl.* VI, q. 5, a. 1.
112. *In I Sent.*, d. 36, q. 1, a. 3; *QD de veritate*, q. 4, a. 6, s.c. 1: "Creatura in Creatore est creatrix essentia."
113. *In I Sent.*, d. 38, q. 1, arg. 3.

The consideration of our human will occupies an important place in the writings of Anselm. The will, he writes, moves all our faculties and also all the virtues.[114] "I think because I want to think."[115] Free will is the power man has to preserve righteousness in his actions and his life[116] and to do what is good.[117] Justice is the rectitude of the will.[118] Sins are only found in the will.[119] Thomas quotes several times the following saying of Anselm: If some people do not receive grace from God, this is not because God does not want to give it, but because they do not want to receive it.[120]

In several texts Anselm recalls that the possibility of sinning does not flow from the nature of the will.[121] If this were the case, God would not have a free will.[122] Our will retains always the possibility of acting in conformity with the law of God.[123] The central place which the will occupies in the thought of Anselm is also visible in a sentence of his *De conceptu virginali*: original justice had in the first place to do with the will, and this is also the case for the original sin opposed to it.[124]

Anselm thought that if our proto-parents had not sinned, their descendants would have their free will confirmed in the good, but Thomas writes that this is just an opinion of Anselm, which should be put aside. If the situation were the way Anselm suggests, the descendants of Adam and Eve would have had a greater perfection than Adam and Eve themselves.[125] In this connection Anselm also speaks of a "necessity to commit sins" as the effect of original sin, but Thomas notes that there is no question of a necessity.[126] Anyway Anselm himself writes that all who have free will have the power to conserve the rectitude of their will.[127] He compares free will as it is present in God, in the angels, and in man, and

---

114. *ST* I, q. 82, a. 4; *In I Sent.*, d. 3, q. 3; d. 38, q. 1, a. 1; *QD de veritate*, q. 10, a. 2, ad 4; q. 14, a. 1.
115. Thomas refers to the beginning of the book *De similitudinibus*, compiled by the monk Eadmer of Canterbury (PL 159: 605). Cf. Anselm, *Monologion*, chap. 11: "Solum iustum est quod vis"; *QD de potentia*, q. 2, a. 3, arg. 3: "Intelligo enim quia volo."
116. *QD de veritate*, q. 24, a. 3, s.c. 1.
117. Ibid., q. 24, a. 14, arg. 8.
118. *ST* II-II, q. 58, a. 4.
119. *QD de malo*, q. 7, a. 1, arg. 16.
120. *In II Sent.*, d. 28, q. 1, a. 4, s.c.
121. *In III Sent.*, d. 12, q. 2, a. 2, arg. 2; *QD de malo*, q. 16, a. 5, arg. 15.
122. *QD de veritate*, q. 24, a. 2, s.c. 1.
123. *QD de malo*, q. 16, a. 5, ad 19; *QD de veritate*, q. 24, a. 10, ad 18.
124. Anselm, *De conceptu virginali*, chap. 3; cf. *ST* I-II, q. 83, a. 3, s.c.
125. *ST* I, q. 100, a. 2, ad 2.
126. Ibid., ad 3.
127. *QD de veritate*, q. 24, a. 10, ad 6.

explains what is common to all three, but Thomas observes that there is only a question of an analogous correspondence and that freedom of will does not have the same properties in God, the angels, and man.[128] The devil no longer has the rectitude of the will proper to the angels and therefore cannot act in conformity to it.

Moral Life and the Virtues

In the *Summa theologiae* I-II, Anselm is mainly quoted in the difficulties put forward in the beginning of the articles. His definition of justice as the rectitude of the will, which it observes because of what the will itself is, is well-known.[129] Does justice depend only on the will? Anselm seems to affirm it, but Thomas explains how we must understand these words. Justice is indeed the rectitude of the will, but the order of things we have to observe depends on God, who has placed things in a certain order. Justice is therefore a rectitude which depends on that which constitutes it, namely, the rule of reason.[130]

According to Anselm prudence would be in the will as its subject,[131] but Thomas reaffirms that it is in our reason, which can issue commands through the will. An opponent mentions that Anselm distinguishes between seven degrees in the virtue of humility, but Thomas says that all these degrees are already contained in the sixth degree.[132] In the question on beatitude in the *Scriptum super libros Sententiarum*, book IV, d. 15, q. 1, a. 1, a reference to Anselm says that he mentions several qualities which characterize humility. But Thomas says that these qualities accompany this virtue rather than being humility itself.

The references to the writings of Anselm in the works of Aquinas hardly show the importance of this great and intrepid theologian for the development of theology: he sought the truth on the basis of an unshakable faith and with total confidence in the value of our reason.

---

128. Anselm, *De libero arbitrio*, chap. 1; *QD de veritate*, q. 24, a. 10, ad 18, and ad 6.
129. *ST* II-II, q. 58, a. 4, s.c.; Anselm, *Monologion*, chap. 30.
130. *QD de veritate*, q. 23, a. 6, s.c. 2.
131. *In III Sent.*, d. 33, q. 2, a. 4, qc. 4, arg. 1.
132. *ST* II-II, q. 161, a. 6, arg. 3, and ad 3.

14 ~ AVICENNA

For several decades the relations between the thought of Thomas Aquinas and the philosophy of Avicenna (Ibn Sina) have been studied by philosophers in the West. Avicenna is one of the great names of Arab philosophy. In the Middle Ages he was first known as a medical doctor—his *Canon* served for quite a while as an established manual in teaching medicine—before he became an authority in philosophy. For one year Avicenna studied medicine, possibly at Jundi-Sapur north of the Persian Gulf, not far from the estuary of the Euphrates, where a great center of medical studies was established, directed by Greek professors.

Born in 980 in the Persian Empire, he studied literature, mathematics, and medicine while still very young. He read the *Isagoge* of Porphyry, the *Geometry* of Euclid, and the *Almagest* of Ptolemy. At the age of eighteen he practiced medicine and began to study the *Metaphysics* of Aristotle, but he found its reading very difficult until a treatise of Al-Farabi put him on the way of understanding the text. Al-Farabi (870–950), who lived in Bagdad, wrote commentaries on the writings of Aristotle, while he himself was close to Neoplatonism in his philosophy. Ever since that contact with metaphysics, Aristotle remained the eminent master for Avicenna. He and Averroes after him played an important role in bringing the thought of Aristotle to the Latin West in the Middle Ages.

The works of Avicenna which have influenced scholars in the West are the following: the *Al-Shifa* (an encyclopedia of philosophy in which Avicenna comments and explains the texts of Aristotle according to his own personal interpretation, influenced by Neoplatonism and Islam); the *Logic*, the *Mathematics*, the *Sufficientia* (the philosophy of nature, of which *Liber VI naturalium*, is an exposé of psychology), and the *Metaphysica*. Thomas examined the doctrine of these last books, and several sentences of these works are quoted in the arguments or difficulties of the *Scriptum super libros Sententiarum*, and the *Quaestiones disputa-*

tae.¹ During the last years of his life, Avicenna wrote some other books, among them the *Book of Science*, a summary of the themes he had treated in his *Al-Shifa*.²

With regard to logic, we should notice that, with Aristotle, Avicenna affirms the existence of universal concepts, but assigns a greater ontological stature to them: they are the essences of things, have a sort of immaterial reality,³ and constitute a mental universe. As such these essences are only the contents of things and must be placed between universality and singularity. Individual beings constitute the object of the natural sciences, whereas the essences are the object of metaphysics. The universal, the object of our intellect, is virtually contained in the individuals.

Thanks to the activity of our external senses, there is a substructure in our imagination that, on the level of sense knowledge, corresponds to the different species of things in our world. The intelligent being that has its seat in the last cosmic sphere that surrounds the earth radiates and transmits these intelligible forms to us. These forms which that intelligent being (the *Dator formarum*) transmits are deprived of all matter. This theory recalls Plato's view of the world of Ideas (forms) which the human souls have known for ever, since they already existed before entering a body on the earth. According to Avicenna the *Dator formarum* is the source of the intellectual knowledge of all men. At first our intellect does not have a single idea. When sense knowledge develops, our intellect, called the *intellectus possibilis*, begins to acquire the needed dispositions to receive from the *Dator formarum* the ideas which correspond to the sensitive representations of things. By repeatedly considering these ideas, one gets a certain facility to absorb them and so what is called "science" is formed.

It must, however, be noted that each time that our intellect is inter-

---

1. See Louis Gardet, "Saint Thomas et ses prédécesseurs arabes," in *Thomas Aquinas, 1274–1974: Commemorative Studies*, ed. A. Maurer (Pontifical Institute of Medieval Studies, Toronto 1974), 419–48. Gardet mentions three main groups among the Arab sources of Aquinas: a) the *mutakallimûn*, or the *loquentes in lege maurorum*; b) Algazel; c) the Hellenistic philosophers of Islam, the *falâsifa*, in two groups: the orientals, Avicenna; the Westerners or Maghrebins, in particular Averroes. The first Latin translations of their works were done by Ibn Daud and Gundisalvi. Then there was a second series of translations made directly from Arabic by Gerard of Cremona. Finally, about 1220, Michael Scot (in Toledo and in Naples) and Herman the German in Toledo made a series of translations, among them those of the commentaries of Averroes which then spread through the Latin West.

2. Cf. Avicenna, *Le livre de science, I. (Logique, Métaphysique)*, trans Mohammed Achena and Henri Massé (Paris: Societe d'Edition Les Belles Lettres, 1955), 17; in vol. II (Paris: Societe d'Edition Les Belles Lettres, 1958), mathematics and natural philosophy are treated. This shorter Persian encyclopedia was not translated into Latin.

3. One might think here of a sort of a meta-physical reality, which, however, is not that of God and the intelligent beings nor that of the material things.

ested in other things, it loses the idea which it had before and must turn again to the *Dator formarum* to acquire it. Thomas draws attention to this aspect of the theory which says that we lose the ideas each time we cease thinking of them. Avicenna notes that people have different intellectual capacities to open themselves to the *Dator formarum*. In his view our universal concepts are not obtained by abstraction from the representations of the imagination.

The first idea which we acquire is that of being (*ens*), a discovery of Avicenna which Thomas appreciates, but as we shall see, Thomas points out certain particularities of Avicenna's conception of being and of the one. Beings are divided, he writes, into necessary and contingent (or possible) beings. Possible beings do not have the ground of their existence in themselves but need a cause. From this point of departure Avicenna constructs a proof of the existence of God, the absolutely necessary being. For Avicenna the subject of metaphysics is not God (as Averroes holds) but being.[4] All other things except God are composed of an essence and of the act of being.

As a believing Muslim Avicenna accepts the doctrine of creation, but influenced by the Neoplatonism of Plotinus he sees creation as a series of emanations issuing from the First Cause.[5] From God flows forth a first intelligent being which produces the intellect of the first sphere of the cosmos, as well as its soul and body. In its turn the intelligent being of the first sphere continues this process of creation-fabrication until we arrive at the last cosmic sphere which surrounds the earth. The intelligent being of this sphere, called as we have seen *Dator formarum*, radiates the forms (essences) to the material substances of the sublunar world and the concepts-essences to the intellects of human beings. This entire process of creation-emanation is necessary. The *Dator formarum* not only radiates the universal concepts in the intellect of human beings, but confers also the essences to the matter of those things on the earth which are capable of receiving them.[6]

Although Avicenna adheres to the Aristotelian doctrine of matter, the human soul does not form one substance with the body. The soul is a

---

4. See Dimitri Gutas, *Avicenna and the Aristotelian Tradition: Introduction to Reading Avicenna's Philosophical Works* (Leiden: E.J. Brill, 1988), 288f.

5. Cf. R. E. Houser, "Avicenna, Aliqui and Thomas Aquinas's Doctrine of Creation," *Recherches de Théologie et Philosophie Médiévales* 80, no. 1 (2013): 17–55.

6. "Avicenna conceives this *Dator formarum* as a reservoir full of intelligible forms." Gérard Verbeke, Introduction to *Liber de Philosophia prima sive Scientia divina I-IV*, ed. Simone van Riet (Leuven: Peeters, 1977), 26.

spiritual substance, equipped with several faculties. Animating—giving life to a body—is only one of its functions.

Despite being imbued by Platonist and Neoplatonist doctrines and a certain essentialism, Avicenna considered Aristotle his foremost master, so that in the Latin West he was considered the great spokesman of Aristotle until Averroes overshadowed him toward the end of the twelfth century. Avicenna was far removed from professing an Aristotelianism faithful to the great Master. To qualify the massive presence of Plotinus's Neoplatonism in Avicenna's philosophy, L. Gardet qualifies it as "an essentialism which ends in monism."[7] But with respect to his doctrine of God, Avicenna holds the Aristotelian doctrine of the First Principle which is thought of thought (νοήσεως νόησις), and is the First Mover. To Avicenna himself, God is the first efficient and final cause. As for this point Avicenna sets aside the description Plotinus gives of the first principle, the One, as being above all knowledge. For Plotinus knowledge consists in the duality of the subject who knows and the object known, a duality Avicenna does not accept. Thomas has a certain appreciation for Avicenna and uses some of his definitions, but, as we shall see, on many points he keeps his distance from him. Avicenna died in 1037.[8]

The purpose of this chapter is to draw attention to the presence of Avicenna in the works of Aquinas. The reader will not find a reconstruction of the whole thought of the Persian philosopher. While almost all references to the doctrines and theories of Avicenna have been taken into consideration, a considerable number of them have been ordered according to a set of themes characteristic of his philosophy, and with regard to which Thomas has taken a position.

In Thomas's works there are a small number of references to other Arab philosophers, whom L. Gardet calls "minor," such as to the *mutakallimûn* Al Kindi, Al Fârabi, Algazel, and Avempace, of whom Thomas has a limited knowledge.[9] The great Arab philosophers are for Thomas the Platonizing Avicenna and the Aristotelian Averroes. In the writings of Thomas there are more than 340 references to theories of Avicenna.[10]

---

7. Gardet, "Saint Thomas et ses prédécesseurs arabes," 444.

8. For the history of the studies on the relation between the philosophy of Avicenna and the thought of Aquinas, see Georges C. Anawati, "Saint Thomas d'Aquin et la Métaphysique d'Avicenne," in *St. Thomas Aquinas, 1274–1974. Commemorative Studies*, ed. A. Maurer (Toronto: Pontifical Institute of Mediaeval Studies, 1974), 450–53.

9. Gardet, "Saint Thomas et ses prédécesseurs arabes," 421.

10. Vansteenkiste has given us a list of these references, see his "Avicenna-citaten bij S. Thomas," *Tijdschrift voor Philosophie* 15 (1953): 437–507.

In the *Scriptum super Libros Sententiarum* and also in the *De ente et essentia* and in the *QD de veritate* these are numerous, but there are very few in the *Summa contra gentiles*, a few in the first part of the *Summa theologiae*, very few in the *prima secundae*, and none in the *secunda secundae* and the third part. There are some references in the *Quaestiones disputatae*, but very few in Thomas's commentaries on the works of Aristotle. There are, however, a number of passages in which theories of Avicenna are implicitly present. Our overview begins with mentioning some doctrines which Thomas appreciated and referred to several times.

Being (*ens*) and the One

In several texts Thomas recalls that according to Avicenna being (*ens*) is the first concept to enter into our intellect, in which all other concepts are resolved,[11] but Thomas noticed that this doctrine of being has its defects: for Avicenna *ens* and *unum* are accidental predicates, which do not signify the substance of things, but something added.[12] According to Avicenna, when we qualify something as a being, we signify a state, a kind of logical existence contrary to non-being, but not the reality and the act of the essence. Thomas observes that this applies also to the definition Avicenna gives of the One, a concept which according to Avicenna is convertible with being, but which adds something to being. This is wrong, "*hoc manifeste falsum est*," says Thomas,[13] since a being in that case would be one by something added to it. If a thing is one by its essence, nothing is added to it. A further difficulty is that the One which is added to a being, is one as the principle of numbers.[14] It is precisely this assimilation of the One to one as the principle of numbers which caused this error, says Thomas ("*deceptus fuit ex aequivocatione unius*").

While the word "being" (*ens*) is derived from the verb "to be," the word "thing" (*res*) is from the essence.[15] Whatever we conceive, we con-

11. *In I Sent.*, d. 38, q. 1, a. 4; *QD de veritate*, q. 1, a. 1; *De ente et essentia*.
12. *In IV Metaph.*, lesson 2, no. 9; *In X Metaph.*, lesson 3, no. 21: "Significant naturam superadditam super ens de quibus dicuntur."
13. *ST* I, q. 11, a. 1, ad 1: "... unum addit aliquam rem super entem, sed hoc manifeste falsum est." Cf. also *Quodl.*, X, q. 1, a. 1.
14. *In I Sent.*, d. 24, q. 1, a. 3, ad 3. See, however, Thomas O'Shaughnessy, "St. Thomas and Avicenna on the Nature of the One," *Gregorianum* 41, no. 4 (1960): 665–79. who suspects that the interpretation of Thomas may have been influenced by a less correct translation.
15. *In I Sent.*, d. 12, q. 1, a. 4, arg. 3.

ceive it as something which exists. "Being" and "thing" accompany all our concepts. Corresponding to this distinction between *ens* and *res*, for which Thomas is grateful to Avicenna, there is a real distinction between the being (*esse*) and the essence in all things. In all created beings their being differs from their essence and does not enter into their definition, as Avicenna says.[16] Whatever has being, has a certain potentiality.[17] But Thomas conceives this composition differently than Avicenna.[18] For Avicenna the essence—the central content of a thing—has already a certain reality, let us say that it is a "real possibility," but then it is placed in the physical world where it undergoes a sort of injection of being. Being (*esse*) is conceived by him as an accident which is added to the essence, based on *Metaphysics* VIII, chapter 4, whereas Thomas stresses that being is not something of the class of accidents: it is the act, the reality of the essence.[19] For Thomas the essence without the act of being has no reality at all; it is a potency, which is realized by the act of being.[20]

According to Avicenna the essences are outside God; they form an eternal ensemble in the flow of emanation which issues from God to pass through the successive intelligent beings. The essences are not altogether simple and have a certain potentiality. God knows them, thinks them and places them in the world by giving them existence.[21] Avicenna leaves Aristotle when he professes a "certain creation" of things by God, but contrary to what the Bible teaches, this creation is eternal. Since there is emanation from a first principle, Avicenna privileges the univocity of things and does not consider the analogy of being.

The concept of being comprises necessary and possible being. We live amidst possible beings, but if there were only possible beings, nothing would exist. What is possible does not have the reason of its existence in itself, contrary to a necessary being; it has no cause.[22] One must notice however that this contingence is quite relative, since once a cause is ac-

---

16. *Quodl.*, IX, q. 4, a. 1, arg. 4.

17. *In I Sent.*, d. 3, q. 4, a. 1, ad 2. See, on this theme, M. D. Roland-Gosselin, *Le De ente et essentia de S. Thomas d'Aquin: texte établi d'après les manuscrits parisiens* (Paris: Librairie philosophique J. Vrin, 1948): 150–56.

18. Cf. *Quodl.* IX, q. 4, a. 1, arg. 4: "In omni creatura esse est aliud ab essentia eius nec intrat in definitionem ut Avicenna dicit."

19. *QD de potentia*, q. 5, a. 4 arg. 3, and ad 3; *In IV Metaph.*, lesson 2, no. 556.

20. *ST* I, q. 3, a. 4: "Oportet igitur quod ipsum esse comparetur ad essentiam quae est aliud ab ipso sicut actus ad potentiam."

21. *QD de veritate*, q. 23, a. 5, arg. 1.

22. Avicenna, *Metaphysica*, I, 6, in Riet, *Liber de philosophia prima, I-IV*, 44; 31–33.

tive, the effect follows necessarily, Avicenna says, in his *Metaphysics* IV, chapter 1. Thomas observes that the argument does not apply to a cause which itself determines the way in which it will produce the effect, as is the case with God's will.[23] This theme is important, and Thomas comes back to it several times in his works; his concern is to preserve God's freedom in his dealings with the world.[24]

Truth

The truth of things is a property of their being which is something determinate, for example, this tree, this man, and which has been ascertained.[25] This definition seems to concern both the logical truth (what one has determined with respect to a thing, *stabilitum*) and the ontological truth in so far as is meant the property of a being to let itself be known. Everything has its being (exists) in some species and has an essence. We cannot make statements except about that which is. Hence it is evident that what is true, is being in one way or another.[26] Avicenna says that which exists is necessarily the very truth.[27]

God

In his *Scriptum super libros Sententiarum*, book II, d. 1, q. 1, a. 1, Thomas quotes Avicenna's demonstration of the existence of God: none of the things in the world is its own being, since we can conceive its quiddity without thinking of it as existent; therefore it is necessary that they receive their being from another, and in this way we arrive at a being whose essence is its being. God is therefore conceived as the only basis and source of the existence of all things.[28] On the other hand, the First Way (of the Five Ways of Thomas), which shows the existence of a First Unmoved Mover, is based on the principle that whatever is moving is moved

---

23. *QD de veritate*, q. 23, a. 5, arg. 1.
24. *QD de potentia*, q. 3, a. 17, arg. 4, and ad 4.
25. *SCG* I, 60; *Quodl.* VIII, q. 8, art unic.: "Veritas uniuscuiusque rei, ut dicit Avicenna, nihil est aliud quam proprietas sui esse quod stabilitum est ei."
26. *QD de veritate*, q. 1, a. 1, ad 7.
27. Avicenna, *Metaphysica*, VIII, 6.
28. Thomas concludes that this is the way to God that Avicenna follows ("et haec est via Avicennae").

by another, and that in this way we arrive at a being which is immobile. Avicenna objects that Aristotle's argument is not solid, since Aristotle reasons that a thing that moves by itself, must be divisible: under one aspect it is itself, but under another aspect it changes. Since there is in material things an infinite divisibility, there is no first of which the movement would not depend on another.[29] However, no single thing of which a part is in movement and another not, moves primarily and by itself. Avicenna rejects Aristotle's argument by rejecting the division in parts; a being which moves by itself must move in its entirety and in its parts. Thomas replies that in a thing, of which we suppose that it moves itself, some part must be immobile and so it does not move by itself. Avicenna suggests the opposite. Therefore, Thomas says, Avicenna's criticism of this proof is wrong.[30]

Since in God there is no composition of being and essence, God is not in the predicament of substance.[31] He alone is necessary by himself.[32] Contrary to Plotinus, who excludes knowledge from God, Avicenna follows Aristotle in his affirmation that God knows himself: God is knowledge of himself in the highest degree, since there is no matter in him.[33] In so far as God knows himself and wills his essence as the principle of things, beings and the forms and matter proceed from him,[34] but he does not know them individually, except in a general way.[35] God operates by his essence, as Avicenna says.[36]

Are the *rationes* (essential contents) of things present in God? Avicenna and Maimonides deny it. God is just his own essence. The *rationes* of all other things are attributed to him in so far as he is their cause, or by the way of negation.[37] Avicenna does not use and does not even seem to accept the *via affirmationis*, which proceeds from the perfections found in

---

29. Cf. *In VII Phys.*, lesson 1, no. 889.
30. *SCG* I, 13: "... ut Avicenna calumniatur." Thomas defends the argument against Avicenna in *In VII Phys.*, lesson 1.
31. *In II Sent.*, d. 3, q. 1, a. 1, ad 1. Cf. *In Boetii De Trin.*, q. 6, a. 3: "Deus in nullo genere est."
32. *QD de veritate*, q. 24, a. 10, arg. 4; *QD de potentia*, q. 2, a. 3: "Deus per se necessarium est esse ut Avicenna probat."
33. Ibid., q. 2.
34. *In I Sent.*, d. 38, q. 1, a. 1.
35. *In I Sent.*, d. 36, q. 1, a. 1; *In II Sent.*, d. 3, q. 3, a. 3; *QD de veritate*, q. 2, a. 5: "Deus cognoscit unumquoque singularium quasi in universali, ut Avicenna et sequaces dicunt;" q. 8, a. 1: "Avicenna writes in his *Metaphysica* that God and the angels know the individual things in a universal way."
36. *In I Sent.*, d. 42, q. 1, a. 1, arg. 2. But, as Thomas explains in his answer to this text of the *Metaphysica* of Avicenna, the word *potentia* is used by Avicenna in its secondary meaning, that is, potentiality.
37. *In I Sent.*, d. 2, q. 1, a. 3.

created beings to ascribe them to God. God gives directly only being to the creatures.

On the other hand, Thomas quotes repeatedly and with appreciation the sentence of Avicenna with which he affirms that God is the only perfectly liberal and generous being in the highest degree.[38]

Creation

Adhering as he does to the emanation theory of Plotinus, Avicenna affirms that from the One, only what is one proceeds. This means that from God only a first intelligent being proceeds, from which a second flows forth, and from this intellect the world soul and the body of the first heaven.[39] This process is repeated eight times until, in the last cosmic sphere the intelligence called the *Dator formarum* appears, from whom the universal concepts of human beings and the matter of physical things proceed. For Avicenna creation is a series of emanations, in which God provides the being of what proceeds but not the essence, whereas for Thomas creation is a pure efficient causality. With regard to this theory Thomas observes that it cannot stand (*"non potest stare"*) for two reasons: creation is strictly the work of God alone which he cannot share with others. An instrumental causality, exercised by creatures, though subordinated to God, is impossible: everything must be willed and done by God.[40]

In another text Thomas writes that the theory of Avicenna, according to which a first intelligent being proceeds from God and from this flow the soul and the matter of the first heaven, is wrong and contrary to the faith.[41] Avicenna lets everything come forth from the First Principle in a certain order: the soul exists because of the celestial bodies, and the matter of the elements is caused by the substance of the heaven. The souls exist because of the mediation of the intelligent beings, corporeal beings come into being from spiritual realities, and corruptible things from in-

38. *In II Sent.*, d. 3, q. 4, a. 1, arg. 1; *SCG* I, 93; *QD de potentia*, q. 7, a. 10.
39. *ST* I, q. 45, a. 5: "Et sic ponit Avicenna quod prima substantia separata creata a Deo creat aliam post se, et substantiam orbis et animam eius; et quod substantia orbis creat materiam inferiorum corporum."
40. *ST* I, q. 47, a. 1; q. 45, a. 5. Houser, "Avicenna, Aliqui and Thomas Aquinas's Doctrine of Creation," note 4, chooses to read in the text of *ST* I, q. 44, a. 2 ("et ulterius aliqui erexerunt se") a reference to Avicenna, but Avicenna's concept of creation is still so defective (see note 43 below) that it is hardly probable that Thomas had Avicenna in mind. He may have thought of Maimonides.
41. *In II Sent.*, d. 15, q. 1, a. 2.

corruptible beings.[42] According to this view all things would not exist by God's causality alone but by the concourse of several causes and would be a product of chance.[43] Thomas also observes that according to this opinion God does not begin to act, since his will remains the same and creation as the act of God takes place from all eternity.

This duality in the creation of the world—God gives being, and the intelligent beings cause the essences—is easier to understand when one takes into account that Avicenna's view of the real distinction (between being and essence) is not the same as the doctrine of Thomas. According to Avicenna being is not the act, the actualization of the essence, but is rather a kind of accident added to the essence which places it in the physical world.

With regard to the problem of evil, Thomas mentions that according to Avicenna there is no evil in the universe above the earth and the sphere of the elements.[44] But Avicenna proposes a "practical" (*perutilis*) division of evil in his *Metaphysica* which Thomas quotes: a first division is between evil by itself and evil *per accidens*. Evil as such is either the privation of a necessary perfection, or that of a perfection that is not necessary for all. Evil *per accidens* is the subject of a privation or its cause.[45]

The Intelligent Beings, the Souls of the Heavenly Spheres, and Their Causality

The intelligent beings connected with the different celestial spheres are simple beings without matter.[46] Among them there are as many individuals as there are species.[47] They are possible beings. These theses Thomas accepts, identifying the intelligent beings with the angels of Christian revelation. For Avicenna, the forms present in the intellect of these intelligent beings are active (*factivae*), and sensible matter obeys them more than any of the active and passive qualities. In this way transmutations

---

42. Ibid.: "... sed hae positio erronea est et contra fidem."
43. *ST* I, q. 47, a. 1: "... secundum hanc positionem non proveniret ex intentione primi agentis universitas rerum, sed ex concursu multarum causarum agentium; tale autem dicimus provenire a casu."
44. *QD de veritate*, q. 5, a. 4; q. 21, a. 2, arg. 1; *In II Sent.*, d. 5,q. 1, a, 1, arg. 1.
45. *In II Sent.*, d. 34, q. 1, a. 2.
46. *In II Sent.*, d. 178, q. 1, a. 2; *QD de spir. creat.*, a. 1, s.c. 5: Avicenna and Algazel say that the separate substances are without any matter.
47. *De ente et essentia*, chap. 5.

take place in the lower bodies, which are not due to material causes. In addition to this causality, there is also that of the motion of the celestial spheres. Thomas notes that this opinion contradicts what Augustine writes in the third book of his *De Trinitate*: the matter of the bodies is not subject to the arbitrary intervention of the angels. Avicenna's opinion is also, in Thomas's view, contrary to reason.[48]

According to Avicenna we would know things by cognitive species (*intentiones*) which the intelligent beings, in particular the *Dator formarum*, impress on our intellect, but Thomas does not accept this opinion.[49] The root of this view is the theory that the forms become entities, whereas for Aristotle the forms do not exist by themselves; what exists is the being composed of form and matter.[50] According to Plato, however, the forms of the things on the earth exist by themselves in the world of the Ideas, but according to Avicenna they are in the intelligent beings and the *Dator formarum*. From these forms in the intelligent beings would come all the forms of the material things. Thomas comes back repeatedly to this error according to which the natural agents in our material world would have no other role than that of making dispositions for the reception of the form. Another consequence of this opinion would be that the sciences and virtues would proceed from this *Dator formarum*, and that we would not acquire the virtues by our actions.[51] Moreover, according to this view it would be the form and not the composite thing which comes to be. Spiritual substances, Thomas says, can exercise a causality which reduces matter to act and brings it so to its form, but they do not produce the forms.[52]

In connection with the theory that the intelligent beings are involved in the creation-emanation of the successive orders of creatures, Avicenna thought that they exercise dominion over the material world and that

---

48. *Quodl.* IX, q. 4, a. 5. Thomas writes that according to Averroes these intelligent beings cannot directly influence the bodies at the lower levels in the universe.

49. *In IV Sent.*, d. 49, q. 2, a. 1, ad 9: "Dictum Avicennae quantum ad hoc (sc. per intentiones impressas) non sustinemus de cognitione substantiarum separatarum;" *In Boetii De Trin.*, I, 1, 2: "... quando res est simplicior quam similitudo per quam cognoscimus, sicut Avicenna dicit quod intelligentias congnoscimus per impressiones earum in nobis."

50. *ST* I, q. 65, a. 4.

51. *In III Sent.*, d. 33, q. 1, a. 2, qc. 2: "Haec positio tollit naturalem virtutem." Cf. *QD de virtutibus*, q. 1, a. 8: "Our actions would only prepare us for receiving the virtues." According to Avicenna a virtue is a power which is mainly given to us to execute operations. But, says Thomas, this is only true for the first beginning of the natural virtues in our faculties.

52. *ST* I, q. 91, a. 2, ad 2. Thomas criticizes Avicenna for imagining (*fingit*) that even the form of the perfect animals can be engendered by the power of the celestial bodies, and recalls as contrary to this view the saying of Aristotle "Homo generat hominem ex materia et sol."

matter obeys them, but, Thomas writes, material things obey only the one who made them, God.[53]

Augustine did not answer the question whether the celestial bodies have a soul, but Avicenna gives an affirmative answer. But he not only attributes thought to these souls, but also imagination, which enables them to understand individual things: they make the heavens turn and be in one place and then in another, and must know where they are at a given moment. But Thomas thinks that this is not necessary, since the movement of the heavens is uniform.[54]

According to Avicenna the celestial bodies produce their effects necessarily; all natural or voluntary causality in the world must be reduced to a celestial principle. According to him, when one considers the question attentively, one must conclude that the effects of the celestial bodies are necessary. Avicenna gives the following argument: if an effect of a celestial body would be impeded, this would have to be through the intervention of one or another voluntary or natural cause. But all of these depend on celestial causes, and an impediment would also be produced by these causes. But, Thomas writes, this argument has already been refuted by Aristotle.[55]

The Human Soul

Like the souls of the celestial spheres, the souls of human beings are also produced by an intelligent being, namely, the *Dator formarum*, who, however, produces them only when their bodies have been prepared. "From the intelligent being which moves the last cosmic sphere proceed or flow forth the human souls."[56] "Avicenna says that the human soul as well as all other substantial forms proceed from this acting intellect,"[57] although in another text he expresses himself more vaguely: the lower souls proceed from the superior ones, hence they are open to impressions coming from above, but, Thomas says, this theory is impossible from the point of view of the Catholic faith (*"secundum fidem catholicam hoc stare non*

---

53. *In III Sent.*, d. 16, q. 1, a. 3, and ad 3.
54. *QD de anima*, a. 8, ad 3.
55. *SCG* III, 86.
56. *In II Sent.*, d. 18, q. 2, a. 3.
57. *In II Sent.*, d. 18, q. 2, a. 2.

potest"), because the human souls are created immediately by God.[58] Since according to Avicenna the souls are not the forms of their bodies and do not constitute with them one substance, they do not depend on the bodies for their being nor with regard to their end or destination, but there is a certain dependence on matter for their individuation, which is realized by their relation to a body.[59] Consequently, Avicenna holds a certain dualism of the body and the soul: the soul cannot be the substantial form of the body, since if it were, it would lose its immaterial nature.[60] But the soul gives being to the body and uses it for its cognitive activities.[61] In his *De anima*, III, chapter 8, and V, chapter 8, Avicenna writes that the "spirits" (i.e., as causes in the material world and instruments of the soul) which spread though the members of the body, are of the nature of light, but Thomas thinks that Avicenna did not want to say that these spirits are of the nature of the *quinta essentia*.[62] In another text we read that the power of the seed is rooted in the "spirit," contained in it and that almost all of the seed is transformed in spirit.[63]

Avicenna defends the immateriality of the human soul: the soul is not a form submerged in matter.[64] In his *De unitate intellectus contra Averroistas*, article 5, Thomas writes that several philosophers defend the theory that there is only one possible intellect, common to all men, but that among the Arab philosophers Algazel and Avicenna teach the plurality of intellects according to the number of human beings. According to Avicenna, indeed, each soul has its intellect, which receives its concepts from the *Dator formarum*. But, as we have pointed out before, our intellect does not conserve the knowledge of the concepts it receives once it ceases considering them.[65] Yet there remains a certain residue in the sensitive part of man,[66] and a repeated consideration creates something like the habitus of a science. In that case our possible intellect no longer needs the sense faculties to think its concepts, but this is wrong, Thomas

---

58. *In II Sent.*, d. 25, q. 1, a. 2, ad 5.
59. *In II Sent.*, d. 17,q. 2, a. 2, ad 4; *De ente et essentia*, chap. 4.
60. See Noriko Ushida, *Étude comparative de la psychologie d'Aristote, d'Avicenne et de St. Thomas d'Aquin* (Tokyo: Keio Institute of Cultural and Linguistic Studies, 1968), 94f.
61. Cf. M. D. Roland-Gosselin, "Sur les relations de l'âme et du corps d'après Avicenne," in *Mélanges Mandonnet*, vol. 2 (Paris: Librairie philosophique J. Vrin, 1930), 47–54.
62. *In II Sent.*, d. 1117, q. 3, a. 1, ad 3.
63. *QD de potentia*, q. 3, a. 11, ad 8.
64. *In III Sent.*, d. 19, q. 1, a. 1.
65. *In II De anima*, lesson 13, no. 3:"Species non conservantur in intellectu possibili."
66. *QD de veritate*, q. 10, a. 2.

notes.[67] According to Avicenna matter is more obedient to the soul of a spiritual man than to contrary powers in nature.[68]

Avicenna holds that besides the five external senses man has also five internal senses, although Aristotle only accepts four of the latter. Avicenna adds a fifth special faculty which has as its task to combine and to separate the forms in our imagination, but Thomas writes that the imagination by itself is sufficient to carry out these tasks.[69] We are given the senses to allow us to acquire a more complete knowledge of things, but the senses do not know their own nature.[70] The cognitive species of sensible things can reduce the senses in act, but not completely, by producing dispositions in them—Avicenna calls that "to be in reserve" or "to be in the treasure," and this can cause a more perfect actualization when the sensible species actually impress themselves on the sense powers. Then there is what is called apprehension.[71]

From the perspective of Avicenna, we no longer need the senses, once the *Dator formarum* has given us the concepts according to the images of the senses. The situation is then that of a person who has finished his voyage: he must no longer seek a change of place. The senses prepare for knowledge, but do not make an essential contribution to it.[72] Thomas, however, reminds us that according to Aristotle the things represented in our imagination are the proper object of the intellect. The intellect must turn to these images, not only when we acquire them, but also when we use them. This is evident, since when the organ of the imagination has been damaged, a man can no longer have recourse to the knowledge he had acquired before. Avicenna's theory, Thomas says, is valid only for the soul separated from the body.[73]

Since our concepts are given us by the *Dator formarum*, the celestial bodies and the other intelligent beings also have a certain influence on what our will chooses. This is not a direct influence, but the impressions which they leave behind in our bodies are as dispositions, and we move

---

67. *In III De anima*, lesson 13, no. 6.
68. *In III Sent.*, d. 16, q. 1, a. 3, arg. 3.
69. ST I, q. 78, a. 4. In his *Commentary on the De memoria et reminiscentia*, lesson 2, Thomas writes that "Avicenna rationabiliter ostendit esse diversas potentias sensitivas;" and in lesson 3 we read: "Avicenna convenienter dicit quod memoria respicit intentionem, imaginatio vero formam per sensum apprehensam."
70. *QD de veritate*, q. 18, a. 4, arg. 2; and q. 1, a. 9.
71. *Quodl.* VII, q. 1, a. 2.
72. *QD de anima*, a. 15.
73. *QD de veritate*, q. 18, a. 8, ad 4.

ourselves in a certain way according to these dispositions—as the passions of our sensitive appetite can exercise a certain influence on our reason. In his *Metaphysica*, X, 1, Avicenna writes that the variety of the acts of our will are reduced to the influence of the celestial bodies as to their cause, although these have themselves a uniform motion. Thomas observes that this theory is false and contrary to the faith.[74] Somewhat further on in the *Scriptum*, Thomas quotes Ptolemy who says that the celestial bodies do not have a compelling influence on the senses, but he adds that Avicenna seems to hold the theory that our will depends on the souls of the celestial bodies as on its guiding rule, since it owes its origin to these heavenly souls.[75] Thomas comes back to this theme in the *QD de veritate*, question 6, article 6: according to certain authors the order which God has established is entirely immutable, whereas the Stoics thought that what has been defined can be modified by prayer and sacrifices; Avicenna appears to have taken over the former view, in that he ascribes to the celestial souls an influence on our bodies; all that happens in our sublunar world follows the impressions and the images which these souls send us.

Thomas notes that this opinion is in disagreement with the faith.[76] It also excludes all contingence in the world.[77] With regard to the different acts which the will can perform, Avicenna distinguishes between: to move, to conduct to an end, to dispose, to command, and to counsel.[78] Further on in his *QD de veritate*, Thomas comes back to the question and concedes that the celestial bodies can exercise some influence on the human body, and that in this way those who follow the inclinations of their bodies are influenced by them, but this does not apply to those who resist to those inclinations.[79]

Since the souls are not their being, but receive it from God, they are marked by potentiality. They do not depend on the body with respect to their being, but in a certain way they depend on it for their individualization—not in the sense that their individuality would be a particular determining factor of their substantial being, but rather that it is consti-

---

74. *In II Sent.*, d. 15, q. 1, a. 3.
75. *In II Sent.*, d. 25, q. 1, a. 2, ad 5.
76. *QD de veritate*, q. 6, a. 6. With respect to this theory, Thomas refers to the *Metaphysica* of Avicenna, X, 1.
77. Cf. *SCG* III, 86 and 87.
78. *ST* I-II, q. 17, a. 1, arg. 1.
79. *QD de veritate*, q. 22, a. 9. A.-M. Goichon notes that for Avicenna magic is a scientific theme. Avicenna, *Livre des directives et remarques*, trans. A.-M. Goichon (Paris: Vrin, 1951), 5.

tuted by its characteristic accidents.[80] As we have seen, each soul has its possible intellect, which receives its concepts from the *Dator formarum*.[81] The soul does not reach its perfection until it has been delivered from the body. In this connection one may recall another theory of Avicenna, that is, that after their death the souls of villains will not be punished by fire, but by likenesses of bodies, which will be like dreams.[82]

Moral Doctrines

When Thomas discusses the election of an action and the passing to its execution, he quotes a text from Avicenna: it is not necessary that during the execution of an action one has always the original intention present in act. Avicenna explains this with the example of a handicraftsman who during the execution of his task does not always think of his initial plan.[83]

In the works of Thomas there are very few references to Avicenna's moral doctrine. The reason for this absence might be that those works in which Avicenna deals with this subject had not been translated into Latin. Those in the Latin West were acquainted with his books on the philosophy of nature, the soul, and metaphysics. This explains why there are hardly any references to Avicenna in the second part of the *Summa theologiae* and in the *Commentary on the Nicomachean Ethics*. There are a few scattered sentences, mentioned by Thomas:

- "Without hope anger is not possible";[84]
- "Joy is a kind of pleasure";[85]
- "Pleasure comes when one perceives something agreeable which accompanies what we are doing or are looking for."[86]

Thomas observes that there is something of a contradiction between what Avicenna writes in the fifth book of his *De natura* and in his *Metaphysica*, where he seems to downgrade the passions in comparison with spiritual joys.

---

80. Cf. Roland-Gosselin, "Sur les relations de l'âme et du corps d'après Avicenne," 60 ff.
81. *In I Sent.*, d. 3, q. 4, a. 1, ad 1; *In II Sent.*, d. 17, q. 2, a. 2, ad 4: "Anima esse individuatum non possit habere nisi secundum quod coniungitur corpori."
82. *In IV Sent.*, d. 44, q. 3, a. 2.
83. *In IV Sent.*, d. 15, q. 4, a. 2, qc. 2, arg. 2.
84. *In III Sent.*, d. 26, q. 1, a. 3, s.c. 3.
85. *In IV Sent.*, d. 49, q. 3, a. 1, qc. 4, s.c. 1; *ST* I-II, q. 31, a. 3.
86. *In IV Sent.*, d. 49, q. 3, a. 2, arg. 1.

- "All passions are characterized by surges and easing down";[87]
- "The reason why people are talking so much is the great number of their desires which spring from their numerous defects";[88]
- "To take shape passions require certain dispositions in our body";[89]
- "Anger is not the most important passion, because it presupposes sadness and hope.[90]

Thomas notes that Avicenna speaks only of the irascible appetite when there is a connection with anger.[91]

- "Our body does not change by fear, envy or anger alone, but by a certain infection which comes from the mind and has a repercussion on the body."[92]

The Cosmos according to Avicenna

Avicenna accepts the model of the cosmos as elaborated by Aristotle: the sphere of the first heaven, the spheres of the planets, and the central place of the earth in the middle of the universe, surrounded by the layers of the elements. But he does not admit Aristotle's ingenious hypothesis of some forty additional spheres which by their revolutions explain the apparently irregular motions of the planets. According to Avicenna there are as many moving substances as there are planets, to which we must add the sphere of the fixed stars and a sphere which has no stars.[93] All celestial bodies are inside the sphere of the first heaven. By the motion of this sphere all revolutions take place. The celestial bodies are composed of a body and a soul.[94] But he notes that the philosophers admitted the existence of two groups of spirits moving the celestial spheres: a first group is formed by the souls of those spheres, of which thought is determined and concerns particular beings; the second group comprises the intelligent beings, whose thought concerns the universal and what is simple.[95]

---

87. ST I-II, q. 23, a. 2, arg. 3.
88. QD de veritate, q. 9, a. 4, arg. 10.
89. Ibid., q. 25, a. 4, arg. 5.
90. Ibid., q. 26, a. 5, ad 3.
91. QD de malo, q. 8, a. 3, ad 5.
92. Ibid., q. 16, a. 9, ad 13.
93. De substantiis separatis, chap. 2.
94. QD de veritate, q. 5, a. 10.
95. In II Sent., d. 10, q. 1, a. 2.

Avicenna reduces the role of the First Principle, God, when he writes that the first sphere is not moved by Him, but by the intelligent being caused by Him.[96] We notice here the influence of Plotinus's Neoplatonism. But Thomas writes that it is more probable that between the first immaterial substance and the first heaven, there are several orders of immaterial substances. The spiritual substance (the intelligent being) which moves the heavens, does so not only by giving it the motion of the revolution of the heaven, but also by an action which goes beyond corporeal causality. Avicenna thinks, in fact, that bodily matter obeys much more the thoughts and orders of this substance than of contrary agents in the physical world. According to him, this explains certain changes, cures, etc. which occur on the earth. The celestial bodies, their souls, and the intelligent beings are in charge of all inferior bodies and are the causes of the matter of the sublunar world and of all the processes of transformation of the elements, of life, and of knowledge.[97]

According to Thomas this was the common opinion of the Platonists. Avicenna distinguishes himself from their common view in so far as he made the last intelligent being, the *Dator formarum*, the cause of the forms of the beings in our sublunar section of the world. This comprises matter, the forms of material things, the impressions on our sense faculties, and the concepts of the intellect.[98] This theory, says Thomas, agrees quite well with the principles of his philosophy, since it affirms that the natural agents do not do more than dispose matter, and that the substantial forms come from this intellect which he calls the *Dator formarum*. If matter obeys it to receive its form, it is no longer surprising that the *Dator formarum* can also introduce certain forms in matter only by its command. But Thomas says, this theory does not hold up against the analysis which Aristotle gives of the causality of the celestial bodies.[99]

In his *Commentary on the Physics* of Aristotle, Thomas quotes some difficulties raised by Avicenna against the Aristotelian theory of motion. Avicenna's argument is that each movement belongs to one or another species of motion, such as local motion. A difficulty looms up with regard to the last sphere which executes its revolution around the center of the universe.

---

96. *In XII Metaph.*, lesson 9, no. 7.

97. *ST* I, q. 110, a. 1; Cf. *QD de veritate*, q. 5, a. 9: the circular movement, common to all the celestial bodies, produces what is common to all things here below, that is, primary matter.

98. *In II Sent.*, d. 15, q. 1, a. 2: "... materiam elementorum a substantia caeli causari." See above the section "creation."

99. *QD de potentia*, q. 6, a. 3 ("non potest stare").

It does not seem to be in a place, if one defines "place" in the way Aristotle says, since that sphere no longer has a surface that surrounds it. Avicenna suggests that it is per accidens in a place, but Thomas raises an objection and prefers to say with Themistius that it is in a place through its parts.

On the principle that whatever moves is moved by another, Avicenna writes that one should not speak of parts when there is question of a being that moves itself. In Book VIII of Aristotle's *Physics*, in the section covered by lesson 21 of the commentary of Thomas, Avicenna raises a difficulty: it is not possible that a finite mover moves during an infinite time.

Matter, Form, and the Body

In Avicenna's philosophy matter does not have the same function nor the same nature as primary matter has for Aristotle. Avicenna seems to have conceived of matter in the way that the Platonists did of their second principle. According to them this principle receives different forms and is not—as it is according to Aristotle—the principle from which the forms are drawn. This explains why Avicenna protests against the way in which, in his *Physics* I, chapter 9, Aristotle speaks of matter. According to Avicenna matter cannot desire a form (as Aristotle writes that it does), since it does not have a nature which inclines it to a form. Moreover, the desire which Aristotle attributes to it, would result from the fact that it has enough of its present form and would want another one, but that is in vain. Thomas, in his turn, gives a fine explanation of what Aristotle means by noting that this desire for something is nothing else but that matter is ordained to it.[100]

Thomas notes that according to Plato and Avicenna, all forms come from outside the receiving being. They base this view on two arguments: the forms do not have matter, and for this reason they can only be produced by agents outside matter; the second argument which they use to ascribe the origin of forms to a cause that is above our sublunar world is that in our material world they do not see other factors at work except active and passive qualities, which are insufficient to produce the forms of material things. Thomas objects that becoming is not proper to forms, but to the composed beings and that the forms are drawn from the potentiality of matter.[101]

100. *Quodl.* IX, q. 5, a. 1.
101. *Quodl.* IX, q. 5, a. 1.

According to Avicenna the human body resembles the celestial bodies. For this reason it is well composed[102] and formed immediately after the formation of the heavens.[103] Avicenna does not follow Plato's theory that the forms of sensible things exist as ideas, but he says that these forms preexist in an immaterial way in the intelligent beings.[104] With regard to the formation of man, Avicenna thinks that what a mother does is just to enhance what she has conceived.[105]

In accordance with this different view of the function of primary matter, Avicenna affirms that the forms of the elements remain actually present in the being which is composed of them. He thinks that they obtain an intermediary position between the substantial forms and the accidents, but Thomas replies that we must say with Aristotle that they remain only virtually present in such accidents as quality.[106]

Another particular opinion mentioned by Thomas is that Avicenna thought that several forms can coexist in material things. The forms of the elements are present in act in the composed being.[107] Avicenna rejects Avicebron's theory of corporeity in its crude form according to which there is present in material things, beside their own specific form, a form which is common to all and constitutes their corporeity. But this cannot be true because a form gives complete substantial being.[108] On the other hand, Avicenna maintains that matter is not deprived of its form of bodily being.[109] Thomas refers to *Sufficientia* II, chapter 3, where one reads that in fire there is the form fire and the form by which it is a body.

That corresponds with another theory of Avicenna, namely, that the elements remain in the composed thing with their substantial forms, according to what they were before, but that they change to a second being by the active and passive qualities.[110] Because of the corporeity of matter, there is only one matter of all bodies, Avicenna says, a view criticized by Averroes.[111] Primary matter, Avicenna says, is the effect of the common circular

---

102. *In II Sent.*, d. 1, q. 2, a. 5.
103. *In II Sent.*, d. 15, q. 2, a. 2, arg. 7.
104. *ST* I, q. 76, a. 4, ad 4.
105. *In III Sent.*, d. 3, q. 2, a. 1.
106. In this theory of Avicenna, there is no longer any contingency in the cosmos. Cf. *Quodl.* I, q. 4, a. 1, ad 3; *ST* I, q. 76, a. 4, ad 4.
107. *QD de anima*, a. 9, ad 10.
108. *In II Sent.*, d. 12, q. 1, a. 4.
109. *In II Sent.*, d. 18, q. 1, a. 2. Cf. Avicenna, *Metaphysica*, II, 3 (van Riet, *Liber de philosophia prima, I-IV*, 89, 76):"Restat ergo ut materia non spolietur a forma corporali."
110. *In II Sent.*, d. 12, q. 1, a. 4. Thomas refers to the *Metaphysica*, II, 11.
111. *In II Sent.*, d. 12, q. 1, a. 1.

movement of all celestial bodies.[112] Primary matter is never without a form. If it loses one, it has immediately another, as Avicenna writes.[113]

Since the form constitutes the substance and form as such is without matter, all substances are intelligible.[114] In the processes of generation and corruption in our world, the corporeal agents act on the basis of their accidental forms and dispose the matter for the substantial form, but as we have seen above, it is an immaterial cause which introduces the substantial form,[115] for corporeal matter is of such a nature that it obeys the immaterial agents more than contrary natural agents.[116] With respect to the natural things of which our world is composed, Aristotle thought that their existence was evident to the senses, but Avicenna wanted to demonstrate it with his general theory of a quasi-necessary emanation. Thomas thinks such a demonstration is irrational (*"Avicenna irrationaliter conatus est..."*).[117]

Scattered over the works of Thomas, we find some quotations of Avicenna's theory of light, a lively debated theme in the Middle Ages. In *In II Sent.*, d. 13, q. 1, a. 3, where Thomas mentions several theories on the nature of light, he quotes Avicenna six times. According to Avicenna light is a quality of the shining body, that is, the sun, which the other bodies receive.[118] The superior bodies do not act on what is on a lower level without the mediation of light. According to some authors light would not add anything to colors. For them, the very visibility of colors is called light, but this opinion is rejected by Avicenna, who advances several proofs. In connection with these theories about light, Thomas mentions the problem of whether God can create things from nothing or needs matter. According to Aristotle the agent and the one who receives his actions (patient) must be of the same genus. But between non-being and God, there is no correspondence, and this seems to exclude creation from nothing. An opponent in the disputed question about this difficulty of the *De potentia* suggests the following solution: Avicenna says that if warmth were deprived from matter as its subject, it would nevertheless remain and be (a form of) matter (itself) on which one can act, but the

---

112. *QD de veritate*, q. 5, a. 9.
113. *In II Sent.*, d. 12, q. 1, a. 4.
114. *QD de spir. creat.*, a. 11, arg. 17 (Avicenna, *Metaphysica*, VIII, 6).
115. *ST* I, q. 115, a. 1.
116. *ST* I, q. 117, a. 3, ad 2.
117. *In II Phys.*, chap. 1.
118. *In Boetii De Trin.*, II, 4, 3, ad 3.

case is different for the passing from not being to being. According to Aristotle the agent and the patient must belong to the same genus. But non-being and God do not correspond at all. Passing from non-being to finite being is not impossible, for being is not a genus.[119]

The Animals

Avicenna thinks that all animals can be engendered by a certain mixing of the elements without an intervention of the seed, but, Thomas says, this does not work (*inconveniens*), because nature always uses determinate means. Neither earth nor water have the power to produce animals.[120] In another text about this subject, we read that according to Avicenna all animals produced from the seed can also be formed in the same species by putrefaction or by another mixture of earthly material.[121]

Conclusion

The frequent references to Avicenna show that he is quite present in the works of Aquinas, in particular in those which go back to his first stay at Paris between 1252 and 1259. During the first decades of the thirteenth century before the overwhelming entrance of Averroes among the masters of the Faculty of Arts, Avicenna was considered a philosopher of great value who helped them to understand Aristotle better. Avicenna provided also a general framework for the organization of philosophical studies: metaphysics should be studied after mathematics and the philosophy of nature.[122] On certain points of doctrine Thomas followed the views of Avicenna, as, for instance, that being (*ens*) is our first concept and that being qua being is the subject of metaphysics and is acquired by a judgement which separates it from all materiality.[123] We have seen, however, that in a good number of references Thomas distances him-

---

119. *QD de potentia*, q. 3, a. 1, arg. 5, and ad 5.
120. *ST* I, q. 71, a. 1.
121. *In VII Metaph.*, lesson 6, no. 1399.
122. *In Boetii de Trin.*, III, 5, 1, ad 9.
123. John F. Wippel, "The Latin Avicenna as a Source for Thomas Aquinas's Metaphysics," *Freiburger Zeitschrift für Philosophie und Theologie* 37 (1990): 51–90. The author refers to *In VI Metaph.*, lesson 6, no. 1165.

self from what Avicenna holds or rejects his theories in strong terms.

G. C. Anawati has summarized the main points where Thomas criticizes Avicenna.[124] A first point mentioned by Anawati is that the bodies in our world exercise only an accidental causality on each other; the introduction of forms is the work of the intelligent beings or of the *Dator formarum*—they come from outside;[125] man does not himself form his concepts; his science is not based on his perception of the beings in our world, but he must receive his knowledge from the *Dator formarum*.[126]

As we have seen above, Avicenna accepts a form of creation-emanation, but the causality of God is a necessary and eternal emanation, and the world has existed for ever. God works through created beings, the intelligent beings. Thomas opposes these theories and presents several arguments in order to show that God creates beings through a decision of his will and not by a process of natural necessity. He is the First Cause, and he himself gives being to all existing things. As John Wippel has pointed out, for Thomas this free choice in the creation of things renders possible the great variety of things in our world.[127] Another point of opposition is that Avicenna excludes from God the knowledge of individual things. Thomas rejects this view: the universal is not the singular, and whatever is real is made by God, who knows it in his causality.[128]

In Avicenna's philosophy the human will is deprived of its freedom of choice, in so far as the intelligent beings and other causes in the celestial sphere exercise a decisive influence on the will, as they do on the physical bodies in the world. Thomas points out that this theory is contrary to the faith which teaches that God is the end of man and that he alone moves our will by a motion which nevertheless lets our choices be free.[129] Another important point of difference between Avicenna and Thomas is the accidental character of the existence of things. To summarize we must say that instead of speaking with Wippel of the writings of Avicenna as a source of the metaphysics of Thomas, it seems more prudent to agree with G. C. Anawati that we have here totally different positions with regard to the foundation of metaphysics.[130]

---

124. Anawati, "Saint Thomas d'Aquin et la Métaphysique d'Avicenne," 460–63.
125. *QD de virtutibus*, q. 1, a. 8.
126. *SCG*, II, 74.
127. Wippel, "The Latin Avicenna as a Source for Thomas Aquinas's Metaphysics," 81; *QD de potentia*, q. 3, a. 15.
128. *QD de veritate*, q. 8, a. 11.
129. *QD de veritate*, q. 5, a. 10; q. 22, a. 9; *SCG* III, 87.
130. Anawati, "Saint Thomas d'Aquin et la Métaphysique d'Avicenne," 464.

15 ~ AVERROES

In the thirteenth century a saying circulated among the academics that Aristotle was the interpreter of nature, but Averroes of Aristotle. Invited by the caliph Abu Ya'qub Yusuf, Averroes undertook writing texts to explain the works of Aristotle. This brought him to compose three series of commentaries on the so-called school writing of Aristotle: a series of paraphrases, a commentary of medium length, and the great commentary. Because of the last two series of commentaries, Averroes was considered the great specialist on Aristotelian philosophy and as such was consulted by the learned in the West. He helped them to understand better the texts of Aristotle, which in their Latin translations were not always very clear. In view of the importance which the books of Aristotle had in university circles and for Thomas in particular, the question of the relation of Thomas with the Arab commentator deserves to be examined from close quarters.

Abu 'l-Walid Muhammed ibn Ahmad ibn Roshd, who in the West is called Averroes, was born in 1126 at Cordova to a family of lawyers. In his youth he was instructed in Islam, studied medicine and law, and was well known in Mohammedan society, but was considered a freethinker. This explains why his works have not had much influence in the Arab world. This becomes clear from the fact that of his great commentary on the works of Aristotle in thirty-eight books, thirty-four of them exist only in their Latin translation.[1] Only in the twentieth century did Arab scholars begin to be interested in the great philosopher. Victim of an outburst of religious fanaticism, Averroes had to leave Cordova; he went to Morocco and died in 1198 in exile.

According to L. Gardet and G.-C. Anawati, one of the main reasons Averroes had for writing his Aristotelian commentaries was to refute the materialistic interpretation which Alexander of Aphrodisias had given of

---

1. We do have, however, the Arab text of his great commentary on the *Metaphysics*.

Aristotle's epistemology.[2] Alexander was well known to the Arab commentators because several of his commentaries on Aristotle's main works had been translated into Arabic, and also through Themistius. Alexander gives a materialistic explanation of Aristotle's philosophy of man. Another objective of Averroes was to replace the mixture of Aristotelianism, and Platonist and Neoplatonist theories propagated in the widely diffused writings of Avicenna by an exposition of what he considered to be the true doctrine of Aristotle.[3]

Toward 1230 the greater part of the Aristotelian commentaries of Averroes had been translated into Latin by Michael Scot, who worked first in Toledo and later at the court of Emperor Frederic II in Palermo. Several years earlier Western scholars had come to know Avicenna, but Latin translations of the commentary by Averroes were only available about 1230. Toward the middle of the thirteenth century, Herman the German, bishop of Astorga, translated or had translated into Latin the Middle Commentaries of Averroes.[4] There existed also a Latin translation of the important treatise *De substantia orbis*, but another book of Averroes, the *Destructio destructionum* on the philosophy of Algazel was only available in Latin in 1328, although its existence was known through the *Guide of the Perplexed* of Maimonides.[5]

The relation of Averroes's philosophy with the Mohammedan faith is a difficult question to which there is no easy answer. In order to explain his position to the faithful of the community of Cordova, he formulated an original theory about the attitude which one can adopt with regard to the Koran: there are three irreducible categories of people: those who are well instructed and have a profound knowledge of the universe, namely, the philosophers, who understand the deeper sense of the texts of the Koran; a second group are those who are satisfied with reading the Koran, the practice of the different prescriptions, and getting acquainted with the prophets; finally there are the faithful who live on images and symbolic explanations. The Koran is the Book of God and therefore true,

---

2. Louis Gardet and Georges C. Anawati, *Introduction à la théologie musulmane: Essai de théologie comparée* (Paris: J. Vrin, 1948), 268.

3. See Dag N. Hasse, "Latin Averroes Translations of the First Half of the Thirteenth Century," in *Universality of Reason, Plurality of Philosophies in the Middle Ages*, vol. 1, ed. Alessandro Musco (Palermo: Officina di Studi Medievali, 2012), 149–77.

4. See Roland de Vaux, "La première entrée d'Averroès chez les latins," *Revue des sciences philosophiques et théologiques* 22 (1933): 199–219.

5. Averroes, *Averroes' "Destructio destructionum philosophiæ Algazelis" in the Latin Version of Calo Calonymos*, ed. Beatrice H. Zedler (Milwaukee: Marquette University Press, 1961).

and Averroes had always considered himself a believer. He attempts to show that the Islamic religion is not contrary to a philosophical study of nature. According to him philosophers are the only ones who read the texts of the Koran with an open mind, and analyze and use rigorous arguments, whereas the officials of the religious community are content with probable explications, and the people are nourished with images and feelings. According to Averroes a philosophical explication and interpretation of the texts of the Koran is possible, independently from Mohammedan theology. Because of the absence of a competent magisterium in the communities of faithful believers, Averroes could defend theories which contradict certain doctrinal points of Islam, such as the negation of the creation from non-being and of the unfathomable will of God. One may add the absence of an opening to the supernatural and the conviction that what the Koran teaches does not go beyond the domain of our reason. He considers Aristotle's doctrine as the truth, although it is on certain points in conflict with the teachings of the Koran.

In the Latin West the entrance and spreading of the writings of Averroes soon gave rise to difficulties. From 1270 the bishop of Paris, Étienne Tempier, published a decree which condemned some theories of the philosopher of Cordova: determinism, the eternity of the world, the universal agent intellect, the negation of the survival of individual souls after death. The condemnation of 1277 also quoted textually some doctrines of Averroes.[6]

With regard to Thomas Aquinas one can say that his interest in the thought of Averroes is understandable given his intention to develop a coherent philosophy on the basis of Aristotle's thought, in order to serve the truth and help us better understand the world and our Christian faith. Therefore Thomas wanted to present as the true philosophy what to him was certain in the doctrine of Aristotle. The commentaries of Averroes could be useful not only for the reading of certain difficult passages of Aristotle to help us understand them better, but also, as G. Théry says, in certain questions "Thomas had to save Aristotle against his commentator,"[7] or, as Gardet and Anawati write, "Thomas saved Aristotle from Averroes but he also saved the positive contribution of Averroes."[8]

---

6. Cf. Roland Hissette, *Enquête sur les 219 articles condamnés à Paris, le 7 mars 1277*, (Louvain: Publications universitaires, 1977), 76 ff. Cf. the propositions 9, 25, and 30, etc.

7. Gabriel Théry, *Entretiens sur la philosophie musulmane et la culture française* (Oran: n.p., 1945), 94.

8. Gardet and Anawati, *Introduction à la théologie musulmane*, 280. See also Leo Elders, "Averroès et saint Thomas d'Aquin," *Doctor communis* 45 (1992): 46–56.

With respect to the presence of texts of Averroes in the works of Aquinas, there are references to his theories without Averroes being named. For instance, in chapters 18 and 32 to 34 of the second book of the *Summa contra Gentiles*, Thomas analyzes objections against the Christian doctrine of creation, without quoting the names of the philosophers who raised these difficulties. All through his works Thomas mentions Averroes ninety times by name and more than three hundred times as the Commentator. We must however note that the word "commentator" may also designate other authors, such as Alexander of Aphrodisias and Simplicius, and the commentators on the writings of Pseudo-Dionysius and of the *Liber de causis*. In the *Scriptum super libros Sententiarum*, Averroes is treated courteously, and Thomas calls him Aristotle's commentator; in the *Summa contra Gentiles* II, 70, we read "commentator Averroes," but in his later works and in his Aristotelian commentaries, Thomas is sometimes severe and seems to reduce Averroes's authority.

As for the important doctrines of Averroes, he comments on Aristotle's treatises on logic following the text to the letter. In the philosophy of nature and in metaphysics, he rejects the Platonic theory of the Ideas, and stresses the doctrine of a substance and its accidents. Each thing is its being, and Averroes opposes the doctrine of the real distinction between the essence of things and their act of existing. According him it is a mistake to hold with Avicenna that being is added to the essence from the outside as an accident. An essence as such, apart from the question whether it exists or not (as Avicenna conceives it), is nothing but a certain content of our thought which we attribute to the word which expresses it; the essence is the contents of a nominal definition, but if one conceives it as real, being does not add anything, we consider true that of which we think. If one says that "to be" is added to the essence, one reduces being to an accident.[9] When one rejects with Averroes the real distinction, which for St. Thomas is characteristic of beings other than God, how does one then explain the difference between the First Mover and the immaterial substances, in particular the intelligent beings in the cosmic spheres? The answer of Averroes is that although these beings are simple, they are nevertheless less simple than God. Contrary to what Avicenna thought, Averroes says that the One, predicated of being (*ens*), is

---

9. See M. D. Roland-Gosselin, *Le De ente et essentia de S. Thomas d'Aquin: texte établi d'après les manuscrits parisiens* (Paris: Librairie philosophique J. Vrin, 1948), 157–59.

this very being, whereas the one as the principle of numbers adds something to a being and places it in a category.[10]

God, His Perfection, and His Science in the Writings of Averroes

According to Averroes the demonstration of the existence of God is not a theme of metaphysics, but of the philosophy of nature. To establish the existence of God, he much prefers the proof from motion. On the other hand the teleological argument has only a slight probability. He gives a new formulation to Avicenna's argument which takes the possible and the necessary as its starting points.[11] Certain beings, such as the immaterial substances, have no possibility not to be at all; because of the absence of matter they have a necessary existence, which, however, does not exclude that their being, although necessary, depends on God. God is the First Unmoved Mover. But what moves without being moved, moves by being desired. The heavens desires him and in this way they are moved by God.[12] The motion of which God is the cause is of infinite duration because of the infinite power of the Mover,[13] and spreads in the universe: the tidal motions of the water in the oceans are the effects of the celestial bodies.[14] The separate substances move the heavenly bodies as efficient and final causes. Thomas complains that Averroes does not always say the same with regard to the question how they move the heavenly bodies, that is, as final or as efficient causes. In his *De substantia orbis* Averroes would have said that this comes down to the same thing.[15] Thomas speaks of a gross mistake (*valde erroneum est*), since according to this text God would be the soul of the first heaven.

In the treatise of the divine perfections, Thomas appreciates several affirmations of Averroes: all forms are in act in the First Mover, they are

---

10. *In I Sent.*, d. 24, q. 1, a. 3. Cf. also *Quodl.* X, q. 1, a. 1: "Unum quod convertitur cum ente, non addit enti."

11. See Léon Gauthier, *Ibn Rochd (Averroès)* (Paris: Presses universitaires de France, 1948), 144 ff.

12. *SCG* II, 70.

13. *In II Sent.*, d. 1, q. 1, a. 5, ad 8. In this article of the *Scriptum*, there are two series of answers: (1) those participants in the debate who disagree with what (2) a first group said. At the end, Thomas himself discusses the latter's arguments.

14. *QD de potentia*, q. 1, a. 3, ad 1.

15. *QD de spir. creat.*, a. 6, arg. 10, and ad 10.

in his intellect.[16] In another quotation we read that all the forms which are in potency in the first matter, are present in the First Mover.[17] God is most perfect since the perfections of all things are present in him.[18]

In medieval Islamic philosophy the question whether the attributes of God must be distinguished from his essence was answered in different ways. Certain authors did not attribute any reality to the attributes, while others accepted that several are real, such as divine perfection and omnipotence. In their attempt to remove from God all composition, certain Moslem theologians saw only a negative value in the attributes, while others thought that they express a certain reality in God.[19] Averroes's doctrine of the divine attributes is not very much different from that of Aquinas,[20] since their plurality is according to our way of conceiving them[21] and they are said of God appropriately.[22] According to Averroes there are in God a great number of forms which are all in act in him,[23] and therefore the names of God are not synonyms.[24] Thomas quotes also a text in which Averroes declares that the divine substance is the measure of all substances.[25]

In several articles of the seventh question of the *De potentia*, texts of Averroes are quoted, such as all forms are present in act in the First Mover (a. 1, arg. 8); that by which all substances are measured is God (a. 3, arg. 7); God possesses in himself the perfections of all the genera of beings (a. 5.); in God there is only multiplicity according to the differences which our intellect distinguishes (a. 6); God is the measure of all things (a. 10, s.c. 2). We may add that Averroes points out that time is one because of the unity of the First Mover.[26]

In the question on God's power an opponent in the dispute quotes a text in which Aristotle affirms that an infinite power is not possible be-

---

16. *In I Sent.*, d. 36, q. 2, a. 1, s.c., and ad 1.
17. *QD de veritate*, q. 2, a. 9, s.c. 5.
18. Ibid., q. 2, a. 11, s.c. 1.
19. Cf. Louis Gardet, *Études de philosophie et de mystique comparée* (Paris: J. Vrin, 1972), 82–86.
20. Cf. Alfonso García Marqués, "Averroës, una fuente tomista de la noción metafísica de Dios," *Sapientia* 37 (1982): 94 ff.
21. *In I Sent.*, d. 2, q. 1, a. 3, arg. 2.
22. Ibid., ad 3: "... nullo modo ponitur in Deo quasi ipse secundum rem est multiplex; sed tamen ipse secundum suam simplicem perfectionem, multitudini istorum attributorum correspondet, ut vere de Deo dicantur et hoc intenndit Commentator."
23. *QD de potentia*, q. 7, a. 1, arg. 8.
24. *In I Sent.*, d. 22, q. 1, a. 3, arg. 4.
25. *Quodl.* V, q. 4.
26. *In II Sent.*, d. 2, q. 1, a. 2.

cause it would have to move outside time. In his answer to this objection Thomas quotes Averroes: Aristotle is thinking of a power of infinite magnitude which operates in infinite time. But we are speaking of an infinite power *outside* the order of magnitude and time.[27]

Concerning the divine science, the basis of God's knowledge of beings outside himself is that He is the cause of their being. But Averroes says that in so far as God knows his own being, he does not know the essences of things.[28] A criticism which often comes back in Thomas's writings is that Averroes excludes from God the knowledge of individual things, except with regard to what they have in common with other beings.[29] According to Averroes in knowing his own essence God does not know exactly (*determinate*) the singular effects in the way they exist in their own nature.[30]

In connection with removing the knowledge of singular things from divine science, God's Providence is also excluded in the writings of Averroes.[31] According to the Arab philosopher, in his divine goodness God does not occupy himself with individual things except for what they have in common with others.[32] This position is shared by many authors of that time. Opposing the determinism of the Stoics, they argue that God takes no interest in individual events. Averroes also adopts this position and denies that God knows the evil in the world: His intellect, always in act, does not know privations, since a privation cannot be known except by the absence of the form, something which does not occur in God.[33] Thomas dismisses the argument: when something is known, then a privation present in it is also known.[34] On the other hand, Thomas quotes a text of Averroes in which we read that in order to obtain that different things cooperate with one another in preserving a certain order, the highest government must direct the individual things so that they tend toward a determinate end.[35]

---

27. *QD de potentia*, q. 1, a. 2, ad 2.
28. *In I Sent.*, d. 33, q. 1, a. 3, ad 1: "Sed haec positio est dupliciter falsa."
29. *QD de veritate*, q. 2, a. 3, ad 1: "Quidam ut Commentator simpliciter negaverunt Deum singularia cognoscere nisi forte in universali volentes naturam intellectus divini ad mensuram nostri intellectus coarctare."
30. Ibid., q. 2, a. 15, ad 3.
31. Ibid, q. 5, a. 2.
32. *QD de veritate*, q. 5, a. 2; and *In I Sent.*, d. 36, q. 1, a. 1: "Videtur expresse negare Deo particularium cognitionem."
33. *QD de veritate*, q. 2, a. 15, arg. 3; Cf. *In I Sent.*, d. 16, q. 1, a. 2.
34. Ibid., ad 3.
35. *SCG* I, 13.

In his commentary on the *De anima* 430b, Averroes takes this theme up again and writes that God does not know the evil in the world and that divine providence in our world must be excluded. Thomas mentions this view in several texts, such as *In I Sent.*, d. 36, q. 1, a. 2, ad 1; *QD de veritate*, q. 2, a. 15, and the *Summa Contra Gentiles* I, 71. Elsewhere he quotes a text in which Averroes writes that God does not know the things of our world except in so far as they are beings, because he is the cause of their being, but he does not know their essential nature.[36]

In the *Summa theologiae* I, question 14, article 11, Thomas mentions an opinion that God would have a certain knowledge of individual things, in so far as he applies universal causes to them of which they are particular effects, but this solution is inadequate, since universal causes do not give knowledge of *this* particular being, since what constitutes the individuality depends on matter but not on universal causes. Thomas himself proposes another solution: God's science extends as far as his causality. But the latter extends to whatever exists, even to matter, and so also to what constitutes the individual.

Creation

In the previous chapter Avicenna's theory of the creation of the world was dealt with: whatever exists "after" God, has been created, even matter. But for Avicenna "to create" means to give existence: the essences as such are not made by God, they exist as possible entities (*possibilia*).[37] Moreover God's causal influence passes through intermediaries. By emanation a first intelligent being comes into being who, by contemplating God, produces a second intelligent being; and in this way the stream of being continues until the sphere of the moon, where the *Dator formarum* has its seat.

At first Averroes seems to have taken over this theory and professed an eternal creation, but contrary to Avicenna he thought that there must be a substratum—eternal matter—for things to be made. Thomas refers to the *De substantia orbis*, chapter 2, where Averroes writes that Aristotle considered God to be not only the cause of the revolution of the heavens but also of their substance.[38] But later Averroes would abandon this

---

36. Cf. *In I Sent.*, d. 35, q. 1, a. 3. Thomas refers to the commentary of Averroes on *Metaphysics* II.
37. Louis Gardet, *La pensée religieuse d'Avicenne* (Paris: J. Vrin, 1951), 58–68.
38. *In II Sent.*, d. 1, q. 1, a. 5, ad 1.

scheme and would even identifi God with the first intelligence, whose causality with regard to the world would not have been more than an exemplary and final causality.[39]

In his commentary on the first book of the *De caelo et mundo*, Averroes argued that if the world did begin to exist, there would have been a void before, but the void does not exist. Hence the world did not begin to exist.[40] Thomas answers that, indeed, the void does not exist. If one speaks of the void, one presupposes a place which becomes empty by being deprived of the presence of a body. But God's causality is different and does not presuppose anything.

According to Averroes the creation of the world from non-being is impossible, since every change needs a subject, but Thomas criticizes him for not understanding that divine causality differs from that of created beings. The First Cause does not need matter to produce beings.[41] Another difficulty raised against the creation at the beginning of time, of which Averroes is probably the author, argues that a succession in time needs a succession in motion, but the will cannot begin to will something new, if first there is not another motion.[42] The answer to this difficulty is that the will of God is unmoved and does not begin to act.[43] Another objection put forward by Averroes in his commentary on *Physics* VIII, is that from a will which is eternal, nothing new can come forth.[44] Averroes conceived creation as an eternal causality that gives being to all things which exist. The answer of Thomas is that God knows all things simultaneously; the fact that the world began to exist in time, is willed by God. To create is proper to God alone. This is why Averroes criticizes Plato who wrote that God first made the angels to charge them with making material things.[45] Thomas says again that to create is proper to God alone.

---

39. Cf. Barry Sherman Kogan, "Averroes and the Theory of Emanation," *Mediæval Studies* 43, no. 1 (1981): 384–404; Kogan, *Averroes and the Metaphysics of Causality* (Albany: State University of New York Press, 1985).
40. *In II Sent.*, d. 1, q. 1, a. 5, arg. 4.
41. Ibid.
42. Ibid., args. 9, 12–14.
43. Ibid., arg. 12.
44. Ibid., arg. 14.
45. QD *de potentia*, q. 3, a. 18, ad 10.

The Intelligent Beings, the Souls, and the Celestial Bodies

We have mentioned already Avicenna's theory of the successive spheres of the celestial bodies and some modifications Averroes introduced. Averroes accepts the existence of immaterial substances which are the immediate cause of the motion of the celestial spheres. In their cognitive life these substances do not reason by going from one theme to another, as human beings do.[46] The object of their thought is their own being; what they think and that by which they think are the same.[47] The natural intellect of these immaterial substances is not limited to created forms of its class, so that it is capable of knowing God. Thomas notes that we must understand this sentence of Averroes as applying to immaterial beings.[48]

Are these heavenly intelligent beings united to souls? According to Averroes they are in the best position to move the heavenly bodies. This would not be the case if they were not connected to souls; therefore they have a soul, as the circular movement of the celestial bodies indicates, since this is an expression of thought.[49] This question whether the heavenly bodies are ensouled remained problematic for Averroes, since he proposed different solutions.[50] We must distinguish, Thomas writes, between the efficient cause of the motions of these bodies—their souls—and the separate Good which moves these souls as a final cause.

To explain the presence of universal concepts in us, we must admit, Averroes writes, the existence of an intellect which gives them to us and in which we can know and think them. This is the unique possible intellect of all of us.[51] We come to know these immaterial substances the more we know this possible intellect.[52] The intelligent beings of the heavenly spheres do not receive their objects from material and divisible things, as we do. While in God his intellect and the known object are identical, in the other intelligent beings there is a difference between what they are

---

46. *QD de veritate*, q. 8, a. 15.
47. Ibid., q. 10, a. 8.
48. *In IV Sent.*, d. 49, q. 2, a. 6, ad 3: "Dictum autem Commentatoris intelligitur de intelligibilibus creatis."
49. *De spir. creat.*, a. 6, args. 10–13.
50. Ibid., ad 10: "Super hoc invenitur Averroes varie locutus."
51. See below under the section "The Unique Possible Intellect and the Agent Intellect."
52. *In II Sent.*, d. 3, q. 1, a. 3. For the doctrine of the possible intellect, cf. below. Avempace thought that by the study of the theoretical sciences we can obtain the knowledge of separate beings, but Averroes rejects this solution (*In IV Sent.*, d. 29, q. 2, a. 7, arg. 12).

and the object of their thought.[53] But when a separate substance thinks itself, it does not need an intelligible species. Its form is sufficient for thinking and knowing itself.[54]

Averroes makes his own the Aristotelian theory of the difference between the separate substances and material beings: the word "essence" has a different meaning for each of these.[55] Because of the difference we cannot know the separate substances in this life, contrary to what Averroes holds, according to an opponent in *QD de veritate*, q. 18, a. 5, ad 8. Thomas dedicates a whole chapter to this question which Aristotle had left open.[56] According to Averroes there is an intellect, called the possible intellect, which is imperishable and separated from us in its being, as there is also an agent intellect which actualizes the intelligible things and makes us know the first principles. He gives the following explanation: when the speculative intelligibles are thought by us—something which happens when their substratum is present in our imagination—the agent intellect actualizes them, so that we know them in the possible intellect, which is also separate from the material world. When all the intelligibles in this possible intellect have been actualized, the agent intellect is united with us so that we come to know the separate substances, which will be our ultimate happiness. According to this theory there is a mysterious continuity between us and the common possible intellect.

Thomas refutes the opinion of Averroes that in this life we can come to know the separate substances: the possible intellect and the agent intellect are not substances separated from us. Moreover, Thomas says, according to Averroes, the agent intellect produces the intelligibles in us, but it does not make separate substances of them. We do not have any special leaning or ordination to them. The question is not without importance, because the philosophers who defended the thesis that we know all things in this common possible intellect, thanks to the agent intellect, believed that man's ultimate happiness consists in the contemplation of these intelligent beings.[57] Anyhow according to the theory of Averroes our place in the order of intelligent beings is comparable to that of primary matter to sensible forms.[58]

---

53. Ibid., d. 3, q. 3, a. 1.
54. *QD de veritate*, q. 8, a. 7: Averroes wants to say that it does not need an impressed cognitive species such as our senses and intellect need them.
55. Ibid., q. 18, a. 5, ad 6.
56. *SCG* III, 43: in this life we cannot know the separate substances.
57. *SCG* III, 48. Alexander and Averroes indeed placed man's supreme happiness in the knowledge of the separate substances.
58. *QD de veritate*, q. 10, a. 8, ad 6.

The Unique Possible Intellect and the Agent Intellect

These texts of Averroes confront us with the theory of the uniqueness of the possible intellect. According to Averroes certain philosophers have developed the theory that the possible intellect is in its being separate from the body[59] and that it is the same for all men. This is also the view of Averroes himself.[60] Thomas discusses this theory "which Averroes has imagined" in a long text.[61] Averroes thought that he had found confirmation in some lines of a text of Aristotle: the possible intellect "is not mixed (with the body), it is impassible and separate," but these words of Aristotle do not oblige us to say that according to him the intellectual substance is not united with the body as the form which gives it being, says Thomas.[62]

Thomas answers these arguments of Averroes in the same chapter of the *Summa contra gentiles*. The possible intellect is individualized, as is the soul by its relation with a body numerically different from other bodies. The second argument of Averroes does not distinguish that by which one thinks and that which one thinks; the third argument (the science of the master and of the disciple are the same, and so the intellect is common), Thomas says, shows that at best the knowledge of them is numerically the same as for its contents, but that there is a difference by that by what they think, that is, their concepts and acts of thinking.

With regard to question of the uniqueness of the possible intellect, we find in the works of Thomas the description of a theory of Averroes of a unique possible intellect, the same for all men. This theory is very problematic. Averroes speaks repeatedly of a *continuation* of this (common) possible intellect with us, without telling how from an ontological viewpoint this continuation must be conceived. At the University of Paris various masters thought that Averroes taught the uniqueness of this possible intellect, but perhaps less precise translations led them into error and the theory of one unique intellect is not what Averroes really holds But according to the purpose of this study we present the theory as Thomas has formulated it.

---

59. *SCG* II, 59.
60. *ST* I, q. 117, a. 1.
61. *SCG* II, 73: "Averroes in III *De anima* fingit..."
62. *SCG* II, 69.

Averroes argues as follows to establish his theory: for an immaterial intellect it would be impossible to be individualized, because it is without matter. Therefore it cannot be particular for each human being. If it were proper to every human being, the cognitive species would also be individualized in each of us, but in reality they are universal concepts.[63] Another argument for the uniqueness of the possible intellect is based on the fact that the master causes in his disciple the same science which he has himself.[64]

Thomas refutes the theory of Averroes by several arguments: man is a thinking substance; but a form is the form of one matter only. The operation proper to a being shows its specific nature. The operation proper to man is thought. An individual man is an animal because of his sense knowledge, but is a man because of his thought. So he is this individual by his possible intellect. Averroes tries to avoid this conclusion by saying that the unique possible intellect of all men is continuous with us (*continuatur nobiscum*) by the intelligible cognitive species, of which an image (*phantasma*) in us is, each time, its point of attachment. Since these images are different in each of us, one can speak of different possible intellects in people, although it is one by what it is, argues Averroes.[65]

With regard to the argument that the science of the disciple and of the master are the same Thomas answers that a master brings his disciple to learn what was unknown to him, by presenting sensible images which correspond to the problem and, secondly, by showing him the principles which will lead him to the right conclusions. Averroes's theory is wrong inasmuch as he says that the concepts are the same in the master and in the disciple.[66]

According to Averroes it is, each time, the agent intellect, which is one and the same for all of us, which actualizes for us the intelligible species in the possible intellect. Thomas writes that for Averroes the possible intellect seems to be composed of the agent intellect and the "passive intellect" (that is, the image in our highest sense faculty, the so-called *cogitativa*),[67] so that the agent intellect would function as its form. In another

---

63. *In II Sent.*, d. 17, q. 2, a. 1. The same argument is also reproduced in *QD de spir. creat.*, a. 2: if the possible intellect were individualized in us, we would not have the same universal concepts as others.

64. *SCG* II, 75.

65. Ibid., 73; *QD de spir. creat.*, a. 9.

66. *ST* I, q. 117, a. 1.

67. *SCG* II, 60. According to Averroes it is through the *cogitativa* that man differs from the animals: the *cogitativa* knows the individual cognitive intentions and compares them with each other.

text, however, Averroes compares the relation between the two intellects to that between the artisan and the matter on which he is working.[68]

Thomas observes that according to the theory of Averroes, the possible and the agent intellect must possess forever this treasure of intelligible species. This means that sense knowledge is not really necessary for a man to be able to think. Averroes answers this by saying that the intelligible species have a dual subject—the possible intellect and the sense image:[69] from the one they have eternity, from the other novelty—but Thomas rejects this answer: "*Haec autem responsio stare non potest.*" It is impossible that what is eternal depends of an image marked by time. It is impossible that the intelligible species, by which the possible intellect is actualized and thinks, should depend on the images which are connected with our senses. Moreover our ancestors in the past have already thought these intelligibles, which means that the possible intellect has them already and that they are not reduced in act by contact with the sense images of contemporary men.[70]

According to Averroes the agent intellect reduces in act the intelligible species in the possible intellect in so far as the latter communicates with us. He writes on the agent intellect that it uses the first principles to develop thinking, to introduce order, and to combine the intelligibles: the first principles are as instruments of the agent intellect.[71] According to Averroes, the agent intellect is separated from us, but Thomas shows with several texts that Aristotle himself did not think that the agent intellect is a separate substance not interlaced with us. When he writes that it is like a "habitus," like a light, he indicates that it does not exist by itself, but belongs to the class of qualities-powers. Aristotle's words, which say that it is separate and not mixed with the body, must be understood in this way, that it does not have a special organ.[72] Somewhat further on in this same chapter, Thomas quotes Averroes again who says that the agent intellect and the possible intellect are distinguished in so far as in the agent intellect the one who thinks and what he thinks are identical, which is not the case in the possible intellect, but Thomas replies that this is contrary to what Aristotle says: in beings without matter, the intellect

---

68. *In II Sent.*, d. 17, q. 2, a. 1.
69. *SCG* II, 73.
70. Ibid.
71. *QD de veritate*, q. 9, a. 1, ad 2; *In II Sent.*, d. 28, q. 1, a. 5; *Quodl.* X, q. 4, a. 1, ad 2.
72. *SCG* II, 78.

and that which is known are identical.[73] The central argument of Thomas against the uniqueness of the agent intellect for all men is the following: in nature each being is equipped to perform the operations which are natural to him. Therefore it must have the faculties needed to form his thoughts.[74]

As for the number of the heavenly bodies, Averroes writes that just as there are a great number of human bodies, there are also many heavenly bodies and movers,[75] but these heavenly bodies are not produced by generation,[76] whereas material forms proceed by generation from forms without matter.[77] If the power of the heavenly bodies is finite, can they continue to exist forever? The Platonists answered that they receive the perpetuity of their being from another, but according to Averroes it is impossible that something which of itself can also not be, should receive its perpetuity from another. According to Averroes there is in those heavenly bodies no potency to non-being, and so they continue to exist. But, says Thomas, this answer is not sufficient: the act of being has no quantitative length as such. It is not necessary that these bodies be ordained to last infinitely, although they will do so in fact since their being is not affected by time.[78]

A stream of causal influence flows from the first heaven to the sublunar world. The light of the celestial bodies influences the generation of inferior bodies.[79]

The Philosophy of Nature, Matter, and the Elements

In general terms Averroes kept to the cosmological system of Aristotle. With regard to the accident of quantity he maintains the anteriority of the circle and the sphere; circular movement is most perfect. Averroes and Maimonides affirm that the celestial bodies and the sublunar elements do not have the same matter.[80] Nevertheless there is no break be-

---

73. Ibid.
74. *QD de spir. creat.*, a. 10.
75. Ibid., a. 9, s.c. 3.
76. *In II Sent.*, d. 1, q. 2, a. 5, ad 1.
77. Ibid., d. 15, q. 1, a. 2.
78. *SCG* I, 20.
79. *In IV Sent.*, d. 48, q. 1, a. 4, qc. 2, arg. 2.
80. *In II Sent.*, d. 3, q. 1, a. 1.

tween both, since the movements of the four elements of the sublunar world follow the impressions of the heavenly bodies.[81] Elements like air and water can partly interpenetrate each other.[82] Plato, Themistius, and Avicenna thought that the causes active in our world—the accidental forms—are incapable of producing living beings. According to them, a separate principle would produce the substantial forms. But according to Averroes all material forms, even souls capable of sense knowledge, are drawn from the potentiality of matter by the power of natural agents.[83]

The forms of bodies presuppose that there are in matter no terminated dimensions.[84] As did Aristotle, Averroes thinks that the matter of material substances is in flux, whereas the substantial forms are permanent.[85] While according to Avicenna there is only one matter for all bodies, Averroes rejects this opinion: the matter of the celestial bodies is different, and primary matter by itself has no form at all, being in potency to all forms. The oneness of matter in all bodies in the entire world is only by analogy.[86] Each body has its natural place according to the requirements of its form.[87]

The first disposition (*habilitas*) of matter is that for the forms of the four elements; there are no intermediary forms between these and the potency of matter, and matter is not potentially disposed to other forms than to those of our sublunar world.[88] According to Averroes the forms of the four elements are, because of their imperfect nature, placed half way between substantial and accidental forms.[89] His line of thinking probably was that matter receives first the more universal forms before the particular ones, for instance, first the form of a body before it acquires the form of a living being,[90] but Thomas says that this concerns only the order of thought. In the matter of a being which results from a process of generation, we must, in thought, assign to it the so-called undetermined dimensions before the arrival of the substantial form.[91]

---

81. Ibid., d. 14, q. 1, a. 4, ad 4. Cf. *In IV Sent.*, d. 33, q. 1, a. 1, ad 4.
82. *Quodl.* I, q. 10, a. 1.
83. *In II Sent.*, d. 18, q. 2, a. 3.
84. *QD de veritate*, q. 5, a. 9, arg. 6.
85. *In II Sent.*, d. 30, q. 2, a. 1.
86. Ibid., d. 12, q. 1, a. 1, ad 1.
87. Ibid., d. 14, q. 1, a. 5, arg. 2.
88. Ibid., d. 12, q. 1, a. 4; d. 30, q. 2, a. 1.
89. *ST* I, q. 76, a. 4, ad 4.
90. *QD de spir. creat.*, a. 3, arg. 17.
91. *In IV Sent.*, d. 12, q. 1, a. 2, qc. 4.

According to Averroes the way in which matter receives forms differs from the manner in which the possible intellect receives the forms.[92] The "appetite" of matter, about which Aristotle speaks in *Physics* I, chapter 9, is not an activity, but an aptitude for receiving forms.[93] In this connection Thomas quotes a text from the *De substantia orbis* of Averroes in which he says that the dimensions exist beforehand (*praeexistunt*) in matter before the forms of the elements, but Thomas observes that when one conceives matter as being already in a perfect state according to the way the corporeal things are, one may conceive as present the dimensions which are accidents typical of this class of being and this specific form.[94]

A question, which in the Middle Ages was of considerable importance for philosophers and also for scientists at the beginning of modern science, was that of the movement of bodies in the void. Averroes thought that a text of *Physics* IV[95] formulates an argument of Aristotle himself, when it affirms that every motion needs a medium and that therefore motion in the void is impossible. But as early as the writing of the *Scriptum in libros Sententiarum*, Thomas understood that this passage does not express the thought of Aristotle himself, but an opinion which was later proposed by Avempace. The question of the medium is not important, and the arguments of Averroes are frivolous.[96]

In several places Thomas quotes a text of Averroes in which the Commentator says that mice engendered in a process of putrefaction differ from those that are born in the ordinary way because a different type of generation leads to the formation of a new species.[97] The forms of natural things are produced from already existent forms. Averroes says that in fact demons cannot transform material bodies,[98] since there is no passive potency in nature without a corresponding active power.[99]

---

92. *QD de veritate*, q. 2, a. 2.
93. *QD de potentia*, q. 4, a. 1, sc. 2.
94. *QD de spir. creat.*, a. 3, ad 16.
95. Aristotle, *Physics* IV, 215a24–216a6.
96. *In IV Phys.*, lesson 12. See, on this question, James A. Weisheipl, "Motion in a Void: Aquinas and Averroes," in *St. Thomas Aquinas, 1274–1974. Commemorative Studies*, ed. A. Maurer (Toronto: Pontifical Institute of Mediaeval Studies, 1974), 467–88.
97. *QD de veritate*, q. 12, a. 2, arg. 4; *In VII Metaph.*, lesson 6.
98. *QD de malo*, q. 16, a. 9, s.c. 2.
99. *QD de veritate*, q. 18, a. 2.

Metaphysical Problems

We have already noted that according to Averroes the One does not add any form to being (*ens*) and that it concerns indifferently the act of being and the essence.[100] As for the definition of the Good—that which all things desire—Averroes notes that what all want is to be, as Aristotle also says.[101] Plato wrote that the First Mover moves himself, something which seems impossible for an Aristotelian. Averroes thinks that he can make sense of these words, if one understands them as presupposing the identity of what one wishes and one's will. The First Mover moves himself in so far as he knows himself and wills himself, but this does not mean that he is moved by creatures because he wants them.[102]

A thing which by itself can be and can not be cannot obtain from another the necessity of being. Certain creatures, however, do not have the possibility of not being, Averroes says. But Thomas observes that they receive this necessary being from God. Connected with this question the following problem presents itself: in order to exist always, the celestial bodies must have an infinite power. But according to Averroes all potencies inherent in bodies are finite, but it would not follow that their power to exist is limited. As for this question Thomas answers that the potency to be is not only relative to the matter of a being, but also to the active power of its form, which in incorruptible things cannot fail. It follows that, as Averroes writes, the celestial bodies have no possibility of perishing, but their motion depends on another cause and therefore it can be stopped. In the bodies composed of contrary elements, there is, as Averroes says, a passive principle of corruptibility. But the process of corruption of the elements stops when the outside cause which produces the corruption stops working.[103]

Can God work in creatures independently of their natural forces or even act contrarily to them? According to Averroes we find in natural beings only passive potencies to which correspond active powers. With regard to what is against nature, there is no active natural power. This means that there is no passive potency either. This means that changes against the nature of a being are not possible, although God can produce them by his power. Thomas answers this argument by saying that all

---

100. Ibid., q. 21, a. 5, arg. 7; ad 8.
101. Ibid., q. 22, a. 1, arg. 7; a. 2, arg. 2.
102. Ibid., q. 23, a. 1, ad 7.
103. *QD de potentia*, q. 5, a. 4, ad 1; a. 5, ad 9; a. 7.

created things are subject in their potency to what a much higher power, such as that of the Creator, can do. An example illustrates this: nature (and God) can bring about effects which man's art cannot produce.[104]

Man

Averroes follows Aristotle in his doctrine of matter and form and of the hylomorphic composition of man. With regard to sense knowledge, he accepts the same faculties as Aristotle. All the faculties of nutrition are active powers, whereas the sense faculties are passive; in the intellect there is both a passive and an active faculty.[105] The sense faculty called *cogitativa*, called by some the passive intellect, would give to man his specific character and distinguish him from the animals. According to Averroes this *cogitativa* would let us distinguish from each other individual cognitive contents and compare them with each other. In this way the *cogitativa* would render the images (of the imagination) capable of receiving the action of the agent intellect, which gives to the possible intellect (united to it) the intelligible contents, in continuity with the *cogitativa*. These intelligible contents, that is, concepts, acquire a dual being, in the possible intellect (common to all men) and in the sense images of the individual man. It is, indeed, a central theory of Averroes, that a spiritual substance cannot unite itself as a form to matter.[106] This excludes that an immaterial soul can be the substantial form of man.

The so-called passive intellect (the images in the *cogitativa*) is already present in the child, although it cannot yet think. The possible and the agent intellects enter into contact with us through the images of the imagination. But Thomas rejects this theory: the intellect is the form which determines our being. It is not an efficient, but a formal cause of our being.[107]

As for the question of what is Averroes's theory of the human soul, we do not find a clear answer in Thomas's writings. In his *Scriptum super libros Sententiarum*, book II, d. 19, q. 1, a. 1, where there is a question of the eventual corruption or survival of the human soul, he quotes different theories attributed to Averroes, mentioning a theory which holds that

---

104. Ibid., q. 6, a. 1, arg. 18.
105. *In III Sent.*, d. 3, q. 2, a. 1, arg. 5. Cf. *QD de veritate*, q. 26, a. 3.
106. *QD de spir. creat.*, a. 2.
107. *SCG* II, 68.

under one aspect the soul is incorruptible, but corruptible under another. It is incorruptible in so far as it signifies the intellect which according to its being (*quantum ad substantiam*), in so far as it is common to all men, is incorruptible.[108] Certain authors say that Averroes is speaking here of the active intellect, others of the passive, because these authors affirm that in its being (*quantum ad substantiam*) this intellect is one in all men. But what are proper to each of us are the images of the imagination which are illuminated by the light of the agent intellect which actualizes the intelligible species in the possible intellect. By these "illuminated" images we think, in so far as through them we are in continuity with the separate intellect. This implies that what is proper to each of us is destroyed when we die, and that what remains of all of us after our death is no more than a common substance. In the text of the *Scriptum super libros Sententiarum*, book II, d. 19, q. 1, a. 1, this theory is not ascribed to Averroes. Somewhat before, Thomas quoted the passage of the *Liber de causis*, proposition 15, on the return to ourselves in our knowledge, a return which is explained by the fact that this intellect exists by itself and is not subject to death.[109]

In the *QD de spir. creat.*, a. 2, Thomas comes back to the question of the human soul and its origin. An opponent recalls that according to Averroes the soul would be united to the body through the mediation of images of the senses, which implies that it is not the form of the body.

Thomas says that, indeed, we have a difficulty here, in as much as the human soul is an immaterial reality which exists by itself, yet is being united with a body as its form. Thomas himself insists on the saying that "this individual man is the one who is thinking" to demonstrate the union of the immaterial soul with the human body. Averroes, who said that the soul is separate, was nevertheless looking for a way to bring the soul into relation with the individual human body, in the sense that the (universal) soul would be in contact with each of us by a "continuity," thanks to the images of our imagination. But Thomas notes that this continuity is not sufficient: the fact that (by the sole common intellect) a cognitive species (concept) is drawn from an image, does not make us think. To make us think we have within ourselves the possible intellect. The theory of Averroes is impossible.[110] In this connection we should re-

108. "Ponunt enim intellectum esse unum in substantia omnium."
109. This observation is attributed to the Commentator. Apparently Thomas did not want to put Averroes in contradiction with himself.
110. *QD de spir. creat.*, a. 2, c., and ad 17: "Positio Commentatoris est impossibilis."

member that Aristotle himself counts the intellect among the faculties of the soul and says that it is the soul which thinks.[111]

In Thomas's treatise *De unitate intellectus*, the criticism of the theory of a sole possible intellect of all is also addressed to those Latin masters in Paris and authors who divulged this theory, saying that it was the theory of Aristotle himself. In five different texts he reproaches Averroes for having given a perverse presentation of the doctrine of Aristotle, as well as of that of Theophrast and Themistius, when he tries to show that the intellect which Aristotle calls possible is a separate substance in its being and not united with the body as its form. Averroes is a *"philosophiae peripateticae depravator."* According to Averroes this (common) intellect becomes active when our senses begin to function.[112]

According to Averroes the human soul does not continue to exist after the death of the body; that means that the sensitive and vegetative souls, which constitute the body, perish together with it. According to Averroes the common possible intellect as well as the agent intellect survive after the death of the body.[113] Thomas's central argument against this theory is that it is this individual man who thinks and that as in nature beings are ordered, he must be equipped with the faculties needed to perform his actions. This means that he himself must have his own intellect.[114] If one were to let the possible intellect exist as a being by itself, as Averroes does, and not as a faculty in the human soul, it would let us know reality in all its extension and also the separate substances, in the knowledge of whom our happiness would consist. Averroes thinks in fact that at the end of our life we can arrive at the knowledge of these separate substances.[115] Thomas shows by quoting some texts that Averroes misunderstood what Aristotle is saying; his theory of the possible intellect contradicts Aristotle's doctrine, is wrong, and is a fiction.[116]

---

111. *SCG* II, 61.
112. *De unitate intellectus*, chap. 3.
113. *SCG* II, 80. There is no survival of an individual spiritual soul.
114. *SCG* II, 60: "Cuiuscumque competit aliqua operari secundum naturam, sunt ei attributa ea sine quibus illa operatio complere non potest."
115. *ST* I, q. 68, a. 1.
116. *SCG* II, 61.

The Moral Life

There are relatively few references to the moral doctrine of Averroes in the writings of Thomas. We quote the following theses: the moral virtues, and in particular chastity, promote the intellectual life and the study of the sciences.[117] Prudence must be placed between the intellectual and the moral virtues.[118] Averroes gives two definitions of love: (a) love is the bond which unites all the beings in the universe; (b) love is the natural movement of all things which are active, is their end and rest which have been assigned to them, and beyond which none of them can go.[119] It is by his virtues that man is best disposed for the contemplative life, and chastity is of the greatest value for the study of the theoretical sciences.[120] According to Averroes movement is essential to life. If beatitude includes immutability, it cannot be the eternal life.[121] Freshness and quietness of the appetite are called pleasure. Pleasure is a super-flowering of nature.[122]

According to Averroes all moral virtues—therefore also justice—are located in that part of the soul which is deprived of reason, but Thomas observes that this holds only for the virtues which moderate the passions.[123] According to Averroes it is permissible to commit adultery if it is the way to eliminate a tyrant, but Thomas writes that one must not commit an evil act for whatever advantage might result from it.[124] Averroes defines the virtues as habits which one can use whenever one wants.[125] For him the ultimate happiness of man consists, as we have seen, in the contemplation of the separate substances. He believes that in a certain way we could reach this knowledge during our life on earth.[126]

---

117. *In II Sent.*, d. 39, q. 3, a. 3.
118. *In III Sent.*, d. 23, q. 1, a. 4, qc. 2, ad 3.
119. Ibid., d. 27, q. 1, a. 2, arg. 2.
120. Ibid., d. 35, q. 1, a. 3, qc, 1, arg. 1; *In IV Sent.*, d. 33, q. 3, a. 3.
121. *In IV Sent.*, d. 49, q. 3, a. 1.
122. Ibid.
123. *QD de malo*, q. 4 a. 5, arg. 4, and ad 4.
124. Ibid., q. 15, a. 1, ad 5: "... pro nulla utilitate."
125. *QD de virtutibus*, q. 1, a. 1.
126. *SCG* III, 44 and 48.

The Presence of Averroes in the Aristotelian Commentaries of Thomas

At the end of our survey of the texts of Averroes quoted by Thomas in his different works, we must examine whether Thomas has used his interpretations of Aristotle's philosophy in his own Aristotelian commentaries. Somewhat surprisingly we notice that there are practically no references to the commentaries of Averroes in Thomas's expositions on the *De anima*, the *Nicomachean Ethics*, *De sensu et sensato*, and *De memoria et reminiscentia*. But Thomas consulted the commentaries of Averroes on the *De caelo*, the *Metaphysics*, and the *Physics*.

In Thomas's commentary on the *Metaphysics*, we read the following remark by Averroes: the Platonists made the genera and species into universal subsistent principles, but the real principles of things are matter and form.[127] Averroes writes that Aristotle does not demonstrate that it is impossible for us to think of abstract beings. In fact, this would not be right, because there are intelligibles and thus the intellect must be able to know them. But Thomas calls this argument ridiculous (*valde derisibilis*), because our intellect does not have as its end the knowledge of the separate substances. Rather the opposite is the case.[128]

In the generation of animals through the process of putrefaction, the power of the heavenly bodies replaces what the seed does in normal generation.[129] Matter and form are the natural principles in the generation of the simple bodies.[130]

Averroes and those who follow him say that the entire essence of things is constituted by their form which brings them into actual existence. Matter should not be placed in their definitions, but Thomas notes that this theory is against the doctrine of Aristotle, who affirms the opposite.[131] At the beginning of Book XII, Aristotle writes that our inquiry concerns the substance and that, if the universe is assumed to be a (organic) whole, substance is its first part, and if it is one only by composition, substance again is first, before quality or quantity. Averroes explains this text in a sense contrary to its obvious meaning (*divertit a plano sensu litterae*): if the only genus were the genus of being and if all things were of

---

127. *In III Metaph.*, lesson 8.
128. *In II Metaph.*, lesson 1.
129. *In VII Metaph.*, lesson 6.
130. Ibid., lesson 8.
131. Ibid., lesson 9.

the same nature or, as an alternative, if things had nothing in common, substance would still have the first place.

In his commentary on the *De caelo et mundo*, Averroes writes that the first heaven has the potency to move with local motion, but not a potency to being, because he thinks, says Thomas, that potency to being is proper to matter alone, while in reality it is proper to the form. On this point Averroes differs clearly from Aristotle (*in hoc manifeste dixit contra Aristotelem*),[132] According to Averroes a body in motion would be heated. The cause of this would be the light, but Thomas doubts this and points to the daily revolution of the first heaven.[133] According to Averroes all the stars are specifically the same, and he says that it is worthwhile to study this kind of question.[134] In lesson 19 of this same second book of the *De caelo*, the power of the First Mover is discussed. According to Averroes what this First Mover gives to the first heaven is limited, except that this movement (of the first heaven) lasts forever. But according to Thomas, Aristotle teaches that the power of the First Mover surpasses infinitely the body of the first heaven.[135] In another text there is a question if the air contributes accessorily to the natural movement of light and heavy bodies. According to Averroes the air would do so because of a natural necessity, but, says Thomas, this is erroneous.[136]

In Thomas's commentary on the *Physics*, Averroes is mentioned more than thirty times. This commentary not only intended to explain what Aristotle says, but also presents what Thomas knew of the interpretations of the text by the Greek commentators on Aristotle. But let us pass in review what Thomas says about observations of Averroes. At the beginning of the *Physics* I, chapter 1 (184a16), Aristotle explains how to proceed in the study of nature: we must go from what is general to more particular things, while at the same time Aristotle also indicates how we proceed in our knowledge of nature, but Averroes considers this phrase a reference to how to formulate definitions. According to Thomas, this is the subject of the second book. In lesson 6 Averroes summarizes what Aristotle tells us about the theory of Parmenides concerning the unity of all things, but Thomas thinks that the exposé of Averroes is twisted (*extorta*) and contrary to the intention of Aristotle.[137]

---

132. *In I De caelo*, lesson 6.
133. *In II De caelo*, lesson 10.
134. Ibid., lessons 16 and 17.
135. Ibid., lesson 19: "Ex quo patet falsum esse quod Averroes dicit."
136. *In III De caelo*, I, lesson 7.
137. *In I Phys.*, lesson 6, no. 11.

In Book IV Aristotle writes that if the void existed, bodies would not move faster or slower in it. Thomas expresses a doubt, but according to Averroes what Aristotle says applies only to those light or heavy bodies which have no other mover but their own form; the void does not slow them down. Thomas considers this observation frivolous (*omnino frivola*: a body which is in a place which is not natural to it, has something unnatural in itself and will move to the place which is in agreement with its nature.[138]

In Book VI Aristotle writes that a thing which changes is partly in its previous state, and partly already in its new one. Averroes raises an objection: substantial changes are instantaneous, but Thomas replies that one can say that the moment the change begins, the thing is at rest, as it also is when it is completely at the terminus of the change. When it changes, it is therefore partly in its previous state, partly in its last.[139]

In Book VII, lesson 1, the principle is formulated that whatever moves, is moved by another. Aristotle tries to show that the principle applies also to living beings: whatever moves is divisible; if one part is at rest, other parts will be in motion, and if so, the living being is not moving primarily by itself. Averroes has his doubts about the validity of the argument, but Thomas gives an ingenious explanation: what is by itself the cause of something must have this in the first place, since what is first in a genus is the cause of what comes later. But there is no first in movement, because of the infinite divisibility of movement, time, and magnitude. We cannot in fact find a first whose movement would not depend on another.[140]

After having rejected Averroes's critique of what Aristotle writes in the first chapter of Book VIII—motion in general is perpetual—Thomas passes to the second chapter, where Aristotle reasons as follows: every motion requires a subject which is in motion, and this subject is by nature earlier. Averroes avails himself of this statement to declare that creation from nothing is impossible and ridicules those who accept it: when simple people do not see from where something comes, they suppose that it comes from nothing. But, Thomas observes that Averroes is mistaken when he thinks that since a particular agent needs matter to make something, the First Cause must also have a subject on which it can exercise its causality.[141] In this same lesson Thomas quotes Averroes who tries to

---

138. *In IV Phys.*, lesson 12, no. 534.
139. *In VI Phys.*, lesson 5, nos. 797–800.
140. *In VII Phys.*, lesson 1, nos. 885–86.
141. Ibid., lesson 2, no. 974.

defend the view of Aristotle that there is no first instant in the succession of time.[142] Thomas dissociates himself from the argument of Aristotle, in order to keep open the possibility that the world had an absolute beginning. With regard to the difficult problem of the way in which a finite mover, for instance, the soul of the first heaven, would be able to move during an infinite time, Thomas in his solution considers the problem from the side of God: a motion caused by a Mover without magnitude, but of infinite power, will produce its effect in agreement with what it has in mind and in conformity with the nature of the moved body.[143] In the same lesson an objection of Averroes is mentioned, in which the latter affirms that the first heaven does not receive the perpetuity of its movement from another. It does not need it, since there is no potency in it to nonbeing. This answer, Thomas says, is contrary to the faith and also opposed to Aristotle's intention.

When, in Thomas's *Exposition in libros Physicorum*, we study the texts where Thomas examines observations and comments of Averroes, his most fundamental criticism appears to be that Averroes thinks it impossible that a thing receive the perpetuity of its being from another, although it may very well receive its perpetual movement from an external cause: the first heaven has no potency not to be and does not need to receive the perpetuity of its being from the First Cause.

Thomas has undoubtedly found many valuable explications in the commentaries of Averroes, but the fact that certain positions of the Arab philosopher have led several Christian masters into error may have made him more critical with regard to the whole of the doctrines of the "Commentator," in particular after 1260.

---

142. Ibid., lesson 2, nos. 892–896: "Averroes autem, volens salvare Aristotelis rationem...."
143. Ibid., lesson 21, nos. 1149–50.

16 ~ JEWISH PHILOSOPHY

Avicebron and Maimonides

In twelfth-century Spain a vast dialogue was carried on between Arab philosophers of the school of Aristotle and Jewish scholars. In a first stage Christians with the assistance of learned Jews or Arabs, translated texts from Arabic into Latin. This translation work was done at Toledo and some other Spanish towns, and also in Italy, in Naples and at the court of the Emperor Frederick.

Avicebron

Among the first of these authors to exercise a considerable influence on the scholars in the Latin West was Avicembron or Avicebron (Solomon ibn Gabirol). Born at Malaga, Spain (1021–22), ibn Gabirol did his studies at Zaragoza, where he worked as a philosopher and poet. His main book, the *Fons vitae*, was translated into Latin by ibn Daud and Gundisalvi.[1] At the center of his philosophy is the theory that all things, except God, are composed of matter and form. Even the spiritual substances, and also the angels, are composed of this fundamental matter,[2] which is the principle of their distinction and to which a specific, spiritual form is added.[3] The corporeal substances all have matter determined

---

1. This Latin text of the twelfth century was published by Cl. Bäumker, in *Beiträge zur Geschichte der Philosophie des Mittelalters. Texte und Untersuchungen*, vol. I (Münster: Aschendorff, 1892).

2. *QD de anima*, a. 6. Avicebron's argument is as follows: if in a being one finds the properties of matter—namely, being, receiving, to be in potency—there is also matter in it. Thomas calls it a frivolous argument, since "receiving" and "being a substrate" are not said in the same way.

3. *In II Sent.*, d. 3, q. 1, a. 1. It is a theory, Thomas writes, which many have adopted. See James A. Weisheipl, "Albertus Magnus and Universal Hylomorphism: Avicebron," *Southwestern Journal of Philosophy* 10 (1979): 21–47: for a certain time Avicebron's book was very popular. William of Auvergne borrowed several ideas from it (courtesy of J. Vijgen).

by the form of corporality. It is this form which reduces matter in them to act and becomes the basis, the subject of later forms which are added. Avicebron conceives the universe according to Neoplatonist theories: on this corporality as a base, other more particular forms are added successively to constitute the bodies of our physical world.

In his treatise *De substantiis separatis* which he composed in the second part of 1271 or somewhat later, Thomas devotes several chapters to the analysis and discussion of the theory of the learned Jewish author. The two ideas underlying the thought of Avicebron are: (a) what we call the genus and the species of things, as, for example, "animal" and "man," are real constituents of the individual being, so that in man the genus has the role of matter, the species of form; (b) a second supposition of Avicebron is that "being in potency" has in all beings the same sense, so that there is no difference between the potency of primary matter and other forms of potentiality. Taking these theories as his point of departure Avicebron saw a series of successive forms in the beings of our world: universal matter (the corporality), the forms of the four elements and the forms of natural things, such as stones and iron. He also made a distinction between (a) the celestial bodies, the matter of which does not receive contrary qualities, and (b) beings which have this universal matter and a spiritual form—the spiritual substances which are distinguished from one another by their forms in different degrees of perfection and of which the least perfect (the human souls) unite themselves to bodies. All these beings must be composed to distinguish themselves from God who is one. In natural bodies the spatial dimensions function as the form of the underlying substance.[4]

A first criticism by Thomas of the system of Avicebron is that in the method he follows the Jewish philosopher starts from what is lowest in the world to go from there to the beings on higher levels, whereas he should have started his analysis from the higher beings. In this way he falls into the error of the first philosophers, who thought that all things were just forms of a single primitive matter. His theory contradicts the concept of primary matter which is in potency and cannot therefore be considered as an actual form of what exists. Avicebron also undermines the very foundation of the philosophy of nature by removing real generation and corruption from things. Finally his theory also destroys the basis of metaphysics by depriving things of the unity of their being and

4. *De substantiis separatis*, chap. 5.

their diversity. Thomas shows that matter is not one and the same for all things, but is distinct according to the different things in which it exists.[5]

Thomas rejects next the theory of Avicebron in which he attributes matter to the separate substances. If these substances have this matter in common with the material beings in our world, they no longer seem to be distinguished. He adds that the matter in our world receives particularized or individualized forms, and not forms in their total amplitude, as do the separate substances. Thomas points out also that the superior beings have a higher degree of realization and that therefore the matter or potency which Avicebron assigns to them is a being in act and a subsistent form or act. Consequently what Avicebron calls the matter of the separate substances is those substances themselves, which therefore are no longer composed of matter and form.

Thomas next refutes the arguments which have been advanced in defense of Avicebron's theory. Forms are different from one another by their more or less greater perfection. One is simply more perfect than another form. In material and spiritual substances, it is not an addition which renders them either material or spiritual, but their own substance does so. The different classes of substances do not exist in the same way: those substances which participate most perfectly in being have in themselves the power to act, but do not have matter. These are the immaterial substances. On a lower level are the substances which have matter in themselves, but their matter is completely actualized by a form, so that there is no potentiality in them for another form: these are the incorruptible heavenly bodies. There are, in the last place, the corruptible substances, which have a matter which, when determined by a form, still remains in potency to other forms.

An argument of Avicebron in favor of his theory was that if the spiritual substances did not have matter, they would not be distinguished from one another. The answer to this argument is simple: they receive the act of being as adapted to their essence, which by itself differs from that of the other spiritual substances.[6]

Another aspect of Avicebron's theory is his doctrine in which he affirms that the forms, which in concrete beings are added to each other, are present in divine science, from which they originate in successive de-

---

5. Ibid., chap. 6. See also *SCG* II, 50–51.

6. On the refutation of Avicebron's theory by Thomas, see Ferdinand Brunner, *Platonisme et aristotélisme: La critique d'Ibn Gabirol par Saint Thomas d'Aquin* (Louvain: Publications universitaires de Louvain, 1965).

grees: the form of corporality, the forms of the simple substances, the accidents, the mathematical dimensions, etc. This emanation which recalls the Neoplatonist system, proceeds from the supreme divine will. Under its impulsion the forms give being to all things, but in order to do so they need the matter which receives and sustains the forms, and then, thanks to the forms, things exist. Being is, therefore, not a fundamental act, but arises at the end of the process of the formation of individual things. As Kohlmeier says, the system of Avicebron results from the attempt to combine a cascade of forms in a Neoplatonist vision of things with the Aristotelian doctrine of primary matter which renders possible the existence of individual things.[7]

By recurring to the creative will of God, Avicebron returns to the biblical doctrine of God, the Creator of the world. The angels are also composed of this universal matter and a specific form. Our human intellect sees a community between the spiritual beings and material things, namely, universal matter. Thomas rejects this view: it is impossible that a spiritual form would determine the same matter as a corporeal form.[8] According to Avicebron there is in one and the same thing an order or succession of several substantial forms.[9] A certain being, for instance, is a thing, a substance, a body, this animal,[10] but such a piling up of forms, Thomas says, does not result in a being. According to Avicebron a person who studies such things, passes from the consideration of sensible forms to that of intelligible forms. In this way the material creation becomes a book for him which takes him to more profound considerations and intuitions. Gilson saw traces of this theory in the Augustinianism of the thirteenth century.[11] But Thomas notes that according to Aristotle the natural movement of the heavenly bodies differs from that of the four elements and that therefore their nature is also different. This excludes a form of corporality which would be common to them and to the elements on earth.[12]

Another particularity of the doctrine of Avicebron is that all activity

---

7. Johann Kohlmeier, "Der Seinsbegriff Ibn Gabirols," *Freiburger Zeitschrift für Philosophie und Theologie* 13/14 (1966–67): 161–97.

8. ST I, q. 50, a. 2.

9. QD de spir. creat., a. 1, ad 9: "Materia prima primo recipit formam substantiae et super hanc formam aliam formam."

10. *In II De anima*, lesson 1.

11. Étienne Gilson, *La philosophie au Moyen âge: Des origines patristique à la fin du XIV siècle*, 2nd rev. ed. (Paris: Payot, 1952), 372.

12. ST I, q. 66, a. 2.

is excluded from bodies. When bodies seem to act, these actions are the work of a spiritual force which passes through all bodies. This power is not that of fire, but a spiritual energy.[13] In order to show that bodies do not act by themselves, Avicebron gives this argument: all agents, except God, need a certain matter as a subject, but corporeal substances do not have a matter as their subject and therefore cannot act. Quantity with its dimensions, characteristic of bodies, impedes action and movement; material substances are furthest removed from God.[14] In the text we quoted from the *QD de potentia*, Thomas rejects this theory: material substances are not all equal, and certain among them are closer to the First Mover and are able to act on others. Thomas adds that the matter of a material substance has the potency for other forms; there will be interaction between these substances. Although quantity is not a principle of activity, one does not see why it would prohibit operations as Avicebron says it does.

Maimonides

Like Averroes, Rabbi Moyses[15] (Maimonides) was a native of Cordova. He was born between 1135 and 1138 to a Jewish family which was forced to leave the city in 1148 because of a persecution organized by the Mahometan government. They went first to Fez in Morocco, then in 1165 to Alexandria, and a few years later to Cairo, where Maimonides became the physician of the sultan. After the tragic death of his brother in a shipwreck with the ensuing loss of the fortune of his parents, Maimonides was obliged to work to sustain his family by practicing medicine. He wrote several books on medical questions: his *Regimen sanitatis*, a book in which he gives advice on how to lead a healthy life, was known in the West. His *Mishneh Torah*, which Maimonides wrote for the Jews in Egypt after he had become a rabbi, knew a wide diffusion among the Jewish communities in the Middle East. In this book Rabbi Moyses gives an an-

---

13. *SCG* III, 69: "Nullum corpus est activum sed virtus substantiae spiritualis pertransiens per corpora agit." *ST* I, q. 115, a. 1: according to Avicebron only God moves, whereas all other beings are moved, but Thomas writes that only primary matter has no activity.

14. *QD de potentia*, q. 3, a. 7. For more details on the life and doctrine of Avicebron, see S. Munk, "Ibn Gabirol, ses écrits et sa philosophie," in *Mélanges de philosophie juive et arabe* (Paris: J. Vrin, 1955), 1–306; H. Simon, "Das Weltbild Gabirols. Seine Bedeutung für die Geschichte der Philosophie," *Wissenschftliche Zeitschrift der Humbold-Universität* 6 (1956–1957): 199–205.

15. Thomas refers to him by this name.

swer to a great number of questions, as, for instance, on the Messiah. This book was written in Hebrew about 1180. Maimonides explains his own philosophical position which takes over the central doctrines of Aristotle. And he adds some advice for conserving one's health. Toward 1190 he finishes his main philosophical work, the *Guide of the Perplexed*, in which he presents texts on philosophical themes, but also exposés on medical, astronomical, and mathematical questions.[16] He dies in 1204.

In the important *Guide of the Perplexed*, Maimonides also wanted to show that it is possible to adhere to both the true philosophy and the teachings of the Bible. It was his intention to explain how to understand certain texts in the writings of the prophets of Israel. This famous book was translated into Latin under the title *Dux neutrorum*.[17] One can read it from a somewhat skeptical perspective—we cannot know God and must respect his transcendence—and also, from a philosophical point of view, read in it the science which leads us to illumination and an experience of the divine. Maimonides shows that the eternal existence of the world, as Aristotle teaches it, has not been demonstrated and that one may therefore accept the biblical story of the creation of the world at the beginning of time. He accepts the cosmological system of Aristotle with its nine spheres, in each of which resides an intelligence, while a tenth intelligence, the agent intellect, illuminates us and gives us our universal concepts. This agent intellect is unique for all men. We should notice that for Rabbi Moyses there is no supernatural life grafted upon our natural thought and elevating it. The intellect receives only an illumination. After our death we preserve the knowledge which we acquired during our life on earth. Maimonides stresses our free will, which allows us to determine the direction of our life. Important is the practice of the virtues, which makes intellectual life possible.

Michael Scot, the well-known translator of the works of Averroes, considers Maimonides in the first place an astronomer; and this reputation of his is still found in the writings of Meister Eckhart. Hasselhoff gives a survey of the presence of certain texts of Maimonides in the writings of Christian authors of the thirteenth and fourteenth centuries.

Rabbi Moyses is quoted more than eighty times in the works of Aquinas. Most of these references are in the *Scriptum super libros Sententiarum*

---

16. For an excellent overview of this period of Maimonides's life, see Görge K. Hasselhoff, *Dicit Rabbi Moyses, Studien zum Bild von Moses Maimonides im lateinischen Westen vom 13. bis zum 15. Jahrhundert* (Königshausen & Neuman, 2004): 22–36.

17. One also finds the titles *Dux errantium* and *Liber perplexorum*.

and in the *Quaestiones disputatae*.[18] Thomas mentions Maimonides as an author who believes what Holy Scripture says[19] and in the God of Israel and who accepts the creation of the world. Maimonides elaborated several proofs of the existence of God, among which the proof from motion occupies the first place. God exists and he is a necessary being, but we do not know what he is. As Gilson writes, God is at the center of the thought of Maimonides.[20]

As we shall see, Thomas refers to Maimonides in the study of certain themes, such as the question of the divine attributes, providence, the angels, cosmological subjects, and the significance of numerous ceremonial laws of the Old Testament, as well as his theory of prophetical knowledge. Our series of quotations is not meant to be an inventory of the entire thought of Maimonides, but is intended to show its presence in the works of Thomas.

God and the World

In his *Guide of the Perplexed*, Maimonides takes over Aristotle's demonstration of the existence of a First Mover, God, adding also other arguments. He himself, as well as Avicenna, holds that God's existence is not immediately evident to us, but must be shown by arguments. For some, he says, his existence is only known by faith.[21]

The best name of God is that of being.[22] But the other names said of him signify that he is not non-wise, non-just, non-merciful.[23] In God there is no other essence except to be.[24] Whatever is said affirmatively of God is said to remove from him the contrary of these predicates. According to Maimonides there is no analogy between the perfections of the creatures and God. We do not know anything positive about him, except the fact that he is being itself. Avicenna and Maimonides affirm that God is subsistent being and that nothing else is in God but being. All other names used to designate God have a certain value, that is, (a) in so

---

18. We notice, however, that in the *QD de potentia* Augustine is quoted 150 times, Averroes twenty-five and Maimonides ten. Apparently the latter's texts had less importance for Thomas.

19. *QD de potentia*, q. 6, a. 7: "Quidam eorum qui sacrae Scripturae credunt ... sicut patet de Rabbi Moyses."

20. Étienne Gilson, "Maïmonide et la philosophie de l'Exode," *Mediæval Studies* 13, no. 1 (1951): 223–25.

21. *QD de veritate*, q. 10, a. 12.

22. *In I Sent.*, d. 8, q. 1, a. 1.

23. *ST* I, q. 13, a. 2.

24. *QD de potentia*, q. 7, a. 2, s.c. 2.

far as they remove the opposed defect; (b) in so far as something follows from a negative statement, for example, that God is not divided, he is one. The attributes which are said of God are only in our intellect, and not in God.²⁵

Whatever we say affirmatively of God is said in order to remove these predicates from him, and not to affirm that God possesses these perfections.²⁶ There is no analogy between God and his creatures, but Thomas says that this opinion of Maimonides cannot be true.²⁷ One can however, understand these names (attributes) as showing a resemblance between what God has done and what we do. When one says, for instance, that God is wise, one can understand it as affirming that there is a wisely established order among his effects, like the order which a wise man tries to establish; but this attributes absolutely nothing to God himself, and these names do not indicate the divine substance. Thomas notes that this explanation by means of a twofold meaning of our sentences about God fails and is misplaced. It is not the same thing when we say that God is wise and that he is choleric.²⁸ According to Maimonides there would not be any relation between the creatures and God, since he accepts only those relations which follow from quantity, but not the relations which follow from action and passions.²⁹ In a few texts, quoted by Thomas, Maimonides criticizes the theory of certain Mohammedan authors who deny that creatures act by themselves: according to them it is God who acts and does everything immediately by himself.³⁰

Maimonides affirms that God knows perfectly the things which he has made, and also their individuality; and he refutes the contrary position that the divine science is entirely different from our knowledge. We find this confirmed, he says, by Psalm 93:9: "Is he who invented the ear unable to hear, the creator of the eye unable to see?"³¹

Connected with the theme of divine science is that of divine providence. Maimonides affirms that divine providence concerns all things,

25. *In I Sent.*, d. 2, q. 1, a. 3.
26. *QD de potentia*, q. 9, a. 7.
27. Ibid., q. 7.a. 7: "Haec opinio non potest esse vera."
28. *QD de potentia*, q. 7, a. 5. According to Seymour Feldman this would be a wrong interpretation of the theory of Maimonides. Feldman, "A Scholastic Misinterpretation of Maimonides' Doctrine of Divine Attributes," in *Studies in Maimonides and St. Thomas Aquinas*, ed. Jacob I. Dienstag (New York: KTAV Publishing House, 1975), 58–74. It is, however, difficult to see where Thomas would have misrepresented the theory of Maimonides.
29. *QD de potentia*, q. 7, a. 10.
30. Ibid., q. 3, a. 7.
31. *In I Sent.*, d. 36, q. 1, a. 1.

also particular beings.³² Thomas even says that Maimonides calls heretics those who restrict God's providence to the universal. Several schools of philosophers refuse to accept divine providence. Maimonides follows a rather common view: in general things are not the object of a special providence, but he makes an exception for men because of their dignity and the splendor of their intellect. Thomas notes that it is true that man with his free will is in a special way the object of divine providence, but that one cannot say with Maimonides that the irrational creatures are not the object of God's providence.³³ On the other hand Maimonides rejects the fatalism of those theologians who follow the law of the Saracens and think that whatever God decides happens necessarily.

Has the World Existed Forever?

Thomas examines this question in *QD de potentia*, question 3, article 17, and reviews the different theories of the philosophers on this point. The existence of the world depends only on God's will and power. Maimonides proposes an interesting explanation: there are people who think that the world has always existed and do not ask where it comes from. That is what a young man would think who, shortly after his birth, would have been brought to a solitary place, would never have heard anything about his own birth, and would not know where he comes from.³⁴ If one looks for reasons which can make people think that the world has begun to exist, one must look around oneself; and that is the reason why Holy Scripture invites us to consider the heavenly bodies, all of which are subject to God's will and providence.³⁵ The matter of the celestial bodies differs from that of the sublunar things. He formulates an objection against the view of the eternity of the world: if the world were infinite, there would now be an infinite number of (immortal) souls, but an infinite number is not possible. Maimonides says that this argument is not a demonstration.³⁶ He accepts creation at the beginning of time instead of the theory of an eternal existence of the world, taught by philosophers.³⁷

The easiest way of demonstrating the existence of God is the supposition of the novelty of the world.³⁸ As for the question whether the world,

---

32. *In I Sent.*, d. 39, q. 2, a. 2.
33. *ST* I, q. 22, a. 2, ad 5.
34. *In Symb. Apostolorum*, a. 1.
35. Ibid.
36. *In II Sent.*, d. 1, q. 1, a. 5, ad 6.
37. Maimonides, *Guide of the Perplexed*, II, 23.
38. *In II Sent.*, d. 2, q. 1, a. 3, ad 2.

created by God from nothing, began to exist in time, Maimonides gives an affirmative answer, notwithstanding Aristotle's theory of an eternal world.[39] But Thomas expresses himself with some reservations: in the texts of the Bible on the creation of the world, Maimonides reads an invitation to consider that everything is subject to God's will, which is true,[40] but he does not think that the world was made in view of man. The grandeur of the universe and of the celestial spheres in Aristotle's cosmology had impressed him so much that he could not believe that the world was made in consideration of man. What the Old Testament says of a renewal of the world and the prophecy of Isaiah about the end Maimonides sees as metaphor.[41]

Nature and the Supernatural

Even according to the Philosopher, coming to know God is the end of human life, but, Thomas says, there is another knowledge of God which goes beyond our nature, that is, the vision of God in his essence. Nature cannot render us capable of this vision. This is the reason why faith is necessary. Concerning the obstacles which one encounters when trying to reach God through knowledge, Thomas quotes a text of Maimonides in which he lists the difficulties which can render it difficult to make progress on this road:[42] (a) this knowledge is far above the level of the senses, therefore, one must leave behind the level of sensitive knowledge; (b) our intellect is by its nature ordained to the knowledge of God, but needs God's illumination; (c) to reach this (natural) knowledge of God, a long preparation is required, such as the study of philosophy; (d) certain people have a slow-working mind and must be brought to familiarize themselves with the study of God; (e) people are busy with taking care of their daily lives and are turned away from the study of divine things. The supernatural, however, does not enter into the considerations of the learned Rabbi Moyses.[43]

---

39. Maimonides, *Guide of the Perplexed*, II, 23.
40. *QD de potentia*, q. 3, a. 17.
41. *In IV Sent.*, d. 48, q. 2, a. 3, ad 6.
42. *In III Sent.*, d. 24, q. 1, a. 3, qc. 1. See also *In Boetii De Trin.*, q. 3, a. 1; *QD de veritate*, q. 14, a. 10; and without mentioning Maimonides, *SCG*, I, 4; *ST* I, q. 1, a. 1; II-II, q. 2, a. 4 (courtesy of J. Vijgen).
43. See Ruedi Imbach, "Ut ait Rabbi Moyses. Maimonidische Philosopheme bei Thomas von Aquin und Meister Eckhart," *Collectanea Franciscana* 60 (1990): 106: "Während also Maimonides mit diesen Gründen seine esoterische Auffassung der Philosophie stützen will, bedient Thomas sich dieser Argumente zur Begründung seiner Theorie der Offenbarung" (courtesy of J. Vijgen).

The Angels

In many passages Sacred Scripture mentions angels who are sent by God to men, especially as guides and messengers. Maimonides has a tendency to reduce the angels to the status of the intelligences mentioned by the philosophers and so to restrict their number to that of the celestial spheres.[44] About this theme Thomas quotes a text of Maimonides, where he says that in beings without matter, multiplication only takes place with regard to the relationship of a cause with its effects. There will not be multiplication, or, if there is some, one angel is the cause of another, says Maimonides. But Thomas explains that the angels are not the causes of other angels and that their number depends on God's wisdom.[45]

According to Maimonides the angels mentioned in the Bible are not separate substances, but powers or spirits.[46] Real angels can never adopt a body.[47] Maimonides attempts to explain what the Scriptures say about the appearances of angels by calling these texts prophetical visions, but Thomas says that this explanation does not do right to the truth of Holy Scripture.[48]

Cosmological Questions

With regard to the question whether matter is different according to the region of the universe in which it is located, Maimonides accepts the position of Avicenna: there is no matter in the immaterial substances, but he follows Aristotle in that he stresses that the heavenly bodies and the elements do not have a common matter.[49] Maimonides is also cited a few times for his explanation of the different cosmic zones described on the first page of the Bible.[50] Thus he says that the darkness of the story of the creation signifies the fourth element, that is, fire; in this way the four elements would have been present on the day of the creation.[51] Thomas also quotes other explanations Maimonides gives of Moses's story of the creation: he places the water above the firmament, whereas Thomas says that according to the text God has suspended two great lamps and stars

---

44. *In II Sent.*, d. 3, q. 1, a. 3.
45. *QD de spir. creat.*, a. 8, arg. 16. Cf. also *QD de anima*, a. 3, arg. 6.
46. *SCG* II, 92.
47. *QD de potentia*, q. 6, a. 7.
48. Ibid.
49. *In III Sent.*, d. 3, q. 1, a. 1.
50. Ibid., q. 4, a. 1.
51. *In II Sent.*, d. 14, q. 1, a. 2, ad 2; *QD de potentia*, q. 4, a. 1, ad 2.

in the firmament. Maimonides suggests that by "firmament" we must understand the cosmic space where the air has it place, close to the earth.[52] With respect to Genesis 1:1—"And God's spirit hovered over the water"—Maimonides thought that by "spirit" the air is meant, but Thomas says that "according to the saints" it is the Holy Spirit.[53]

Has God first made unformed matter before creating the different things? Thomas answers that it is only by thought that one can imagine unformed matter. He does not accept all the explanations Maimonides gives of the narrative of the creation, because Maimonides tries to construct a relation between what the Bible says and Aristotle's cosmology. Maimonides is fond of comparing the first heaven with the human heart: just as the first heaven has the function to move the other celestial spheres and whatever moves in the world, the human heart is the center of the motions of all processes in the human body.[54]

With regard to Psalm 9:1, "The heavens chant your majesty," Maimonides says that in order to do so they must have an intellect. So he believes that he has found confirmation in the Bible of Aristotle's theory of the presence of intelligences in the heavenly spheres, but Thomas says that this "proof" is naive (*frivola*), even if it is Maimonides who formulates it.[55] In his commentary on Psalm 18 (19) Thomas writes that the heavens do not praise the glory of God since then they would be living beings, as Maimonides says, but rather it is their beauty which refers us to their Creator. According to Plato there are as many separate substances (the Ideas) as there are essences, but for Aristotle they have a function in the world such as the causes of movement or as final causes. Therefore their number corresponds to the movements of the spheres, Maimonides says, wanting to reconcile what the Bible says with this theory.[56]

---

52. *QD de potentia*, q. 4, a. 1, ad 5, and ad 15.
53. *ST* I, q. 74, a. 3, ad 4. Cf. also Thomas's general reflections on the possible cosmological meaning of the description of the creation, in *ST* I, q. 68, a. 1, ad 1, where Thomas assigns a certain value to the suggestions of Maimonides.
54. *In II Sent.*, d. 14, q. 1, a., 1 ad 2; *QD de veritate*, q. 5, a. 9, s.c. 5; *QD de potentia*, q. 5, a. 7, arg. 7.
55. *QD de anima*, a. 8, ad 19.
56. *ST* I, q. 50, a. 3.

Man

As for his doctrine of man, Maimonides confirms that we are composed of a body and a soul, and endowed with an intellect and a will, sense appetite, and five external senses. A universal agent intellect, which exists outside us, illuminates our possible intellect and renders the knowledge of abstract concepts possible. According to Maimonides, however, we cannot say that the celestial bodies, each of which is endowed with an intellect, have been created for the sake of man. Thomas says that although it is true that they are much larger than our body, we surpass them, thanks to our spiritual soul; and that for this reason one can say that they have been made for man.[57]

The Meaning of the Ceremonial Laws

Thomas refers repeatedly to Maimonides in order to clarify the meaning of certain texts of Holy Scripture. On the ceremonial laws of the Old Testament, Maimonides says that these are prescriptions whose sense is not evident,[58] but Thomas thinks that there are probable, or sometimes even evident, reasons which led to their redaction, as is the case for the observation of the Sabbath and the feast of Easter. But were so may laws needed? Maimonides says that the (Old) Law had already reduced the external cult, but the cult of God should not be reduced to the point that people turn to the veneration of the demons.[59]

Sometimes Maimonides gives surprising explanations of certain prescriptions; among pigeons the small ones are better, and that is why they should be offered to God, but that is not the case with turtle doves. We must offer the best to God.[60] Maimonides also says that the Law prescribes a way to kill the animals, so that they suffer less. This excludes cruelty in those who are going to kill them and avoids the deterioration of the killed animals.[61] As for the ceremony of the expiation of sins, the animal which was sacrificed was of lesser value the more serious the sins were.[62] Why did the Jews before the construction of the Temple in Jerusalem not have a precisely determined place for offering these sacrifices?

---

57. *In IV Sent.*, d. 48, q. 2, a. 3, ad 6.
58. *ST* I-II, q. 101, a. 1, arg. 4.
59. *ST* I-II, q. 102, a. 3, ad 2.
60. Ibid., ad 4.
61. Ibid., ad 6.
62. Ibid., ad 12.

Maimonides thinks that the reason was that so their enemies could not seize and destroy it, and also to avoid rivalries between the tribes.⁶³

In the eyes of God many of the things declared impure by the Law are not sordid. As Maimonides says, there are practical and symbolic reasons for these laws: by contact with certain contaminated persons and even by looking at them, one may incur a contamination, such as by contact with a woman during her menstrual period. Thomas adds that all this shows in a mystical way that impiety is odious to God.⁶⁴ Why was it forbidden to consume fat and blood? Maimonides says that this was because they were not good nourishment. Thomas thinks that by all those animals and products sins are indicated.⁶⁵ According to the Law we must also turn our eyes away from animals which are coupling, since this view could stimulate the passions, says Maimonides.⁶⁶

When a murder has been committed by an unknown murderer, a calf must be sacrificed in a place that could no longer be used for agriculture, as a deterrent.⁶⁷ The law of the observation of the Sabbath reminds us that the world has a beginning.⁶⁸ Thomas also mentions Maimonides's view on the question of sexual intercourse outside marriage. Maimonides justifies the relation of Judah with Tamar, because it took place before the proclamation of the Law, whereas Thomas considers it in the light of the natural law. Thomas borrows from Maimonides what the latter says about the regulations which forbid marriage between relatives, but abbreviates them.⁶⁹ Maimonides also provides explanations of some judiciary laws.⁷⁰

As for the spiritual meaning of the ceremonial laws, Thomas adds a few words to the explanations given by Maimonides, to whom he ascribes a special competence to explain the meaning of these laws which, for Thomas, were characteristic of the Old Testament as preparatory for the New Law. The way in which Thomas quotes Maimonides and refers to him on this question is unparalleled for its time.⁷¹

---

63. Ibid., a. 4, ad 2.
64. *ST* I-II, q. 102, a. 5, ad 4.
65. Ibid., a. 6, ad 1.
66. Ibid., a. 8.
67. *ST* I-II, q. 105, a. 2, ad 12.
68. *In II Sent.*, d. 15, q. 3, a. 3, arg. 3; *In III Sent.*, d. 37, q. 1, a. 5, s.c. 2.
69. *In IV Sent.*, d. 40, q. 1, a. 4.
70. *ST* I-II, q. 105, a. 2, ad 12.
71. See Hasselhoff, *Dixit Rabbi Moyses*, 88.

Maimonides's Doctrine of Prophecy

In discussions on a possible dependence of Thomas on Maimonides, the doctrine of prophecy occupies a central place. Some authors have suggested that Thomas is indebted for his doctrine to the learned Jewish author, but that sometimes he neglects to mention his source.[72] Although Merx is disgusted with this alleged plagiarism, he says that there is a mitigating circumstance: at the time Thomas wrote his *Summa*, it was prudent not to mention the author, whose books had been burned in public. The learned Jew Jakob Guttmann wrote in 1890 that the influence of Maimonides on Thomas can hardly be exaggerated.[73] These accusations provoked reactions from such Catholic authors as Wehofer and Mausbach. Bruno Decker made what one may call a definitive study of the theme in his magisterial work on the treatises of prophecy in the twelfth and thirteenth centuries.[74] This author shows that the thought of Christians on prophecy was nourished by an assiduous reflection on Holy Scripture and the writings of the Fathers, as well as on the experience of the Christian people. Their important insights were taken entirely from the Bible.

Maimonides examines prophecy in the second part of his *Guide of the Perplexed*. He brings together texts on the anthropomorphisms in the language of the biblical prophets and themes of a more speculative nature such as creation, the nature of the angels, and the destruction of the universe. The prophets announced, indeed, a destruction of the world, and so Maimonides was led to treat of their respective prophecies. He considered prophecy as a stream of light which comes from God and penetrates into the intellect of a prophet, in order to establish itself in his imagination, where the essential act of a prophet takes place, either during his sleep or while he is awake. The external senses do not collaborate with this process. This illumination is the highest perfection which man can reach. To receive it one must have a good intelligence and a fine imagination, in a highly developed body. People who are not very talented can never become prophets.

---

72. Adalbert Merx, *Die Prophetie des Joel und Ihre Ausleger* (Halle, Germany: Buchhandlung des Waisenhauses, 1879), 367: "Die ganze Theorie des Prophetismus bei Thomas erweist sich so auf Maimonides begründet, in den Einzelkeiten wie in den Grundgedanken."

73. Jakob Guttmann, *Das Verhältnis des Thomas von Aquino zum Judentum und zur jüdischen Literatur* (Göttingen: Vandenhoeck & Ruprecht, 1891), 31.

74. Bruno Decker, *Die Entwicklung der Lehre von der prophetischen Offenbarung von Wilhelm von Auxerre bis zu Thomas von Aquin* (Breslau: Müller & Seiffert, 1940).

This description shows that we have to do with a theory which casts the data of the Bible in the framework of the philosophy of Avicenna. Prophecy is no longer supernatural knowledge, and we no longer see what its relation with supernatural salvation is. There is no act of faith in the message which God reveals. Thomas could not but reject this theory. For him prophecy is a charism, a gratuitous gift in view of salvation, which consists in a transitory impression of truths which are above the range of natural reason. Thomas also rejects that the external senses are necessarily at rest during the reception of this illumination, except in those cases where the prophetic revelation brings visions in the imagination with it.[75]

Let us consider a few quotations from the *Guide of the Perplexed* in Thomas's works. With regard to what a prophet knows by prophetical illumination, his mind is in a different situation from that of one who knows something by a demonstration. The prophet knows, but in a different way. The judgment of the prophet is the same as the conclusions reached by other persons. Thomas says that by this remark Maimonides does not want to exclude the possibility of a prophetic revelation, although the knowledge he is here speaking about lies on the natural level.[76] In another text Maimonides sees in the pursuit of pleasures and in the worldly undertakings (of a prophet)[77] a sign indicating that he is a bad prophet. Further on in this disputed question, a participant quotes a sentence of Maimonides affirming that prophecy begins in the intellect but that it is completed in the imagination, but Thomas replies that this remark is not acceptable, since the prophet David would then be inferior to the other prophets, while the Church Fathers say the contrary. Yet this opinion has a grain of truth, since in order to judge something about a person it is better to have him before oneself. So the intellectual vision may be completed by the imagination.[78]

In question 13 of the *De veritate*, rapture is dealt with. In 2 Corinthians 12:2, St. Paul describes what happened to him: a new form of knowledge of God was given to him. An opponent in the discussion suggests that this experience is a prolongation of natural knowledge. The remark

---

75. See Jean-Pierre Torrell, "Le traité de la prophétie de s.Thomas d'Aquin et la théologie de la révélation," in *La doctrine de la revelation divine de saint Thomas d'Aquin*, ed. Leo Elders (Vatican City: Libreria Editrice Vaticana, 1990), 171–95.
76. *QD de veritate*, q. 12, a. 2, arg. 6, and ad 6.
77. Ibid., q. 12, a. 5.
78. Ibid., q. 12, a. 12, ad 6.

makes us think of the theory of Maimonides, but Thomas answers that what happened to Paul was a divine intervention which our nature obeys. He quotes a text from Maimonides which says that our knowledge corresponds to the state of development of our mind: for a child it is different than that of an adult. Thomas uses these words to say that the natural knowledge of God which we can obtain in this life is acquired through the mediation of creatures, but that in heaven it will be different, direct and perfect. This heavenly knowledge would not fit in with our actual state, just as for a boy it would be against nature to have a beard.

Maimonides's theory of prophecy was influenced by the thought of Avicenna: a stream of light flows from the first being and is communicated, through the agent intellect as intermediary, to our possible intellect. The mind of the prophet becomes a mirror of intelligible forms. This scheme is characterized by a certain rationalism. On the other hand, in Thomas's text, the theological tradition occupies an important place: we come across twenty-five references to Augustine, fifty-six to other Fathers, and twenty-two to Pseudo-Dionysius.[79] In his answer to the question whether the prophets know what, in their visions and sayings, comes from God and what results from their natural knowledge, Thomas quotes Augustine twice.

One case where Thomas would have borrowed from Maimonides, and on which an author like Merx insists, is found in the question whether a prophet is certain of the supernatural origin of his knowledge. In his answer Thomas proposes the same example as Maimonides: if Abraham had not been certain that the order came from God himself, he would not have decided to sacrifice Isaac. While for this article the borrowing of the example from Maimonides is possible, there is on the other hand a long tradition among Christian authors who used it.[80] Thomas would also have taken over from Maimonides the scheme of the division of prophecies which for Maimonides was essential, since it concerns the way in which the stream of light arrives in man: a sub-prophetic inspiration; the emergence of a vision; hearing a voice; hearing a voice while the prophet also sees the person who speaks; finally, the apparition of an angel who speaks to the prophet. When this happens while the prophet is awake, the illumination has a greater power. In this way Maimonides distinguishes

---

79. On this theme, cf. Leo Elders, "Les rapports entre la doctrine de la prophétie de saint Thomas et le Guide des égarés de Maïmonide," *Divus Thomas* 78 (1975): 449–56.

80. Augustine, *De Gen. ad litt.*, XII, 14 and 26; Gregory the Great, *Hom. in Ezech.* (PL 76: 793).

two series of four degrees each, according to whether the prophecy is giving during the sleep of the prophet, or when he was vigilant.[81]

The enumeration is clear and classifies quite well the numerous biblical descriptions of prophetic knowledge. Nevertheless Thomas remodels it.[82] The difference becomes already visible in the description of the first two degrees of a sub-prophetic illumination/inspiration, where Thomas changes the examples and excludes the so-called hagiographic inspiration.[83] More important is that Thomas also knows other divisions, for example, according to the different ways of revelation, or to the cognitive faculties of man.[84] The fundamental division of prophecies, however, remains the division according to the object of prophecies: a prophecy of predestination, a prophecy of prescience, and a prophecy of threats.

What carries weight is the illumination of the intellect, but since this illumination is withdrawn from our knowledge, we cannot speak of its greater or lesser perfection except by referring to its repercussion in our imagination. What is more, Thomas presents a total reconstruction of the division by substituting the successive degrees by four principles according to which a revelation can be said to be more or less perfect: Is a prophecy received during the prophet's sleep or when he was awake? Is there just a vision or does one also hear words? Is there an interlocutor? Is it a man, an angel, or God? This division does justice to the descriptions of Holy Scripture, where the borderlines between the different types are fluid. Contrary to what Maimonides says, Thomas affirms that prophets other than Moses can also, when awake, see or listen to God. In this way Thomas avoids the rationalism of Maimonides who reduces the degrees of prophecies received when the prophet is awake to those of the illumination received during his sleep, for according to Maimonides there is no interlocutor nor a voice which addresses itself to the external senses of a prophet.

While in *In IV Sent.*, d. 49, q. 2, a. 7, ad 2, Thomas mentions Maimonides as his source, he does not refer to him in the questions on prophecy of the *Summa theologiae*. It has been suggested that the reason was that the *Guide of the Perplexed* was suspected of heresy, and there was much

---

81. Maimonides, *Guide of the Perplexed*, II, 45.
82. *ST* II-II, q. 174, a. 3.
83. The example of Judges 14:19 is replaced by the passage from Judges 15:14. As for the second degree, in the example of King Solomon, Thomas says that the king's science concerned profane knowledge and abstracts from an inspiration by God.
84. *ST* II-II, q. 174, a. 1, ad 3.

opposition to Maimonides in the circles of orthodox Jews in France, and, toward 1230, at the request of certain Jewish communities, the church authorities had his works publicly burned.[85] But these circumstances did not influence Thomas because in the *prima pars* of the *Summa theologiae* and in the *prima secundae* he quotes Maimonides some twenty times, sometimes under the title *Doctor dubiorum* or *Dux Neutrorum* or *Errantium*, and sometimes under that of the books of the *Perplexorum* or *Prophetarum*. In the *aecunda secundae* and the *tertia pars*, Maimonides is no longer mentioned. Our examen of these quotations has shown that except for the doctrines of the *creatio in tempore* and divine providence and the interpretation of the ceremonial laws of the Old Testament, Thomas rejects the position of Maimonides, for example, in his explanation of the divine attributes and the mission and number of the angels. Twice he reproaches Maimonides with having interpreted biblical texts wrongly in order to make them agree with doctrines of Plato or Aristotle, but in general he shows respect for the learned Jewish author.[86]

This suggests that Thomas considered Maimonides to be a specialist in the field of the pre-theological and scientific explanation of Holy Scripture, but that he does not consider him an authority in questions of theological doctrine. It is perhaps also for this reason that he does not mention him in his treatise on prophecy, even if he borrows two or three texts from him. Rather than a lack of respect, we see here a preoccupation with reminding the reader that the Christian doctrine of prophecy is radically different from that of the famous Jewish philosopher. The "silence" of Thomas about certain parts of the doctrine of prophecy of Maimonides signifies that Thomas wanted to suggest that prophetical knowledge cannot be described in terms taken from a psychology and cosmology marked by rationalism.

---

85. See Georges Vajda, *Introduction à la pensée juive du moyen âge* (Paris: J. Vrin, 1947), 147–51.
86. On the theme of this chapter, see also Avital Wohlman, *Thomas d'Aquin et Maimonide. Un dialogue exemplaire* (Paris: Cerf, 1988).

WORKS CITED

Translations throughout the text are by the author unless otherwise noted. Published full English translations of these works are mentioned below for the use of readers. The Aquinas section of the bibliography was developed from the longer list of sources in Pasquale Porro, *Thomas Aquinas: A Historical and Philosophical Profile*, trans. Joseph G. Trabbic and Roger Nutt (Washington, D.C.: The Catholic University of America Press, 2016).

Works of Aquinas

The following list presents Thomas's works based on their type. Within the types, the works are alphabetically ordered by the Latin titles, with any available English translations (complete or partial) appearing after the Latin. But first, some general observations about the Latin and English texts.

Latin: Versions of most of Aquinas's Latin texts are available online at http://www.corpusthomisticum.org/. This site links to some but not all of the definitive critical Latin editions of his works, which are published by the Leonine Commission in conjunction with various publishers (Sancti Thomae de Aquino doctoris angelici, *Opera Omnia*, iussu impensaque Leonis XIII P.M. edita, cura et studio fratrum praedicatorum). The first texts established by the commission were published in 1882, and more texts are released as they are completed. Where no Leonine edition yet exists, another Latin edition is mentioned in the bibliography below. Texts not mentioned by Leonine edition or specific alternate Latin edition can still be found in one of these two historic sources:

Parma: *Sancti Thomae Aquinatis Doctoris Angelici Ordinis Praedicatorum Opera Omnia ad fidem optimarum editionum accurate recognita*. 25 vols. Parma: Typis P. Fiaccadori, 1852–73. Reprint: New York: Musurgia, 1948–50.

Piana: *Divi Thomae Aquinatis Opera Omnia*. 15 vols. Gratiis privilegiisque Pii V, Pont. Max., excusa. Rome: 1570. Vives: *Doctoris Angelici divi Thomae Aquinatis sacri Ordinis F. F. Praedicatorum Opera Omnia sive antehac excusa, sive etiam anecdota ..., studio ac labore Stanislai Eduardi Frette et Pauli Mare sacerdotum, Scholaeque thomisticae Alumnorum*. 34 vols. Paris: apud Ludovicum Vives, 1871–72.

English: There is a large (although not complete) collection of Thomas's works in English translation presently available online at http://dhspriory.org/thomas; this collection can be consulted if no published English version of a work is listed below. The only comprehensive project to translate Thomas's entire *Opera Omnia* into English is being directed and published by the Aquinas Institute for the Study of Sacred Doctrine, in Lander, Wyoming. To date, the entire *Summa theologiae* and many of Thomas's commentaries on the New Testament are available. The volumes are hard cover and include the Latin text with the English translation on the facing pages. Another resource is Thérèse Bonin, "Thomas Aquinas in English: A Bibliography.":http://www.home.duq.edu/~bonin/thomasbibliography.html.

Theological Syntheses

Compendium theologiae. Part 1, *De fide*. Edited by H.-F. Dondaine. Part 2, *De spe*. Edited by G. de Grandpre. *De articulis fidei*. Leonine Commission 42. Rome: Editori di San Tommaso, 1979.

Compendium of Theology. Translated by Richard Regan. Oxford: Oxford University Press, 2009.

The Compendium of Theology. Translated by Cyril Vollert. St. Louis: B. Herder, 1947. Reprinted as *Light of Faith: The Compendium of Theology*. Manchester, N.H.: Sophia Institute, 1993.

Compendium of Theology. Translated by Lawrence Lynch. New York: McMullen, 1947.

Summa contra Gentiles or *Summa contra Gentiles cum commentariis Ferrariensis*. Leonine Commission 13–15. Rome: Typis Riccardi Garroni, 1918–30.

Summa contra Gentiles. Edited by A. C. Pegis, J. F. Anderson, V. J. Bourke, and C. J. O'Neil. 5 vols. Notre Dame, Ind.: University of Notre Dame Press, 1975.

Summa theologiae or *Summa theologiae cum Supplemento et commentariis Caietani*. Leonine Commission 4–12. Rome: Ex Typographia Polyglotta S. C. de Propaganda Fide, 1888–1906.

Summa theologiae. Complete set, Latin-English. Lander, Wy.: The Aquinas Institute, 2012.

Summa theologica. Edited by the Fathers of the English Dominican Province. 5 vols. Westminster, Md.: Christian Classics, 1981. Another Latin-English version, *Summa Theologiae*, edited by T. Gilby and T. C. O'Brien. 60 vols. Cambridge: Cambridge University Press, 1964–73.

Scriptum super libros Sententiarum. Books I–II, 2 vols. Edited by P. Mandonnet. Paris: Lethielleux, 1929. Book III to distinction 22 of Book IV, 2 vols. Edited by M. F. Moos. Paris: Lethielleux, 1922–37.

On Love and Charity: Readings from the "Commentary on the Sentences of Peter Lombard." Translated by Peter A. Kwasniewski, Thomas Bolin, OSB, and Joseph Bolin. Washington, D.C.: The Catholic University of America Press, 2008.

Thomas Aquinas's Earliest Treatment of the Divine Essence: Book I Distinction 8. Translated by E. M. Macierowski and Joseph Owens. Medieval Studies Worldwide. Center for Medieval and Renaissance Studies. Albany: State University of New York Press, 1997.

Biblical Commentaries

Catena aurea in quattuor evangelia. Vol. 1, *Expositio in Matthaeum et Marcum*; vol. 2, *Expositio in Lucam et Ioannem.* Edited by A. Guarienti. Turin-Rome: Marietti, 1953.

Catena Aurea: Commentary on the Four Gospels Collected Out of the Works of the Fathers by S. Thomas Aquinas. 4 vols. Translated by John Henry Newman. Oil City, Penn.: Baronius Press, 2009.

Expositio super Iob ad litteram. Edited by A. Dondaine. Leonine Commission 26. Rome: Ad Sanctae Sabinae, 1965.

The Literal Exposition on Job: A Scriptural Commentary Concerning Providence. Translated by Anthony Damico. Classics in Religious Studies 7. Atlanta, Ga.: Scholars Press, 1989.

Expositio super Isaiam ad litteram. Edited by H.-F. Dondaine and L. Reid. Leonine Commission 28. Rome: Editori di San Tommaso Ad Sanctae Sabinae, 1974.

Lectura super Ioannem. 2 vol. Lander, Wy.: The Aquinas Institute, Aquinas Institute for the Study of Sacred Doctrine, 2013. (Latin-English, includes the Greek text of the gospel.)

Commentary on the Gospel of John. 3 vols. Translated by James A. Weisheipl and Fabian R. Larcher. Edited by Daniel Keating and Matthew Levering. Thomas Aquinas in Translation. Washington, D.C.: The Catholic University of America Press, 2010.

Commentary on the Letters of Saint Paul: Complete Set. 5 vols. Edited by John Mortensen. Lander, Wy.: The Aquinas Institute, 2012. (Latin-English edition, includes Greek text of the epistles.)

Super I Epistolam B. Pauli ad Corinthios lectura.

Super I Epistolam B. Pauli ad Thessalonicenses lectura.

Super I Epistolam B. Pauli ad Timotheum lectura.

Super Epistolam B. Pauli ad Colossenses lectura.

Super Epistolam B. Pauli ad Ephesios lectura.

Commentary on St. Paul's Epistle to the Ephesians. Translated by Matthew L. Lamb. Aquinas Scripture Commentaries 2. Albany: Magi Books, 1966.

Super Epistolam B. Pauli ad Galatas lectura.

Commentary on St. Paul's Epistle to the Galatians. Translated by Fabian R. Larcher. Aquinas Scripture Commentaries 1. Albany: Magi Books, 1966.

Super Epistolam B. Pauli ad Hebraeos lectura.

Commentary on the Epistle to the Hebrews. Translated by Chrysostom Baer. South Bend, Ind.: St. Augustine's Press, 2006.

Super Epistolam B. Pauli ad Philemonem lectura.

Super Epistolam B. Pauli ad Romanos lectura.

Super Epistolam B. Pauli ad Titum lectura.

Commentary on St. Paul's Epistles to Timothy, Titus, and Philemon. Translated by Chrysostom Baer. South Bend, Ind.: St. Augustine's Press, 2006.

Super Evangelium S. Matthaei lectura.
Commentary on the Gospel of Matthew. 2 vols. Translated by Jeremy Holmes and Beth Mortensen. Lander, Wy: The Aquinas Institute, 2013.
Postilla super Psalmos.

Commentaries on Aristotle

Commentaria in octo libros Physicorum Aristotelis. Leonine Commission 2. Rome: Ex Typographia Polyglotta S. C. de Propaganda Fide, 1884.
Commentary on Aristotle's Physics. Translated by Richard J. Blackwell, Richard J. Spath, and W. Edmund Thirlkel. Aristotelian Commentary Series. Notre Dame, Ind.: Dumb Ox Books, 1999.
Expositio Libri Peri hermeneias [*Expositio libri Peryermenias*]. Rev. ed. Edited by R.-A. Gauthier. Leonine Commission 1/1. Rome: Vrin, 1989.
Commentary on Aristotle's On Interpretation. Translated by Jean Oesterle. Notre Dame, Ind.: Dumb Ox Books, 2004.
Expositio libri Posteriorum. Rev. ed. Edited by R.-A. Gauthier. Leonine Commission 1/2. Rome: Vrin, 1989.
Commentary on Aristotle's Posterior Analytics. Translated by Richard Berquist. South Bend, Ind.: St. Augustine's Press, 2007.
Commentary on the Posterior Analytics of Aristotle. Translated by F. R. Larcher. Albany: Magi Books, 1970.
In duodecim libros Metaphysicorum Aristotelis exposition. 3rd ed. Edited by M.-R. Cathala and R. M. Spiazzi. 1950. Turin-Rome: Marietti, 1977.
Commentary on Aristotle's Metaphysics. Translated by John P. Rowan. Aristotelian Commentary Series. Notre Dame, Ind.: Dumb Ox Books, 1995.
In libros Aristotelis Meteorologicorum exposition. Leonine Commission 3. Rome: Ex Typographia Polyglotta S. C. de Propaganda Fide, 1886.
In libros Aristotelis De caelo et mundo expositio. Leonine Commission 3. Rome: Ex Typographia Polyglotta S. C. de Propaganda Fide, 1886.
Exposition on Aristotle's Treatise on the Heavens. 2 vols. Translated by Fabian R. Larcher and Pierre H. Conway. Columbus, Ohio: College of St. Mary of the Springs, 1964.
In librum primum Aristotelis De generatione et corruptione expositio. Leonine Commission 3. Rome: Ex Typographia Polyglotta S. C. de Propaganda Fide, 1886.
Sentencia libri De anima. Edited by R.-A. Gauthier. Leonine Commission 45/1. Rome: Vrin, 1984.
Commentary on Aristotle's De anima. Translated by Robert C. Pasnau. New Haven, Conn.: Yale University Press, 1999.
Sentencia libri De sensu et sensato cuius secundus tractatus est De memoria et reminiscencia. Edited by R.-A. Gauthier. Leonine Commission 45/2. Rome: Vrin, 1985.
Commentaries on Aristotle's On Sense and What Is Sensed *and* On Memory and Recollection. Translated with introductions and notes by Kevin White and

Edward Macierowski. Thomas Aquinas in Translation. Washington, D.C.: The Catholic University of America Press, 2005.
Sententia libri Ethicorum. 2 vols. Edited by R.-A. Gauthier. Leonine Commission 47. Rome: Ad Sanctae Sabinae, 1969.
Commentary on Aristotle's Nicomachean Ethics. Translated by C. I. Litzinger. Aristotelian Commentary Series. Notre Dame, Ind.: Dumb Ox Books, 1993.
Commentary on Aristotle's De Anima. Translated by Kenelm Foster and Silvester Humphries. Aristotelian Commentary Series. Notre Dame, Ind.: Dumb Ox Books, 1994.
Sententia libri Politicorum. Edited by H.-F. Dondaine and L-J. Bataillon. Leonine Commission 48. Rome: Ad Sanctae Sabinae, 1971.
Commentary on the Politics. Translated by Richard Regan. Indianapolis: Hackett, 2007.

Other Commentaries

Expositio libri Boetii De Hebdomadibus. Edited by L.-J. Bataillon and C. A. Grassi. Leonine Commission 50. Rome: Cerf, 1992.
An Exposition of the On the Hebdomads *of Boethius*. Latin-English. Translated by Janice Schultz and Edward Synan. Thomas Aquinas in Translation. Washington, D.C.: The Catholic University of America Press, 2001.
In librum Beati Dionysii De divinis nominibus exposition. Edited by C. Pera, with historical introduction and doctrinal synthesis by P. Caramello and C. Mazzantini. Turin-Rome: Marietti, 1950.
In Librum de causis expositio: Cura et studio Ceslai Pera. Edited by Ceslas Pera. Taurini: Marietti, 1955.
Sancti Thomae de Aquino super Librum de causis Expositio. Edited by Henri-Dominique Saffrey. Textus philosophici friburgenses, Seriem moderatur, 4–5. Fribourg: Societe Philosophique, 1954.
Super librum de causis expositi,. Edited by Henri-Dominique Saffrey. Textes philosophiques du Moyen Age. Paris: Vrin, 2002.
Commentary on the Book of Causes. Translated by Vincent A. Guagliardo, Charles R. Hess, and Richard C. Taylor. Thomas Aquinas in Translation. Washington, D.C.: The Catholic University of America Press, 1996.
Commento al Libro delle Cause. Edited by Cristina D'Ancona Costa. Milano: Rusconi, 1986.
Super Boetium De Trinitate. Edited by P.-M. J. Gils. Leonine Commission 50. Rome: Cerf, 1992.
The Division and Methods of the Sciences: Questions V and VI of His Commentary on the De Trinitate *of Boethius*. 4th ed. Translated by Armand Maurer. Mediaeval Sources in Translation 3. Toronto: Pontifical Institute of Mediaeval Studies, 1986.
Faith, Reason and Theology: Questions I–IV of His Commentary on the De Trinitate

of Boethius. Translated by Armand Maurer. Mediaeval Sources in Translation 32. Toronto: Pontifical Institute of Mediaeval Studies, 1987.

Disputed Questions

Quaestiones disputatae de malo. Edited by P.-M. Gils. Leonine Commission 23. Rome: Vrin, 1982.

The De malo of Thomas Aquinas. Latin-English. Translated by Richard Regan. Oxford: Oxford University Press, 2002.

On Evil. Translated by John A. and Jean T. Oesterle. Notre Dame, Ind.: University of Notre Dame Press, 1995.

On Evil. Translated by Richard Regan. Edited by Brian Davies. Oxford: Oxford University Press, 2003.

De unione verbi incarnati. Latin-English. Dallas Medieval Texts and Translations 21. Translation, introduction, and notes by Roger W. Nutt. Latin Text by Walter Senner, OP, Barbara Bartocci, and Klaus Obenauer. Louvain: Peeters Press, 2014.

Quaestiones disputatae de virtutibus.

Disputed Questions on Virtue. Translated by Ralph McInerny. South Bend, Ind.: St. Augustine's Press, 1998.

Disputed Questions on Virtue. Translated by Jeffrey Hause and Claudia Eisen. Indianapolis: Hackett, 2010. *On the Virtues (in General).* Translated by John Patrick Reid. Providence: Providence College Press, 1951. (Includes *On the Virtues in General, On Fraternal Correction, On Hope,* and *On the Cardinal Virtues.*)

On Charity. Translated by Lottie H. Kendzierski. Mediaeval Philosophical Texts in Translation 10. Milwaukee: Marquette University Press, 1960.

Quaestio disputata de spiritualibus creaturis. Edited by J. Cos. Leonine Commission 24/2. Rome: Cerf, 2000.

On Spiritual Creatures. Translated by Mary C. Fitzpatrick and John J. Wellmuth. Mediaeval Philosophical Texts in Translation 5. Milwaukee: Marquette University Press, 1949.

Quaestiones disputatae de potentia. In *S. Thomae Aquinatis, Quaestiones disputatae.* 2 vols. Edited by P. M. Pession. Turin-Rome: Marietti, 1965.

The Power of God. Abridged. Translated by Richard Regan. Oxford: Oxford University Press, 2012.

On the Power of God. Translated by Laurence Shapcote. Reprint: Eugene, Ore.: Wipf and Stock, 2004.

On Creation: Quaestiones Disputatae de Potentia Dei, Q. 3. Translated by Susan C. Selner-Wright. Thomas Aquinas in Translation. Washington, D.C.: The Catholic University of America Press, 2010.

Quaestiones disputatae de anima. Edited by B.-C. Bazan. Leonine Commission 24/1. Rome: Cerf, 1996.

Questions on the Soul. Translated by James H. Robb. Mediaeval Philosophical Texts in Translation 27. Milwaukee: Marquette University Press, 1984.

The Soul. Translated by J. P. Rowan. St. Louis: B. Herder, 1949.
Quaestiones disputatae de veritate. Edited by A. Dondaine. Leonine Commission 22. Rome: Editori di San Tommaso, 1970–76.
Truth. 3 vols. Translated by Robert W. Mulligan, James V. McGlynn, and Robert Schmidt. Library of Living Catholic Thought. Chicago: Regnery, 1952–54. Reprint: Indianapolis: Hackett, 1994.

Quodlibetal Questions

Quaestiones de quolibet. Edited by R.-A. Gauthier. Leonine Commission 25. Rome: Cerf, 1996.
"Faith, Metaphysics, and the Contemplation of Christ's Corporeal Presence in the Eucharist: Translation of St. Thomas Aquinas' Seventh *Quodlibetal Dispute*, Q. 4, A. 1 with an Introductory Essay." Translation and introduction by Roger W. Nutt. *Antiphon: A Journal of Liturgical Renewal* 15, no. 2 (2011): 151–71.
Quodlibetal Questions 1 and 2. Translated by Sandra Edwards. Mediaeval Sources in Translation 27. Toronto: Pontifical Institute of Mediaeval Studies, 1983.

Other Writings

Contra doctrinam retrahentium a religione homines a religionis ingressu. Edited by H.-F. Dondaine. Leonine Commission 41. Rome: Ad Sanctae Sabinae, 1969.
An Apology for the Religious Orders. Translated by John Procter. London: Sands, 1902. Reprint: Westminster, Md.: Newman, 1950.
Contra errores Graecorum ad Urbanum papam. Edited by H.-F. Dondaine. Leonine Commission 40. Rome: Ad Sanctae Sabinae, 1969.
Ending the Byzantine Greek Schism: Containing the 14th c. Apologia of Demetrios Kydones for Unity with Rome and St. Thomas Aquinas' "Contra Errores Graecorum." Translated by Peter Damian Fehlner. Edited by James Likoudis. 2nd ed. New Rochelle, N.Y.: Catholics United for the Faith, 1992.
Contra impugnantes Dei cultum et religionem. Edited by H.-F. Dondaine. Leonine Commission 41. Rome: Ad Sanctae Sabinae, 1969.
De aeternitate mundi [On the Eternity of the World]. Edited by H.-F. Dondaine. Leonine Commission 43. Rome: Editori di San Tommaso, 1976.
De articulis fidei. Edited by H.-F. Dondaine. Leonine Commission 42. Rome: Editori di San Tommaso, 1979.
The Aquinas Catechism: A Simple Explanation of the Catholic Faith by the Church's Greatest Theologian. Manchester, N.H.: Sophia Institute Press, 2000. (Includes *Collationes de decem praeceptis, Collationes super Pater Noster, Collationes super Ave Maria, De articulis fidei et Ecclesiae sacramentis,* and *Collationes super Credo in Deum.*)
De duabus praeceptis caritatis et decem legis praeceptis (or *Collationes de decem praeceptis*).
De ente et essentia. (Attributed to Thomas.) Edited by H.-F. Dondaine. Leonine Commission 43. Rome: Editori di San Tommaso, 1976.

Aquinas on Being and Essence: A Translation and Interpretation. Translation by Joseph Bobik. Notre Dame, Ind.: University of Notre Dame Press, 1965.

Concerning Being and Essence. Translated by G. G. Leckie. New York: Appleton-Century-Crofts, 1937.

De forma absolutionis paenitentiae sacramentalis ad Magistrum Ordinis. Edited by H.-F. Dondaine. Leonine Commission 40. Rome: Ad Sanctae Sabinae, 1969.

De mixtione elementorum ad magistrum Philippum de Castro Caeli. Edited by H.-F. Dondaine. Leonine Commission 43. Rome: Editori di San Tommaso, 1976.

De modo studendi. *How to Study: Being the Letter of St. Thomas Aquinas to Brother John.* Latin-English. Translated by Victor White. London: Blackfriars, 1953.

De principiis naturae ad fratrem Sylvestrum. Edited by H.-F. Dondaine. Leonine Commission 43. Rome: Editori di San Tommaso, 1976.

Aquinas on Matter and Form and the Elements: A Translation and Interpretation of the De Principiis Naturae *and the* De Mixtione Elementorum *of St. Thomas Aquinas.* Latin-English. Translated by Joseph Bobik. Notre Dame, Ind.: University of Notre Dame Press, 1998.

De perfectione spiritualis vitae. Edited by H.-F. Dondaine. Leonine Commission 41. Rome: Ad Sanctae Sabinae, 1969.

De rationibus fidei ad Cantorem Antiochenum. Edited by H.-F. Dondaine. Leonine Commission 40. Rome: Ad Sanctae Sabinae, 1969.

De substantiis separatis ad fratrem Raynaldum de Piperno. Edited by H.-F. Dondaine. Leonine Commission 40. Rome: Ad Sanctae Sabinae, 1969.

De unitate intellectus contra Averroistas. Edited by H.-F. Dondaine. Leonine Commission 43. Rome: Editori di San Tommaso, 1976.

Aquinas against the Averroists: On There Being Only One Intellect. Translated by Ralph M. McInerny. Purdue University Series in the History of Philosophy. West Lafayette, Ind.: Purdue University Press, 1993.

The Trinity and the Unicity of the Intellect. Translated by Rose W. Brennan. St. Louis: B. Herder, 1946.

The Aquinas Prayer Book: The Prayers and Hymns of Saint Thomas Aquinas. Translated by Robert Anderson and Johann Moser. Sophia Institute, 2000. (Includes *Officium de festo Corporis Christi* and many of the prayers composed by St. Thomas, such as *Adoro te devote* and *Pange lingua.*)

The Letter of Saint Thomas Aquinas De Occultis Operibus Naturae ad Quemdam Militem Ultramontanum. Translated by J. B. McAllister. Washington, D.C.: The Catholic University of America, 1939.

Expositio super primam et secundam Decretalem ad archidiaconum Tudertinum. Edited by H.-F. Dondaine. Leonine Commission 40. Rome: Ad Sanctae Sabinae, 1969.

In Symbolum Apostolorum.

Responsio ad magistrum Ioannem de Vercellis de 108 articulis and *Responsio ad magistrum Ioannem de Vercellis de 43 articulis.* Edited by H.-F. Dondaine. Leonine Commission 42. Rome: Editori di San Tommaso, 1979.

Responsio ad lectorem Venetum de 36 articulis. Edited by H.-F. Dondaine. Leonine Commission 43. Rome: Editori di San Tommaso, 1979.
Sermones. Edited by L. J. Bataillon. Leonine Commission 44/1. Paris: Cerf, 2014.
The Academic Sermons. Translated by Mark-Robin Hoogland, C.P. Fathers of the Church Mediaeval Continuation 11. Washington, D.C.: The Catholic University of America Press, 2010.

Primary Sources

Albert the Great. *Physica* [Commentary on the Physics]. Edited by Paul Hossfeld. Alberti Magni Opera Omnia 4, 1–2. 1987. Münster: Aschendorff Verlag, 1993.
Ambrose. *De fide ad Gratianum* [On Faith, to Gratian Augustus]. PL 16: 527–698C.
Anselm. *Proslogion*. PL 158: 223–248. Translated by M. J. Charlesworth, in *The Major Works*, edited by Brian Davies and G. R. Evans, 82–104 (Oxford; New York: Oxford University Press, 1998).
Anonymous. *Liber de causis*. Translated by Dennis J. Brand as *The Book of Causes*, Mediaeval Philosophical Texts in Translation 25 (Milwaukee, Wis.: Marquette University Press, 1984).
Anselm. *De conceptu virginali et originali peccato*. PL 158: 431B–462. Translated by Camilla McNab as "On the Virgin Conception and Original Sin," in *The Major Works*, ed. Brian Davies and G. R. Evans (Oxford; New York: Oxford University Press, 1998), 357–389.
———. *Monologion*. PL 158: 141C–224A. Translated by Simon Harrison, in *The Major Works*, ed. Brian Davies and G. R. Evans (Oxford; New York: Oxford University Press, 1998), 5–81.
Aristotle. All works: see the series Scriptorum classicorum bibliotheca Oxoniensis. London: Oxford University Press. For those omitted therein, *Aristotelis Opera, ex recensione Immanuelis Bekkeri, edidit Academia regia borussica; accedunt fragmenta scholia index Aristotelicus* (Berlin: De Gruyter, 1960–87). Translated as *The Basic Works of Aristotle*, edited by Richard McKeon (1941; New York: Random House, 2001).
———. *Analytica Priora et Posteriora*. Edited by Sir David Ross and Lorenzo Minio-Paluello. Scriptorum classicorum bibliotheca Oxoniensis. London: Oxford University Press, 1981.
———. *De anima*. Edited by Sir David Ross. Scriptorum classicorum bibliotheca Oxoniensis. London: Oxford University Press, 1956.
———. *De caelo et mundo*. Edited by D. J. Allan. Scriptorum classicorum bibliotheca Oxoniensis. London: Oxford University Press, 2005.
———. *Ethica Nicomachea*. Edited by Ingram Bywater. Scriptorum classicorum bibliotheca Oxoniensis. London: Oxford University Press, 1920.
———. *Metaphysica*. Edited by Werner Jaeger. Scriptorum classicorum bibliotheca Oxoniensis. London: Oxford University Press, 1957.
———. *Physica*. Edited by Sir David Ross. Scriptorum classicorum bibliotheca Oxoniensis. London: Oxford University Press, 1951.

Augustine. *Confessiones*. PL 32: 657–868. Translated by Vernon J. Bourke as *Confessions*, Fathers of the Church 21 (1953; Washington, D.C.: The Catholic University of America Press, 2008).

———. *Contra Faustum*. PL 42: 207–518. Translated by Roland J. Teske as *Answer to Faustus, a Manichean*, The Works of Saint Augustine I/20 (Hyde Park, N.Y.: New City Press, 2007).

———. *De civitate Dei*. PL 41: 13–804. Translated by Gerald G. Walsh, Demetrius B. Zema, and G. Monahan as *The City of God*, 3 vols., Fathers of the Church 12–14, 1950–54 (Washington, D.C.: The Catholic University of America Press, 2008).

———. *De doctrina christiana*. PL 34: 15–122. Translated by John J. Gavigan as "Christian Instruction," in *Christian Instruction; Admonition and Grace; The Christian Combat; Faith, Hope and Charity*, Fathers of the Church 2 (1950; Washington, D.C.: The Catholic University of America Press, 2002), 19–235.

———. *De duabus animabus*. PL 42: 93–112. Translated by Roland J. Teske as *The Two Souls*, The Works of Saint Augustine III/1–19 (Hyde Park, N.Y.: New City Press, 2006).

———. *De Genesi ad litteram*. PL 34: 245–486. Translated by Roland J. Teske as *On the Literal Interpretation of Genesis*, Fathers of the Church 84 (1990; Washington, D.C.: The Catholic University of America Press, 2001).

———. *De immortalitate animae*. PL 32:1021–34. Translated by Ludwig Schopp as "The Immortality of the Soul," in Augustine, *The Immortality of the Soul; The Magnitude of the Soul; On Music; The Advantage of Believing; On Faith in Things Unseen*, The Fathers of the Church 4 (Washington, D.C.: The Catholic University of America Press, 1947).

———. *De libero arbitrio*. PL 32: 1219–310. Translated by Robert P. Russell, O.S.A., as *On the Freedom of the Will*, Fathers of the Church 59 (1968; Washington, D.C.: The Catholic University of America Press, 2004).

———. *De natura boni*. PL 42: 551–72. Translated by Roland J. Teske as *The Nature of the Good*, The Works of Saint Augustine III/1–19 (Hyde Park, N.Y.: New City Press, 2006).

———. *De natura et gratia*. PL 44: 247–90. Translated by John A. Mourant as "On Nature and Grace," in *Four Anti-Pelagian Writings*, Fathers of the Church 86 (1992; Washington, D.C.: The Catholic University of America Press, 2002), 22–90.

———. *De sermone Domini in monte*. PL 34: 1229–307. Translated by Denis J. Kavanagh as "Commentary on the Lord's Sermon on the Mount," in *Commentary on the Lord's Sermon on the Mount with Seventeen Related Sermons*, Fathers of the Church 11 (1951; Washington, D.C.: The Catholic University of America Press, 2001), 19–199.

———. *De Trinitate*. PL 42: 819–1098. Translated by Stephen McKenna as *On the Trinity*, Fathers of the Church 45 (1963; Washington, D.C.: The Catholic University of America Press, 2002).

———. *De vera religione*. PL 34: 121–72. Translated by Edmund Hill, OP, Ray Kearney, Michael G. Campbell, and Bruce Harbert as *On True Religion*, The Works of Saint Augustine, vol. I/8 (Hyde Park, N.Y.: New City Press, 2005).

———. *Epistulae*. PL 33: 13–1094. Translated by Wilfrid Parsons, SND, as *Letters of Saint Augustine*, 5 vols., Fathers of the Church 12, 18, 20, 30, 32 (1951–56; Washington, D.C.: The Catholic University of America Press, 2008).

———. *In Ioannis Evangelium*. PL 35: 1379–976. Translated by John W. Rettig as *Tractates on the Gospel of John*, 5 vols., Fathers of the Church 78–79, 88, 90, 92 (1988–95; Washington, D.C.: The Catholic University of America Press, 2000–2014).

———. *Retractationes*, PL 32: 581–656. Translated by Mary Inez Bogan, RSM, as *The Retractations*, Fathers of the Church 60 (1968; Washington, D.C.: The Catholic University of America Press, 1999).

———. *Sermones*. PL 39; PL 40; PL 46; PL 47. Translated by Edmund Hill, OP, as *Sermons*, The Works of Saint Augustine III/1–11 (Hyde Park, N.Y.: New City Press, 1990–94, 1997).

———. *Soliloquia*. PL 32: 867–904. Translated by Ludwig Schopp as *Soliloquies*, Fathers of the Church 5 (1948; Washington, D.C.: The Catholic University of America Press, 2008).

Avicenna. *Livre des directives et remarques*. Translated with introduction and notes by A.-M. Goichon. Paris: Vrin, 1951. Translated by Shams Constantine Inati as *Remarks and Admonitions* (Toronto: Pontifical Institute of Mediaeval Studies, 1984).

———. *Metaphysica* [Metaphysics]. In *Liber de philosophia prima, I-IV*. Edited by Simone van Riet. Peeters-Brill, Louvain-Leiden 1977. Translated by Parviz Morewedge as *The Metaphysica of Avicenna [Ibn Sina]* (New York: Columbia University Press, 1973).

Averroes. *Averroes' "Destructio destructionum philosophiæ Algazelis" in the Latin Version of Calo Calonymos*. Edited by Beatrice H. Zedler. Milwaukee: Marquette University Press, 1961.

Boethius. *De consolatione philosophiae*. PL 63: 579–870A. Translated by P. G. Walsh as The Consolation of Philosophy (Oxford: Clarendon Press, 1999).

———. *De Hebdomadibus*. PL 64: 1311–1314.

———. *De Interpretatione* [Commentary on Aristotle's *De Interpretatione*]. PL 64: 293–640A. Translated by Andrew Smith, David L. Blank, and Norman Kretzmann as *On Aristotle On Interpretation*, Books 1–3; Books 4–6; Book 9, Ancient Commentators on Aristotle (London; New York, NY: Bloomsbury Academic, 2014).

———. *De Trinitate* [On the Trinity]. PL 64: 480–524. Translated by H. F. Stewart, E. K. Rand, and S. J. Tester as "The Trinity Is One God Not Three Gods," in *Theological Tractates; The Consolation of Philosophy*, Loeb Classical Library 74 (Cambridge, Mass.: Harvard University Press, 2014), 3–31.

Cassiodorus. *De artibus ac disciplinis liberalium litterarum*. PL 70: 1149–1220.

Cicero. *De finibus*. Translated by Harris Rackham as *On Ends*, Loeb Classical Library 40 (Cambridge, Mass.: Harvard University Press, 1914).

———. *De inventione*. Translated by H. M. Hubbell as "On Invention," in *On Invention; The Best Kind of Orator; Topics*, Loeb Classical Library 386 (Cambridge, Mass.: Harvard University Press, 1949).

———. *De re publica*. Translated by Clinton W. Keyes as "On the Republic," in *On the Republic; On the Laws*, Loeb Classical Library 213 (Cambridge, Mass.: Harvard University Press, 1928).

———. *De Tusculanis disputationibus*. Translated by J. E. King as *Tusculan Disputations*, Loeb Classical Library 141 (Cambridge, Mass.: Harvard University Press, 1927).

———. *Pro Milone*. Translated by N. H. Watts as "On Behalf of Titus Annius Milo," in *Pro Milone; In Pisonem; Pro Scauro; Pro Fonteio; Pro Rabirio Postumo; Pro Marcello; Pro Ligario; Pro Rege Deiotaro*, Loeb Classical Library 252 (Cambridge, Mass.: Harvard University Press, 1931).

Eadmer of Canterbury [attrib.]. *De similitudinibus Anselmi*. PL 159: 605A–708D.

Gregory the Great. *Dialoguorum*. PL 77: 149–430A. Translated by Odo John Zimmerman as *Dialogues*, Fathers of the Church 39 (1959; Washington, D.C.: The Catholic University of America Press, 2002).

———. *Magna moralia*. PL 75: 509–1162B; and 76: 9–782A. Translated by Brian Kerns, OCSO, as *Moral Reflections on the Book of Job*, 3 vols., Cistercian Studies 249, 257, 258 (Collegeville, Minn.: Liturgical Press/Cistercian Publications, 2014–16). (Volumes 4 through 6 are still forthcoming.)

———. *Liber regulae pastoralis*. PL 77: 13–128A. Translated by George E. Demacopoulos as *The Book of Pastoral Rule*, Popular Patristics 34 (Crestwood, N.Y.: St. Vladimir's Seminary Press, 2007).

———. *Homilae xl in evangelia*. PL 76: 1075–312C. Translated by David Hurst, OSB, as *Forty Gospel Homilies*, Cistercian Studies 123 (Kalamazoo, Mich.: Cistercian Publications, 1990).

———. *Homilae in Ezechielem* Prophetam Libri Duo. PL 76: 785–1072C. Translated by Theodosia Gray as *Homilies on the Book of the Prophet Ezekiel* (Etna, Calif.: Center for Traditionalist Orthodox Studies, 1990).

Hugh of Saint-Victor. *Didascalicon*. PL 176: 739–838D. Translated by Jerome Taylor as *The Didascalicon of Hugh of Saint Victor: A Guide to the Arts* (1961; New York: Columbia University Press, 1991).

Jerome. *Adversus Jovinianum* [Against Jovinianus]. PL 23: 205–384.

———. *Commentariorum in Ezechielem*. PL 15: 490D. Translated by Thomas P. Scheck as *Commentary on Ezekiel*, Ancient Christian Writers 71 (New York: Newman Press, 2017).

Maimonides. *Guide of the Perplexed*. Translated by Shlomo Pines. Chicago: University of Chicago Press, 1963.

Plato. *Timaeus*. Platonis Opera recognovit Ioannes Burnet. Scriptorum Classicorum Bibliotheca Oxoniensis. 1905–13. London: Oxford University Press, 1953. Translated by D. J. Zeyl, in *Plato: Complete Works*, edited by John M. Cooper (1997; Indianapolis: Hackett, 2009).

Proclus. *Elementatio theologica*. Translated by E. R. Dodds as *The Elements of Theology*. Revised with translation, introduction, and commentary by E. R. Dodds. 2nd ed. Oxford: Clarendon Press, 1963.

Pseudo-Dionysius. *De divinis nominibus*. PG 3: 585–996. Translated by John D. Jones as "The Divine Names," in *The Divine Names; The Mystical Theology*, Mediaeval Philosophical Texts in Translation 21 (Milwaukee, Wis.: Marquette University Press, 1980).

———. *De mystica theologia*. PG 3: 997–1064. Translated by John D. Jones as "The Mystical Theology," in *The Divine Names; The Mystical Theology*, Mediaeval Philosophical Texts in Translation 21 (Milwaukee, Wis.: Marquette University Press, 1980).

———. *De Coelesti Hierarchia*. PG 3: 115–369. Translated by Colm Luibheid as "The Celestial Hierarchy," in *Pseudo-Dionysius: The Complete Works*, ed. Paul Rorem, Classics of Western Spirituality (New York: Paulist Press, 1987).

Seneca. *De ira*. Translated by John W. Basore as "On Anger," in *Moral Essays, Volume I: De Providentia; De Constantia; De Ira; De Clementia*, Loeb Classical Library 214 (Cambridge, Mass.: Harvard University Press, 1928).

———. *Epistulae morales ad Lucilium* [Letters on Morals to Lucilius]. Translated by Richard M. Gummere as *Epistles 1–65*, Loeb Classical Library 75 (Cambridge, Mass.: Harvard University Press, 1917); *Epistles 66–92*, Loeb Classical Library 76 (Cambridge, Mass.: Harvard University Press, 1920); *Epistles 93–124*, Loeb Classical Library 77 (Cambridge, Mass.: Harvard University Press, 1925).

Secondary Sources

Anawati, Georges C. "Saint Thomas d'Aquin et la Métaphysique d'Avicenne." In *St. Thomas Aquinas, 1274–1974. Commemorative Studies*, edited by A. Maurer, 449–65. Toronto: Pontifical Institute of Mediaeval Studies, 1974.

Anderson, James F. *St. Augustine and Being: A Metaphysical Essay*. The Hague: M. Nijhoff, 1965.

Angelou, Athanasios. *Nicholas of Methone: Refutation of Proclus' Elements of Theology: A Critical Edition with an Introduction on Nicholas' Life and Works*. Corpus philosophorum Medii Aevi., Philosophi Byzantini 1. Leiden: Brill, 1984.

———. *Liber de Philosophia prima sive Scientia divina I–IV*. Edited by Simone van Riet; introduction by Gérard Verbeke. Leuven: Peeters, 1977.

Backes, Ignaz. *Die Christologie des hl. Thomas von Aquin und die griechischen Kirchenväter*. Forschungen zur christlichen Literatur und Dogmengeschichte 17. Paderborn, Germany: Schöningh, 1931.

Baguette, Charles. "Une période stoïcienne dans l'évolution de la pensée de saint

Augustin." *Revue des Études Augustiniennes et Patristiques* 16, no. 1–2 (1970): 44–77.
Bassler, Wolfgang. "Die Kritik des Thomas von Aquin am ontologischen Gottesbeweis." *Franziskanische Studien* 55 (1973): 97–190.
Bardenhewer, Otto. *Die pseudo-aristotelische Schrift über das reine Gute, bekannt unter den Namen* Liber de causis. Fribourg i. Br.: Herdersche Verlagshandlung, 1882. Later edition, Frankfurt: Minerva, 1961.
Boyer, Charles. *L'idée de vérité dans la philosophie de saint Augustin*. Paris: Gabriel Beauchesne, 1920.
Brunner, Ferdinand. *Platonisme et aristotélisme: La critique d'Ibn Gabirol par Saint Thomas d'Aquin*. Louvain: Publications universitaires de Louvain, 1965.
Carroy, Bertrand. "Héritage et différences: Thomas d'Aquin et Albert le Grand, commentateurs du *De generatione et corruptione*." In *Lire Aristote au Moyen Âge et à la Renaissance. Réception du traité sur la Génération et la corruption*, edited by Joëlle Dacos and Violaine Giacomotto-Chorra, 102–17. Colloques, congrès et conférences 10. Paris: H. Champion, 2011.
Casazza, Fabrizio. "Il *Commento di San Tommaso d'Aquino alla* Politica *di Aristotele*." *Archivio teologico torinese* 10, no. 2 (2004): 325–42; 11, no. 1 (2005): 97–110; 12, no. 1 (2006): 63–80.
Chadwick, Henry. *Boethius: The Consolations of Music, Logic, Theology and Philosophy*. Oxford: Clarendon Press, 1981.
Chaix-Ruy, Jules. *Saint Augustin. Temps et Histoire*. Paris: Études augustiniennes, 1956.
———."La Cité de Dieu et la structure du Temps chez saint Augustin." In *Augustinus Magister Congrès international augustinien, Paris, 21–24 septembre, 1954*, vol. 2, 923–931. Paris: Etudes augustiniennes, 1954.
Cheneval, Francis and Ruedi Imbach, eds. *Thomas von Aquin: Prologe zu den Aristoteles-Kommentaren*. KlostermannRoteReihe 69. Frankfurt am Main: Klostermann, 1993.
Chenu, Marie-Dominique. *Introduction à l'étude de saint Thomas d'Aquin*. 2nd ed. Paris: Vrin 1954. Translated by A.-M. Landry and D. Hughes as *Towards Understanding St. Thomas* (Chicago: H. Regnery Co, 1964).
Colish, Marcia L. *The Stoic Tradition from Antiquity to the Early Middle Ages, 2: Stoicism in Christian Latin Thought through the Sixth Century*. Studies in the History of Christian Thought 35. Leiden: Brill, 1990.
Courcelle, Pierre. *Les lettres grecques en occident de Macrobe à Cassiodore*. Bibliothèque des écoles françaises d'Athènes et de Rome 159, part 1. Paris: E. de Boccard, 1948.
D'Ancona Costa, Cristina. *Recherches sur le Liber de Causis*. Etudes de philosophie médiévale 72. Paris: J. Vrin, 1995.
———. "Saint Thomas, lecteur du Liber de causis." *Revue thomiste* 92, no. 4 (1992): 785–817.

Dauphinais, Michael, Barry David, and Matthew Levering, eds. *Aquinas the Augustinian*. Washington, D.C.: The Catholic University of America Press, 2007.
Decker, Bruno. *Die Entwicklung der Lehre von der prophetischen Offenbarung von Wilhelm von Auxerre bis zu Thomas von Aquin*. Breslauer Studien zur historischen Theologie 7. Breslau: Müller & Seiffert, 1940.
de Couesnongle, Vincent, OP. "La causalité du maximum." *Revue des sciences philosophiques et théologiques* 38 (1954): 433–44.
de Vaux, Roland. "La première entrée d'Averroès chez les latins." *Revue des sciences philosophiques et théologiques* 22 (1933): 193–243.
des Places, Édouard. *Syngeneia. La parenté de l'homme avec Dieu d'Homère à la patristique*. Etudes et commentaires 51. Paris: C. Klincksieck, 1964.
Dillon, John M. *The Middle Platonists*. London: Duckworth, 1977.
Doig, James. *Aquinas on Metaphysics: A Historico-doctrinal Study of the Commentary on the Metaphysics*. The Hague: Nijhoff, 1972.
———. *Aquinas's Philosophical Commentary on the Ethics*. New Synthese Historical Library 50. Dordrecht: Kluwer Academic Publishers, 2001.
Dondaine, Antoine, and Louis-Jacque Bataillon. "Le commentaire de saint Thomas sur les *Météores*." *Archivum fratrum praedicatorum* 36 (1966): 81–152.
Dodds, E. R. "Numenius and Ammonius." In *Les sources de Plotin*, 3–32. Entretiens sur l'Antiquité classique V. Geneva: Fondation Hardt, 1960.
———. *The Greeks and the Irrational*. Sather Classical Lectures 25. Berkeley: University of California Press, 1951.
Elders, Leo. *Aristotle's Cosmology. A Commentary on the De Caelo*. Wijsgerige teksten en studies 13. Assen: Van Gorcum, 1966.
———. *Autour de saint Thomas*. Vol. 1, *Les commentaires sur les oeuvres d'Aristote; La métaphysique de l'être*. Paris: Fac-Editions, 1987.
———. *Faith and Science: An Introduction to St. Thomas'* Expositio in Boethii De Trinitate. Studia Universitatis S. Thomae in Urbe 3. Rome: Herder, 1974.
———. "Les rapports entre la doctrine de la prophétie de saint Thomas et le Guide des égarés de Maïmonide." *Divus Thomas* 78 (1975): 449–56.
———. "Le commentaire sur le quatrième livre de la *Métaphysique*." In *San Tommaso d'Aquino nel suo settimo centenario. Atti del Congresso Internazionale Roma-Napoli, 17–24 aprile 1974*, vol. 1, 207–18. Naples: Edizioni domenicane italiane, 1975–76.
———. "Structure et fonction de l'argument *Sed contra* dans la *Somme théologique*." *Divus Thomas* 80 (1977): 245–60.
———. "Le commentaire de saint Thomas d'Aquin sur le De caelo d'Aristote." In *Proceedings of the World Congress on Aristotle (Thessaloniki, August 7–14, 1978)*, 173–87. Athens: Ministry of Culture and Science, 1981.
———. "St. Thomas Aquinas's Commentary on the Metaphysics of Aristotle." *Divus Thomas* 86 (1983): 307–26.
———. "La doctrine de la conscience de saint Thomas d'Aquin." *Revue thomiste* 83 (1983): 533–57.

———. "St. Thomas Aquinas's Commentary on the Nicomachean Ethics." In *The Ethics of St. Thomas Aquinas*, edited by Leo Elders and Klaus Hedwig, 9–49. Vatican City: Libreria Editrice Vaticana, 1984.

———. "Les citations de saint Augustin dans la *Somme théologique* de saint Thomas d'Aquin." *Doctor Communis* 40 (1987): 115–67.

———. "St. Thomas Aquinas' Doctrine of Conscience." In *Lex et libertas. Freedom and Law According to St. Thomas Aquinas. Proceedings of the Fourth Symposium on St. Thomas Aquinas' Philosophy*, 125–134. Vatican City: Libreria Editrice Vaticana, 1987.

———. "Saint Thomas d'Aquin et Aristote." *Revue thomiste* 88, no. 3 (1988): 357–76.

———. "Saint Thomas d'Aquin et la métaphysique du Liber de Causis." *Revue thomiste* 89 (1989): 427–42.

———. *The Philosophical Theology of St. Thomas Aquinas*. Studien und Texte zur Geistesgeschichte des Mittelalters 26. Leiden: Brill, 1990.

———. "Averroès et saint Thomas d'Aquin." *Doctor communis* 45 (1992): 46–56.

———. "The Greek Christian Authors and Aristotle." In *Aristotle in Late Antiquity*, edited by Lawrence P. Schrenk, 111–42. Washington, D.C.: The Catholic University of America Press, 1994.

———. "L'acédie, un vice capital." *Nova et Vetera* 69 (1994): 175–84.

———. *La théologie philosophique de saint Thomas d'Aquin*. Paris: Téqui, 1995.

———. "Thomas Aquinas and the Fathers of the Church." In *The Reception of the Church Fathers in the West: From the Carolingians to the Maurists*, edited by Irena Backus, 338–66. Leiden: E.J. Brill, 1997.

———. "The First Principles of Being in the Philosophy of St. Thomas Aquinas." *Doctor Angelicus* 3 (2003): 59–95.

———. "The Aristotelian Commentaries of St. Thomas Aquinas." *The Review of Metaphysics* 63, no. 1 (2009): 29–53.

———. *Sur les traces de saint Thomas d'Aquin théologien*. Paris: Presses universitaires de l'IPC, 2009.

———. "St. Thomas Aquinas's Commentary on Aristotle's *Physics*." *The Review of Metaphysics* 66, no. 4 (2013): 713–48.

———, ed. *La doctrine de la revelation divine de saint Thomas d'Aquin*. Vatican City: Libreria Editrice Vaticana, 1990.

Endress, Gerhard. *Proclus Arabus. Zwanzig Abschnitte aus der Institutio Theologica in arabischer Übersetzung*. Beiruter Texte und Studien 10. Wiesbaden: im Kommission bei F. Steiner, 1973.

Feldman, Seymour. "A Scholastic Misinterpretation of Maimonides' Doctrine of Divine Attributes." In *Studies in Maimonides and St. Thomas Aquinas*, edited by Jacob I. Dienstag, 58–74. New York: KTAV Publishing House, 1975.

Festugière, A.-J. *La révélation d'Hermès Trismégiste*. Vol. 1, *L'Astrologie et les sciences occultes*. Paris: J. Gabalda, 1950.

García Marqués, Alfonso. "Averroës, una fuente tomista de la noción metafísica de Dios." *Sapientia* 37 (1982): 87–106.

Gardet, Louis. *La pensée religieuse d'Avicenne*. Etudes de philosophie médiévale 41. Paris: J. Vrin, 1951.

———. *Études de philosophie et de mystique comparée*. Bibliothèque d'histoire de la philosophie. Paris: J. Vrin, 1972.

———. "Saint Thomas et ses prédécesseurs arabes." *St. Thomas Aquinas, 1274–1974; Commemorative Studies*, edited by A. Maurer, 419–48. Toronto: Pontifical Institute of Mediaeval Studies, 1974.

Gardet, Louis, and Georges C. Anawati. *Introduction à la théologie musulmane: Essai de théologie comparée*. Etudes de philosophie médiévale 37. Paris: J. Vrin, 1948.

Gauthier, Léon. *Ibn Rochd (Averroès)*. Les Grands philosophes. Paris: Presses universitaires de France, 1948.

Geenen, J. G. "Le fonti patristiche come 'autorità' nella teologia di S. Tommaso." *Sacra doctrina* 20 (1975): 7–67.

Gigon, Olof. "Cicero und Aristoteles." *Hermes* 87, no. 2 (1959): 143–62.

Gilson, Étienne. "Pourquoi saint Thomas a-t-il critiqué Augustin?" *Archives d'Histoire doctrinale et littéraire du Moyen-Age* 1 (1926–27): 5–127.

———. *La philosophie de Saint Bonaventure*. Etudes de philosophie médiévale 4. Paris: J. Vrin, 1953. Translated by Illtyd Trethowan and Francis Joseph Sheed as *The Philosophy of St. Bonaventure* (Patterson, N.J.: St. Antony Guild Press, 1965).

———. "Maïmonide et la philosophie de l'Exode." *Mediæval Studies* 13, no. 1 (1951): 223–25.

———. *La philosophie au Moyen âge: Des origines patristique à la fin du XIV siècle*. 2nd rev. ed. Bibliothéque historique. Paris: Payot, 1952.

———. *The Philosopher and Theology*. New York: Random House, 1962.

Grabmann, Martin. *Die Werke des hl. Thomas von Aquin*, 3rd ed. Beiträge zur Geschichte der Philosophie und Theologie des Mittelalters 22:1–2. Münster: Aschendorff, 1949.

———. *Die Geschichte der scholastischen methode*. 2 vols. Graz: Akademische Druck und Verlagsanstalt, 1957.

Gutas, Dimitri. *Avicenna and the Aristotelian Tradition: Introduction to Reading Avicenna's Philosophical Works*. Islamic Philosophy and Theology 4. Leiden: E.J. Brill, 1988.

Guttmann, Jakob. *Das Verhältnis des Thomas von Aquino zum Judentum und zur jüdischen Literatur*. Göttingen: Vandenhoeck & Ruprecht, 1891.

Hadot, Pierre. "La métaphysique de Porphyre." In *Porphyre*, edited by Heinrich Dörrie, 125–63. Entretiens sur l'Antiquité classique 12. Geneva: Vandœuvres, 1965.

———. "La distinction de l'être et de l'étant dans le *De Hebdomadibus* de Boèce." In *Die Metaphysik im Mittelalter: ihr Ursprung und ihre Bedeutung*, edited by Paul Wilpert, 147–53. Miscellanea mediaevalia 2. Berlin: De Gruyter, 1963.

Hankey, Wayne J. "Aquinas, Plato and Neoplatonism." In *The Oxford Handbook to*

Aquinas, edited by Brian Davies and Eleonore Stump, 55–64. Oxford: Oxford University Press, 2011.

Hasse, Dag N. "Latin Averroes Translations of the First Half of the Thirteenth Century." In *Universality of Reason, Plurality of Philosophies in the Middle Ages*, vol. 1, edited by Alessandro Musco, 149–77. Palermo: Officina di Studi Medievali, 2012.

Hasselhoff, Görge K. *Dicit Rabbi Moyses, Studien zum Bild von Moses Maimonides im lateinischen Westen vom 13. bis zum 15. Jahrhundert*. Königshausen & Neuman, 2004.

Hayen, André. *Saint Thomas d'Aquin et la vie de l' Église*. Essais philosophiques 6. Louvain: Publications universitaires, 1952.

Henle, R. J. *Saint Thomas and Platonism: A Study of Plato's and Platonic Texts in the Writings of Saint Thomas*. The Hague: M. Nijhoff, 1956.

Hissette, Roland. *Enquête sur les 219 articles condamnés à Paris, le 7 mars 1277*. Louvain: Publications universitaires, 1977.

Houser, R. E. "Avicenna, Aliqui and Thomas Aquinas's Doctrine of Creation." *Recherches de Théologie et Philosophie Médiévales* 80, no. 1 (2013): 17–55.

Imbach, Ruedi. "Ut ait Rabbi Moyses. Maimonidische Philosopheme bei Thomas von Aquin und Meister Eckhart." *Collectanea Franciscana* 60 (1990): 99–115.

Isaac, Jean. "Saint Thomas, interprète des œuvres d'Aristote." In *Scholastica ratione historico-critica instauranda*, 353–63. Bibliotheca Pontificii Athenaei Antoniani 7. Rome: Pontificium Athenaeum Antonianum, 1951.

———. *Le Peri Hermeneias en Occident de Boèce à saint Thomas*. Bibliothèque thomiste 29. Paris: J. Vrin, 1953.

Jaffa, Harry V. *Thomism and Aristotelianism: A Study of the Commentary by St. Thomas Aquinas on the Nicomachean Ethics*. Chicago: University of Chicago Press, 1952.

Jenkins, John, CSC. "Expositions of the Text: Aquinas's Aristotelian Commentaries." *Medieval Philosophy and Theology* 5, no. 1 (1996): 39–62.

Jolif, Jean-Yves. "Le sujet pratique selon saint Thomas d'Aquin." *Saint Thomas d'Aquin aujourd'hui*, edited by Association des Professeurs de Philosophie des Facultés catholique de France, 13–44. Recherches de philosophie 6. Paris: Desclée de Brouwer, 1963.

Jordan, Mark D. "Thomas Aquinas's Disclaimers in the Aristotelian Commentaries." In *Philosophy and the God of Abraham: Essays in Memory of James A. Weisheipl, OP*, edited by R. James Long, 99–112. Papers in Mediaeval Studies 12. Toronto: Pontifical Institute of Mediaeval Studies, 1991.

Judycka, Joanna. "L'attribution de la *Translatio nova du De Generatione et corruptione* à Guillaume de Moerbeke." In *Guillaume de Moerbeke: Recueil d'études à l'occasion du 700e anniversaire de sa mort*, edited by Josef Brams and Willy Vanhamel, 247–52. Ancient and Medieval Philosophy (Series 1) 7. Leuven: Leuven University Press, 1989.

Kaczor, Christopher. "Thomas Aquinas's Commentary on the *Ethics*: Merely an

Interpretation of Aristotle?" *American Catholic Philosophical Quarterly* 78, no. 3 (2004): 353–76.

Kogan, Barry Sherman. "Averroes and the Theory of Emanation." *Mediæval Studies* 43, no. 1 (1981): 384–404.

———. *Averroes and the Metaphysics of Causality*. Albany: State University of New York Press, 1985.

Kohlmeier, Johann. "Der Seinsbegriff Ibn Gabirols." *Freiburger Zeitschrift für Philosophie Und Theologie* 13/14 (1966–67): 161–97.

Lafranque, Marie. *Poseidonios d'Apamée*. Publications de la Faculté des lettres et sciences humaines de Paris-Sorbonne 13. Paris: Presses universitaires de France, 1964.

Matthen, Mohan, ed. *Aristotle Today: Essays on Aristotle's Ideal of Science*. Edmonton: Academic Printing & Publishing, 1987.

McInerny, Ralph. *Boethius and Aquinas*. Washington, D.C.: The Catholic University of America Press, 1990.

———. *Aquinas on Human Action: A Theory of Practice*. Washington, D.C.: The Catholic University of America Press, 1992.

Merx, Adalbert. *Die Prophetie des Joel und Ihre Ausleger*. Halle, Germany: Buchhandlung des Waisenhauses, 1879.

Munk, S. "Ibn Gabirol, ses écrits et sa philosophie." In *Mélanges de philosophie juive et arabe* (Paris: J. Vrin, 1955), 1–306.

Neumann, Siegfried. *Gegenstand und Methode der theoretischen Wissenschaften nach Thomas von Aquin, auf Grund der Expositio super librum Boethii De Trinitate*. Beiträge zur Geschichte der Philosophie und Theologie des Mittelalters 41. Münster: Aschendorff, 1965.

O'Shaughnessy, Thomas. "St. Thomas and Avicenna on the Nature of the One." *Gregorianum* 41, no. 4 (1960): 665–79.

Patfoort, Albert. "L'unité de la 'Ia Pars' et le mouvement interne de la Somme théologique de S. Thomas d'Aquin." *Revue des sciences philosophiques et théologiques* 47, no. 4 (1963): 513–44.

Pattin, Adriaan. "Over de schrijver en de vertaler van het *Liber de causis*," *Tijdschrift voor Filosofie* 23, no. 2 (1961): 323–33; no. 3 (1961): 503–36.

———. "Le Liber de Causis. Édition établi à l'aide de 90 manuscrits avec introduction et notes." *Tijdschrift voor Filosofie* 28, no. 1 (1966): 90–203.

Pierce, C. A. *Conscience in the New Testament*. Studies in Biblical Theology 15. London: SCM Press, 1955.

Prantl, Karl. *Geschichte der Logik im Abendlande*. Leipzig: Verlag von S. Hirzel, 1870.

Pohlenz, Max. *Die Stoa. Geschichte einer geistigen Bewegung*. Göttingen: Vandenhoeck & Ruprecht, 1948.

Portalupi, Enzo. "Gregorio Magno nelle 'Quaestiones disputatae de veritate' di Tommaso d'Aquino." *Rivista di filosofia neo-scolastica* 77 (1985): 556–98.

———. *Studi sulla presenza di Gregorio Magno in Tommaso d'Aquino*. Dokimion:

Freiburger Zeitschrift für Philosophie und Theologie 10. Freiburg, Switzerland: Universitätsverlag, 1991.

Puech, Henri-Charles. "La ténèbre mystique chez le Pseudo-Denys l'Aréopagite et dans la tradition patristique." *Études carmélitaines* 23, no. 2 (1938): 33–53.

Rand, Edward K. *Cicero in the Courtroom of St. Thomas Aquinas*. The Aquinas lecture, 1945. Milwaukee: Marquette University Press, 1946.

Reale, Giovanni and Samuel Scolnicov, eds. *New Images of Plato: Dialogues on the Idea of the Good*. Sankt Augustin, Germany: Academia Verlag, 2002.

Rich, Audrey N. M. "The Platonic Ideas as Thoughts of God." *Mnemosyne* 7 (4th series), no. 4 (1954): 123–33.

Rist, John. *Stoic Philosophy*. London: Cambridge University Press: 1969.

———. "Augustine, Aristotelianism and Aquinas." In *Aquinas the Augustinian*, edited by M. Dauphinais, Barry David, and M. Levering, 77–99. Washington, D.C.: The Catholic University of America Press, 2007.

Robin, Léon. *La pensée grecque et les origines de l'esprit scientifique*. Évolution de l'humanité, synthèse collective 1. Paris: A. Michel, 1948. Translated by Marryat Ross Dobie as *Greek Thought and the Origin of the Scientific Spirit* (New York: Russell & Russell, 1967).

Roland-Gosselin, M. D. *Le De ente et essentia de S. Thomas d'Aquin: texte établi d'après les manuscrits parisiens*. Bibliothèque thomiste 8. Paris: Librairie philosophique J. Vrin, 1948.

———. "Sur les relations de l'âme et du corps d'après Avicenne." In *Mélanges Mandonnet*, vol. 2, 47–54. Bibliothèque thomiste 14. Paris: Librairie philosophique J. Vrin, 1930.

Ross, W. David. *Plato's Theory of Ideas*. Oxford: Clarendon Press, 1951.

Saffrey, Henri-Dominique. "Allusions antichrétiennes chez Proclus: le diadoque platonicien." *Revue des Sciences Philosophiques et Théologiques* 59, no. 4 (1975): 553–63.

Schurr, Viktor. *Die Trinitäts Lehre des Boethius im Lichte der skytischen Kontroversen*. Forschungen zur christlichen Literatur- und Dogmengeschichte, 18. Paderborn, Germany: F. Schöningh, 1935.

Souchard, Bertrand. "Le commentaire de Thomas d'Aquin du *De generatione et corruptione* d'Aristote: de la critique aristotélicienne des matérialistes à la critique thomasienne des spiritualistes." In *Lire Aristote au Moyen Âge et à la Renaissance. Réception du traité sur la Génération et la corruption*, edited by Joëlle Dacos and Violaine Giacomotto-Chorra, 55–83. Colloques, congrès et conférences 10. Paris: H. Champion, 2011.

Spanneut, Michel. *Permanence du Stoïcisme. De Zénon à Malraux*. Gembloux, Belgium: Duculot, 1973.

———. "Influences stoïciennes sur la pensée morale de saint Thomas d'Aquin." In *Ethics of St. Thomas Aquinas*, edited by Leo Elders and Klaus Hedwig, 50–79. Studi tomistici 25. Vatican City: Libreria Editrice Vaticana, 1984.

Stewart, Hugh Fraser. *Boethius: An Essay*. London: W. Blackwood and Sons, 1891.
Stiglmayr, Josef. "Der Neuplatoniker Proklos als Vorlage des sog. Dionysius Areopagita in der Lehre vom Übel." *Historisches Jahrbuch* 16 (1895): 253–73; 717–48.
Taylor, Richard C. "The Liber de causis: A Preliminary List of Extant MSS." *Bulletin de philosophie médiévale* 25 (1983): 63–84.
———. "The *Kalam Fi Mahd Al-Khair (Liber de causis)* in the Islamic Philosophical Milieu." In *Pseudo-Aristotle in the Middle Ages: The Theology and Other Texts*, edited by Jill Kraye, W. F. Ryan, and Charles B. Schmitt, 37–46. Warburg Institute Surveys and Texts. London: Warburg Institute, University of London, 1986.
Theiler, Willy. *Die Vorbereitung des Neuplatonismus*. Berlin: Weidmann, 1934.
Théry, Gabriel. *Entretiens sur la philosophie musulmane et la culture française*. Oran: n.p., 1945.
Thijssen, Johannes M. M. H. "The Commentary Tradition on Aristotle's *De Generatione et corruptione*: An Introductory Survey." In *The Commentary Tradition on Aristotle's De Generatione et corruptione*, edited by Johannes M. M. H. Thijssen and Henricus A. G. Braakhuis, 9–20. Turnhout: Brepolis, 1999.
Torrell, Jean-Pierre, OP. "Le traité de la prophétie de s.Thomas d'Aquin et la théologie de la révélation." In *La doctrine de la revelation divine de saint Thomas d'Aquin*, edited by Leo Elders, 171–95. Vatican City: Libreria Editrice Vaticana, 1990.
———. *Initiation à saint Thomas d'Aquin*. 3rd ed. 1993; Paris: Éditions du Cerf, 2015. Translated by Robert Royal as *St. Thomas Aquinas: The Person and His Work*, 2nd ed. Washington, D.C.: The Catholic University of America Press, 2005.
Ushida, Noriko. *Étude comparative de la psychologie d'Aristote, d'Avicenne et de St. Thomas d'Aquin*. Studies in the Humanities and Social Relations. Tokyo: Keio Institute of Cultural and Linguistic Studies, 1968.
Vajda, Georges. *Introduction à la pensée juive du moyen âge*. Paris: J. Vrin, 1947.
Van Camp, Jean, and Paul Canart. *Le sens du mot theios chez Platon*. Recueil de travaux d'histoire et de philologie. Louvain: Bibliothèque de l'université, 1956.
Van Steenberghen, Fernand. *Aristotle in the West*. Louvain: Nauwelaerts, 1970.
Vansteenkiste, Clemens. "Procli elementatio theologica translata a Guilelmo de Moerbeke (Textus ineditus)." *Tijdschrift voor Philosophie* 13 (1951): 263–302, and 491–531.
———. "Avicenna-citaten bij S. Thomas." *Tijdschrift voor Philosophie* 15 (1953): 437–507.
———. "Il Liber de Causis negli scritti di San Tommaso." *Angelicum* 35 (1958): 325–74.
———. "Cicerone nell'opera di S. Tommaso." *Angelicum* 36 (1959): 343–382.
Verbeke, Gérard. *The Presence of Stoicism in Medieval Thought*. Washington, D.C.: The Catholic University of America Press, 1983.

Vijgen, Jorgen. "Aquinas' Use of Aristotle in the Sacramental Theology of the *Summa theologiae* III, qq. 60–90." *Divinitas* 57, no. 2 (2014): 187–241.
von Ivanka, Endre. "Aristotelische und thomistische Seelenlehre." In *Aristote et saint Thomas d'Aquin; journées d'études internationales,* edited by Paul Moraux, 221–28. Louvain: Publications universitaires de Louvain, 1957.
Waldmann, Michael. "Synteresis oder Syneidesis? Ein Beitrag zur Lehre vom Gewissen." *Theologische Quartalschrift* 119 (1938): 33–37.
Wallis, Richard T. *Neoplatonism.* London: Scribner's, 1972.
Weisheipl, James A. "The Commentary of Saint Thomas Aquinas on the *De caelo* of Aristotle." *Sapientia* 29 (1974): 11–34.
———. "Motion in a Void: Aquinas and Averroes." In *St. Thomas Aquinas, 1274–1974. Commemorative Studies,* edited by A. Maurer, 467–88. Toronto: Pontifical Institute of Mediaeval Studies, 1974.
———. "Albertus Magnus and Universal Hylomorphism: Avicebron." *Southwestern Journal of Philosophy* 10 (1979): 21–47. Reprinted in *Albert the Great Commemorative Essays,* edited by Francis J. Kovach and Robert W. Shahan, 239–60. Norman, Okla.: University of Oklahoma Press, 1980.
White, Kevin. "Three Previously Unpublished Chapters from St. Thomas Aquinas's Commentary on Aristotle's *Meteora,*" *Medieval Studies* 54 (1992): 49–93.
Wippel, John F. "The Latin Avicenna as a Source for Thomas Aquinas's Metaphysics." *Freiburger Zeitschrift für Philosophie und Theologie* 37 (1990): 51–90. Reprinted in Wippel, *Metaphysical Themes in Thomas Aquinas II.* Washington, D.C.: The Catholic University of America Press, 2007.
———. "Thomas Aquinas' Commentary on Aristotle's *Metaphysics.*" In *Uses and Abuses of the Classics: Western Interpretations of Greek Philosophy,* edited by Jorge J. E. Gracia and Jiyuan Yu, 138–64. Burlington, Vt.: Ashgate, 2004.
Wohlman, Avital. *Thomas d'Aquin et Maimonide: Un dialogue exemplaire.* Paris: Cerf, 1988.

INDEX OF NAMES

Abelard, 181
Adam, 119
Al Fârabi, 24, 283, 286
Al Kindi, 242, 286
Alanus van Lille, 242
Albert the Great, 24, 65, 220, 242
Alexander of Aphrodise, 41, 46, 51, 83, 306, 309, 316
Alexander of Hales, 243, 286, 295, 307
Algazel, 286, 295, 307
Ambrose, saint, 70, 130, 144, 159, 173, 295
Ammonius, 84, 178
Anawati, G. C., 286, 337
Anawati, M.-M, 305f., 307
Anaxagoras, 6
Anderson, J. F., 106
Angelou Athanasios D., 245
Anselm, saint, 274f.
Apuleus, 88
Architas of Tarento, 2
Arius, 150
Aspasius, 41
Athanasius, saint, 136, 144
Aulus Gellius, 73
Avempace, 286, 315, 322
Avendauth, 284
Averroes, 45, 51f., 149, 253, 306f.
Avicebron, 97, 332f.
Avicenna, 51, 183, 242, 267, 283f.

Backus, Ignaz, 103
Backus, Irena, 103
Bacon, Roger, 243
Baeumker, C., 332
Baguette, C., 70
Bardenhewer, O., 3, 241
Barnes, J., 43
Basil, saint, 21, 169, 227, 271

Basilides, 86
Bassler, W., 277
Bataillon, L.-J., 50
Berangar of Tours, 274f.
Bernard of Clairvaux, saint, 128, 181
Boethius, 9, 40f, 71, 178
Bonaventure, saint, 23, 34
Boyer, C., 126
Braakhuis, H., 49
Brunner, Fernand, 334
Burgundio, John, of Pisa, 40, 49, 157

Calippus, 46
Canart, P., 95
Carroy, Bertrand, 49
Casazza, Fabrizio, 66
Cassiodorus 184 186
Chadwick, H., 192
Cheneval, F., 43
Chenu, M.-D., 90
Chrysippus, 69
Chrysostom, John, saint, 86f., 95, 102, 144, 154
Cicero, 33, 62, 71f
Cleanthes, 70
Clement of Alexandria, 21, 70
Colish, Marcia L., 70
Couesnongle, V., de, 90, 98
Courcelles, P., 178
Cyril of Alexandria, 262

Dacos, Joelle, 49
Damascene, John, saint, 101f., 262f.
D'Ancona Costa, Christina, 241
Dauphinais, M., 106, 113, 120
David, Barry, 106
De Ghellink, J., 92
Decker, B., 346

374 ∽ INDEX OF NAMES

Democritus, 8
Dillon, J., 86
Dionysius the Areopagite (Pseudo-Dionysius), 4, 212, 220f., 260f.
Dodds, E. R., 84, 245, 248
Doig, James, 56, 60
Donatus, 129
Dondaine, A., 50

Empedocles, 86
Endress, G., 270
Epicurus, 70f.
Eudoxus, 46, 97

Fabro, C., 1
Feldnan, S., 339
Festugière, A.-J., 85

García Marqués, A. 311
Gardet, Louis, 284f 306, 308, 311, 313
Gauthier, R. A., 41, 59
Geenen, J. G., 102
Gerard of Cremona, 3, 46, 242, 284
Giacomotto-Chorra, Violine, 49
Gigon, Olaf, 72
Gilbert of Portiers (de la Porrée), 96, 179
Gilson, E., 23, 39, 220, 277, 338
Godefroy of Saint-Victor, 184
Goichon, A. M., 297
Grabmann, Martin, 45f, 101, 180
Gregory of Nazianzus, saint, 128, 133, 227
Gregory the Great, 33, 37, 110, 120, 193
Grosseteste, Robert, 43, 46
Gundisalvi, 242, 284, 332
Gutas, D., 285
Gutmann, J., 346

Hadot, P., 188f
Hankey, Wayne J., 90
Hannibaldus de Hannibaldis, 180
Hardon, J., 125
Hasse, D., 307
Hasselhoff, G. K., 337f., 345
Hayen, A., 90
Hedwig, K., 65, 71
Henle, R. J., 5, 7
Heraclitus, 5

Herman the German, 307
Hilary, saint, 144, 173, 179
Hilduin, 220
Hissette, Roland, 27, 35, 308
Houser, R. E., 285
Hugh of Saint-Victor, 41, 181

Imbach, Rudi, 43, 341
Irenaeus, saint, 86
Issac, J., 25
Isidore of Seville, 101, 114
Ivanka, E., von, 36

Jaffa, H. V., 58f
James of Venice, 42f
Jenkins, J., 40
Jerome, saint, 70, 80, 86, 89, 127f.
John Scotus Eriugena, 220 239
John the Baptist, saint, 155, 159
John the Evangelist, saint, 169
Jolif, J.-Y., 62
Jordan, M. D., 60
Judycka, J., 49

Kackzor, Christophor, 60
Kogan, B. Sherman, 314

Lactantius, 88, 98
Lanfranque, M., 82
Laertin, M.-J., 96
Leo the Great, saint, 130
Levering, M., 106, 113, 120
Longinus, 85
Louis of Valence, 65

Macierowski, E. M., 54
Macrobius, 35f., 73, 97
Maimonides, 320, 332f., 336f.
Mani, 87
Marcus Aurelius, 70, 76
Marshall, Bruce, 113
Massé, H., 316
Mary of Bethany, 166
Mausbach, J., 346
McInerny, Ralph, 60, 192
Mers, A., 346
Michael Scot, 284 307
Michael the Stutterer, 220

INDEX OF NAMES 375

Minio-Paluello, L., 41
Munk, S., 336

Nemesius, 14, 71, 205, 270, 271
Neumann, S., 180
Newman, J. H., 21
Numenius, 84

Origenes, 97, 101, 139
Otte, J. R., 49
Owens, J., 56, 59

Panetius, 70
Parmenides, 182
Patfoort, A., 91
Pattin, A., 242f.
Peckham, John, 35
Pera, C., 241
Philoponus, 16, 48
Pierce, C. A., 80
Peter of Auvergne, 65
Peter of Poitiers, 180
Places, E., des, 85
Plotinus, 15, 51, 89, 93, 182, 188, 290
Pohlenz, Max, 68, 70
Porphyrius, 51, 89, 91, 178, 184, 283
Portalupi, Enzo, 193
Possidonius, 51, 70
Prantl, K., 3, 241
Proclus, 2, 80f., 183, 188, 220, 222, 228, 248, 258f., 285
Pseudo-Andronicus, 71
Ptolemy, 283
Puech, H., 11, 239
Pythagoras, 84

Rand, E. K., 71
Reale, Giovanni, 4
Rich, Audrey N. M., 7
Richard of Saint-Victor, 211
Rist, John M., 74
Roland of Cremona, 243
Roland-Gosselin, M.-D., 288, 295, 298, 309
Ross, David, 9
Rowson, E., 242
Ruffinus, 103, 132
Ryan, W. F., 242

Saffrey, H. D., 241f., 245
Schmitt, C. B., 242
Schurr, V., 179
Schenk, L. P., 1
Sconicov, S., 20
Seneca, 7, 72
Sheldon-Williams, P., 221
Sherman Kogen, B., 314
Sherwin, Michael S., 120
Siger of Brabant, 44, 241, 243
Simon, H., 336
Simplicius, 46f., 88f., 309
Socrates, 6
Souchard, Bertrand, 50
Spanneut, Michel, 70, 78f.
Speusippus, 92
Stewart, H. F., 184
Stiglmayr, J., 270
Syrianus, 41

Taylor, R. C., 242f.
Tempier, Etienne, 308
Tertullian, 70
Theiler, W., 7
Themistius, 51, 178, 307, 326
Theodore of Mopsuestia, 128
Theophrastus, 326
Théry, G., 308
Thierry of Chartres, 223
Thijssen, Johannes, 49
Torrell, Jean-Pierre, 54, 59, 65, 347

Ushida, Noriko, 295

Vajda, G., 350
Valentinus, 86, 150
Van Camp, J., 95
Vansteenkiste, C., 21, 241, 243, 286
Van Steennerghen, E., 46
Vaux, P., de, 307
Velásquez, H., 66
Verbeke, G., 75, 285
Vijgen, Jörgen, 38, 332

Waldmann, M., 80
Wallie, R. T., 95
Wehofer, F., 346
Weisheipl, James, 49, 322, 332

White, Kevin, 50, 54
William of Auvergne, 332
William of Auxerre, 243
William of Moerbeke, 41f., 49, 53f., 241
William of Saint-Thierry, 181
Wippel, J. F., 55, 59, 304f
Wohlman, A., 350

Xenocrates, 92

Zedler, B. H., 307
Zeno, 67, 70

GENERAL INDEX

abstraction, 52, 179, 185, 328
Academy, the Ancient, 92
accidents, 38, 288, 309
acedia, 208
act and potency, 250
active life, 211
ἀδιάφορα, 69
affirmations are incongruous, 239
allegory, 196f.
Al-Schifa, 283
alteration 49
alteritas, 182
analogy, 14, 32
angels, 94, 100, 114, 134f., 139, 169, 199, 201f., 224, 252, 267
anger, 73, 134, 196, 272, 298
animalia aerea, 14
animals, 202, 250, 303
animation of the heaven, 47
ἀντακολουθία, 79
ἀπάθεια, 82
appetite: concupiscible, 191; irascible, 191
Arians, 21, 157
assensio, 68
atomism, 14
attributes, divine, 235f., 275, 311, 338f.
Augustinism, 233
authority, 128

baptism, 200
beatitude, 23, 34f., 60, 117, 316
beauty, 225f., 229
becoming: of substances, 185
being, 41, 223, 248, 285; act of (*esse*), 41f., 287; being and essence, 249; first, 57; immaterial, 249; necessary and possible, 288; qua being, 55; to be, 30
body, 143, 301

capital sins, 174, 208
categories, 14
Catena aurea, 195, 197
causality, divine, 10, 222, 230, 258
cause, 22; exemplary, 232; first, 55, 246f., 250
charisms, 209
charity, 120, 250
chastity, 327
Church Fathers, 20, 101f
circumstances, 270
clemency, 72
cognitive species, 239
commentaries on Aristotle, 39, 306, 325
composite things, 189
concepts, forming, 52
concupiscence, 174, 272
conflagration, 134
conformity with nature, 78
conscience, 80
contemplation, 23, 60, 122, 202, 226
contingency, 42, 75, 288, 297
corporeity, 30, 202
corruption, 334
cosmology, 16, 46f.; of Plato, 16; of the Stoa, 82
cosmos, model of, 299
creation, 11, 169, 223f., 246, 255, 285f., 291, 305, 313f., 342; through intermediaries, 293
criteria of morality, 61
cult of God, 344
culture, profane, 129
curse, 174

Dator formarum, 284f., 293, 300, 305, 316
De anima, 51
De causis, 3, 10, 241f.,
De caelo et mundo, 25, 46, 48, 329

377

De divinis nominibus, 221f.
De fide orthodoxa, 103
De generatione et corruptione, 5, 49
De hebdomadibus, 9
De malorum subsistentia, 220
De natura hominis, 14
De potentia, 12
De spiritualibus creaturis, 325
De substantia orbis, 310
De substantiis separatis, 3, 20, 28, 91, 333
De unitate intellectus, 295
death, 30, 62, 81, 96, 336; life after, 210, 269, 298
demiurge, 10
determinism, 312
devil, 137, 227, 268
dialectics, 274f.
disciple and master, 318
dimensions, indeterminate, 32
disciplinaliter, 186
distinction, the real, 288
diversity of things, cause of, 254
divided line, 250
divination, 121
divine causality, 230
dreams, 92
dualism, 86, 248, 295
Dux neutrorum, 337
dyad, indeterminate, 93, 182

earthquakes, 5
ecstasy, 226
effect: returns to its cause, 99
Elementatio, 241, 243f., 260
elements, the four, 49f., 320f., 333
emanation, 222, 254, 275, 293, 303, 335
empiricism: of Aristotle, 53
end, 117; last, 60, 117
ἔννοιαι, 68
entity, mathematical, 13
envy, 298
ἐπέκεινα, 4
episcopate, 245
ἐποπτικόν, 188
eschatology 141 210
esse existentibus, 251
essence, 251, 284, 288
essentialism, 286

eternity, 47, 179, 247; of motion, 58; of the world, 20, 23, 35, 340
ethics, philosophical, 58
Eucharist, 125, 172, 200
evil, 227f., 292; not a being, 229; not a first principle, 229; problem of, 107, 227f., 289, 312
exemplaria, 230f.
existence of God, 275

faculties of the soul, 30, 324
faith, 48, 119, 198, 232, 341
fasting, 148, 175, 200
fatalism, 74
fear, 298
fides quaerens intellectum, 275
fire, 211
firmament, 343
flux, 321
forms: of beings, 185, 293, 311; subsistent, 2, 7; theory of, 5, 33, 190, 301f., 318, 333
fortune, 75
fraternal correction, 132
freedom of choice, 230, 264

generation, 328, 401
geocentrism, 46
gifts of the Holy Spirit, 209
glosses, 103, 127
gnosis, 85
Gnosticism, 21, 85f., 92
God, 11f., 48, 136, 222f., 228, 278, 289, 310, 313; as being of existing things, 230, 251; goodness of, 226; knowledge of, 263f., 313
Good, the, 4, 55, 191, 223, 247, 323; and being, 192, 223
goodness, 192, 226
Great, the: and the Small, 11, 93
Guide of the Perplexed, 337, 347, 350

habilitas, 321
habit 206
happiness, 64. See also beatitude
harmony, 68, 225
heart, human, 343
heaven: animation of, 343; the first, 17, 320, 329, 343
heavenly bodies, 320

hegemonikon, 68
heretics, 120, 135, 148f.
hierarchy, 12, 95, 222, 228f.; of angels, 228; of beings, 95; ecclesiastic, 239
Holy Spirit, 173, 280f.
hope, 298
humility, 63, 207, 282
hylomorphism, 63, 212, 250
hyperdea divinitas, 221
hypostasis, 136, 222f., 250

ideas: of accidents, 7; causality of, 9, 11, 94; in God's intellect, 58, 112; and numbers, 93; theory of, 6f., 57, 231, 309
illumination, 222, 246, 250, 337, 349
image of God, 188, 269
imagination, 52, 284, 296, 349
immaterial, 55, 295; substances, 9, 213
immateriality, 253, 257
immisor malarum, 268
immortality, 267
immutability of God, 112, 235
imperialism, 121
imperishable, 10
incarnation, 123, 135, 265
inclinations, natural, 68f.
incompactus, 239
individuation, 183
induction, 4
infinite ocean of being, 263
informitas materiae, 169
ingenerate, 183
intellect, 52, 252, 295, 326; agent, 30, 52, 316, 318f., 324; passive, 52; possible, 52, 284, 315f., 324; theoretical, 187; unique, 317
intellectualia, 224
intellectualiter, 186
intelligences, 225, 249f., 315
intermediaries, 247

judgment, 53, 161
justice, 62; divine, 234; legal, 62; natural, 62

knowledge, 6, 255; divine, 312f., 332; origin of our, 6; as remembering, 7; scientific, 22; self-, 116; sense, 8
Koran, 307

language, 251
law, 119; ceremonial laws, 344f.; cosmic, 78; positive, 62, 119; Jewish, 111, 142, 160, 165; natural, 76, 346; New Law, the, 110f., 119, 239
liberality, 63
Liber de causis, 241f.
life, 121f.; active, 211; contemplative, 211
light, 251f., 305, 348
lightning, 51
littera, sensus, sententia, 41
logic, 68, 309
logica nova, 179
logos, 67, 233
love, 174, 226f.; of the good, 236
lying, 134

magic, 85
magnanimity, 13, 63
magnificence, 27, 63
man, 105, 269, 280, 324f., 344
Manicheism, 87, 108
marriage, 173
Mary. *See* Virgin
Mary of Bethany, 166
material beings, 290
mathematical entities, 13
mathematics, 41, 84
matter, 10f., 35, 104, 224, 301, 311, 320; and form, 190, 301; primary, 333
mean, theory of the, 61
memory, 53
metaphysics, 54f.
Meteora, 50f.
method in the sciences, 65, 180, 186f.
Middle Platonism, 4
miracle, 157, 160
Misneh Torah, 336
monism, 85, 254, 286
monk, 176
moral life, 143, 173f., 271, 290f., 327
moral teachings of Platonism, 18f., 97
moral theology, 59
mother of Christ, 197
motion, 58, 300, 320
move, to, 301
Mover, First, 27, 55f., 57, 310

Monologion, 275
mutakallimûn, 284

name, 9; divine, 222, 224, 263
nature, 143, 341
necessary, 74, 288
negation, the way of, 238f.
negationes in divinis sunt verae, 269f.
negative theology, 221
Neoplatonism, 4, 13, 24, 71, 92, 95, 98, 189, 220, 222, 237, 281, 285, 333
Nestorians, 264
Nicomachean Ethics, 58
non-being, 3
νοῦς, 6, 23, 85, 275
numbers, 93

oath, 145
obedience, 148, 207
οἰκείωσις, 68
omnipotence, 235
ὁμολογουμένως ζῆν, 68
One, the, 13, 94, 287, 222, 275, 323; as a cause, 95, 247; and the Good, 247; and numbers, 95
ontological argument, 276
order in the universe, 254
ordo amoris, 118
otherness, 182, 237

parables, 163, 197
participation, 9f., 189f., 247
passions, 69, 73, 205, 229, 272, 298f.,
patience, 121, 207
peace, 236f.
penance, 125, 148, 173
perfections, 235, 311
Peri Hermeneias, 29
perpetuity, 320, 331
persons, divine, 113, 123, 213
phantasma, 318
philosophy, 130; first, 55, 188
physics, 64, 184
piety, 146
place, 183, 301, 321
planets, influence of, 92, 299
Platonism, 98, 100, 220f.; Middle, 4
Platonists, 17, 88, 224, 285, 328

pleasure, 18, 63f., 97, 173, 272, 298
plurality, cause of, 182
pneuma, 67f.
possibilia, 288
potency, 323, 329
potentiality of matter, 323
poverty, 147
power, divine, 231f.
powers of the soul. *See* faculties
prayer, 266
preaching, 205
predestination, 113
preexistence of the soul, 105
prefiguration, 128
presence of God, 224
pride, 122
priest, 172, 176
primacy of Peter, 170
primum creatum est esse, 251
principles: causality of the, 246; of contradiction, 22, 43; first, 22, 43, 98, 319; of the practical intellect, 31, 62
privation, 224
πρόληψις, 68
property, 65
prophecy, 122, 142, 188, 199, 346
Proslogion, 228
providence, 20, 23, 28, 75, 96, 107, 229, 263, 312, 338f.
prudence, 60, 282, 327
psalms, 128, 196
punishment, 169
putrefaction, 322, 328
Pythagoreanism, 15

quality, 50
quantity, 183, 326

rationaliter, 18
rationes rerum, 290
realism, 20
reason (*ratio*), 187, 233; at the service of faith, 32
receptacle, 11
recta ratio, 61
Regimen sanitatis, 336
Registrum, 195
Regula pastoralis, 194

religion, 121
religious life, 84, 146, 214
remember: to know is to, 8
reminiscence, 53
res, 287
resurrection, 163, 210, 231
revelation, prophetic, 65, 186
right by nature, 62
rotation, 48

Sabbath, 345
sacrament, 124, 140, 172, 200
sacrifice, 124, 278
saints, cult of the, 262f.
same, the: and the other, 16
scandal, 144
science: divine, 339; speculative, 184
secundum intentionem Aristotelis, 29
sed contra arguments, 32
self-knowledge, 144, 251, 253
sense organs, 53
sense perception, 8
senses, the external, 52f., 67, 284, 296
sensualism, 76
separatio, 285
serfdom, 66
sin, 119, 173, 207f., 260
soul, the, 13f., 35, 51f., 95, 97, 143, 248, 260, 270, 286, 292, 294, 315; being of, 247; human, 294; is all things, 53; origin of, 116, 325
species, intelligible, 52, 250, 296
spheres, celestial, 4, 57, 292, 300, 340
Spirit, gifts of the, 209
spiritual beings, 202, 333
stars: fixed, 299, 329; shooting, 50
Stoicism, 67f.
strength (*virtus*), 233
striking formulae, 130
study, 304
subsistent, 246
substance, 22, 223, 235, 309, 328; immaterial, 57, 257, 333; separate, 316, 328, 334
συγκατάθεσις, 68
suicide, 27
Sufficientia, 283
συμπαθεία, 67

sun, 225
supernatural order, 36, 273
superstantialis, 221, 223
syllogism, 42
synderesis, 61, 80, 145

tabula, 102
tabula rasa, 252
teaching, 213, 215
temperance, 206
temptation, 127
θεαρχία, 222
theology, 182, 186, 190; monastic, 182; negative, 221; role of philosophy in, 32, 182; status of, 180
thing, 287f.
thought, 51, 185, 318
time, 236, 253; God and, 236, 311
transfiguration, 137, 163
Trinity, the, 113, 278
tripartition: of philosophy, 55, 184; of the soul, 15
truth, 165, 232f., 277, 289

unity, 252; of all things, 237
universal, 6; concepts, 284
unlimited, the, 248

vice, 119, 145, 207f., 272
Virgin, Mary, the, 87, 102, 135, 138, 171, 280
virginity, 27, 121
virtue, 37, 62, 69, 79, 118, 206, 272, 282; cardinal, 37, 72; moral, 79
vision of God, 169
void, 332, 327, 330
voluntary, 270
voluntas consequens, 270

weakness, moral, 64
will, 115, 271, 280, 288; free, 75, 134, 143, 269f.
wisdom, 232
Word, 200; the divine, 169, 279
world, 253, 331, 340f.; eternal, 35, 58, 340; origin of, 10

zones, cosmic, 342

Thomas Aquinas and His Predecessors: The Philosophers and the Church Fathers in His Works was designed in Arno and composed by Kachergis Book Design of Pittsboro, North Carolina.

www.ingramcontent.com/pod-product-compliance
Lightning Source LLC
Chambersburg PA
CBHW030250010526
44107CB00053B/1653